WITHDRAWN
UTSA LIBRARIES

RENEWALS

D0221024

The Daughters of Hāritī

Hāritī is the ancient Indian goddess of childbirth and women healers, known at one time throughout South and Southeast Asia from India to Nepal and Bali. This book looks at her 'daughters' today, female midwives and healers in many different cultures across the region. In some places they are skilled and respected professionals, elsewhere low-caste menials whose primary function is to deal with the 'pollution' of birth.

The Daughters of Hāritī: Childbirth and female healers in South and Southeast Asia also traces the transformation of childbirth in these cultures under the impact of Western biomedical technology, national and international health policies and the wider factors of social and economic change. The authors look at the various situations of birthing mothers in these societies and the choices facing them and their families. They ask what can be done to improve the high rates of maternal and infant death and illnesses still associated with childbirth in most societies in this area. Is the technology necessarily a good thing? Even where it might be, can the delivery of biomedical technology be improved so that it is more accessible and relevant to the needs of birthing mothers?

This fascinating volume combines scholarly analysis with human sensitivity to an area with a direct influence on the lives of hundreds of millions of Asian women. It is the first contemporary survey of childbirth in this region and it adds dramatically to our knowledge of this field. It will be of great use to postgraduate students as well as to professionals.

Santi Rozario and **Geoffrey Samuel** both teach in the School of Social Sciences, University of Newcastle, NSW, Australia. Santi Rozario has researched on women and development, health and Islam. Geoffrey Samuel has researched on Tibetan society, religion and music.

Theory and Practice in Medical Anthropology and International Health

A series edited by Susan M. DiGiacomo, *University of Massachusetts, Amherst*

Editorial Board

H. Kris Heggenhougen
Harvard University, Cambridge, Massachusetts

Daniel E. Moerman
University of Michigan, Dearborn

R. Brooke Thomas
University of Massachusetts, Amherst

International Advisory Board

George Armelagos, Hans Baer, Peter Brown, Xòchitl Castaneda, Deborah Gordon, Xòchitl Herrera, Judith Justice, Montasser Kamal, Charles Leslie, Shirley Lindenbaum, Margaret Lock, Setha Low, Mark Nichter, Duncan Pedersen, Thomas Ots, Nancy Scheper-Hughes, Merrill Singer

Founding Editor

Libbet Crandon-Malamud[†]

The Daughters of Hāritī

Childbirth and female healers in
South and Southeast Asia

Edited by Santi Rozario and
Geoffrey Samuel

London and New York

First published 2002
by Routledge
11 New Fetter Lane, London EC4P 4EE

Simultaneously published in the USA and Canada
by Routledge
29 West 35th Street, New York NY 10001

Routledge is an imprint of the Taylor & Francis Group

© 2002 Taylor & Francis Books Ltd

Typeset in Times by M Rules
Printed and bound in Great Britain by MPG Books Ltd, Bodmin

All rights reserved. No part of this book may be reprinted or
reproduced or utilised in any form or by any electronic,
mechanical, or other means, now known or hereafter invented,
including photocopying and recording, or in any information
storage or retrieval system, without permission in writing from
the publishers.

British Library Cataloguing in Publication Data
A catalogue record for this book is available from the British
Library

Library of Congress Cataloging in Publication Data
A catalog record for this book has been requested

ISBN 0–415–27792–2

Library
University of Texas
at San Antonio

Contents

Illustrations

Figures

Maps

Tables

List of contributors

The editors

Santi Rozario was born in Dhaka, Bangladesh, and completed a BA in Sociology at Dhaka University in 1975. She was subsequently awarded a Ph.D. by the School of Sociology, University of New South Wales, Sydney, in 1989 for research on women in a multi-religious village in Bangladesh. Since then, she has carried out extensive research on women and development, women and health, and women and Islam, primarily in Bangladesh, but also in India, Nepal, Sri Lanka, Australia and the United Kingdom. She is currently Senior Lecturer in the School of Social Sciences, University of Newcastle, NSW, Australia. Dr Rozario is the author of the book *Purity and Communal Boundaries: Women and Social Change in a Bangladeshi Village* (London: Zed Books, also Sydney: Allen and Unwin, 1992) and of numerous articles. She is currently working on a book on microcredit schemes in Bangladesh.

Geoffrey Samuel was awarded a Ph.D. in Social Anthropology from the University of Cambridge in 1975 for research on religion in Tibetan societies. He is currently Professor of Anthropology at the University of Newcastle, NSW, Australia. He has written extensively on issues relating to Tibetan society, religion, music, and anthropological theory. He is the author of *Mind, Body and Culture* (Cambridge University Press, 1990) and *Civilized Shamans: Buddhism in Tibetan Societies* (Smithsonian Institution Press, 1993), and co-editor of *Tantra and Popular Religion in Tibet* (Aditya Prakashan, 1994), *Nature Religion Today* (Edinburgh University Press 1998) and *Healing Powers and Modernity* (Greenwood Press, 2001).

Contributors

Janet Chawla is an American who has lived and worked in India for twenty-three years. For the past four years she has led a research project, MATRIKA (Motherhood and Traditional Resources, Information, Knowledge and Action) documenting and reclaiming indigenous midwifery skills, practices and cultural knowledge. She has a Master of Theology degree from Vidyajyoti Institute of Religious Studies, where she has also taught courses on Goddesses in the Indian traditions. She is currently a research associate at the Five Colleges Women's Studies Research Centre at Mount Holyoke College in Western Massachusetts, working on a book *Matas and Midwives, Dais and Demons: Cultural Images of Birth in India*.

Amanda Harris was awarded a Ph.D. in Anthropology at the University of Newcastle, NSW, in 1999. She has recently carried out field research in Iban longhouse communities in Sarawak, East Malaysia, on the topic of healing, modernity and transformations of Iban identity in the context of the politics of the Malaysian nation-state. She is currently with the Australian Agency for International Development.

Cynthia L. Hunter is Lecturer in Anthropology at Macquarie University, Sydney. She has a Ph.D. in Anthropology from the University of Newcastle, NSW (1997). She has carried out work with non-governmental organisations on maternal and child health projects in Eastern Indonesia. Her chapter is based on fieldwork conducted on the island of Lombok, Indonesia during 1991 and 1992. Her research interests include ritual, illness and healing in contexts of medical pluralism. She has written on the topics of maternal and child health, and national health services in Indonesian communities.

Linda Iltis is Lecturer in Comparative Religion and South Asian Studies at the University of Washington, Seattle. She earned a Ph.D. in 1985 from the University of Wisconsin–Madison. Her research areas include women and religion, Hinduism and Indo-Tibetan Buddhism, and anthropology of South Asia. She has conducted research primarily in Nepal, also in India and Sri Lanka, and among South Asian immigrant communities in the USA. Her research and publications feature studies of goddesses; space, place and identity; expressive culture and ritual performance; and trance and possession. Her most recent publications include *Introduction to World Religions: Eastern Traditions* (University of Washington, 2000).

Patricia Jeffery and **Roger Jeffery** are both Professors in the Department of Sociology, University of Edinburgh, Scotland. Patricia Jeffery is author of *Frogs in a Well: Indian Women in Purdah* (1979/2000) and Roger Jeffery is author of *The Politics of Health in India* (1988). Since the early 1980s, most of their research has been conducted in Bijnor District in North India where they have focused on aspects of agrarian change, gender politics (including childbearing and family planning) and communal politics. Their publications on Bijnor include *Don't Marry Me to a Plowman! Women's Everyday Lives in Rural North India* (1996) and *Population, Gender and Politics: Demographic Change in Rural North India* (1997). **Andrew Lyon** was a research student in Sociology at the University of Edinburgh in 1982/3, at the time of their first Bijnor research. The three together co-authored *Labour Pains and Labour Power: Women and Childbearing in India* (Zed Books, 1989).

Barbara Johnson is an independent filmmaker who worked for ten years for the Smithsonian Institution's Human Studies Film Center and Archives. In 1978 and 1980 she lived and filmed in a Newar farming village in Nepal, where she shot over fifty-five hours of sync-sound colour film now in the Film Archives. In 1997 she completed an edited videotape of one of the births she filmed in Nepal. Johnson was a documentary film student at Hampshire College in Amherst, Massachusetts, and now lives in Arlington, Virginia with her husband and two children.

Lynda Newland was awarded a Ph.D. in Anthropology in 1999 by Macquarie University for a thesis which analysed the impact of the Indonesian family planning programme on a rural Sundanese community in West Java. Her chapter is based on fieldwork conducted in 1995/6, the last years of the Suharto regime. In 1998, she returned to the field with a video camera and is now in the process of finding funding for post-production and preparing her thesis for publication. She is currently teaching in the Department of Sociology, University of the South Pacific, Fiji.

Maya Unnithan-Kumar's doctoral work was on kinship and gender politics in Southern Rajasthan in India. The research was based on fieldwork among a poor farming community of Girasia 'tribals'. Her monograph *Identity, Gender and Poverty: New Perspectives on Caste and Tribe in Rajasthan* (Berghahn, 1997) discusses Girasia women and men's roles and relationships in the context of their poverty and discussions on tribe–caste distinctions. Currently her research interest is in issues of reproductive health and women's agency in urban and rural Rajasthan. Other interests include micro-level household analysis on scarcity and drought conditions in Rajasthan, and religion, fundamentalism and gender in India and among Indians in Britain. She is Senior Lecturer in Social Anthropology at the School of African and Asian Studies, University of Sussex.

Cecilia Van Hollen is Assistant Professor of Anthropology at the University of Notre Dame. She received her Ph.D. in Medical Anthropology from the University of California at Berkeley (1998). Her forthcoming book, *Birth on the Threshold: Childbirth and Modernity in South India*, will be published by the University of California Press (2002).

Andrea Whittaker is a medical anthropologist who has conducted research on health and illness both in Thailand and in Australia. Her recent book *Intimate Knowledge: Women and their Health in Northeast Thailand* is an ethnographic study on women's health. She has been recently appointed as Lecturer in a joint position at the Key Centre for Women's Health and Melbourne Institute of Asian Languages and Societies at the University of Melbourne.

Acknowledgements

The initial inspiration for this volume came from a session (Birth in South Asia: Midwives and Female Healers) held at the annual meeting of the Association of Asian Studies at Washington, DC in April 1995. Other papers were contributed later. Chapter 4 is reprinted by permission from *Women, State and Ideology: Studies from Africa and Asia*, edited by Haleh Afshar (Macmillan 1987). We thank all the contributors for their generosity and patience.

We wish to acknowledge the assistance, support and encouragement of Susan DiGiacomo and Carol Hollander from Gordon & Breach, and Mark Simon, David Mainwaring and Karen Stenner from Harwood, without whom this book would never have taken shape, and Julene Barnes, Polly Osborn, Liz O'Donnell, Diane Stafford and Mike Hauser, who have seen it through to publication for Routledge. All have made invaluable and much appreciated contributions. We also thank both Tricia Jeffery and Gordon and Breach's anonymous reader for their incisive and helpful comments on an earlier stage of the manuscript, and Stephen Dick for the excellent maps.

Figure 1.1 Statue of Hāritī at Goa Gadja, Bali (photo by Geoffrey Samuel, 1994)

Chapter 1

Introduction

The daughters of Hārītī today

Geoffrey Samuel

The Hārītī of our title is the ancient Buddhist goddess of childbirth (Auboyer and de Mallmann 1950: 225; Strong 1992: 36–7). At one time, her cult seems to have been important through much of the vast area covered by our book, which includes studies located in the modern nations of Nepal, India, Bangladesh, Malaysia, Thailand and Indonesia (Maps 1.1 and 1.2). The 'daughters of Hārītī' are the birth attendants, midwives and female healers of the South and Southeast Asian region. Their fate, in a world very different from that in which the cult of Hārītī took shape, is one central subject of this book. The other, closely related subject is the transformation of childbirth practices now taking place in Asian societies under the impact of modernity and biomedicine.

Hārītī herself is a figure of some interest. Her worship seems to have been particularly important in Gandhāra and Mathura (present-day Pakistan and North India, first century BCE to fourth century CE).[1] Her legend describes her as a child-eating demoness who was converted by the Buddha (Strong 1992: 36). Perhaps, though, this negative depiction reflects a process in which respected *yakṣa* and *yakṣī* (nature spirits, deities of prosperity and fertility) such as Hārītī and her consort Pāñcika were brought into a subordinate relationship with the newly developing Buddhist and Brahmanical pantheons. At any rate, Hārītī received regular offerings in Buddhist monasteries, and her cult became closely associated with Buddhism and Buddhist monasticism as they spread through South and Southeast Asia, the region of our book. Hārītī shrines formed part of the Buddhist cave-temple complexes at Ajanta and Ellora in Western India, the Buddhist monastery of Ratnagiri in East India and the Buddhist complex at Candi Mendut in Java (Cohen 1998: 381–93; Malandra 1997: 76, 104, 115–16). Hārītī also accompanied Buddhism through the trading oases of the Silk Route, where paintings of her have been found, and on to China and Japan (Dhirasekera 1976: 69–70, and see Chapter 3 this volume).

Today, traces of her presence remain throughout South and Southeast Asia. Hārītī's cult is alive in Nepal, where there is a very active temple to her at Swayambhunath, near Kathmandu (see Slusser 1982: I, 329; Anderson

1988: 78; Josephson 1985: part II, 1–2). As Linda Iltis describes in Chapter 3 of this book, women in contemporary Nepal still heal in her name and through her power. At the opposite end of the region, on the island of Bali, a thousand-year-old statue of Hārītī still receives offerings in a small modern shrine next to the cave temple of Goa Gadja (Figure 1.1; see also Kempers 1991: 125, 127 fig. 92).

However, as her legendary origins as a child-eating demoness suggest, Hārītī is a complex figure. The ambivalence which surrounds her and deities like her has something to tell us about the ambivalence with which birth attendants, midwives and female healers are still viewed in many Indic-derived cultures. In Nepal, Hārītī is closely associated with Śītalā, the well-known Hindu goddess of smallpox (Auboyer and de Mallmann 1950). As Strong notes:

> Like other smallpox goddesses of India, [Hārītī] was probably the object of an ambivalent attitude on the part of her worshippers. On the one hand, she was feared as the bringer of the disease and harrier of children. On the other hand, she was worshipped as the one who could spare and, in this sense, give life to those same children.
>
> (1992: 36)

Hārītī's principal Hindu counterpart as patroness of childbirth and small children, Ṣaṣṭhī (Haque 1992: 263–7; and cf. Samuel 1997: 3), seems to have had a similar background (Gadon 1997: 296), as does Śītalā, and the important contemporary Bengali snake goddess Manasā, again both an inflicter of snake bites and protector of children (Haque 1992: 286–95; Gadon 1997; Samuel 1997: 11).

Female 'demons' who attack women in childbirth and young children, but who can also be induced to provide healing, figure prominently in the classical Indian medical tradition as well. As Dominik Wujastyk notes, 'women, especially pregnant women, are especially vulnerable to demonic possession, and [. . .] demons are also the cause of miscarriage' (Wujastyk 1997: 6; see also Wujastyk 1999). In fact, ambivalent female deities, half-demons, half-guardians, inflicters of deadly illness and childbirth mortality who are also invoked for protection, have a very long history in Indian religion. They indicate the concern people must have always felt for the risky situation of childbirth in premodern times. Perhaps, as we shall see, these figures also reflect the negative attitudes of Brahmins and other male clerics and literati towards women and towards an autonomous sphere of women's ritual life.

Thus, in referring to the birth attendants, midwives and female healers of South and Southeast Asia as 'daughters of Hārītī', the editors are also alluding to the ambivalent attitudes towards them witnessed by several of the studies in this book.

These negative attitudes may surprise some Western readers. The idea of midwife-assisted birth, at home or in a clinic or birthing centre, has been revived and actively promoted in Western societies in recent years. This revival developed as a reaction to what was seen as the excessive medicalisation of childbirth, and also as part of a feminist-inspired desire for women to assert control over childbirth, one of the most significant and critical events in most women's lives. While this movement has certainly not removed childbirth as a whole from the sphere of medical dominance, it has led to widespread criticism of the dehumanisation involved in medicalised childbirth, and of earlier dismissive and negative attitudes to midwife-assisted birth. Western readers who are familiar with these criticisms may expect, or at least hope, that South and Southeast Asian societies preserve a more favourable orientation to traditional birthing practices and female healers.

While glimpses of an older, more positive valuation of midwives and traditional female healers can be found in the South and Southeast Asian studies in this book, the dominant attitude portrayed, especially in the North Indian and Bangladeshi chapters, is very different. It is perhaps not surprising that Asian governments, under pressure from international health organisations and foreign-aid donors, strongly endorse the medicalisation of childbirth and regard the replacement of traditional practices by procedures derived from Western biomedicine[2] as a virtually unqualified good.[3] What is more striking is that most indigenous women's movements themselves support such policies. In part this is because they see them as combating the high mortality and morbidity rates still occurring throughout the region for both mothers and children, but it is also because negative images of 'traditional birth attendants' or TBAs (to use the World Health Organisation's jargon) have long been widespread in the region.

Thus, international organisations, national health authorities and indigenous women's movements largely agree in their dismissive attitude to the traditional midwives and birth attendants. While a new generation of modern, medically trained midwives may be viewed as an adjunct to state-endorsed medicalisation, traditional midwives and birth attendants are seen as part of the old order to be superseded. At best, some 'TBAs' may be offered retraining and given a limited role in the new medical order. Such experiments have been tried since the nineteenth century (see Chapter 4 for British India,[4] and Chapter 12 for the Dutch East Indies), and 'TBA retraining' has been part of World Health Organisation policy since the Alma Ata conference of 1978 (e.g. Chapter 12; see also Saunders 1989), but these measures have never been seen as more than a stopgap until the 'TBA' can be phased out completely.

There are some signs of a reaction against excessive medicalisation and of a re-evaluation of traditional birth practitioners, particularly in India,[5] but this has had little effect as yet on childbirth practice or on government and health organisation policies regarding childbirth. Here, the long indigenous history in South Asia of negative and dismissive attitudes to female childbirth specialists arguably poses a major obstacle.

This is not to say that all the women of South and Southeast Asia have embraced the medicalisation of childbirth with an equal degree of enthusiasm. As the studies in this book show, the situation is much more complex, and for a variety of reasons. In some areas (mainly urban) 90 per cent to 95 per cent of births may take place in hospitals or clinics under medical supervision. In many rural areas, however, this proportion is closer to 10 per cent or 20 per cent, with the vast majority of births still taking place at home with the assistance of traditional birth attendants and midwives.

These contrasts relate in part to the differential availability of the modern medical option. In many regions, public hospital facilities are grossly inadequate, underfunded and understaffed. Expense is often a major consideration. Even where public facilities are officially free, using them may involve hidden costs in the form of 'unofficial' payments to staff, purchase of drugs, and the like. In some rural areas, transport difficulties may be a major obstacle, and taking a woman in an advanced state of pregnancy to a distant hospital may be impracticable. Such factors tend to restrict hospital and clinic births to the wealthy who can afford private clinic facilities, 'unofficial' payments and transport expenses.

There are other issues too. Hospital and clinic staff in rural areas often come from educated urban backgrounds, and there may be large gaps in language and culture between them and the village population. Even staff from local rural backgrounds tend to take on the agenda of modernisation and development. A constant theme in the literature, including several of the chapters in this book, is the arrogance of hospital doctors and other staff, their condescending and negative attitudes towards village women and their hostility towards traditional practices of any kind, which they see solely in terms of superstition, ignorance and resistance to modernity.[6] Ironically, as Van Hollen notes in Chapter 8, the supposedly 'scientific' knowledge of these agents of modernity may be less self-critical and less securely founded than the practices they are attacking.

Where hospital practices contravene local norms of decency and modesty (for example in relation to women exposing their bodies to the view of non-relatives, especially men), there is often little or no concern shown by hospital staff to accommodate local attitudes or to avoid causing embarrassment to the women or their families. Traditional practices, such as those relating to the disposal of the placenta, which is an important issue in much of the region, may be interfered with or not allowed, and access by close kin to the birthing mother may be restricted. For these and other reasons, the hospital environment may be perceived as unwelcoming and hostile when compared with giving birth at home among a supportive group of kin and with the assistance of a familiar traditional birth practitioner. In circumstances such as these, hospital birth tends to become a last resort in cases where the birth is not proceeding normally.

As this discussion suggests, the medicalisation of childbirth cannot be disentangled from the more general situation of these mostly postcolonial societies. Throughout the region we find vast gaps between the elites, often including a new, Westernised and mostly urban middle class, and the rural population; an often vastly inadequate provision of public services, which is being further worsened by structural adjustment policies; much of the population engaged in a struggle for day-to-day survival, as traditional subsistence and trading economies are restructured to fit the demands of international capital; and the consequent poverty and inadequate diet of much of the rural population, which can both block access to expensive health care and severely compromise the ability of women to cope successfully with childbirth. To these we can add the dominance of a discourse of modernity and development which holds out the promise of a future in which all will have access to the benefits of progress as portrayed in the fantasy world of Bollywood movies, Western TV soap operas and their local equivalents. There are other competing discourses of modernity as well: those offered by the Hindu right in India or the Islamist movement in Indonesia or Malaysia, in which the new society is based on an idealised vision of a purified religiously based state.

The case studies in this book are of local communities and individual families situated in a variety of different positions in relation to these factors. Consequently, we find a wide range of attitudes to childbirth and modernity, among birthing mothers, traditional birth attendants and female healers, and representatives of biomedicine. It is worth looking here at some of the general regional discourses within which childbirth and birth attendants are viewed.

The discourses of childbirth

We can usefully identify at least six kinds of discourse about childbirth and its practitioners in South and Southeast Asia:

1 In general, where biomedical discourse has not achieved dominance, childbirth is seen as a natural process. It may be facilitated by traditional midwives or birth attendants but should not normally need medical intervention. Childbirth does, however, require appropriate treatment of mother and child in terms of ritual procedures, diet and other physical regimes (massage, post-partum heating, etc.). This is also the realm of traditional midwives, birth attendants and healers, who are mostly though not always female.[7] The physiological process of giving birth is widely described in humoral terms, using the 'hot'/'cold' distinction. Generally speaking, the mother is 'hot' before the birth (in humoral terms, not temperature), and 'cold' afterwards. The 'cold' condition of the mother who has just given birth is associated with weakness and vulnerability, and is

countered through physical heating and through a diet of 'hot' foods. These ideas seem to be particularly significant in Southeast Asia and South India, but they occur throughout the region.[8] Sophisticated humoral theories are present throughout the region in the form of the Galenic-Islamic, Ayurvedic and Chinese medical systems, and these have doubtless interacted with the humoral model of childbirth, for example in South India where Ayurvedic dietary concepts are widespread (see Chapter 8, also Nichter 2001, Ram 2001). However, the widespread folk humoral system may well predate these formalised systems (Manderson 1991).

2   The risk of illness and death to child and mother is also regularly phrased throughout South and Southeast Asia in terms of vulnerability to spirit-attack. The idea of dangerous female deities who can bring both illness and healing, such as Hāritī, Śītalā and Manasā, is widespread in North India particularly, as mentioned above.[9]

3   As is well known, the language of purity and pollution is deeply entrenched in South Asian societies. It forms a central part of the ideological basis for the Hindu caste system and is present in modified forms in Muslim, Buddhist, Jain and Christian communities as well. In North India, Bangladesh and parts of Nepal in particular, the process of childbirth and the physical substances associated with it are widely regarded as highly polluting. Birth attendants from low-status castes carry out the polluting work of helping the mother give birth, and may also have the job of cleaning away the pollution associated with the birth. Ideas of pollution may also mean that medical personnel such as doctors and nurses are unwilling to come into direct contact with birthing women.

4   Ideas of shame, honour and propriety are of considerable importance for female behaviour throughout South and Southeast Asia, particularly in Islamic societies. The system of *pardā*, in which married women are restricted as far as possible to their households, is widespread in North India and Bangladesh and is particularly important in Muslim communities. As already mentioned, this has consequences for childbirth practices, in that families that practice *pardā* are unwilling to have women give birth outside the home or for them to be examined by male medical personnel.

5   Birth attendants themselves may defend against negative stereotypes associated with their role by emphasising their professional skills (Chapters 6, 12) and also by seeing themselves as engaged in a form of religious service. Thus, a lower-caste midwife from South India comments that the way to the 'resting-place of Vishnu' (Heaven) is open for midwives (Viramma, Racine and Racine 1997: 73, and see Chapter 6 in this volume); Muslim *dais* in North India refer to the Prophet's respectful treatment of his mother's midwife (Chapter 4); Muslim birth attendants from Bangladesh say that delivering 101 babies is equivalent

to undertaking the pilgrimage to Mecca (Rozario 1995a: 95 and n. 9, and Chapter 6); and Muslim *paraji* in West Java stress religious aspects of their role (Chapter 12).

6   Discourses of modernity and development, as mentioned above, are pervasive throughout South and Southeast Asia today. Such discourses figure the traditional birth attendant as ignorant, dirty and dangerous, and present clinic or hospital birth as both safer and associated with modernity.[10] Islamist and neo-Hindu discourses on modernity, though typically highly critical of the West and of 'Western values', have much in common with the secularist models. They are equally dismissive of local traditions and folk practices such as those associated with childbirth, though some Islamist movements may endorse the ideas of shame and propriety mentioned previously.

In the individual chapters of this book we see the intersection and dialogue between these various discourses. Each chapter is a specific local manifestation of complex large-scale processes which are ongoing through space and time. Local situations no doubt have always differed from each other, but the differential impact of colonial history, of national health policies, of the 'structural adjustment' of Asian economies, of physical location in relation to urban centres of modernisation, and the like, are markedly present in the contrasting studies in this book. This is particularly noticeable in relation to one of the most contentious and difficult topics in this book, the association between birth pollution and the low status of *dais* (TBAs) in North India and Bangladesh.

Birth pollution and the low status of birth attendants

In the societies of North India and Bangladesh, the birth attendant is often a woman from a low (lit., 'untouchable') subcaste or from an equivalent Muslim background, generally referred to as *dai*.[11] A series of studies from North India (Jeffery, Jeffery and Lyon 1985, 1989, and Chapter 4 this volume; Jeffery and Jeffery 1993) and Bangladesh (Blanchet 1984; Rozario 1995a, 1995b, 1998) have argued that the low status of the *dai* is connected with how her function is understood by the local community. These studies have suggested that villagers view the *dai* as a low-status menial whose role is as much that of cleansing the 'pollution' associated with birth as of helping in the delivery, and that this ideology surrounding the *dai* makes it unlikely that she could be effectively incorporated into a WHO-style scheme for upgrading 'traditional birth attendants' through retraining. They have also suggested that many present-day *dais* do not in fact have high levels of skills. Rather than representing a sophisticated indigenous tradition of midwifery passed down through women over the centuries, many *dais* are largely self-taught.

Other writers have stressed that *dais* do have sophisticated knowledge, and have suggested that dismissive attitudes to the *dais* by the medical establishment and by Western writers are a reflection of the biomedical discourse of modernity (e.g. Chawla 1993, 1994, and Chapter 7 this volume; Ram 2001; Van Hollen Chapter 8 this volume).

The issues here are complex and not easily unravelled. The *dais* in Jeffery et al.'s studies, located in Bijnor District, Uttar Pradesh, are, with a few exceptions (see Chapter 4), impoverished women from 'untouchable' Hindu castes or similar Muslim backgrounds, who undertook this work through lack of other ways of earning an income. The limited knowledge possessed by most of these *dais*, and the low esteem they are held in by the community, may, as Jeffery et al. comment (see Chapter 4), be a product of recent structural changes in the economy.

In addition, the term *dai* itself has led to some confusion. Not all birth attendants in North India or Bangladesh are referred to as *dai*, nor are they all from low-caste backgrounds. Thus, Patel, speaking of Rajasthan, comments as follows:

> Child delivery is usually conducted by some elderly women relatives or neighbours who have the knowledge and prior experience of handling births. A *dai* is also called. The attendants and the *dai* together manage the delivery. The *dai* is rarely considered to be such an expert that her every advice has to be followed.
>
> (Patel 1994: 111)

Unnithan, again speaking of Rajasthan, similarly notes that Nagori Sunni births in Rajasthan are 'usually attended by two kinds of "midwives" – midwives who are kin, and lower Hindu caste midwives' (Chapter 5 this volume). Unnithan notes that only the lower-caste midwives are referred to as *dai*, but also says that both kinds of midwife describe their work as *dai ka kaam*, which she glosses as 'the work of the midwife'. She comments that knowledge about birthing is not regarded as specialist knowledge, but is widely distributed throughout the community. The low status of the *dai* (i.e. lower-caste midwife) reflects this, but also reflects villagers' perception of her knowledge as limited and incomplete in comparison with medically trained women gynaecologists or religious healers (Chapter 5).

Rozario, working in rural Bangladesh, found impoverished, low-status birth attendants similar to those described by Jeffery et al., and originating from Muslim and Christian as well as low-caste Hindu backgrounds. In the villages in Dhaka district where she carried out most of her research, they were usually referred to as *dai,* but in a study of childbirth in Noakhali, in southern Bangladesh, she found that local women, including the birth attendants themselves, use alternative terms such as *dhatri* and *dhoruni*. Here the term *dai* is avoided, because it is associated with the particularly despised task of cutting the cord (Rozario 1995a: 92–3). In North India, however, *dais* do not necessarily cut the cord, a task which, as in Bangladesh, may be left to the mother herself (Chapter 5 this volume).[12] In a study of a caste Hindu community from Western Nepal by Mary Cameron we again find a lower-caste midwife (Cameron does not use the term *dai*), assisted by the birthing woman's mother-in-law (Cameron 1998: 257–61). This midwife is clearly a skilled person whose expertise is recognised by the other women present; Cameron notes that she 'control[s] the entire event' (1998: 259). Again, the birthing woman is made to cut the cord herself (1998: 260).

As Cecilia Van Hollen notes in Chapter 8 of this volume, the image of the *dai* as a 'highly stigmatised low-caste, filthy, vermin-ridden women whose main function [is] to deal with the "pollution" of childbirth' has a long history in British colonial health policy. There seems little doubt that it also corresponds to a significant strand in indigenous South Asian discourses concerning childbirth, at least in the northern part of the subcontinent. We should be wary nevertheless of taking this dismissive discourse at face value. As I have noted above, it is one of a number of discourses, and by no means always the dominant one. Thus, studies from South India and Sri Lanka, including Van Hollen's own work (Chapter 8 this volume)[13] and that of Kalpana Ram (1988a, 1988b, 2001), Inge Hutter (1994) and Daya de Silva (1997) consistently point to a more positive conception of the indigenous birth practitioner.[14] The same is true for the Newars of Nepal (Chapters 2 and 3 this volume).

Yet the negative discourse about the *dai* is real – and influential. *Dais* in North India and Bangladesh may in fact have significant expertise in childbirth (Anand 1994; Chawla 1993, 1994, and Chapter 7 this volume; Patel 1994; Radhika and Balasubramaniam 1990; Rozario Chapter 6 this volume). Their knowledge, however, is not necessarily respected or regarded as authoritative, and their role in relation to 'pollution' remains in many ways definitive of their status.

Certainly 'pollution' is a major concern in North India and Bangladesh, and is associated with the risk of attack by malevolent spirits. For high-caste Hindu families, birth is a problematic and difficult situation, and one which threatens the purity and integrity of the high-caste household. The involvement of the untouchable *dai* at the moment of birth seems to symbolise and underline these concerns (Cameron 1998: 261). Much the same is true in the Muslim society of Bangladesh. Here, the former Hindu subcaste from which the *dais* came has largely vanished in the post-Partition population movements, but pollution concerns are extremely significant, and the women who act as birth attendants, whether called *dai* or by other names, still come from the lowest social strata (Blanchet 1984; Rozario 1995a, 1995b, 1998, see also Chapter 6 this volume).

Modern developments in health policy, abetted in part by the residual effects of British colonial attitudes such as those referred to by Van Hollen, have undoubtedly worsened the situation of the *dais*. As Ram has noted, following Shetty (1994), this has not simply been a question of a male-dominated medical profession dismissing the expertise of traditional female healers. The campaign against traditional birth practices was initially promoted largely by white women doctors, and was enthusiastically adopted by early Indian female medical graduates. These attitudes 'continue to shape contemporary discourses on the *dai*' (Ram 2001: 67). While most childbirths in North India and Bangladesh are still today home births attended by the *dai* and/or the mother's female relatives rather than by biomedically trained personnel, the *dais*' position in relation to the new biomedical technology is weak and threatened, and such knowledge as they have is increasingly devalued. Attempts to integrate them into the biomedical system have been largely unsuccessful (see Chapter 6 this volume).

In studies from South India and Sri Lanka, as noted above, there are strong indications that traditional birth attendants (generally not called *dai*) are more highly valued. Pollution appears to be a less overriding concern, and its removal is not necessarily the function of the traditional birth attendant. In addition, while some traditional birth attendants come from 'untouchable' castes (e.g. Viramma, Racine and Racine 1997, McGilvray 1982: 57), others do not (Hutter 1994: 182; de Silva 1997: 18–19, 21), and the connection with the 'polluting' role of cleaning up is also often absent.

In place of the dominance of the discourse of pollution and danger, the most characteristic theme in South India and Sri Lanka is diet. While diet is an important theme in North India and Bangladesh, the emphasis is mostly on food restrictions, especially after birth (e.g. Jeffery, Jeffery and Lyon 1989: 128–30; Rozario 1998: 154–6). Thus, in handling childbirth, South Indian societies seem to be as much or more concerned with maintaining and strengthening the health of mother and child through appropriate diet as with managing 'pollution' (e.g. Chapter 8, also Hutter 1994: 149–93; Ram 1998a, 2001; de Silva 1997: 188–200). Although these dietary concerns are phrased in terms of the humoral discourse mentioned before, which can be found throughout South and Southeast Asia, the emphasis on them in South India and Sri Lanka seems to reflect a generally stronger emphasis on diet in this region (e.g. Nichter 2001).[15]

The contrast between both dominant discourses and practices in North and South India, however, also makes some sense in terms of the well-known contrasts in kinship and family structure between the northern and southern parts of South Asia (Trautmann 1981; Kapadia 1995) and the generally more positive attitude to women and to female sexuality in South India and Sri Lanka. Thus, a girl's first menstruation among most South Indian communities (including parts of Orissa) is celebrated through public ritual, and while removal of pollution may be part of the ritual, there is also a positive endorsement of the girl's future role as a fertile woman (see Kapadia 1995: 92–123; Lincoln 1991: 7–16; Apffel-Marglin 1994; Good 1991; Ram n.d.). In

North India and Bangladesh, menarche is neither marked by public ritual nor otherwise treated as an occasion for celebration.

While this overall contrast between North India (including Bangladesh and parts at least of lowland Nepal) and South India (with Sri Lanka) seems to have some validity,[16] not all South Asian societies fit neatly into this opposition. The unusually high status of women among the Newar people of the Kathmandu valley (see Chapters 2 and 3) has been noted elsewhere, although its meaning is subject to dispute (see Gellner 1991). Perhaps it helps to explain the respected role for female healers (*dya: māju*), seen as mediums for the goddess Hāritī, described in Chapter 3. Women who heal as 'vessels' for the deity are not unknown elsewhere in South Asia (e.g. Stanley 1988; Wadley 1980), but the *dya: māju*'s combination of spirit-mediumship with Tantric ritual expertise and a general healing role is less usual. Possibly it reflects older patterns which have been more thoroughly marginalised in other parts of the subcontinent.

Such local patterns, as Arjun Appadurai has recently stressed, are best understood in terms of historical processes rather than permanent traits:

> [W]e need an architecture for area studies which . . . sees significant areas of human organization as precipitates of various kinds of action, interaction and motion – trade, travel, pilgrimage, warfare, proselytization, colonization, exile and the like. These geographies are necessarily large-scale and shifting, and their changes highlight variable congeries of language, history and material life . . . Regions are best viewed as initial contexts for themes that generate variable geographies, rather than as fixed geographies marked by pre-given themes. These themes are equally 'real,' equally coherent, but are results of our interests and not their causes.
>
> (Appadurai 1999: 232)

Appadurai's remarks apply forcibly to such highly provisional entities as 'North India' and 'South India' (and for that matter 'South Asia' and 'Southeast Asia'). We hope that the collection of studies presented in this book, with their many underlying strands of 'action, interaction and motion', will provide stimulating material for rethinking regional contrasts along other lines. In particular, the common experience of the impact of modernity and the transition to biomedicine has marked all of the studies in this book, and provides a theme which, while affected by national and sub-national health policies, cuts across all of the conventional boundaries of these regions. The next section discusses this transition in more detail.

The transition to biomedicine

The question of the adoption of biomedical approaches is critical for almost all the studies in this book, and it is worth considering what it might imply. On the face of it, there is a dramatic difference between a world in which

Table 1.1 Figures from World Health Organisation poster

	Lifetime risk of maternal death (1 in)	Perinatal deaths per 1,000 births	Skilled attendant at delivery (%)
Sri Lanka	230	25	94
Thailand	180	20	71
India	37	65	35
Bangladesh	21	85	14
Nepal	10	75	8

Source: World Health Organisation 1997.[17]

childbirth is dominated by concerns with supernatural pollution, spirit affliction and humoral medicine, and one where it is conceived in terms of biomedicine. The contrast between the childbirth mortality and morbidity rates for mothers and for children between countries and regions where biomedicine has been widely adopted (Sri Lanka, Thailand) and those where it has not (Bangladesh, Nepal) provides a very strong and compelling argument for the value of biomedicine. Consider Table 1.1, which shows the figures from a WHO poster, the text of which implies a direct correlation between the presence of a (biomedically) skilled attendant at delivery, the lifetime risk of maternal death and the perinatal death rate (stillbirths and infants in the first week of life).

While the accuracy of statistics such as these is often questionable, the overall contrast shown in Table 1.1 is doubtless valid enough. The strength of the implied causal relationship, between the presence of the biomedically trained attendant and the lower risks of mother and infant death, may still be questioned. As mentioned above, it is not always easy to separate out the effects of biomedical health care from other factors, such as general improvements in nutrition or sanitation.

In addition, not all elements of the traditional situation are negative. The transition to biomedical approaches involves loss as well as gain. Many authors have argued for the traditional skills and supportive atmosphere of the indigenous approach to childbirth (Vincent-Priya 1991, 1992; Anand 1994; Chawla 1993, 1994; Patel 1994; Radhika and Balasubramaniam 1990, and see Chapters 3, 7, 8, 11 and 12 in this volume). In the Western context, and especially the United States, there has been an extensive literature criticising the over-medicalisation of childbirth (e.g. Martin 1987; Raymond 1993; Diamond 1994), and widespread moves to counter these developments and to move to more woman-friendly approaches. As noted earlier, this critique has barely begun to make inroads into South and Southeast Asia, but viewing the dehumanising and objectifying nature of obstetric care in many hospitals in the region, it is arguable that many of the worst features of Western childbirth practices are being replicated in Asia.

How similar are the social and cultural processes which generated modern childbirth practices in Western societies and those which South and Southeast Asian societies have been undergoing in more recent times? Here, in addition to the critical literature on the extreme medicalisation of childbirth referred to above, we might consider the debate about the transition in Europe and North America from midwives to biomedical personnel (Merchant 1980; Ehrenreich and English 1973; Achterberg 1990; Harley 1990; Purkiss 1996). The issues are complex, and much basic research still needs to be done. Clearly, there were several different aspects to the transition in Europe and North America, as there are in contemporary South and Southeast Asia. Among these we can distinguish:

- the adoption of biomedical techniques and approaches itself;
- the shift in the locus of decision making from the family to health professionals;
- the relocation of birth from home to hospital or clinic;
- the management of the birthing process in ways that suit the requirements of biomedical procedures and biomedical ideology;
- the marginalisation or exclusion of traditional midwives, birth attendants and other female healers.

Underlying these, both historically in the West and today in Asia, are a series of complex economic, political and social agendas, including negotiations concerning the role of women in society, attempts to impose scientific rationality and economic 'efficiency', and the need for professional organisations (including doctors and medically trained midwives) to create and maintain areas of expertise and control.

These processes have been accomplished to differing degrees and in different ways in various Western countries, with some health systems (e.g. the UK or Netherlands) retaining a significant place for biomedically trained midwives, while others (e.g. much of the USA) have been much less tolerant towards them. 'Healthy' birthing practices have often come at the price of radical disempowerment and dehumanisation for birthing mothers, but this does not necessarily have to be the case. Western societies themselves have arrived at a wide range of solutions, and the extreme medicalisation of much of the US system is neither universal nor uncontested.

Modern South and Southeast Asia too presents a variety of local histories and developments, as the studies in this book demonstrate. It is important to recognise this variety of local situations, especially as there is still the possibility in many parts of South and Southeast Asia of avoiding some of the worst problems of the Western transition.

It might be hoped that the WHO's policy of giving biomedical training to traditional birth attendants and retaining them as part of the health system, at least as part of a transitional arrangement, would offer opportunities to counter the uncritical dominance of biomedical discourse. While the WHO policy was adopted primarily for the pragmatic reason that there were insufficient biomedical personnel to impose an immediate transition to biomedical birthing, it has provided an officially sanctioned space in which old and new practices might interact and inform each other.

In reality, it is all too clear from the studies in this book that the interaction does not take place on equal terms. The biomedical approach dominates throughout. Retrained traditional birth attendants are seen by health authorities as at best a temporary expedient. Training programmes vary from a few days of workshops to more substantial courses, but few trainers recognise that many of the women they are 'training' may already have a very substantial body of knowledge and experience (see Chapter 7). Nevertheless, as the studies here show, the WHO policy has resulted in a variety of quite different situations 'on the ground', depending on how it has been implemented locally as well as on local social, cultural and economic factors.

We can usefully distinguish between two aspects of the biomedical transition: the effects of national policy, including international health agencies such as the WHO and in many cases also local and international non-governmental organisations (NGOs), and the extent to which local populations are themselves actively seeking out biomedical alternatives.

South and Southeast Asian states vary considerably both in the material resources available to them and in the extent to which they have been politically willing to take on an actively interventionist role in health care. Governments such as Malaysia or Indonesia have been at the interventionist end of the policy spectrum; others, such as Bangladesh or Nepal, are much less so. The actual provision of biomedical facilities can also vary greatly. Large towns and cities throughout the region have public hospitals, and many of these institutions are in theory at least available for free or at nominal charge to poor urban and rural families, but the facilities can range from the excellent to the truly appalling. While some facilities are genuinely free, others may not be. 'Unofficial' charges levied by underpaid medical and nursing personnel may mean, as in much of rural Bangladesh, that the hospital system is barely available in practice to poorer families (see Rozario 1995b; Leppard 1997).

As noted earlier, the cultural distance between city-trained hospital staff and rural families may be vast, and can manifest as rudeness and hostility to village people and unwillingness to accommodate their concerns, a theme which appears in one form or another in almost every study in this book. Dealing with the local hospital staff can be a difficult and frustrating experience, particularly when there is also a significant language or dialect barrier involved. In addition, where communities are at some distance from the nearest hospital, the hidden costs involved in transport to and from the hospital and in making family members available to care for the patient while in hospital may be prohibitive (see Rozario 1995a, 1995b).

Private clinics and hospitals, run on a charitable or commercial basis, form an essential component of biomedical care in many regions. Some mission-run and other charitable facilities provide an excellent service and are genuinely available to the poorer sections of the community (e.g. Rozario 1995a). Often, though, private facilities offer a way for wealthier families to avoid low-quality public facilities. At the same time, the level of service offered by many of the smaller commercial clinics may also be very questionable.

All this means that the willingness of families to adopt biomedical practices for childbirth may depend in large part on pragmatic questions of accessibility and expense, as well as on more or less realistic judgments of the quality of health care provided. Cultural factors such as the attitude of hospital staff and their unwillingness to cater to local concerns (for example regarding 'shame' or privacy) can also be major barriers. However, the message that clinic and hospital births are safer has been very effectively propagated in many parts of South and Southeast Asia, and this in itself means that many families will use them if they can. In addition, the prestige and status attached to 'modernity' in all its forms in many communities may have the effect of encouraging the adoption of biomedical practices, particularly among more prosperous and 'modern' families (see Chapter 13 for one example), irrespective of their actual value.[18] The desire to determine the sex of children in South Asian societies has also led to pressure for greater biomedical intervention, understandable in a society where having female rather than male children may have dramatic financial consequences for the family concerned.

Overall, while we can speak in a very broad sense of a continuum between populations where medicalisation is more advanced and those where it is less so, this would override many of the significant differences between these societies. In practice, issues of physical access and expense, of the quality of the biomedical alternative as locally provided, of the attitude and behaviour of biomedical staff, of education, and of access to education, of the political and religious relationship between indigenous groups and the governments of nation-states, of modes of resource allocation in poor rural families, may play as large a part as the actual availability of biomedical technology.

In addition, biomedical intervention does not necessarily involve using hospital services. The use of oxytocin injections to speed up childbirth, for example, has been widely adopted in many communities where childbirth still regularly takes place at home. Biomedicine is present in South and Southeast Asia in numerous forms from large state and private hospitals through to local village practitioners, with facilities and equipment from the most sophisticated international standards to the very basic, and it is delivered with a wide range of levels of competence. However, the effect of biomedicine in specific societies in South and Southeast Asia depends not only on material and economic factors such as the actual presence and affordability of biomedical facilities but also, in many cases quite critically, on the way in which the society views and understands the whole birthing process.

Here, the various forms of discourse referred to above are a critical component, and we can see a wide contrast between South and Southeast Asia (with the Tibetans of Chapter 9 being, in this context, closer to the Southeast Asian pattern). Thus, looking at the studies from North India and Bangladesh, there seems little doubt that the emphasis on pollution and the associated negative attitudes to the birthing process helps to explain why there is little enthusiasm for hospital birth among the poor rural population (see Chapter 9 this volume). The WHO strategy of 'retraining' TBAs (i.e. *dais*) has little chance of success here, since the *dais* are by and large unable, as a result of their low social position, to act as a channel for the introduction of biomedical approaches (Stephens 1992). The negative attitudes to childbirth, however, pervade the biomedical system itself (Jeffery, Jeffery and Lyon 1989; Rozario 1995a; Leppard 1997), and it is these attitudes, as well as the cultural differences between urban doctors and village women, that underlie the frequently appalling behaviour of medical staff in the state hospital system towards birthing women. Doctors and biomedically trained nurses avoid direct physical contact with birthing mothers, leaving these polluting tasks to lower-status nurse aides and orderlies with limited biomedical training. There is often little attempt to achieve basic levels of hygiene within the hospital system.

Consequently, as Rozario and Leppard have shown (Rozario 1995a, 1995b; Leppard 1997), the selective incorporation of elements of biomedical practice does not mean that negative elements of 'traditional' attitudes and orientations disappear. Frequently, they are in fact reinforced by the negative orientations of urban elite doctors towards lower-class village women.

Another critical issue is the discourse on honour and shame referred to above. Male village household heads are reluctant to undergo the embarrassment and 'shame' of exposing their birthing women to the public context of the hospital and its mostly male medical personnel. The *dai* fits into the social norms of the village community, while the hospital rides roughshod over them.

While some of these features are found in South India too, they are more muted. The state of Kerala (in South India) and Sri Lanka provide the most dramatic examples in South Asia of the transition to the biomedical approach. Both have achieved impressive reductions in mortality and morbidity for mothers and children. It may be significant that these are regions where pollution issues are apparently less salient or have (in Kerala) been successfully countered through systematic political action. Sri Lanka and Kerala also have by far the highest levels of female education in the entire South Asian region. Women in these societies are in a much better position to understand the alternatives open to them in childbirth and to have a real influence on decisions as to which alternative is employed. Even so, it is unclear how far the much better health statistics for these areas result from access to 'better' hospital facilities and medical practices, and how far from better levels of female nutrition.[19]

In Southeast Asia, the transition to biomedical approaches is also a key theme. In Malaysia, Thailand and Indonesia the shift to biomedical approaches has not been universally welcomed, for reasons explored in Chapters 11, 12 and 13 among others, but it has gone much further than in most of South Asia. The WHO policy of retraining TBAs in biomedical techniques and approaches also seems to have been more productive than in South Asia (see Chapters 10, 11 and 12). It seems likely that the higher status of traditional midwives and birth attendants, and their greater authority within the community, are important factors here.

The studies in this book

It remains to survey the specific studies which make up the body of this book. Chapters 2 to 9 refer to field studies in South Asia (see Map 1.1). Chapters 2 and 3 are both located among the Newar people of the Kathmandu Valley in Nepal. The bulk of Chapter 2 is a transcript of Barbara Johnson's film of a Newar birth, *We Know How To Do These Things*. The film itself is available from Documentary Educational Resources, and is an excellent introduction to many of the issues surrounding birth in South and Southeast Asian societies.

We Know How To Do These Things presents a home birth, in which Jolmaya, a Newar woman giving birth, is assisted by a neighbour, Chirimaya, as midwife; the others present are close female relatives of Jolmaya. Chirimaya is not a low-status *dai*, but a member of the birthing woman's own Jyapu caste. Her advice is obviously valued and followed, although the other women in the situation are by no means just spectators. The role played by food, a theme in many later chapters, is noticeable here: Johnson comments in her introduction that 'much of the focus of the birth attendant and female relatives is on feeding the laboring woman', and she explains the role of the appropriate foods in managing the spiritual forces on which the birth depends. Chirimaya also organises and directs the ritual offering which is made to help the birth take place.

The conversation between the women at the birth brings up the question of hospital births. The women see biomedicine as appropriate in difficult cases, but the hospital is a problematic environment. Some of the nurses are 'screaming crazy women' and birthing women at the hospital have to conform to medical norms, including the extreme embarrassment of being undressed completely in a public place. Yet a neighbour at the end of the film comments, when the baby is being washed, that 'We people don't know much': at the hospital they would know how to wash the baby properly.

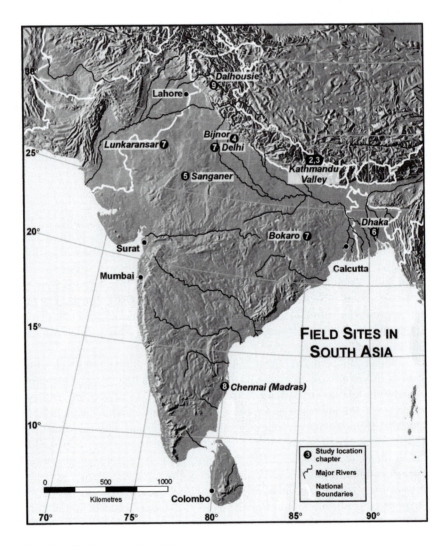

Map 1.1 Field sites in South Asia

Chapter 3, by Linda Iltis, is a study of the *dya: māju*, women healers who act as mediums for the Grandmother Goddess, Hāritī, also known as Ajimā ('Grandmother'), and who are particularly concerned with illnesses of children and with problems of fertility and childbirth. The *dya: māju* are not merely passive spirit-mediums, but Tantric ritual specialists, who may choose to take on this role voluntarily through Tantric initiation and study. Like the *balian* of Bali (Connor, Asch and Asch 1986), the *dya: māju* are ritual experts with a wide range of competence, and they allow their clients to undertake direct dialogue with the gods in order to resolve their problems. Iltis contrasts their 'inclusive, friendly' interaction with their clients with that of Western-trained Nepali doctors, who 'use the lowest of familiar forms in addressing . . . patients, and display one of the most exclusionary and ill-received styles of bedside manner I have seen'. She takes issue with earlier writers who have portrayed the *dya: māju* as 'peripheral', have marginalised Hāritī as a 'wild goddess' and dismissed female viewpoints as inevitably subordinate and 'subaltern':

> If cultures are changing and fluid . . . then the dualism of rigid, dominant power and authority and an essentially separate, subjugated and antithetical resistance should also be questioned . . . If we . . . attempt to see women as women see themselves, describe what they do and what they say, and work outwards from the subject of inquiry . . . we can begin . . . to solicit data that is less the product of external discourses, and more the voice of an experienced grandmother.
>
> (Chapter 3)

Chapters 4 to 7 are all located in North India and Bangladesh. Chapter 4 is a reprint of an article dating from 1987 by Patricia Jeffery, Roger Jeffery and Andrew Lyon, based on fieldwork in Bijnor District, Uttar Pradesh in 1982/3. It provides an important supplement to their well-known book (1989), focusing in much more detail on the women who act as *dais* and the effects of state policy since the nineteenth century on their role. In Chapter 4, Jeffery et al. suggest that '[s]hame and pollution are dominant features of childbirth in rural Bijnor' and that 'the role of village *dais . . .* is virtually limited to the removal of childbirth pollution'. Government *dai* training schemes, in their opinion, are unlikely to make much difference to maternal and child health.

While Jeffery et al.'s 1989 book has sometimes been taken as a reified and universalised account of *dais* as low-status, untrained menials, this was not their intention. In particular, it is important to note that there, as in the present volume, they were representing the views of the local community, not giving their own evaluation of the *dais'* expertise.[20] In Chapter 4, they stress specific factors underlying the situation in Bijnor during their fieldwork. They mention that government health workers such as the ANMs (auxiliary nurse midwives) were resented and mistrusted as a result of the sterilisation campaign during the Emergency (1975–1977) and of other government initiatives clearly aimed more at population limitation than at mother and child health, so destroying the viability of *dai* training schemes. They also speculate that the Green Revolution, which has worsened the situation of the poorest women by eliminating various other possible means of supplementing their incomes, may have propelled some of these women into the role of *dai*, and that the relative lack of knowledge of many of the Bijnor *dais* might reflect their recent recruitment to the role. These *desi dai* (village *dais*) do not, with occasional exceptions, come from family backgrounds with a tradition of midwifery and other medical practice. By their own account, they mostly acquired their skills through witnessing several deliveries. However, even in Bijnor, as Jeffery et al. note, there are some *dais* (referred to as *hoshiyar dai*, 'intelligent *dai*' by contrast to the *desi dai* or 'village *dai*'), whom local people regard as having more ability and knowledge.

Chapter 5, by Maya Unnithan, is also based on fieldwork in Rajasthan, here mostly with Muslim women in villages near Jaipur city, and again focuses on questions of indigenous knowledge. Unnithan gives a detailed description of the birth of the ninth child of a 35-year-old woman, Jetoon, attended by two 'kin midwives' and one 'lower-caste midwife' (i.e. *dai*). That three 'midwives'[21] were present reflects the mother's fears that this would be a difficult birth. Each of the midwives regularly attends births on her own, but in this case they have complementary roles, with the lower-caste midwife massaging and stretching the vaginal opening and helping the baby to emerge, under the general direction of the senior kin-midwife.

Unnithan stresses that much of the knowledge regarding female health and childbirth is widely shared within the community. Midwives are consulted for some kinds of reproductive illness, but so are religious healers (men possessed by healing spirits) and private women gynaecologists, both of whom are regarded, unlike the *dais*, as having a specialist competence. Village women used the services of the private gynaecologists as a way of spacing children through abortion. Although Unnithan's work was carried out about fifteen years after Jeffery et al.'s research, and some twenty years after the Emergency and the forced sterilisation campaign, distrust of government health workers was still an issue, and villagers consulted the ANMs neither for contraception nor for midwifery services.[22]

Unnithan emphasises the importance of the mostly kin-based support networks between women in determining why women seek particular kinds of health care. She agrees with Jeffery et al., Rozario and others that the *dais* are not in a position to transform maternal morbidity and infant mortality by themselves. She suggests that 'an extension of delivery facilities and antenatal and postnatal care at the level of the primary health centre' might be one way to improve the situation by providing a context where gynaecologists could work together with lower-caste and kin midwives 'so as to be socially connected with their patients while at the same time providing inexpensive, yet expert services'.

In Chapter 6, Santi Rozario looks at the predicament of the *dais* in rural Bangladesh, using field material from her research in villages in Dhaka district. Most births in rural Bangladesh still take place at home, and the government has neither the resources nor the political will to bring about a massive shift to biomedical birthing practices. However, the *dais*, already undervalued in the 'traditional' system through their association with the pollution of childbirth, are now further devalued both morally and economically by the increasing presence of biomedicine. For the *dais* themselves, mostly poor and uneducated women who are heavily reliant on the limited income they gain through their practice, the situation is increasingly difficult, since clients today may refuse even the small traditional payments associated with the work. Rozario examines how they cope with this constant denigration of their skills and status through an assertion of their professional expertise, and of the charitable and spiritually sanctioned nature of their work.

If Jeffery et al. are right about the specific historical situation underlying the low level of knowledge of most Bijnor *dais*, we might expect that *dais* elsewhere may have more knowledge and more skills. Chapter 7, by Janet Chawla, argues that some *dai*, at least, are part of a genuine tradition of ethno-medical knowledge and practice. Chawla accepts the 'subaltern' label rejected by Iltis, but her position is in fact close to Iltis's, in that both seek to present indigenous female health specialists as possessing genuine knowledge and skills which have been ignored and marginalised by biomedicine and Western academic knowledge. Chawla and her MATRIKA group organised a series of workshops with *dai* in three parts of North India (Bokaro Dist., Bihar; Lunkaransar in Bikaner Dist., Rajasthan; and slum areas of Delhi) with a view to documenting and understanding their knowledge. Chawla's sensitive account deciphers the sophisticated imagery used by *dais* to describe the processes of birth, stressing that the imagery needs to be seen in holistic terms; it refers to energy and sensation at least as much as to anatomy and physiology. She also suggests that 'pollution' language should not be taken at face value: 'ritual uncleanness is the language of Brahmanic sacerdotal and textual tradition [while] women's work of birth involves different forms of sacrality and ethno-medical rite and practice'. Women use the term *narak* (usually glossed as 'hell' or 'filth') in relation to both the post-partum period and the lower part of the body, but *narak* here refers to the 'fertility or fruitful potential of the earth and the female body' and does not have the pejorative associations of its Brahmanical usage.

In Chapter 8, Cecilia Van Hollen describes the conflict between 'traditional' and 'scientific' approaches at a hospital in Madras (Chennai) in South India. For the medical officer at the hospital, as for so many others, '[t]he women who come here are mostly illiterates, you see. So they don't know what is best for them.' Van Hollen describes the hospital and the medicalisation of childbirth more generally as part of the apparatus of 'development'. Childbirth is both a context in which 'modern subjects' should be fashioned, but also the location of a discourse which local people must choose to collude with, resist or otherwise manoeuvre their way around. Indigenous humorally derived notions of how to care for the newborn child and its mother are dismissed and overridden in the name of modern biomedical knowledge.

Van Hollen notes the irony of this situation. Indigenous approaches to matters such as diet, based on oppositions between 'hot' and 'cold', 'wet' and 'dry' foods, are applied in a flexible and experimental way. By contrast, biomedical injunctions, at any rate as presented by the MCH (Mother and Child Health) development workers, are almost entirely lacking in self-criticism regarding their knowledge claims. Here she cites Nandy and Visvanathan's suggestion that modern medicine was 'the first major system of healing to try to do away with this element of scepticism and self-criticism' (Nandy and Visvanathan 1990: 147).

In the South Asian context, currently endorsed biomedical norms (for example, long-term breastfeeding rather than infant formula, however impractical in the mother's actual circumstances, or policies on washing the baby after birth) become a factor in the power relations inherent in the development process as a whole. Mothers who fail to conform are accused of immoral behaviour. They are not doing what is unquestionably best for their child.

Some women have the class and caste status to resist this discourse and interact with the hospital staff on their own terms. In one of Van Hollen's examples, a middle-class Brahmin mother accused of stunting the development of her child's 'brain cells' by depriving her of bananas and other 'cold' foods during her first three years refuses to be intimidated. Her daughter is doing very well in her studies at an English medium school and clearly has not suffered from her early diet! However, Van Hollen suggests that 'many lower class women in Tamil Nadu may not use government allopathic MCH services . . . in part because of the forms of condescension, blame, and discrimination which they experience'.

Chapter 9, by Santi Rozario and myself, takes up some of the issues regarding North Indian concepts of 'pollution' in a cross-cultural context. The chapter discusses a hospital birth which took place in the Tibetan refugee community in Northern India during our fieldwork there in 1996. Our observations, and the general literature on Tibetan societies, points to the importance of an indigenous concept, *drip*, which might be rendered as 'pollution'. There is certainly *drip* associated with childbirth, but how does this 'pollution' compare with the childbirth pollution of North India or Bangladesh? For that matter, how does the 'pollution' of childbirth in North India relate to the principle of purity and pollution which form the ideological basis of the Hindu caste system? How do South Asian societies resolve the conflict between the negative associations of childbirth pollution (the 'worst of all kinds of pollution' according to some writers) and the very positive value attached to fertility and the birth of children?

The chapter suggests that Tibetan and North Indian-Bangladeshi cultures both see 'pollution' or 'impurity' as an everyday part of human existence, but that they situate it differently. For the Tibetans, pollution is primarily an intrusion from outside the social world, to be avoided as far as possible and ritually countered where unavoidable. Birth pollution is part of this pattern, with childbirth itself an event that is placed as far as possible outside the social world, but birth pollution is not otherwise particularly problematic. Within North Indian and Bangladeshi discourse about pollution, however, pollution is central to the social world, above all through its association with biological process. Birth pollution is its most extreme form

> For Hindu India (and the same is essentially true for Muslim India and Bangladesh as well), impurity is not something at the edge of society, but something which is right at its centre, in the intrinsic identity of women, their polluted and fertile nature, without which human life could not continue.
>
> (Chapter 9)

It is the working out of this tension within Brahmanical discourse which led to the devaluation of the *dais* and other 'lower-caste' members of Hindu society, a devaluation which has been taken over and rephrased in other forms by North Indian and Bangladeshi Muslims and by contemporary elite groups.

The remaining four chapters are based on field research in Southeast Asia (Map 1.2). Andrea Whittaker's study of birth attendants in a village in Northeast Thailand (Chapter 10), describes a community where most births now take place in hospital. Women, however, remain ambivalent about the unfriendly and alienating way they are treated in the hospital, the low level of personal care provided, and the lack of co-operation with local practices, such as those regarding the disposal of the placenta. Two remaining traditional birth attendants (*mor tam yae*) in the community continue to deliver a substantial proportion of local births, in part because local women value the close nurturing relationship which forms part of the traditional birthing situation. However, hospitals are perceived to offer safer births, and most women use them for this reason, even though they dislike the way they are treated there.

Whittaker notes the importance of the post-partum period as a time when traditional practices are still extensively employed. As in much of Southeast and South Asia, this is a time of danger and vulnerability for mother and child, countered both by ritual precautions and by such humorally derived practices as heating the mother by a fire (*yuu kam*). Several *mor tam yae* who no longer deliver children still help women with these post-partum practices.

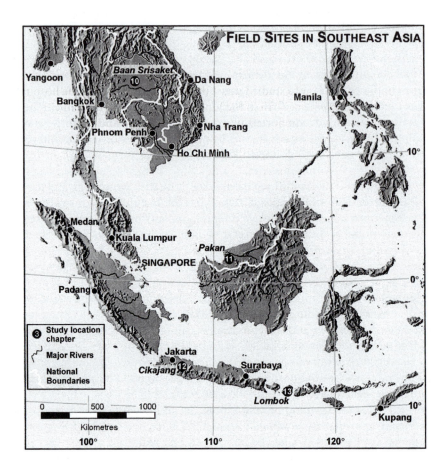

Map 1.2 Field sites in Southeast Asia

Amanda Harris's study of childbirth and traditional healing practices among rural Iban women in Sarawak, Malaysia (Chapter 11) has parallels to Whittaker's. A system of government clinics and hospitals has made biomedical approaches available to the villagers, and there is strong government pressure for births to take place in these facilities, which are staffed by government-trained midwives and doctors. If a birth takes place at home, the parents may not be able to secure a birth certificate for the child, who will then have difficulty obtaining the identity card needed for employment. Almost all births in the village Harris studied now take place at the clinic or the hospital.

Yet the transition from birth in the longhouse to birth in the clinic or hospital, however heavily supported by government policy and rhetoric, is not unproblematic. Harris's study focuses on conversations about birthing among Iban women, and subtly draws out the changing understandings of the body and of childbirth within this community. Many women see the past as a time of greater health. They still regard the traditional longhouse as a place of safety and security and the ideal location for childbirth, and want to keep traditional practices, such as *bekindu'*, the local version of the post-partum 'heating' of the mother. The clinic and hospital are uncomfortable and threatening locations where the birthing woman is isolated from her kin and subjected to episiotomies, injections to bring on contractions, and other unwelcome and weakening technological interventions. Modernity provides opportunities for outside employment for village men, but biomedical discourse tends to recreate village women as an 'ailing collectivity' subject to progressive limitation and increased debility.

Elsewhere, however, at a 'model' Iban longhouse that has received exceptional benefit from development and modernity, with easy access by road to clinic and hospital, women are more enthusiastic about biomedical birthing, and more negative about birth in the longhouse.

Lynda Newland's study of traditional village midwives (*paraji*) and biomedically trained midwives (*bidan*) among the Sundanese people of West Java, Indonesia (Chapter 12), again describes a society with high levels of government intervention, much of it concerned primarily with reducing population growth through contraception. West Java is one of the most 'developed' parts of Indonesia, but there has been only limited adoption of biomedical approaches to childbirth. The traditional midwives (*paraji*) are older women who have themselves had many children, and are integral members of the village community. Their practice emphasises ritual, divine sanction and defence against the *kuntilanak* (ghosts of women who have died in pregnancy). By contrast, the newly introduced medical midwives (*bidan*) are mostly young women, often unmarried and from outside the village, and they employ a highly medicalised and objectifying discourse and practice. While some younger village women use the *bidan*, whom they see as more modern and efficient, for their childbirths, others actively avoid involvement with the Government's health apparatus, and at least 80 per cent of births are still carried out by the *paraji*.

Newland suggests that the *bidan*, who charge for their services at a fixed rate, belong to the logic of commerce, while the *paraji*, with their close connections to the religious and mystical, are part of a less formal and more fluid realm of transactions with a deep basis in the village community. While the *paraji* are required to undergo biomedical training and are supposed to co-operate with the *bidan*, they are not always impressed by the *bidan*'s competence and emphasise the superiority of their own approach. The two forms of knowledge associated with the two types of practitioners also reflect 'different priorities accorded to mother and child': the *bidan* is primarily concerned with the baby, while the *paraji* emphasises the post-partum care of the mother through massage and herbal treatment.

The Indonesian rural health system is based on the *puskesmas* or community health centres; in Java and Bali in 1974, one *puskesmas* existed for each 40,000 inhabitants. An outreach programme, the *posyandu* (Integrated Service Post), begun in 1984, involves sending *puskesmas* staff out into the villages to deliver services such as vaccinations, baby weighing, and the checking of pregnancies.[23] Newland notes how the *posyandu* provides greater biomedical assistance, but also subjects village women to the 'medical gaze' of the national health bureaucracy. Forms of biomedical intervention, such as oxytocin injections to speed up labour, are becoming widely adopted, but undermine village conceptions of pregnancy and childbirth as 'natural and expected processes' which should not need biomedical intervention.

Cynthia Hunter's field location among the Sasak people of Lombok, also in Indonesia (Chapter 13, see also Hunter 1996, Grace 1996), has some similarities to Newland's, but in this relatively remote community, few of the indigenous midwives (*belian ranak*) have received clinic training, and the government-trained medical midwives at the village level (*bidan desa*) have yet to establish themselves as a real alternative. Here childbirth is still viewed as 'a natural, if dangerous process . . . it is a time to be safe amongst family members, sympathetic friends and trusted healers who will guide the woman through the birthing process.' In the Sasak village, it is only wives of wealthy, upwardly mobile families who desire to be seen as 'modern' who are likely to opt for a *bidan* birth, let alone for confinement at the relatively distant *puskesmas* clinic under the care of the *puskesmas bidan*, a biomedically trained nurse with midwifery qualifications. The case study on which Hunter's chapter is based is a study of one such *puskesmas* birth, that of the seventh child of Inaq Kariati, the 42-year-old wife of a retired government bureaucrat and minor aristocrat with 'reformist' ideas. The clinic birth in Hunter's description is a largely successful compromise between Sasak *adat* (customary practice) and the biomedical approach, in part because the *puskesmas* and its nurse-midwife, herself a Sasak woman, are prepared to accommodate to the family's ritual and other requirements. At the same time, while a clinic birth made sense for Inaq Kariati and her family, it is unlikely to be an option for most Sasak village births in the foreseeable future.

Conclusion

Overall, the studies included in this volume provide a much more comprehensive view of childbirth in South Asia than has previously been available, and add significantly to the previously available studies for Southeast Asia.[24] They range from situations that could be regarded in general as successes for biomedicine, if qualified in some respects (e.g. Chapter 10) to others where the biomedical promise of safe birthing is still far from being effectively delivered (e.g. Chapters 5 and 6). In between, we find a variety of partial incorporations of biomedical approaches, with communities often caught between supportive and culturally appropriate traditional approaches and potentially safer, but also often alienating, objectifying and culturally inappropriate biomedical alternatives. However, as we have stressed above, 'traditional' practices throughout the region also vary greatly, and need to be understood also in terms of the general conceptions of gender and the body within specific societies.

The importance of childbirth practices in relation to the ongoing health of South and Southeast Asian women can hardly be overemphasised, yet if the studies in this book convey any single message it is the need for the policies of governments, NGOs and other instrumentalities concerned with health issues to understand, respect and work creatively with the very specific needs and situations of the individual communities they are attempting to assist. This involves a readiness to investigate the particular practical and economic factors, such as 'unofficial' fees and expenses, which may (as in much of rural Bangladesh and North India), make supposedly free systems in fact unavailable to those most in need. It also requires a commitment to transform the alienating, hostile and demeaning nature of birth practices in public hospitals and clinics in many parts of the region, and a willingness to co-operate with local culturally perceived needs for traditional practices. As many of our studies demonstrate, these practices are not just a question of 'ritual' narrowly conceived, but typically form part of a wider nurturant relationship, often beginning well before the actual birth and extending long into the postpartum period, which plays an essential part in the physical and psychological well-being of the birthing woman.

There is no doubt that women and their families throughout South and Southeast Asia are concerned about the safety of birth, and that many are prepared to adopt elements of biomedicine if this can lead to a safer delivery. There is little doubt too that some aspects of biomedical practice can and do make a real difference to the ability of Third World women to give birth safely to healthy children. However, the effective delivery of these aspects of biomedical practice is often open to question. Even a limited involvement with the international health aid scene demonstrates the irrelevance of much of what does take place to the needs of many of the poor, frequently undernourished, rural peasant or urban slum-dwelling women who are most at risk during childbirth. In addition, the entanglement of childbirth policy with population control has dominated much of what has happened in recent years. Health policy in many South and Southeast Asian societies cannot be considered independently of the whole process of 'development', with MCH (mother and child health) initiatives often motivated as much by the need to maintain the flow of development funds and to meet international pressure for population control as by a genuine commitment to improve the health situation for birthing women and their children. Here the provision of health care is subject to many of the criticisms which have been developed in recent years in regard to the development process as a whole (e.g. Rahnema 1997).

This complex area is nevertheless of critical importance to the health and well-being of many hundreds of millions of women and their children, and we hope that the studies in this collection will provide the reader both with a much more extensive and comprehensive view of the field than has so far been available, and with a basis of understanding from which more satisfactory and adequate approaches might be developed.

Notes

1 Hundreds of images identified as Hāritī, often alongside her consort Pāñcika, whose iconography overlaps with that of Kubera, god of wealth, have been found in sites from these periods (e.g. Zwalf 1996: I, 44, 48 n. 125, 116ff., pl. 3; Czuma 1985: 156–8, 162–3; Panikkar 1997: 31–53 and pls 12 to 14).
2 The term 'biomedicine' is used here to refer to the modern Western-derived medical system (often referred to as allopathic medicine).
3 The anonymous reader of this chapter for Harwood noted that governments may have little choice in relation to policy: '[d]ebt reduction in the poorest countries has already been tied to "target" increases in the percentage of "institutional births"'.
4 The longer original version of Chapter 4 goes into more detail on this issue (Jeffery, Jeffery and Lyon 1985: 6–8).
5 In the work of Janet Chawla and the MATRIKA group (Chawla 1993, 1994, and Chapter 7 this volume); see also Shodhini 1997; Radhika and Balasubramaniam 1990; Ram 2001.
6 See also Jeffery, Jeffery and Lyon 1989: 115–18, 217; Ram 1998a: 132–3. There are of course exceptions, such as the doctor described by Linda Newland (Chapter 12 this volume).
7 For examples of male birth attendants, see Laderman 1987a (Malay), Vincent-Priya 1991 (Orang Asli in Malaysia) and Chapter 12 this volume (West Java). I do not know of any South Asian examples of male birth attendants, but male religious healers may play an important role (see Chapter 5 this volume).
8 For a North Indian example, see Jeffery, Jeffery and Lyon 1989: 77–8, 104–5, 128–32, 244. For South India, see Chapter 8 this volume and Hutter 1994: 149–93. For Southeast Asia, Manderson 1981 and Laderman 1987b.
9 There are South Indian versions of these deities too, but in South India there seems to be more stress on their positive protective role (see Biardeau 1989).
10 As the anonymous reader noted, many of the practices attacked in such discourses are precisely those prevalent in Western obstetric practice in the recent past.
11 While I use *dai* as a generic term for the low-status or low-caste birth attendant – and the term is widespread – other terms are also sometimes used (e.g. *dhatri*,

dhoruni in parts of rural Bangladesh, Rozario 1995a). *Dai* itself (more correctly *dāī*) is not an Indian term in origin, but a borrowing from Arabic via Persian.

12 According to Rozario, this is sometimes the case in Noakhali as well (1995a: 93).

13 In an earlier and longer version of Chapter 8 Van Hollen suggests that birth pollution might have less significance in Tamil Nadu than in North Indian regions such as that where the Jefferys worked. She argues that the *teeddukkazhittal* (literally, 'removal of pollution') ceremony (see Chapter 8) 'is more about a rite of passage out of a state of extreme vulnerability of the mother and child's health following birth than [about] overcoming the vulnerability of those who might come into contact with the mother's body as a "polluted" space'.

14 McGilvray's account of birth among Batticaloa Tamils and Moors in Sri Lanka is a partial exception, in that it stresses the pollution-removing role of the lower-caste midwife (*maruttuvicci*), although it also refers at length to dietary issues. As McGilvray himself notes, he was unable as a male to attend a childbirth, so his information was necessarily second hand (McGilvray 1982: 57–61).

15 There are some references in material from North India to the regular feeding of 'strengthening' foods after birth, however (*punjeeri* in the Punjab, Gideon 1962: 1230; *ladoo* in Rajasthan, Chapter 5 this volume). In Bijnor, strengthening foods before childbirth were thought of as desirable, but most village women did not receive them. This is partly a matter of poverty but also, as Jeffery, Jeffery and Lyon point out, of family priorities (Jeffery, Jeffery and Lyon 1989: 77–81). Women might receive some special foods after a first delivery, but not generally after later deliveries (128–9).

16 One might expect that much of Pakistan, at least the lowland regions, would be similar to North India and Bangladesh, but I do not know of any studies from Pakistan to confirm or question this. Gideon's account of a birth among Sikh Jats in Ludhiana District, in the Indian Punjab (1962), closely resembles the studies from UP, Rajasthan and Bangladesh (low-caste *dai*, cord-cutting, pollution, etc.).

17 It is not clear from the poster to which years these figures refer, but they appear to be from the early 1990s.

18 Another example here might be the apparently very high rate of Caesarean births in some Sri Lankan hospitals which Santi Rozario and I discovered on a field visit to Sri Lanka in January 1998, and which we were told was in part due to publicity in the local press for 'scientific' findings that Caesarean-born children suffered less birth trauma and were consequently more intelligent.

19 I owe this point, and some other points in the following discussion, to Patricia Jeffery (personal communication, August 2000). According to a recent Bangladeshi study on maternal morbidity, 'even with maintaining safe hygienic practices by trained TBAs, puerperal infection was not significantly reduced'. The study suggested that 'other factors such as the existing unhygienic environment and malnutrition of mothers can also result in infections' (Afsana and Rashid 2000: 61, citing Goodburn 1994).

20 Patricia Jeffery has stressed this in a personal communication (August 2000). See also the introductory note to Chapter 4.

21 It is clear that in Unnithan's account, 'midwife' does not correspond to an indigenous category, although she does stress that each of the three had attended births on her own. One of her main points is that knowledge relating to childbirth is widely distributed through the community and not regarded as specialised knowledge. Thus, a 'midwife' (as distinct from a *dai*) is simply someone recognised as knowledgeable in this area.

22 Patricia Jeffery notes that the ANMs were still not much trusted in Bijnor on her return in 1990 (personal communication, August 2000).

23 For the *puskesmas* and *posyandu* in Lombok, see Grace 1996, Hunter 1996.
24 On Southeast Asia, in addition to Laderman's study (1987a) and the more popu-
    lar works of Vincent-Priya (1991, 1992), see the recent collection edited by Rice
    and Manderson (1996).

References

Achterberg, J. 1990. *Woman as Healer.* Boston and Shaftesbury: Shambhala.
Afsana, K. and S.F. Rashid. 2000. *Discoursing Birthing Care: Experiences from Bangladesh.* Dhaka: University Press Limited.
Anand, R. 1994. The rebirth of ancient wisdom. *Down to Earth* 15 September 1994: 43–4.
Anderson, M.M. 1988. *The Festivals of Nepal.* Calcutta: Rupa and Co.
Apffel-Marglin, F. 1994. The sacred groves: menstruation rituals in rural Orissa. *Manushi* 82 (May–June 1994): 22–32.
Appadurai, A. 1999. Globalization and the research imagination. *International Social Science Journal* 160: 229–38.
Auboyer, J. and M.-T. de Mallmann. 1950. Śītalā-la-froide: déesse indienne de la petite vérole. *Artibus Asiae* 13: 207–27.
Biardeau, M. 1989. *Histoires de poteaux: variations védiques autour de la déesse hindoue.* Paris: École Française d'Extrême-Orient.
Blanchet, T. 1984. *Women, Pollution and Marginality: Meanings and Rituals of Birth in Rural Bangladesh*, Dhaka: University Press.
Cameron, M.M. 1998. *On the Edge of the Auspicious: Gender and Caste in Nepal.* Urbana and Chicago: University of Illinois Press.
Chawla, J. 1993. A woman-centred revisioning of the traditional Indian midwife: the dai as ritual practitioner. Research paper for Masters of Theology Degree, Vidyajoti Institute of Religious Studies, Delhi.
—— 1994. *Childbearing and Culture: Woman-Centred Revisioning of the Traditional Indian Midwife: The Dai as Ritual Practitioner.* New Delhi: Indian Social Institute.
Cohen, R.S. 1998. Nāga, yakṣiṇī, Buddha: local deities and local Buddhism at Ajanta. *History of Religions* 37: 360–400.
Connor, L.H., P. Asch and T. Asch. 1986. *Jero Tapakan, Balinese Healer: An Ethnographic Film Monograph.* New York: Cambridge University Press.
Czuma, S.J. 1985. *Kushan Sculpture: Images from early India.* Cleveland, OH: The Cleveland Museum of Art in co-operation with Indiana University Press.
de Silva, D. 1997. *Fading Traditions: Memories of Rural Sri Lanka.* Sri Lanka: Sarvodaya Vishva Lekha.
Dhirasekera, J.D. 1976. Hāritī and Pāñcika: an early Buddhist legend of many lands. In *Malalasekera Commemoration Volume*, edited by O.H. de A. Wijesekera. Colombo: Malalasekera Commemoration Volume Editorial Committee.
Diamond, I. 1994. *Fertile Ground: Women, Earth, and the Limits of Control.* Boston, MA: Beacon Press.
Ehrenreich, B. and D. English. 1973. *Witches, Midwives, and Nurses: A History of Women Healers.* New York: The Feminist Press.
Gadon, E.W. 1997. The Hindu goddess Shasthi: protector of women and children. In *From the Realm of the Ancestors: An Anthology in Honor of Marija Gimbutas*, edited by J. Marler. Manchester, CT: Knowledge, Ideas and Trends, Inc.

Gellner, D.N. 1991. Hinduism, tribalism and the position of women: the problem of Newar identity. *Man* (N.S.) 26: 105–25.

Gideon, H. 1962. A baby is born in the Punjab. *American Anthropologist* 64: 1220–34.

Good, A. 1991. *The Female Bridegroom.* Oxford: Clarendon Press.

Goodburn, E.A., A.M.R. Chowdhury, R. Gazi, T. Marshall, W. Graham and F. Karim. 1994. *An Investigation into the Nature and Determinants of Maternal Morbidity related to Delivery and the Puerperium in Rural Bangladesh.* London: Maternal and Child Epidemiology Unit, London School of Hygiene and Tropical Medicine. Dhaka: BRAC.

Grace, J. 1996. Healers and modern health services: antenatal, birthing and postpartum care in rural East Lombok, Indonesia. In *Maternity and Reproductive Health in Asian Societies,* edited by P.L. Rice and L. Manderson. Amsterdam: Harwood Academic.

Haque, E. 1992. *Bengal Sculptures: Hindu Iconography up to c.1250 AD.* Dhaka: Bangladesh National Museum.

Harley, D. 1990. Historians as demonologists: the myth of the midwife-witch. *Social History of Medicine* 3 (1): 1–26.

Hunter, C.L. 1996. Women as 'good citizens': maternal and child health in a Sasak village. In *Maternity and Reproductive Health in Asian Societies,* edited by P.L. Rice and L. Manderson. Amsterdam: Harwood Academic.

Hutter, I. 1994. *Being Pregnant in Rural South India: Nutrition of Women and Well-being of Children.* Amsterdam: Thesis Publishers/PDOD (Netherlands Graduate School of Research in Demography).

Jeffery, P., R. Jeffery and A. Lyon. 1985. *Contaminating States and Women's Status.* New Delhi: Indian Social Institute (Monograph Series, 22).

—— 1989. *Labour Pains and Labour Power: Women and Childbearing in India,* London and New Jersey: Zed Books Ltd.

Jeffery, R. and P.M. Jeffery. 1993. Traditional birth attendants in rural North India: the social organization of childbearing. In *Knowledge, Power and Practice: The Anthropology of Medicine and Everyday Life,* edited by S. Lindenbaum and M. Lock. Berkeley: University of California Press.

Josephson, R. 1985. *Swoyambu Historical Pictorial: A Satya Ho Book* [summarised by N.B. Bajracharya from a Nepali text by H. Shakya, edited and arranged by R. Josephson]. Kathmandu: Satya Ho.

Kapadia, K. 1995. *Siva and her Sisters: Gender, Caste, and Class in Rural South India.* Boulder, CO, San Francisco and Oxford: Westview Press.

Kempers, A.J.B. 1991. *Monumental Bali: Introduction to Balinese Archaeology and Guide to the Monuments.* Berkeley, CA, and Singapore: Periplus Editions.

Laderman, C. 1987a. *Wives and Midwives: Childbirth and Nutrition in Rural Malaysia.* Berkeley: University of California Press.

—— 1987b. Destructive heat and cooling prayer: Malay humoralism in pregnancy, childbirth and the postpartum period. *Social Science and Medicine* 25: 357–65.

Leppard, M. 1997. Embodied understanding: birthing in a Bangladeshi district hospital. Paper for the South Asian Anthropologists' Group Meeting, London, September 1997.

Lincoln, B. 1991. *Emerging from the Chrysalis.* New York and Oxford: Oxford University Press.

McGilvray, D.B. 1982. Sexual power and fertility in Sri Lanka: Batticaloa Tamils and Moors. In *Ethnography of Fertility and Birth*, edited by C.P. MacCormack. London: Academic Press.

Malandra, G.H. 1997. *Unfolding a maṇḍala: The Buddhist Cave Temples at Ellora*. Delhi: Sri Satguru.

Manderson, L. 1981. Roasting, smoking and dieting in response to birth: Malay confinement in cross-cultural perspective. *Social Science and Medicine* 15B: 509–20.

Martin, E. 1987. *The Woman in the Body: A Cultural Analysis of Reproduction*. Boston, MA: Beacon Press.

Merchant, C. 1980. *The Death of Nature: Women, Ecology and the Scientific Revolution*. New York: Harper and Row.

Nandy, A. and S. Visvanathan. 1990. Modern medicine and its non-modern critics: a study in discourse. In *Dominating Knowledge: Development, Culture and Resistance*, edited by F.A. Marglin and S.A. Marglin. Oxford: Clarendon Press.

Nichter, M. 2001. The political ecology of health in India: indigestion as sign and symptom of defective modernization. In *Healing Powers and Modernity: Traditional Medicine, Shamanism, and Science in Asian Societies*, edited by L.H. Connor and G. Samuel. Westport, CT: Bergin and Garvey.

Panikkar, S.K. 1997. *Saptamātṛka Worship and Sculptures*. New Delhi: DK Printworld.

Patel, T. 1994. *Fertility Behaviour: Population and Society in a Rajasthan Village*. Delhi: Oxford University Press.

Purkiss, D. 1996. *The Witch in History: Early Modern and Twentieth-century Representations*. London and New York: Routledge.

Radhika, V.M. and A.V. Balasubramaniam (eds). 1990. *Mother and Child Care in Traditional Medicine. Part II*. Madras: Lok Swaasthya Parampara Samvardhan Samithi (LSPSS Monograph No. 4).

Rahnema, M. with V. Bawtree. 1997. *The Post-development Reader*. London: Zed Books. Halifax, NS: Fernwood.

Ram, K. 1998a. Maternity and the story of enlightenment in the colonies: Tamil coastal women, South India. In *Modernities and Maternities: Colonial and Postcolonial Experiences in Asia and the Pacific*, edited by K. Ram and M. Jolly. Cambridge: Cambridge University Press.

—— 1998b. Maternal experience and feminist body politics: Asian and Pacific perspectives. In *Modernities and Maternities: Colonial and Postcolonial Experiences in Asia and the Pacific*, edited by K. Ram and M. Jolly. Cambridge: Cambridge University Press.

—— 2001. Modernity and the midwife: contestations over a subaltern figure, South India. In *Healing Powers and Modernity: Traditional Medicine, Shamanism, and Science in Asian Societies*, edited by L.H. Connor and G. Samuel. Westport, CT: Bergin and Garvey.

—— n.d. The female body of puberty: Tamil linguistic and ritual perspectives on theories of 'sexuality'. Typescript.

Raymond. J.G. 1993. *Women as Wombs: Reproductive Technologies and the Battle over Women's Freedom*. San Francisco: HarperSanFrancisco.

Rice, P.L. and L. Manderson (eds). 1996. *Maternity and Reproductive Health in Asian Societies*. Amsterdam: Harwood Academic.

Rozario, S. 1995a. Dai and midwives: the renegotiation of the status of birth attendants in contemporary Bangladesh. In *The Female Client and the Health-care Provider*, edited by J. Hatcher and C. Vlassoff. Ottawa: International Development Research Centre (IDRC) Books.

—— 1995b. TBAs (Traditional Birth Attendants) and birth in Bangladeshi villages: cultural and sociological factors. *International Journal of Gynaecology and Obstetrics* 50 (Sup. no. 2): 145–52.

—— 1998. The dai and the doctor: discourses on women's reproductive health in rural Bangladesh. In *Modernities and Maternities: Colonial and Postcolonial Experiences in Asia and the Pacific*, edited by K. Ram and M. Jolly. Cambridge: Cambridge University Press.

Samuel, G. 1997. Women, goddesses and auspiciousness in South Asia. *Journal of Interdisciplinary Gender Studies* 2: 1–23.

Saunders, P.-J. 1989. Midwives and modernization: a feminist analysis of the World Health Organization's suggestion that indigenous midwives be incorporated into primary health care programmes. Honours subthesis, Women's Studies Programme, Faculty of Arts, Australian National University.

Shetty, S. 1994. (Dis)locating gender space. In *Eroticism and Containment: Notes from the Flood Plain*, edited by C. Siegel and A. Kibbey. New York: New York University Press.

Shodhini. 1997. *Touch Me, Touch-me-not: Women, Plants and Healing.* New Delhi: Kali for Women.

Slusser, M.S. 1982. *Nepal Mandala: A Cultural Study of the Kathmandu Valley.* Princeton, NJ: Princeton University Press.

Stanley, J.M. 1988. Gods, ghosts, and possession. In *The Experience of Hinduism: Essays on Religion in Maharashtra*, edited by E. Zelliot and M. Berntsen. Albany: State University of New York Press.

Stephens, C. 1992. Training urban traditional birth attendants: balancing international policy and local reality. *Social Science and Medicine* 35 (6): 811–17.

Strong, J. 1992. *The Legend and Cult of Upagupta: Sanskrit Buddhism in North India and Southeast Asia.* Princeton, NJ: Princeton University Press.

Trautmann, T.R. 1981. *Dravidian Kinship.* Cambridge: Cambridge University Press.

Vincent-Priya, J. [*also* Vincent Priya]. 1991. *Birth without Doctors: Conversations with Traditional Midwives.* London: Earthscan.

—— 1992. *Birth Traditions and Modern Pregnancy Care.* Shaftesbury, Dorset and Rockport, MA: Element.

Viramma, J. Racine and J.-L. Racine. 1997. *Viramma: Life of an Untouchable.* London and New York: Verson. Paris: UNESCO Publishing.

Wadley, S. (ed.). 1980. *The Powers of Tamil Women.* Syracuse, NY: Maxwell School of Citizenship and Public Affairs.

World Health Organization. 1997. Maternal health around the world. Poster. WHO: Maternal and Newborn Health/Safe Motherhood Unit, Division of Reproductive Health.

Wujastyk, D. 1997. Medical demonology in the *Kāśyapasaṃhitā.* Unpublished Ms.

—— 1999. Miscarriages of justice: demonic vengeance in classical Indian medicine. In *Religion, Health and Suffering*, edited by J.R. Hinnells and R. Porter. London and New York: Kegan Paul International.

Zwalf, W. 1996. *A Catalogue of the Gandhāra Sculpture in the British Museum.* London: British Museum Press.

Part 1

South Asia

Chapter 2

'We know how to do these things'

Birth in a Newar village

Barbara Johnson

This chapter comprises an introduction to and transcripts of dialogue from the video We Know How To Do These Things: Birth in a Newar Village *edited from research film shot in Nepal by Barbara Johnson for the Smithsonian Institution.*[1]

Introduction

In 1978 and 1980 I worked in Nepal as a solo research filmmaker for the Smithsonian Institution's Human Studies Film Centre (Wintle and Homiak 1995). The Smithsonian and the Royal Nepal Academy were launching the first of what they hoped would be several projects in Nepal. Living in Thecho, a large Jyapu village in the Kathmandu Valley, I recorded over 50 hours of 16mm film, which is now in the Human Studies Film Archives. The Jyapu are the farming caste of the Newars, the indigenous residents of what is now called the Kathmandu Valley (Nepali 1965; Toffin 1977, 1984; Gellner and Quigley 1995). Nepal was united as a nation over 200 years ago when the three large Newar city/kingdoms of the Nepal Valley – Kathmandu (the Newar city Ye), Patan (Yele), and Bhaktapur (Khopa) – came under the jurisdiction of Nepali-speaking people from the surrounding highlands. Of the twenty-six different ethnic groups in Nepal, each with its own language, and as many different Newar castes, the Jyapu were chosen for the first film project in Nepal because of the proximity of their villages to the capital city, and because the strength of Jyapu agricultural, social and religious traditions may be seen as the foundation of the whole very ancient, highly developed Newar civilisation. To this day, the Newar role in originating, adapting and passing along developments in human culture between Asia's oldest known centres of civilization in India and China poses many intriguing and unanswered questions.

I lived in Thecho for six months in 1978. Returning to Nepal in 1980, I did some comparative filming in the Newar pottery-making village of Thimi, outside of Bhaktapur, and then went back to Thecho for the rest of my nine-month stay. The purpose of my filming was to make a record of Jyapu life, especially of how children were raised to be members of their culture. When I returned to Thecho in 1980 and noticed that several women in the courtyard were pregnant, I hoped that I could film a birth. I was called so late for the first birth I filmed that I didn't see anything leading up to the birth itself. The film described in this chapter is the second birth I filmed, when I was called early enough to see several hours of labour.

Thecho is situated approximately seven miles south of Patan, beyond the village of Sunakothi, on the road to Chapagaon and Lele. Like spokes of a wheel, the roads to Harisiddhi and Godavari to the west and Bungamati across the Nakhu River to the east go out from Patan on either side of the road to Thecho. Footpaths through fields and across rivers between Thecho, Harisiddhi and Bungamati are well travelled in the interconnecting trade and festival life of the Kathmandu Valley.

A village of 1,200 houses and approximately 5,000 people in 1980, Thecho was populated almost exclusively by landowning Jyapu farmers. There was one neighbourhood (around fifty people) of the Newar butcher caste (Nay), a few members of the Newar tailor/musician caste (Kusle), and three households of the Newar Buddhist Priest caste (Gubhaju). Rice, cultivated in irrigated paddies in the summer rainy season, was the main crop, with a secondary crop of wheat grown in the same fields when they were dry in winter. Each family grew vegetables for their own consumption, and the village specialised in two crops used for trading: chilli peppers and mustard seeds (pressed to make oil). Compared to many Jyapu villages, only a small number of people in Thecho engaged in non-farming work. Of the thirty-five families in the courtyard where I lived, only three men left the village to work at jobs in the city. Similarly, Thecho had one of the lowest levels of children in school of all the Jyapu villages. A driveable dirt road from Patan reached Thecho in the late 1950s. A Nepali-language primary school opened in 1958. Electricity was brought in between 1969 and 1970, and a piped water system was put in place after 1972.

Like all Newar villages, Thecho is a densely populated, urban-style community of attached three-story brick houses surrounded by cultivated land. Houses line the narrow brick-paved streets which open into courtyards of varying sizes. The two largest courtyards surround the temples on the north and south sides of the village. Most of my filming took place in Tawnany Tole (big courtyard), where I lived. Tawnany Tole, near the temple on the south side of Thecho, is made up of about twenty-five houses around an open paved square. The square contained an old well, a water tap which ran each morning and evening, a small way-house or *pathi*, used for shelter by adults and children socialising and engaged in a wide variety of activities, and a small four-sided Buddhist *stupa* or *chaitya*. When I was there, approximately150 people lived in Tawnany Tole.

Although Newar city houses often have four floors, most of the houses in Thecho are built with three.[2] The ground floor is used for keeping animals:

chickens, goats, cows or water buffalo. Going up the wooden steps to the first floor, one finds an open sitting/sleeping room (called *mata*), usually bare of furniture except for a straw mat on the mud/dung-coated floor. Off the *mata* are low wooden doors to two tiny rooms which may or may not have a window. The *dyaw kothay* (the god's room) is the location for a shrine to the household deity and is used to store staple crops (in large pottery containers). The second small room is used for sleeping and may contain a lockable wooden chest for storage of good clothing and other valuables. This is the room in which women give birth and remain in seclusion with their baby for the first three post-partum days. Doors to both rooms can be locked when the family is away. Directly above the first flight of stairs is a second set, which leads from the *mata* to the kitchen, a large open room occupying the top floor of the house. There is a mud-coated brick stove built into one corner of the kitchen, with an opening in the ceiling to let smoke rise into the attic and out of the house. There is a large pottery water crock, assorted pots and cooking utensils, a straw mat for sitting (this is where meals are eaten) and sometimes a loom strung across the length or width of the room.

Newar women give birth in their husband's house, which is their official residence after marriage.[3] Actually, the amount of time a woman spends in her husband's house increases gradually after marriage, and substantially after the birth of each child. Giving birth is a women's affair, and men are not usually present. In addition to her mother-in-law, and when possible her own mother and other relatives, a woman giving birth is assisted by a traditional birth attendant, called *aji*, or Grandmother, who is an experienced older relative or neighbour. Each family has a relationship with a particular *aji*, and she is called whenever they have a birth. The birth attendants in the two births I witnessed were both members of the same Jyapu caste as the women giving birth, and lived close to the families where the births took place. My understanding is that a traditional birth attendant usually learns her practice from either her mother or mother-in-law. In return for her birthing and post-partum services a birth attendant is given a new blouse, is fed a meal and served liquor.

Since the 1960s, the relative proximity of hospitals in Patan and Kathmandu has given women with problems during labour the option of hospital care. Although hospital birth was still very much the exception in Thecho in 1980, hospital experiences are discussed at length by the birth attendant and relatives of the labouring woman in the film. The mother-in-law of the woman giving birth asked me to provide a bar of soap to wash the new baby, because soap was used in the hospital, causing a neighbour to comment 'What do we know?'

The traditional Newar view of birth is of an event dependent on powerful benevolent and malevolent spirits. Food plays an important part in managing these forces. From the idea that the child will be greedy in life if he or she is not fed well *in utero*, to the protective power of yoghurt as a 'pure' food, eggs as auspicious and date sugar for strength, much of the focus of the birth attendant and female relatives is on feeding the labouring woman. After the baby is born a neighbour suggests that the mother-in-law give Jolmaya mustard seed oil to keep her uterus from hurting, and the new mother is fed many kinds of special seeds and other foods considered to be beneficial and strengthening. The elements of heat and fire also play an important role in giving birth. A pot of burning embers is kept in the room during labour, and refilled with flaming coals just before the birth.

The birth attendant is also experienced in the use of rituals to manage the spiritual forces that help or hinder birth. In the film, when Jolmaya is in great pain, the birth attendant instructs Jolmaya's mother to prepare a plate of foods and coins (*kisle*) for a ritual offering to be left at the village cross-roads for spirits that may be blocking the birth. There is danger/power associated with the blood of childbirth, and straw contaminated with it is thrown out in the *chwasa*, a ritual disposal place. The birthing mother herself goes out in the evening to wash out the skirt and petticoat in which she gave birth, and the birth attendant purifies the room by putting a fresh coat of clay and cow dung on the birthing room floor.

An unusual feature of Newar birth is the practice of not cutting the umbil-lical cord for three days after birth. The delivery of the placenta is awaited with great anxiety in the film: the birth attendant, mother-in-law and mother all urge the new mother to swallow some of her hair so she can vomit, to help expel the placenta. After it is delivered, the mother-in-law places it in a small clay bowl and covers it with cloth. The new mother stays in the birthing room for three days while her baby is attached to the placenta. On the fourth day a woman of the butcher caste (Nay) is called to cut the cord (*pih dhenegu*) and throw it out to the *chwasa*, the ritual disposal place. Once this is done the childbirth purification ritual (*maca buh byākugu*) and baby naming ceremony can take place. According to Ishii (2000: 375), the birth attendant, new mother, baby and family purify themselves by bathing, and having their nails cut by a member of the barber caste (Nau). The birth attendant re-coats the floor of the birthing room with a new layer of the mud-dung mixture, and performs a purification ritual before the mother and baby go outside for the first time. After the first birth I filmed, I missed the purification ritual but was able to film when all the children from the courtyard were invited into the new baby's house to be treated to handfuls of *dhau-baji*, a mixture of dry pounded rice with yoghurt, raisins and nuts.

Post-partum care for the baby begins as soon as the placenta is delivered and the birth attendant can turn her attention to the newborn. The birth attendant bathes the baby thoroughly, removing all traces of the protective coating with which the baby is born. Mustard seed oil is heated over the pot of coals that has been in the room throughout labour, and the birth attendant gives the baby a vigorous massage. A daily mustard-seed oil massage and sun bath is part of the new mother and baby's routine for the first two to three months after birth. This is a time when Newar mothers are cared for and fed special foods to build up their strength. While the birth attendant is washing and massaging the baby, the new mother puts on a clean skirt (*parsi*) and petticoat, and fresh straw is laid down for her to sit on in a clean spot in the room. After massaging the baby, the birth attendant wraps her snugly in a clean cloth and lays her down next to the mother. When the baby cries the mother will pick her up to hold her and nurse her for the first time.

The birth in the film took place in the household of a family I knew very well, two doors away from where I lived. The parents, Dangopynda and Chirimaya (grandparents of the baby in the film), were in their forties. They had six children, aged from 4 to 20. Jolmaya, the 20-year-old wife of their eldest son, had given birth to a son (her first child), two years before. The birth in the film is of her second child. I was told that Jolmaya's labour started during the night, and that the birth attendant (Tawrimaya Aji) was called at dawn. Chirimaya came to get me around 7 a.m. The film begins at the point when I came into the birthing room and saw the birth attendant sitting with Jolmaya, while her mother-in-law helped the rest of the family get started on their tasks for the day. When the birth attendant went out, Chirimaya took her place sitting with Jolmaya. By 8 o'clock Jolmaya's mother had come from the other side of the village to bring special foods for her daughter. She stayed to help with the birth. Jolmaya's married older sister also joined them for a while and the women exchanged stories about other births.

Jolmaya's sister left while Jolmaya was resting, still in the early stages of labour. Her mother went out for a while, and the birth attendant and I each went home for breakfast. I returned around 10 a.m., to find Jolmaya's mother and mother-in-law quite concerned that the birth attendant wasn't back yet, because Jolmaya was in a lot of pain. Chirimaya finally went to get Tawrimaya, and the baby was born by 11 o'clock. It was almost noon by the time the baby's bath and massage were finished, and I shot the last of my film just before Jolmaya sat down and held her daughter for the first time.

The transcript of the film that follows is illustrated with a series of stills from the video.

We Know How To Do These Things: Birth in a Newar Village (transcript)

Speakers in the film

JOLMAYA, the woman giving birth
Tawrimaya, the traditional BIRTH ATTENDANT (aji)
Chirimaya, Jolmaya's MOTHER-IN-LAW
Dangopynda, Jolmaya's FATHER-IN-LAW
JOLMAYA'S MOTHER
JOLMAYA'S SISTER
NEIGHBOURS

Abbreviations

*   *Indicates dialogue not included in the edited film.*

- - - - - -   *Indicates the camera turning off and then on again. The tape recorder also stopped when the camera was off.*

*JOLMAYA: *Aiya, oof . . . aiya.*
*BIRTH ATTENDANT (*to* MOTHER-IN-LAW) There's no water here.

JOLMAYA: *Aiya . . . aiya . . . oof . . .*
MOTHER-IN-LAW (*to eldest daughter?*): How come? Didn't I tell you to get it? I'm having my meal. Run and get it.
FATHER-IN-LAW (*calling to son from outside room*): Where are you? Upstairs? Are you upstairs, I said?
JOLMAYA: *Aiya, ai . . . ya . . .*

MOTHER-IN-LAW: Narayana![4] Let me rub your back.

JOLMAYA: *Aiya . . . ya . . . ya . . . oof!*

- - - - - -

(*The room is cold, and the* BIRTH ATTENDANT *warms her hands over a pot of coals.*)

BIRTH ATTENDANT: Will she [Barbara] be going to the mustard fields again today?

JOLMAYA: Today? No, she won't go today.

BIRTH ATTENDANT: Will she be going to Yele?[5]

JOLMAYA: She might go there today, or she might go tomorrow.

(JOLMAYA'S MOTHER *is heard calling up to them from the foot of the stairs.*)

JOLMAYA'S MOTHER: Daughter!

JOLMAYA: Yes?

BIRTH ATTENDANT: Come in. She's taking our picture!

MOTHER: *Bhagi ti.*[6]

BIRTH ATTENDANT: *Bhagi ti.*

(JOLMAYA'S MOTHER *has heard that her daughter is in labour, and she comes with gifts of special foods to help make the birth successful.*)

BIRTH ATTENDANT: That might spill.

JOLMAYA'S MOTHER: Where shall I put these eggs?

BIRTH ATTENDANT: I've already fed her once.

JOLMAYA'S MOTHER: I've brought eggs. Two.

BIRTH ATTENDANT: Shall I cook them?

JOLMAYA'S MOTHER: Yes.

JOLMAYA: *Unh, unh . . . oof!*

(*The* BIRTH ATTENDANT *takes the eggs upstairs to the kitchen.*)

JOLMAYA'S MOTHER: Is all the pain in your back, or does it hurt in front too?

JOLMAYA: It hurts in front and in back. It's getting worse.

JOLMAYA'S MOTHER: Is your stomach hurting a lot right now?

JOLMAYA: It gets better for a while, and then it starts hurting again! I can't stand it! *Aiya!*

- - - - - -

JOLMAYA'S MOTHER: You don't show signs of *nhyasu*.[7]

JOLMAYA: *Aiya . . . oof!*

- - - - - -

(*The* MOTHER-IN-LAW *and* BIRTH ATTENDANT *return with eggs.*)

*MOTHER-IN-LAW: Here, take it.

*BIRTH ATTENDANT: What about that dish?

*MOTHER-IN-LAW: Yes, I'll serve it in that.

BIRTH ATTENDANT (*to* MOTHER-IN-LAW): Do you want to serve it or shall I?

MOTHER-IN-LAW (*to* BIRTH ATTENDANT): I'll give it to her.

BIRTH ATTENDANT: That's what I meant. We know how to do these things, don't we?

JOLMAYA'S MOTHER (*to* BIRTH ATTENDANT): Yes

JOLMAYA'S MOTHER (*to* MOTHER-IN-LAW): Take some for yourself too.

(JOLMAYA'S MOTHER *pours out the pounded rice that she has brought in her waist-cloth.*)

BIRTH ATTENDANT (*to* MOTHER-IN-LAW): Take some!

JOLMAYA'S MOTHER: Take some I said.

MOTHER-IN-LAW: I don't need any . . .

JOLMAYA'S MOTHER: She doesn't eat from this dish, I'll put it in that bowl there.

JOLMAYA: I don't want *baji* [dry pounded rice]. I won't eat it.

BIRTH ATTENDANT (*to* JOLMAYA'S MOTHER): Have you already been to Dowkhya?[8]

JOLMAYA'S MOTHER: I went, but they weren't back home yet.

BIRTH ATTENDANT: What did she have?

JOLMAYA'S MOTHER: A girl.

MOTHER-IN-LAW: A girl there too?

JOLMAYA'S MOTHER: Yes, they said, she was born yesterday.

BIRTH ATTENDANT: Was the other one a boy?

JOLMAYA'S MOTHER: No, the one that died was a boy. The one that died was a boy.

BIRTH ATTENDANT (*to* JOLMAYA): Here, take this.

JOLMAYA'S MOTHER (*to* JOLMAYA): After you eat put the dish over there. Put it in the bowl and eat it.

(MOTHER-IN-LAW *leaves the room*)

BIRTH ATTENDANT (*to* JOLMAYA'S MOTHER): She's already eaten one egg.

JOLMAYA'S MOTHER: What?

BIRTH ATTENDANT: She ate one egg already.

(JOLMAYA'S MOTHER *gives* JOLMAYA *yoghurt, and they urge her to take it.*)

JOLMAYA'S MOTHER (*to* JOLMAYA): Here, drink this [yoghurt].

BIRTH ATTENDANT (*to* JOLMAYA'S MOTHER): She keeps refusing, what a person she is! Take it!

JOLMAYA'S MOTHER (*to* JOLMAYA): Here, if you take it my grandchild will be born quickly.

BIRTH ATTENDANT: That's right.

JOLMAYA: Just a little, I don't want a lot.

BIRTH ATTENDANT: That's what you said earlier too.

JOLMAYA'S MOTHER: Here, take half of it.

JOLMAYA: Please, not that much. Just a little bit.

MOTHER-IN-LAW: Eat just this little bit, I haven't given you much.

BIRTH ATTENDANT: Eat, eat.
JOLMAYA'S MOTHER: Gobble it up.

BIRTH ATTENDANT: Earlier, everything had already moved down.
JOLMAYA'S MOTHER: What?
BIRTH ATTENDANT: Everything had already moved down.
JOLMAYA'S MOTHER: Earlier?
(JOLMAYA'S MOTHER *wants to give the* MOTHER-IN-LAW *some of the food she's brought, but Chirimaya is polite and refuses.*)
JOLMAYA'S MOTHER (*to* MOTHER-IN-LAW): Take that piece for yourself.
MOTHER-IN-LAW (*to* JOLMAYA'S MOTHER): No, that's all right.
BIRTH ATTENDANT (*to* MOTHER-IN-LAW): Take it, don't show off.
JOLMAYA'S MOTHER (*to* MOTHER-IN-LAW): Take that little bit.
BIRTH ATTENDANT (*to* MOTHER-IN-LAW): Why not?
JOLMAYA'S MOTHER (*to* MOTHER-IN-LAW): Just take a little bit.
*MOTHER-IN-LAW: (*unintelligible*)
*BIRTH ATTENDANT (*to* MOTHER-IN-LAW): What's on that dish?
*MOTHER-IN-LAW (*to* BIRTH ATTENDANT): This one? I've rinsed it.
*BIRTH ATTENDANT (*to* MOTHER-IN-LAW): It's black.
*MOTHER-IN-LAW (*to* BIRTH ATTENDANT): I just fried an egg in it, on the stove with the cowdung.
(*They hear* JOLMAYA'S SISTER *calling up to them from the foot of the stairs.*)
BIRTH ATTENDANT: Who's there?
JOLMAYA'S MOTHER: My daughter.
BIRTH ATTENDANT: Come in.
- - - - - -
(*The* BIRTH ATTENDANT *tells a story about a baby who died in the hospital to* JOLMAYA'S MOTHER *and* JOLMAYA'S SISTER *as* JOLMAYA *rests quietly.*)

BIRTH ATTENDANT: Now, there was a baby born dead in the hospital, Kansa's baby . . . Well, even though it was born the day before, the next day it was still there. They need money, don't they, to keep it there like that? Then, that next day, I went there . . .

(*Jolmaya's* MOTHER-IN-LAW *can be heard through the thin wooden wall to the next room, as she looks for a hard, brittle sweet made of date sugar.*)

MOTHER-IN-LAW: It's not here.

BIRTH ATTENDANT: Kansa asked me 'What shall we do? Chirima, will you bury it, or should I leave it with them? If I leave it with them it will cost 15 or 16 rupees', he said. 'Now, it's our own child, so I will take it myself', I said. Then they didn't give us the baby. Those people delayed forever! Kansa asked them three or four times, and finally they brought the baby to us. I laid out an old piece of *parsi* [skirt cloth] for it, without even looking to see if it was a boy or a girl.

JOLMAYA'S MOTHER: After it's dead, what does it matter what it is?

BIRTH ATTENDANT: Yes, so I carried it to the Bagmati [River] like that, and Kansa said 'Here, Chirima, leave it here.' I made a place for it on the bank of the Bagmati, and came home. Whatever may happen next, the river will do what it wants. With my part done, I came home.

JOLMAYA'S SISTER: When was it – four or five days ago? Someone told me that two babies were brought to the Bagmati.

JOLMAYA: Were they alive?

JOLMAYA'S SISTER: I don't know if they were alive [or dead].

BIRTH ATTENDANT: Oh, those sisters! Every time they have a baby I have to attend them so, for every baby!

JOLMAYA'S SISTER: And it goes on for days on end!

BIRTH ATTENDANT: Yes, they never . . .

JOLMAYA'S SISTER: They cry like water buffalo.

BIRTH ATTENDANT: And they never ask anyone but me. I'm the only one. Nani Maicha's *dya: dukaya* [ceremony] was done, but it seemed to me that she wasn't able to have the baby, things weren't right.

*BIRTH ATTENDANT: 'Daughter!' I said, 'We should send a *kisli* [offering] to Nani Maicha's *dya: dukaya*.' Nani Maicha was woken up and sent out with the *kisli*, and a little later the baby was born.

- - - - - -

BIRTH ATTENDANT: She gobbled that up too! She ate *ja* [the morning meal] and *baji* [the midday meal] too. All day there wasn't anything that she didn't eat! And then she gave birth at night. And also she didn't give birth in the *kothay*. We brought her to the *mata*, and she gave birth there.[9]

JOLMAYA'S MOTHER: She's yawning now, and she wasn't before.

BIRTH ATTENDANT: Yes she was, she was yawning earlier. When we brought her to the *mata* she gave birth, when the place was changed.

JOLMAYA'S SISTER: Wasn't it like that for Chirima too?

BIRTH ATTENDANT: Yes.

JOLMAYA'S SISTER: The one in Tanbal?[10]

BIRTH ATTENDANT: The baby that died wasn't born upstairs, that one also wasn't born in the usual room. It was born when she was brought to the *mata* [sitting room], the one who died. Oh, giving birth is very hard for these two sisters!

JOLMAYA'S SISTER: Is it so hard for the older one?

BIRTH ATTENDANT: When the older one had her first baby she planted *wala* [a type of rice] all day, and all day she had water discharge. She planted *wala* the whole day. Even with so much discharge, she still couldn't deliver three days later.

JOLMAYA'S MOTHER: Even when there is discharge labour doesn't always start. For me, too, when my son was born, there was discharge . . .

BIRTH ATTENDANT: Three days . . .

JOLMAYA'S MOTHER: Just like you said, I had water discharge on that day from the time of eating *baji* [the midday meal].

BIRTH ATTENDANT: Mmmm.

JOLMAYA'S MOTHER: Then that same day our neighbours from the corner house were winnowing rice outside. I wasn't unwell [in labour], actually, I was fine, but men were tossing the rice [for winnowing], so I was embarrassed.

BIRTH ATTENDANT: Who knows what could happen . . .

JOLMAYA'S MOTHER: Yes, I was so embarrassed, I didn't know what to do. I winnowed with them for two or three piles, then left. This was from the midday meal one day, and the baby was born after the midday meal the next day.

BIRTH ATTENDANT: Now that girl, didn't you see her? She went out threshing rice when her waters came out, all over her *parsi* [skirt]. Oh, she had to go and rinse it so many times, and she was afraid the others would notice, she was so embarrassed, it was a heavy discharge.

JOLMAYA'S MOTHER: And then when the heavy discharge ends, it seems dry, but it doesn't really stop. And when the others were going to the fields she carried the water jar out for them. Ploughing, I think they [were] going to plough.

BIRTH ATTENDANT: She doesn't even get the floor wet. You know, even when it's menstruation time her skirt doesn't get stained.

JOLMAYA'S SISTER: Now both of them, Nani Maicha's too, some time ago . . .

BIRTH ATTENDANT: (unclear)

JOLMAYA'S SISTER: Will everybody do that?

BIRTH ATTENDANT: Three days, three days . . . (unclear)

JOLMAYA'S SISTER: Chirimaya now . . .

*JOLMAYA'S MOTHER: When Nhyathu's baby was born she was pounding rice [to make baji] all day, she pounded rice all day, while inside herself she felt unwell [was in labour].

- - - - - -

(JOLMAYA'S MOTHER tells about having to send her husband away from their bedroom one evening when she knew her labour was starting.)

JOLMAYA'S MOTHER: When he came into the room he bumped into me and said, 'Why are you upstairs?' I didn't say anything. 'It's time for me to go to sleep now, to put out my mattress.' 'Put mine out too', he said. 'You won't need it, you shouldn't stay here, go and sleep outside', I said. Now, if I hadn't told him that he wouldn't have gone to eat his dinner. I said 'Don't stay here, go on, you should sleep outside.' I wanted to say, go sleep upstairs. As he went down the stairs he called 'Hey daughter, go check on what's happening in the kothay [room].' And then he went out. He went out and enjoyed himself, and when he came back to sleep everything was all over. Then my mother-in-law complained that she hadn't had enough sleep, while up to that point I hadn't needed sleep or anything. Our daughter-in-law also, our daughter-in-law, now how long has it been since we brought our daughter-in-law home, this was that long ago, now this was before sakuna buswa [festival], it was a week before suku phuni [a specific full moon], when this one was born. Now, for the festival . . .

BIRTH ATTENDANT: That's when you brought your daughter-in-law home?

JOLMAYA'S MOTHER: Yes, it was around that time that my daughter-in-law, the one who sleeps upstairs, was brought home to be seen. She was brought right after this baby was born, so she could help with the baby, and with the festival, at sukuna phuni time the baby had been born.

BIRTH ATTENDANT: (unintelligible)

JOLMAYA'S MOTHER: It was just the day before baji making [pounding roasted rice] that the baby was born. Now, this daughter-in-law, we brought her in to help with the festival on the day of the full moon. The pene chaigu [ceremony] takes place on the Chwebo day or the full moon day.

BIRTH ATTENDANT: Our nephew had such a great wish this last Mohni [annual festival, called Dasain in Nepali]. He said he wouldn't rest until he took both his aunts to his home, he kept insisting that we visit his home, so both Nhyatukhuncha and I went and drank two to three cupfuls of rice beer and returned.

JOLMAYA'S MOTHER: Now, what can we do? How long will she stay like this?

- - - - - -

*BIRTH ATTENDANT: Now that girl from Tikolon . . .

*JOLMAYA'S MOTHER: I had just arrived there when I met . . .

*BIRTH ATTENDANT: The elder one had a hard time like that

*JOLMAYA'S MOTHER: Now I didn't go there because I thought I shouldn't . . .

BIRTH ATTENDANT: She couldn't have it at home, at their home there, she had a hard time when the second one was born, when she had already started labour she was carried along in a *duli* [traditional carrier] wasn't she? for her second baby, and then . . . I had eaten my evening meal and was just sitting there and talking when the elder sister came to say her younger sister was being carried to the hospital, so I started running so fast, when we were in front of Pukhudai's house, and I was still without my *jani* [long waist-cloth] and my *ga* [outer waist-cloth or shawl], without anything, I rushed out like that, with just a short *jani* tied around me. When I got out there, they put her in a car, the car that carries the vegetables to the market, she wasn't in a *duli*, so we went there, and when we arrived, when we arrived at Thapathali [the maternity hospital] she was put on a stretcher, lying down flat on her back, her clothes were taken off, other clothes were put on her, (now they won't dress her any more) and then she . . .

MOTHER-IN-LAW (*speaking to the* BIRTH ATTENDANT *through the wall*): Tawrima [elder mother]!

BIRTH ATTENDANT: Yes?

MOTHER-IN-LAW: Here, take this.

(JOLMAYA'S MOTHER-IN-LAW *hands a lump of date sugar through the wall to the* BIRTH ATTENDANT.)

JOLMAYA'S SISTER: What about Chirima and the others, where were they?

BIRTH ATTENDANT: And then the nurse – hey, this [sugar lump] has to be broken in half – never mind.

JOLMAYA'S SISTER: They say that in the hospital they undress you completely.

JOLMAYA'S MOTHER: That's right.

BIRTH ATTENDANT: And then . . .

JOLMAYA'S MOTHER: It's very embarrassing.

JOLMAYA'S SISTER: After undressing you they make you lie flat on your back.

BIRTH ATTENDANT: The hand, just a little . . .

JOLMAYA'S MOTHER: How embarrassing it must be!

JOLMAYA'S SISTER: Even if the hand moves a little . . .

BIRTH ATTENDANT: The hand was a little bit out of position, and that nurse moved so roughly that I was disgusted, and then one nurse came back, and another nurse came in, and she looked at the place where the tickets are kept, and after looking there quietly brought her into the room, and when she had been brought into the room, when she got there she gave birth right away.

(*The* BIRTH ATTENDANT *tries to give a piece of the date sugar to* JOLMAYA.)

BIRTH ATTENDANT: Here, take it.

JOLMAYA: No, I don't want any.

BIRTH ATTENDANT: Here, take it, don't show off, I said.

JOLMAYA'S MOTHER: Come on, eat it.

BIRTH ATTENDANT: Here, take it and eat it. And then she had the baby, and after the baby was born we had no place to spend the night.

JOLMAYA'S MOTHER: There was no place to stay?

BIRTH ATTENDANT: No. We couldn't sleep there. Go on, take it, oh what a show-off! And then her brother-in-law, our Harimaya's son, Bekhalal, and the rest of us came and waited, and that nurse was a good one, she brought us to the room.

JOLMAYA'S MOTHER: Some nurses are actually good people, but some of them are crazy screaming women!

BIRTH ATTENDANT: That's right. After the baby was born, they said 'There's no place for you people to sleep here, go home now, and tomorrow . . .'

- - - - - -

JOLMAYA: I don't want it, I don't want it.

JOLMAYA'S MOTHER: Go on and eat it, go on and eat it.

JOLMAYA: I don't want it, I said.

BIRTH ATTENDANT: Go on and take it.

JOLMAYA: I don't want it.

BIRTH ATTENDANT: Eat, eat this one piece.

JOLMAYA'S MOTHER: Just eat this little piece, that's all. Eat this one piece.

BIRTH ATTENDANT: Now I don't have any more. Over there, it seems like two or three people . . .

JOLMAYA'S MOTHER (*to* BIRTH ATTENDANT): Did she eat the medicine?

BIRTH ATTENDANT: What?

JOLMAYA'S MOTHER: Did she eat the medicine?

BIRTH ATTENDANT: I don't know . . . When they had a baby I would always go.

JOLMAYA'S SISTER: You would go that far? You would prepare everything here and take them that far?

BIRTH ATTENDANT: When he was the village leader, I went six times, six times.

*JOLMAYA'S MOTHER: Did it take all day to get there?

*BIRTH ATTENDANT: Yes, and when I got there I heated the meat and stirred it up,

*JOLMAYA'S SISTER: If you leave here in the morning, what time would you arrive there?

*BIRTH ATTENDANT: If you go right after breakfast you get there when the light is about to fade.

*JOLMAYA'S SISTER: Then when you're there the next day, you leave after breakfast . . .

*BIRTH ATTENDANT: I would stay the whole next day, and would leave the day after that. And then when she was sick and was brought to the hospital, he must have lost hope, and called me 'Mother, come, Mother, come.' Now the hospital, at the time of this son's birth, I went and came back the day after the *byākugu* [cleansing ritual], that's when I went.

*JOLMAYA'S MOTHER: Oh.

*BIRTH ATTENDANT: They say he really knows how to care for his wife. He ground half a jar full of *masala* [spices and nuts], and put it where the rice is kept for his wife. Now they say they killed a chicken for the *byākugu*, they don't have a place to get meat like we do here.

*JOLMAYA'S SISTER: Is there no killing there?

*BIRTH ATTENDANT: Yes, they killed a chicken for the *byākugu*, and then rice . . .

- - - - - -

BIRTH ATTENDANT: Then I came here, now you, if it's necessary to make rice beer I had to stay longer, then that rascal grandson said he had to do the ploughing.

JOLMAYA'S SISTER: Is your land all ploughed now?

BIRTH ATTENDANT: What?

JOLMAYA'S SISTER: Aren't you finished ploughing?

BIRTH ATTENDANT: We're bringing in the straw now . . .

- - - - - -

BIRTH ATTENDANT: Why should he get angry and think we were going to take it? Now, he doesn't act like a brother and come to see his sister. He isn't anything like his older brothers. He didn't even feed me during the Mohni festival.

JOLMAYA'S MOTHER: He didn't give you anything to eat?

BIRTH ATTENDANT: No, he didn't. I didn't even go to his house.

*JOLMAYA'S MOTHER: Why should you?

*BIRTH ATTENDANT: I didn't even go in there.

*JOLMAYA'S MOTHER: There's no reason for you to go.

*BIRTH ATTENDANT: During Mohni I went to call Lubdha. My sister-in-law asked me again and again to come upstairs. I went there after I'd eaten lunch, and I didn't go upstairs, I didn't feel like going.

JOLMAYA'S MOTHER: I have to go . . .

BIRTH ATTENDANT: I no longer have a caring brother.

JOLMAYA'S MOTHER: No more.

BIRTH ATTENDANT: Try a bit of the *baja* [water-pipe with sweetened tobacco].

JOLMAYA'S MOTHER: I don't want any.

BIRTH ATTENDANT: It's in the *mata*.[11]

JOLMAYA'S MOTHER: I don't want any.

BIRTH ATTENDANT: Go ahead and smoke a little, I said.

JOLMAYA'S MOTHER (*to* JOLMAYA): What did I step on?

BIRTH ATTENDANT: Why don't you smoke a little bit?

(JOLMAYA'S MOTHER *excuses herself to go outside for a little while, and* JOL-MAYA'S SISTER *leaves. The* BIRTH ATTENDANT *goes home for breakfast and so do I.*)

- - - - - -

(*When I come back* JOLMAYA*'s labour is getting much more difficult. Her* MOTHER *is with her but the* BIRTH ATTENDANT *hasn't come back yet.*)

JOLMAYA (*moaning*): *ai, ai.* . . . oh, I can't bear it, *ai, ai* . . . I can't take it, *e,e,e* . . . Narayana, *aiya* . . . (*yawns*) . . . *ai, ai, ai, aiya* . . .

- - - - - -

JOLMAYA: Now one of my legs has gone to sleep again, *ai* . . .

JOLMAYA'S MOTHER: We're not very strong.

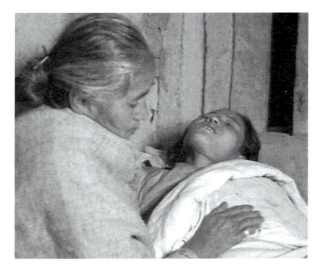

JOLMAYA: *Ufu*, I can't stand this, *aiya* . . .
JOLMAYA'S MOTHER: (*unclear*)
JOLMAYA: Yes.
JOLMAYA'S MOTHER: Here.
(JOLMAYA *sits up with her* MOTHER.)
JOLMAYA: (*unclear*)

JOLMAYA'S MOTHER: Does your back hurt?
JOLMAYA: What?
JOLMAYA'S MOTHER: Does your back hurt?
JOLMAYA: It hurts so much I can't stand it.
- - - - - -
(JOLMAYA *leans against her* MOTHER. *The* MOTHER-IN-LAW *comes in, but the*
    BIRTH ATTENDANT *still isn't back.*)
JOLMAYA'S MOTHER (*to* MOTHER-IN-LAW): We're not very strong, if only she
    were strong.
MOTHER-IN-LAW: I've got some pickled *gundru* [a sour vegetable dish]
    upstairs, would you like some?
JOLMAYA: No, I don't want any.
JOLMAYA'S MOTHER: Why don't you try some?
MOTHER-IN-LAW: (*unclear*) . . . Can I bring you a small portion?
JOLMAYA: I don't want any.
*JOLMAYA'S MOTHER: If you want it you don't have to say you don't.
*MOTHER-IN-LAW: Of course not.
- - - - - -
JOLMAYA: *Oof, aiiii* . . .
JOLMAYA'S MOTHER: (*unclear*)

(MOTHER-IN-LAW *comes in, clears away dish and leaves.*)

JOLMAYA'S MOTHER: (*unclear*) . . . the pain is getting bad and still you don't want to eat anything.

JOLMAYA: *U, u, aiya, aiya, uu,u, aiya, u,u, u* . . . It's getting worse.

JOLMAYA'S MOTHER: (*unintelligible*)

JOLMAYA: *Ts, uf, ai, uf,* . . . *ts, u, u, ts* . . . *Ai, ai,* oh mother, I can't stand it.

JOLMAYA'S MOTHER: Does it hurt up higher than before? God Narayan.

(MOTHER-IN-LAW *comes in again and looks in her change purse for a coin.*)

MOTHER-IN-LAW: Should I make a *kisle* [plate for religious offering]?

- - - - - -

(JOLMAYA'S MOTHER *and* MOTHER-IN-LAW *get more and more worried. They have* JOLMAYA *get into the birthing position, kneeling over an upturned basket covered with bedding.*)

*JOLMAYA: How should I be?

*MOTHER-IN-LAW: Here's the bedding.

*JOLMAYA'S MOTHER: Over on that side . . . put your head down.

*MOTHER-IN-LAW: Is there a blanket there? I'll put a blanket there.

*JOLMAYA'S MOTHER: Has Chanmaya[12] come?

*MOTHER-IN-LAW: She hasn't come yet.

*JOLMAYA'S MOTHER: We don't know how to do anything. I can't do anything.

*MOTHER-IN-LAW: What could we possibly do without the *nhyasu* [sign of imminent birth] coming first?

*JOLMAYA'S MOTHER: The *nhyasu* hasn't come yet.

*MOTHER-IN-LAW: Without the *nhyasu* coming there is nothing we can do.

JOLMAYA'S MOTHER: How are we supposed to know what to do?

MOTHER-IN-LAW: What can we do? If only *nhyasu* would come soon.

JOLMAYA'S MOTHER: Yes, *nhyasu* hasn't come, she says. Has it come yet?

JOLMAYA: No, it hasn't come.

JOLMAYA'S MOTHER: It hasn't come, without *nhyasu* what can we do?

MOTHER-IN-LAW: Until the *nhyasu* comes, until a little water breaks, we can't do anything.

*JOLMAYA'S MOTHER: Until the *nhyasu* comes you need not even sit in that position.

(*The* MOTHER-IN-LAW *goes to get the* BIRTH ATTENDANT.)

- - - - - -

(*The* BIRTH ATTENDANT *returns and takes over.*)

JOLMAYA: *Aiya* . . .

BIRTH ATTENDANT: Her petticoat is too tight around her stomach.

JOLMAYA'S MOTHER: The baby had moved up before. I told her to tie it higher, and she tied it.

BIRTH ATTENDANT: Now it's come down.

*JOLMAYA'S MOTHER: Is it down?

(MOTHER-IN-LAW *brings in a pot of burning corn cobs.*)

BIRTH ATTENDANT: If *nhyasu* comes, then this would be all right.

JOLMAYA'S MOTHER: She says it hasn't come.

*BIRTH ATTENDANT: If only it would come.

*JOLMAYA: I can't stand it, oh mother, Narayan, *aiya*, Narayan, I can't stand it.

*JOLMAYA'S MOTHER: (*some words unclear*) . . . Food . . . she wouldn't eat you know.

*BIRTH ATTENDANT: What?

*JOLMAYA'S MOTHER: When the first one was born . . .

- - - - - -

*JOLMAYA: How can I stand it? How can I stand it? Narayan, it's unbearable, *aiya* . . . Narayan, *aiya* . . .

- - - - - -

*JOLMAYA: I can't stand it, Narayan.

*BIRTH ATTENDANT: A lot of water hasn't come down yet, has it?

*JOLMAYA'S MOTHER: Not yet.

*MOTHER-IN-LAW: Until the water comes . . .

*JOLMAYA: Narayan, I can't stand it, *aiya*, what can I do, *aiya*, what can I do? *Aiya*, what can I do?

BIRTH ATTENDANT: It's moving a lot now.

MOTHER-IN-LAW: What?

BIRTH ATTENDANT: It's moving a lot now.

JOLMAYA: *Aiya*, What can I do?

*MOTHER-IN-LAW: Somewhere, somewhere, it's being blocked.

*BIRTH ATTENDANT: We need to perform *bhagiyana* [a blessing] on this side . . .

*JOLMAYA'S MOTHER: Do it.

*BIRTH ATTENDANT: Look, perform a blessing.

BIRTH ATTENDANT: Perform a *bhagiyana* now, on her side.

MOTHER-IN-LAW: Yes . . .

BIRTH ATTENDANT: Go take it and come back.

(JOLMAYA'S MOTHER *follows the* BIRTH ATTENDANT*'s instructions to prepare an offering plate to lure away evil spirits that may be blocking the birth.*)

JOLMAYA: *Aiya*, what can I do, what can I do? Narayan.

BIRTH ATTENDANT: What's in the way?

JOLMAYA: *Aiya*, what can I do? I can't stand it I say.

BIRTH ATTENDANT: This isn't right.

JOLMAYA: *Aiya – aiya*, oh, I can't bear it.

*BIRTH ATTENDANT: Get up.

- - - - - -

(JOLMAYA'S MOTHER *takes the offering plate and sprinkles water on* JOLMAYA.)

JOLMAYA: Narayan . . . *aiya*.

BIRTH ATTENDANT: Circle it around that side.

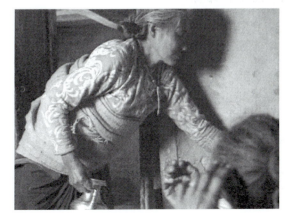

JOLMAYA: Narayan.
BIRTH ATTENDANT: Where shall I put this mat?
JOLMAYA: *Aiya . . .* how can I take this?
(JOLMAYA'S MOTHER *circles the plate over* JOLMAYA. *She takes it out to leave at the crossroads at the edge of the village.*)
BIRTH ATTENDANT: Get up, get up.
- - - - - -

(BIRTH ATTENDANT *stands with legs straddling* JOLMAYA. *She applies pressure to the sides of her belly to help move the baby down.*)
JOLMAYA: *Aiya,* what can I do?
MOTHER-IN-LAW: Pull up the front pleats of her skirt.
BIRTH ATTENDANT: What?

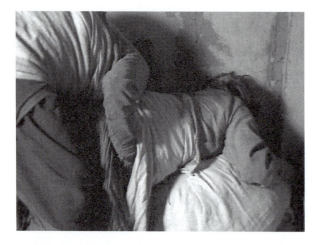

JOLMAYA: What can I do?
MOTHER-IN-LAW: Pull up the front of her skirt, I said.
JOLMAYA'S MOTHER: Pull up the front of her skirt.
BIRTH ATTENDANT: Move up a little. Move your stomach up a little higher. That's right.
(*When* JOLMAYA'S MOTHER *returns the birth comes very quickly.* JOLMAYA *pushes, her waters break, and the baby is born. With just a glance at the baby, they concentrate on delivering the placenta.*)
BIRTH ATTENDANT: Swallow your hair. Make yourself vomit.
JOLMAYA'S MOTHER: Try to vomit.
MOTHER-IN-LAW: How big.[13]
BIRTH ATTENDANT: Watch out for the baby. Make yourself vomit.
JOLMAYA'S MOTHER: Watch out for the baby. Try to vomit.
MOTHER-IN-LAW: Move the baby first I say.
*BIRTH ATTENDANT: What?
*JOLMAYA: How can I stand it?

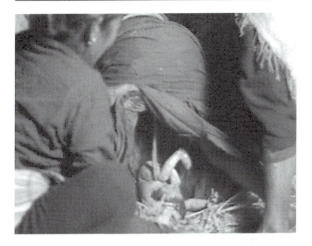

*JOLMAYA'S MOTHER: Move the baby, move the baby.
*JOLMAYA: What can I do? This is awful.
*MOTHER-IN-LAW: Make yourself vomit, swallow your hair and vomit.
*JOLMAYA'S MOTHER: Swallow your hair and try to vomit.
*BIRTH ATTENDANT: Watch out for the baby.
*JOLMAYA'S MOTHER: Put a clump of hair in your mouth and swallow it.

- - - - - -

BIRTH ATTENDANT: It's a girl.
JOLMAYA'S MOTHER: Don't worry, try to vomit, try to vomit.
MOTHER-IN-LAW: Look and see, has it [the placenta] come out?
JOLMAYA'S MOTHER: It doesn't seem to have come out yet.
BIRTH ATTENDANT (to MOTHER-IN-LAW): There must still be something that
    feels like a ball in her stomach.
MOTHER-IN-LAW (to BIRTH ATTENDANT): You know I don't know anything.
BIRTH ATTENDANT: It hasn't come yet.
MOTHER-IN-LAW: I don't know.
BIRTH ATTENDANT: There must be something like a ball in her stomach –
    press it all the way down.

- - - - - -

BIRTH ATTENDANT: Vomit, try to vomit.
MOTHER-IN-LAW: People who have such long hair.
BIRTH ATTENDANT: Rinse some water around on the *hasa* [flat winnowing
    basket]. Rinse some water in the *hasa* and give it to her to drink.
*MOTHER-IN-LAW: The *hasa* isn't here.
*JOLMAYA'S MOTHER: The *hasa*?
*MOTHER-IN-LAW: It's downstairs with mustard seeds in it.
*BIRTH ATTENDANT: Make yourself gag, vomit, vomit . . . It hasn't come out
    yet.

- - - - - -

(*The placenta comes out.*)

JOLMAYA'S MOTHER: Hold still.

BIRTH ATTENDANT: Don't move that way.

JOLMAYA'S MOTHER: Don't move.

BIRTH ATTENDANT: It's come, it's come.

JOLMAYA: It's come.

BIRTH ATTENDANT: It's come, it's come.

MOTHER-IN-LAW: Has it come out?

BIRTH ATTENDANT: Yes. Hey, where are you going? Go the other way.

MOTHER-IN-LAW: Watch out.

BIRTH ATTENDANT: Over there, over there.

JOLMAYA'S MOTHER: Never mind, bring it here.

BIRTH ATTENDANT: Lean back against that. Watch your leg, what kind of a person!

*BIRTH ATTENDANT: Blood is coming out fast.

*JOLMAYA'S MOTHER: We need the box of soap. We have the soap, don't we?

*BIRTH ATTENDANT: Get it, now the one who couldn't wait two months . . .

*JOLMAYA'S MOTHER: She says they don't know how to do it . . . (*unclear*)

- - - - - -

(*The* MOTHER-IN-LAW *puts the placenta in a small clay bowl and covers it with a cloth.*)

JOLMAYA'S MOTHER: Over there.

MOTHER-IN-LAW: Move that, move that over there.

BIRTH ATTENDANT: We have to heat some water for this one [the baby].

(*Hearing the baby cry, several* NEIGHBOURS *who have been sitting outside in the courtyard come in.*)

*FIRST NEIGHBOUR: Did she [Barbara] give you the soap this morning? (*to Barbara*) Did you give them the soap this morning?

SECOND NEIGHBOUR: What is it? A girl or a boy?

BIRTH ATTENDANT: It's a girl.

FIRST NEIGHBOUR: *Bhagi ti.* When it's a girl it's hard.

BIRTH ATTENDANT: Yes. It took a long time.

FIRST NEIGHBOUR: When it's a girl it's hard.

BIRTH ATTENDANT: That's right. The baby was down low since early this morning.

MOTHER-IN-LAW: They say it's always a little harder when it's a girl.

BIRTH ATTENDANT: She [Barbara] brought this soap to give us.

FIRST NEIGHBOUR: That's for washing the baby. Look at her hair!

BIRTH ATTENDANT: As long as she was inside [the womb] she didn't need to cry. Now she's out she cries.

*FIRST NEIGHBOUR: It's finally over, isn't it?

*BIRTH ATTENDANT: From early in the morning . . .

- - - - - -

FIRST NEIGHBOUR (*to* MOTHER-IN-LAW): Pour some mustard oil for her to drink so her womb won't hurt.

MOTHER-IN-LAW (*to* FIRST NEIGHBOUR): Who?

SECOND NEIGHBOUR (*to* MOTHER-IN-LAW): Your daughter-in-law, your daughter-in-law.

BIRTH ATTENDANT (*to* JOLMAYA): Drink some oil, so your womb won't hurt.

FIRST NEIGHBOUR (*to* JOLMAYA): Then it won't hurt, you know. Look, take it in your right hand.

FIRST NEIGHBOUR (*to* MOTHER-IN-LAW): Not your hand – hers.

BIRTH ATTENDANT (*to* JOLMAYA): Drink a little.

FIRST NEIGHBOUR (*to* JOLMAYA): It will still hurt, but the pain won't be as bad.

MOTHER-IN-LAW: Here, drink this.

???: The water is hot.

FIRST NEIGHBOUR (*to* MOTHER-IN-LAW): You must have rushed to get the bowl from my house.

MOTHER-IN-LAW (*to* FIRST NEIGHBOUR): We don't have a single pot here when we need it!

MOTHER-IN-LAW (*to* BIRTH ATTENDANT?): Pour me some water.

FIRST NEIGHBOUR: I'll pour it for you.

MOTHER-IN-LAW: Don't you see my seven hands?

(MOTHER-IN-LAW *is flustered trying to do so much at once.*)

FIRST NEIGHBOUR: Pour the oil in her hand to drink.

BIRTH ATTENDANT: Mmmm.

FIRST NEIGHBOUR: My mother's eldest sister always made me drink oil like that. She would give me three palmfuls.

BIRTH ATTENDANT: I never drank it.

MOTHER-IN-LAW (*to* JOLMAYA): Here, take this.

FIRST NEIGHBOUR (*to* MOTHER-IN-LAW): Give it to her.

JOLMAYA (*to* MOTHER-IN-LAW): That's enough, I don't want any more.

JOLMAYA'S MOTHER (*to* JOLMAYA): Your stomach will hurt, your womb.

- - - - - -

FIRST NEIGHBOUR: They bundled the baby in an old piece of skirt cloth and brought it here in a hurry.

(JOLMAYA'S MOTHER *is looking for thread to tie the umbilical cord.*)

JOLMAYA'S MOTHER: I need more thread.

FIRST NEIGHBOUR: I wonder what all this is on her hair? Look at her yawning away. Look at her hair, and her forehead is so bright and shiny, this little girl's.

MOTHER-IN-LAW: Her hair will be beautiful.

FIRST NEIGHBOUR: I wanted to come up here earlier, but I was too shy. Just like when Chirimaya had her baby. Honestly, first I was too embarrassed, I felt shy, and then I just rushed in here.

BIRTH ATTENDANT: Tulsi says that she came to visit here three times. She says she never goes to anyone's house.

JOLMAYA'S MOTHER: Tulsi who?

BIRTH ATTENDANT: Tulsi from Daigal,[14] she says she came to visit three times.

*FIRST NEIGHBOUR: When their daughter-in-law had her baby.

*BIRTH ATTENDANT: She usually doesn't come down from upstairs.

*FIRST NEIGHBOUR: That's right. You don't need to cover down low. You have so much discharge. As for me, even when I have my period, you can barely see it.

*BIRTH ATTENDANT: Like the mark of a *tika*?

*FIRST NEIGHBOUR: Yes, and when I give birth there's not much either . . .

BIRTH ATTENDANT (*to* MOTHER-IN-LAW): Here, pour me some water.

SECOND NEIGHBOUR: It's a girl, a little girl.

FIRST NEIGHBOUR: Take the bowl.
MOTHER-IN-LAW: It's here already.

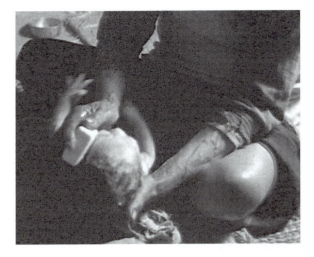

SECOND NEIGHBOUR: You don't have to pour it so low . . .
BIRTH ATTENDANT: I should start washing here first, right?
FIRST NEIGHBOUR: Yes, wash her face all at once. We people don't know much.
*FIRST NEIGHBOUR: When you go there [to the hospital], who knows what
    they do, as soon as the baby is born it's brought out, water is heated, and
    with the hot water . . .

- - - - - -

*BIRTH ATTENDANT: We waited and waited, the baby wasn't born till evening,
    around sunset.
*MOTHER-IN-LAW: I also gave birth at that time.
*BIRTH ATTENDANT: It couldn't move at all, and couldn't see a thing.
*JOLMAYA'S MOTHER: When we brought (unclear) in, I was also telling them . . .
*BIRTH ATTENDANT: When that baby was born it couldn't see a thing, and
    then there was bleeding, clots of blood fell on the floor, I've never seen it
    like that. I mopped it up from the floor and put it in a basket, and the two
    of us put her to sleep and left. We put her to sleep, and then in the
    evening I went back to see if she had been fed or not, and the baby still
    couldn't see, that evening . . .
BIRTH ATTENDANT: . . . and then I told Chiriba to give his mother some warm
    milk to drink, and I myself put it in a glass and gave it to her and left.
BIRTH ATTENDANT (to MOTHER-IN-LAW): Don't you have a bowl?
MOTHER-IN-LAW: Don't pour it on the floor, pour it over the plate.
BIRTH ATTENDANT: Why use a plate if you have a bowl?
BIRTH ATTENDANT: Pour it here.

- - - - - -

BIRTH ATTENDANT: Is there more water left upstairs?
MOTHER-IN-LAW: There's still some left.
BIRTH ATTENDANT: Pour it, pour it here. It's not gone yet is it?
MOTHER-IN-LAW: There's still some left.

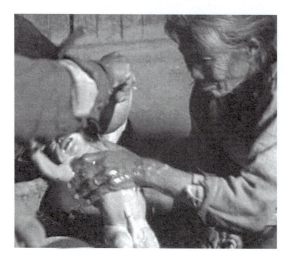

(*The* MOTHER-IN-LAW *pours warm water to rinse off the soap.*)
*BIRTH ATTENDANT: There is hair inside the elbow too.
*MOTHER-IN-LAW: Don't you see the hair?
*BIRTH ATTENDANT: Sure, lots of hair.
*MOTHER-IN-LAW: Ummm.
*JOLMAYA'S MOTHER?: So much hair . . .
*BIRTH ATTENDANT: She has so much hair.
- - - - - -
*MOTHER-IN-LAW: There's water upstairs – everything's over now, I'll go get
     the water.
*BIRTH ATTENDANT: Get it and bring it here.
BIRTH ATTENDANT: Listen to her 'sing'. If only she had a little less . . . ooh,
     look at it roll off, now I'll massage her with oil and wipe off more of it.
(*They warm mustard oil over the hot coals, and when the baby is dry she will
     receive her first massage.*)
*JOLMAYA: Shall I take this off?
*JOLMAYA'S MOTHER: Take it off.
*JOLMAYA: Now do I put this on too?
*JOLMAYA'S MOTHER: Are you going to put on a *parsi* [skirt]?
*JOLMAYA: Yes, if you'd give me the one on top there.
*JOLMAYA'S MOTHER: This one?
*JOLMAYA: Yes.
*JOLMAYA'S MOTHER: I thought you told me to take the one over there.

*BIRTH ATTENDANT: Go ahead, pour more water.

*MOTHER-IN-LAW: You need to wash more around the rectum . . . hair, more hair (*unclear*).

- - - - - -

*JOLMAYA'S MOTHER (*pouring mustard oil*): Will this much be enough?

*BIRTH ATTENDANT: That's not enough.

*JOLMAYA'S MOTHER: Shall I pour some more?

*MOTHER-IN-LAW: Go ahead, pour it.

*BIRTH ATTENDANT: The hair still has to be wiped off, with an oil massage.

*JOLMAYA'S MOTHER: How much shall I put in?

*MOTHER-IN-LAW: I should empty the bowl, shouldn't I?

*BIRTH ATTENDANT: What?

MOTHER-IN-LAW (*to* BIRTH ATTENDANT): You don't need the bowl, do you?

BIRTH ATTENDANT (*to* MOTHER-IN-LAW): No, empty it.

MOTHER-IN-LAW: I'll take these outside, OK?

BIRTH ATTENDANT: Take them.

MOTHER-IN-LAW: This is for you to wash your hands. Now, if it's better we could tie this tightly.

- - - - - -

*BIRTH ATTENDANT: Here, look, it's still not off the armpits. Now I'll have to wipe this all again.

MOTHER-IN-LAW: Move the *maka:* [pot with coals] over a little, that's good.

JOLMAYA: The pants aren't here.

JOLMAYA'S MOTHER: They're here. Here they are.

- - - - - -

*MOTHER-IN-LAW: We'll have to take it out.

*BIRTH ATTENDANT: Take the bedding, it's yours, isn't it?

*MOTHER-IN-LAW: Give it to me, yes.

*JOLMAYA'S MOTHER: I'll move it, OK?

*BIRTH ATTENDANT: Yes, move it.

*JOLMAYA'S MOTHER: Whoever it is.

*BIRTH ATTENDANT (*to* MOTHER-IN-LAW): You're making a shadow [for the filming].

*JOLMAYA'S MOTHER: That's what I was going to say.

*MOTHER-IN-LAW: You sit there in one place somewhere, lay out something to sit on.

- - - - - -

*MOTHER-IN-LAW (*to* JOLMAYA): Now if you put on a *parsi* [skirt] [going to the bathroom?] will be easier.

*JOLMAYA'S MOTHER (*to* JOLMAYA): Yes it will be easier. Step on the bottom of the *parsi* and pull it down.

*JOLMAYA'S MOTHER (*to* JOLMAYA): Wrap yourself in the flannel *ga* [shawl], you don't need to tie it around. Put on the *jani* [waist-cloth] too. Put it on the other way, the other way, lift the *jani* up.

*MOTHER-IN-LAW (*to* BIRTH ATTENDANT): Shall I bring you some warm *ela* [rice liquor]?

*BIRTH ATTENDANT (*to* MOTHER-IN-LAW): You can bring it now.

- - - - - -

BIRTH ATTENDANT: I was sitting out in the sun carding cotton. I went in, and the baby was born as soon as I got upstairs. My mother-in-law was out in front of Bishnu Lal's. There weren't even any children around.

JOLMAYA'S MOTHER: Everyone was working.

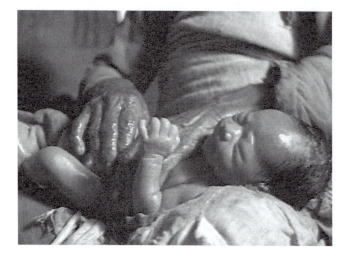

BIRTH ATTENDANT: Yes, so I called out the window to my mother-in-law. She came in and said, 'I just saw you outside, and now the baby is already born.'

- - - - - -

*MOTHER-IN-LAW: Are you finished with it?

*BIRTH ATTENDANT: I'm finished.

*MOTHER-IN-LAW: Do you see, there's still water on her neck? Barbara, I have to go through here.

BIRTH ATTENDANT: . . . and I told her not to wrap it around the stomach, at the store . . .

MOTHER-IN-LAW: We don't need that. Now we have a *parsi* [skirt cloth] (*unclear*).

BIRTH ATTENDANT: Don't you have some old torn *janis* [waistcloths]? If you have a *jani*, it would be good to wrap the baby in.

- - - - - -

JOLMAYA'S MOTHER: We have to tear it.

BIRTH ATTENDANT: OK.

MOTHER-IN-LAW: Tomorrow or the day after we may need . . .

(*The* BIRTH ATTENDANT *wraps the baby in a clean piece of cloth.*)

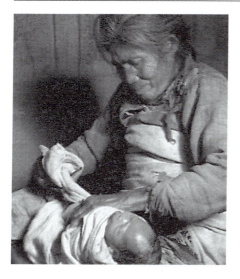

BIRTH ATTENDANT: There, now, where is the baby going to be put?

JOLMAYA: First we have to move the *suku* [straw mat].

(JOLMAYA *is putting on a fresh skirt. When it gets dark she will go out and wash her soiled clothing herself. They push the dirty straw into a corner, and lay out a mat for* JOLMAYA *and the baby.*)

BIRTH ATTENDANT (*to* JOLMAYA): . . . one place that isn't wet, put them in there, and then you can go and rinse them out.

JOLMAYA: I'll go and wash them later. It might show outside.

MOTHER-IN-LAW: Are you going to tie that?

BIRTH ATTENDANT: Yes.

JOLMAYA (*to* BIRTH ATTENDANT): Shall I put them [my dirty clothes] here?
BIRTH ATTENDANT: Put them there, and then you'll take them all . . . Now, where shall I put this one [the baby]?
MOTHER-IN-LAW: Put her over there.

(*My film runs out just before* JOLMAYA *sits down to hold her daughter for the first time.*)

Notes

1 This video is available from DER (Documentary Educational Resources), 101 Morse Street, Watertown, MA 02172, USA (email: docued@der.org).
2 For Newar domestic architecture see Auer and Gutschow 1977; Toffin 1977: 137–60.
3 For other accounts of birth among the Newars see Bomgaars 1976; Dhungel 1980; Lienhard 1986; Toffin 1984, ch. 5.
4 An aspect of the god Vishnu.
5 Yele is the Newar name for Patan, the closest of the three Kathmandu Valley cities to Thecho.
6 A respectful form of greeting.
7 Signs that the birth is imminent
8 Name of a place.
9 The *kothay* is the usual room for birth. The *mata* is the sitting room (see Introduction).
10 Name of a place.
11 The sitting room, just outside the room they are in.
12 Another name for the birth attendant?
13 May refer to the baby's hands, feet or ears.
14 A place in the village.

References

Auer, G. and N. Gutschow. 1977. Domestic architecture of Nepal. *Art and Archaeology Research Papers* 12: 64–8.
Bomgaars, M. 1976. *The Traditional Birth Attendants in Nepal: Existing Practices and Suggestions for Training.* Kathmandu: United Mission to Nepal, Community Health Programme, Shanta Bhawan Hospital.
Dhungel, B. 1980. The Newars. In *Traditional and Prevailing Childrearing Practices among Different Communities in Nepal*, edited by S. Paneru. Centre for Nepal and Asian Studies, Tribhuvan University, Kirtipur.
Gellner, D.N. and D. Quigley (eds). 1995. *Contested Hierarchies: A Collaborative Ethnography of Caste among the Newars of the Kathmandu Valley, Nepal.* Oxford: Clarendon Press.
Ishii, H. 2000. Bon, Buddhist and Hindu life cycle rituals: a comparison. In *New Horizons in Bon Studies*, edited by S.G. Karmay and Y. Nagano. Osaka: National Museum of Ethnology (Bon Studies, 2.)
Lienhard, S. 1986. Dreimal Unreinheit: Riten und Gebrauche des Nevars bei Geburt, Menstruation und Tod. In *Formen Kulturelles Wandels und andere Beiträge zur*

Erforschung des Himalaya, edited by Bernhard Kolver. VGH-Wissenschaftsverlag, Sankt Augustin.

Nepali, G.S. 1965. *The Newars: An Ethno-sociological Study of a Himalayan Community*. Bombay: United Asia Publications.

Toffin, G. 1977. *Pyangaon, une communauté Newar de la Vallée de Kathmandou: la vie matérielle*. Paris: Editions du Centre National de la Recherche Scientifique.

—— 1984. *Société et religion chez les Newar du Népal*. Paris: Editions du Centre National de la Recherche Scientifique.

Wintle, P. and J. Homiak. 1995. *Guide to the Collections, Human Studies Film Archives, National Museum of Natural History*. Smithsonian Institution, Washington, DC.

Chapter 3

Knowing all the gods

Grandmothers, god families and women healers in Nepal[1]

Linda Iltis

South Asian women healers, if they are described at all in Western scholarship, are not infrequently characterised as having less significant roles than male healers. Instances of higher ritual status of women are also described as being temporary reversals of the normal lower status that women have in everyday life.[2] Without denying that women in South Asian society have difficult lives and are victims of male oppression, we can still recognise that women who are primary actors in a variety of contexts may function independently of, and without concern one way or another for, the contextually variable patriarchal system that some Western scholars permanently essentialise. The Buddhist concept of impermanence allows men and women to transcend the notion of permanent suffering and to live a lifestyle organised around the goal of removing suffering of themselves and others. Individual responsibility for this is strongly encouraged, regardless of gender. In a Buddhist world system, then, all must take 'right action' as primary actors. Recent scholarship which identifies women and low-caste groups as 'subaltern', or 'peripheral', and goddesses as 'wild' or 'untamed', seems to remove these individuals from even being considered in the realm of positive actors or subjects, and to marginalise or relegate them to the status of 'vassals', or objects of ongoing oppression. Whose world is it, anyway? In the world of a woman healer, *dya: māju*, who is a medium or human 'vessel' for the tutelary Buddhist Goddess Hāritī, we find an ongoing sense of responsibility to an entire community of people in need of relief from suffering. She harbours a special concern for the health and well-being of children and their young mothers, with whom she can most readily identify, being a grandmother herself.

The Newars of the Kathmandu Valley have an especially deep reverence for the ancestor-god couple, Grandfather and Grandmother, Āju and Ajimā. These two sagacious deities, who are identified with Bhairava and Kālī, teach and protect the community in a way similar to personal family elders.[3] All the people of the locality also feel they are the children of these two. Just as children are guided by grandparents, the gods Āju and Ajimā guide the community through rough moments and times of suffering.

One of the more difficult forms of suffering known to humankind is birth. Suffering is going to happen; it is evident, unpredictable and may escalate into tragedy, even when every precaution is taken. Newar women are psychologically prepared, from childhood on, to accept this eventuality, in part through their early associations with grandparents, and through intersection with and proximity to Ajimā ritual activities, including offering of both after-birth and funeral offerings at the same crossroads site. There is death as surely as there is life. But Ajimā helps remove suffering associated with both. In puberty rituals for Newar girls, *bhārataygu*, where young girls are isolated in a dark room for several days, an image of Ajimā is sometimes drawn on the wall of the room for protection and guidance. This establishes an early association of this goddess with female reproductive abilities in the minds of women. Newar midwife birthing specialists may also be called *aji* or *diri aji* (Toffin 1984: 127–31). Ajimā, in her form of Hāritī, is the tutelary grandmother goddess for Newar women healers called *dya: māju* or Hāritī Mā. This goddess, her god family and her human counterparts serve family and community as healers in contexts ranging from pregnancy and childbirth to disease and village conflicts.

Hāritī in Buddhist legend and history

The Goddess Hāritī is a Buddhist Goddess of protection, sometimes identified in non-Buddhist contexts with Śītalā, Goddess of Smallpox; she is reputedly a goddess who converted to Buddhism from her bloodthirsty habits of eating children (Slusser 1982: 216, 328–9; Dasgupta 1969: 262 n. 1 and 2; Getty 1928: 84–7). Her widespread popularity is partially due to her association with protection from smallpox in a setting of smallpox epidemics. But she is widely worshipped and consulted for removal of both physical and psychological illnesses unrelated to smallpox, and not all early historical references to her mention this particular disease or its symptoms in connection with her. She is considered to be especially efficacious in protecting and curing children, and she is also consulted for problems of fertility and childbirth. Iconographically and culturally, Hāritī is one of the most famous Ajimā goddesses in the Kathmandu Valley, and has early associations with Buddhism dating to 200 BCE. The stories and imagery surrounding Hāritī come from early Buddhist texts. Along with her *yakṣa* husband, Pañcika (later Kuvera), the *yakṣinī* Hāritī is depicted in Gandharan and Mathura sculptures, identified with early stūpa sites, and found in Buddhist monastery refectories of ancient India.[4] There are numerous Buddhist textual sources detailing the conversion of Hāritī, including one that has detailed guidelines for rituals, mantras and mūdras.[5] A now famous ninth-century image from Yarkhoto, Central Asia, of Hāritī surrounded by eight children, one suckling at her breast, was nicknamed the 'Notre Dame de Tourfan' and the 'Buddhist Madonna' (see Figure 3.1; Foucher 1910, 1972:

Figure 3.1 Notre Dame de Tourfan
    Source: Getty 1928, after Foucher 1910.

276).[6] According to Getty (1928: 84), Hārītī's identities in other Buddhist
areas include: Yid-'phrog-ma (Tibetan = 'Heart-ravishing'), Kui-tzū-mu-
shen or Sung-tzu (Chinese = 'Mother of Demons' or 'Giver of Sons'), and
Ki-shi-mo-jin or Koyasu Kwan-non (Japanese = 'Mother of Demons' or
'Giver of Sons').[7]

According to some oral traditions and early Buddhist texts, Hārītī, in a previous lifetime, was made to dance when she was pregnant. She had a
miscarriage as a result. She was so angered and resentful that in her next life
she gradually became an ogress, and had 500 children, but vowed to eat all the
other children of Rājgriha to sustain her own. This earned her the nickname
Hārītī, or 'stealer of children'. Upon hearing this, the Buddha stole her
youngest favourite child, Piṅgala (or Priyaṅkara), and hid him under his beg-
ging bowl. Hārītī was upset when the child went missing and went to the
Buddha for help. He asked, how she could feel bad about losing only one of
her 500 children, when some women had lost their only child? She said it was
her favourite child. Then Buddha showed her the suffering she had caused to
the women whom she had taken children from. He converted Hārītī to
Buddhism, and she vowed to stop killing and start protecting children. The
Buddha also assured her that his monks would make sure that Hārītī and her

children were always fed. The name Hāritī means 'stealer of children', but through conversion to Buddhism she is transformed into the 'remover of suffering'. The Buddha also mandated that Buddhist monks would be responsible for feeding her children. This is why her shrine is located in monastery refectories.

Early Chinese travellers to India, Hiuan Tsang and I-tsing (see Foucher 1901, 1972), mention the Hāritī stūpa *Sare makh Dheri,* located near Peshawar (Chārsadda) in Pakistan, as the site where Hāritī was converted.[8] They also note the presence of Hāritī shrines or images in monastic refectories throughout North India, and identify Chinese names for Hāritī. Foucher (1901), at the turn of the twentieth century, found that Hindus and Muslims in formerly Buddhist areas still believed in the efficacy of dirt from the Hāritī stūpa site for curing childhood illnesses. Gandharan images of Hāritī and her children depict what Foucher (1910, 1972), Waddell (1912) and others call a 'Madonna-like' figure, a woman with six to eight babies on her lap or shoulders, and playing at her feet. Images of Hāritī are also found in China and Japan and at Caṇḍi Mendut near Borobuḍur, Java.[9]

Contemporary representations and meanings of Hāritī

In the Kathmandu Valley of Nepal, Ajimā Hāritī shrines are usually the first to be approached to counter childhood illness and other grave illnesses by both Hindus and Buddhists. She is visited by Newars, Brahmans, Chetris, Tamangs, Gurungs and Tibetans. Newar Vajrācāryā priests conduct special *chāhāykegu pūjās* (see Figure 3.2) for clients at the large Hāritī temple at Svayambhū.[10] Hāritī is worshipped by Tibetan monks at meal time, by making five-finger-fist-squeezed food offerings with rice or *tsampa,* to Hāritī and her children.[11] Hāritī shrines are located adjacent to many Buddhist vihāras in Kathmandu Valley. At the famous Vikramaśila Mahāvihāra in Kathmandu, there is still a ritual teasing of Ajimā's baby during the festival of Indra Jātra. And at Bodhanath Stupa there is an image of Hāritī eating a baby.

Typically, she is represented with at least six, and sometimes eight children, usually with one on her shoulder. At Svayambhū Chaitya in Nepal, the presence of a large Hāritī shrine has the appearance of Hindu hegemony by virtue of associations with the Hindu goddess Śītalā; but in fact the connection to Mahāyakṣiṇī Hāritī and Buddhism has been continuous and the primary focus all along.[12]

Both early textual and contemporary oral traditions[13] refer to suffering and children, especially the loss of them. Suffering is a key Buddhist idea. The physical suffering associated with childbirth is a part of the Life of the Buddha. Loss of a child is one type of suffering that is especially hard to rationalise. So the conversion of Hāritī to help with this common occurrence is a novel Buddhist phenomenon that reaches out to the non-monastic

Figure 3.2 A Vajrācāryā performs the chāhāykegu pūjā, 'pouring ritual' at the Hāritī shrine west of Svayambhū Stūpa (photo by Linda Iltis)

Buddhist and Hindu lay community, particularly to married couples, and especially to women. When Hāritī converts to Buddhism, she takes the three refuges and five precepts and thus becomes a lay follower of the Buddha. She does not become a nun. Buddha also offers to support her children from the monastery of monks. While this tradition is kept by Vajrācāryās and Tibetan monks, the focus on laypeople in the Buddhist Hāritī stories seems to be maintained and intensified in the contemporary human embodiment of Hāritī through her designated 'vessels', the *dya: māju* healers.

Dya: māju: god women vessels for Hāritī

Outside of the formal temple, Ajimā's presence is acknowledged at designated crossroads for quick offerings. The ready availability of Ajimā is significant since it means that potential relief from suffering is never very far away. Hāritī Ajimā may also be cultivated as a tutelary goddess by women who receive tantric initiation from a Vajrācāryā priest and become specialists as human 'vessel' supports for direct consultation with the goddess. These 'god women', called *dya: māju*, may or may not have a spiritual illness prior to becoming a specialist.[14] But they need training in mantra, mūdra, recitation, visualisation and ritual procedure. Through the tutelary goddess Hāritī, a *dya: māju* has access to virtually all the gods and goddesses of the Newar world. Beginning with her own six children – Dhanabhāju, Dhanamayju, Lātibhāju, Lātimayju, Jhilambhāju, Jhilammayju – her sister goddesses and teachers, etc., she also can be possessed by a tiger spirit or Nārāyāna, or any god. The possibility of direct possession-dialogue experience gives other

Figure 3.3 Portrait of a *dya: māju* with one of her *mūdras*
(photo by Linda Iltis)

non-specialist clients personalised access to deities in a way not possible in other public ritual contexts. The rituals of the Vajrācāryā priests are, by contrast, less participatory for a client.[15]

In hearing about a woman becoming a 'vessel' we might flinch at the possible Western association of the 'woman as vessel waiting to be filled', but as we shall see, *pātras*, especially tantric ones, are more than the 'mere vessels' that our narrowly conceived English definition allows for. In both Hindu and Buddhist tantric religious practice, the *pātra*, or ritual vessel, serves as a central focus for ritual action. The 'vessel' into which a deity is invited to temporarily enter and reside may be a clay or metal water pot, an image or a human being.[16] Human *pātras* may be male or female.

The idea of 'vessel' is linked, verbally and conceptually, with concepts of possession expressed in terms of filling the vessel. The Newari term *dubina* refers to the act of possession or 'going inside'. Etymologically, it also has the extended sense of 'surrender' or 'giving in', or 'allowing entrance', *du* = in, and *biye* = give.[17] The amount of control, or volition, is dependent on the context. *Dya: mājus* themselves are sometimes called *Hārītī Mā* after the name of their tutelary goddess. The term *dya: māju* means 'respected god woman', and a male counterpart would be *dya: ju*, or 'respected god man'. Unlike other male *pātras* for ritual dance groups, *dya: mājus* are not made eligible for their *pātra*-ship through residential affiliation, inheritance, or obligatory lottery drawings. However, some may acquire their interest and inspiration from another *dya: māju* in the community, and later resolve to become trained and initiated by a Vajrācārya priest. While male *pātras* get initiation for and possessed by only one god, a *dya: māju* I know used to say, 'I can be possessed by *all* the gods. I know all the gods and goddess' songs, mantras and mūdras'.

The *dya: māju* in everyday life

The primary informant for this study was a *dya: māju* who is a resident of a Newar farming community.[18] Her becoming a *dya: māju* was the result of self-motivated study and initiation with a Newar Buddhist Vajrācārya priest and tantric master from another neighbouring community, about a half a mile away. Her studies began once her children were growing up. When not involved in her rituals, consultations and pilgrimages to Hārītī shrines, she is engaged in agriculture, herding, spinning, weaving and caring for her grandchildren.

Her *pātra*-ship is not a full-time occupation, but a state of always being on call in case of need, and possession is not necessarily a daily event. Dwelling within the lay community, this *dya: māju* lives a life of perpetual readiness. This involves establishing and maintaining an increased level of purity, especially appropriate to the gods or goddesses that will temporarily come in. She and her husband must both observe certain dietary and hygiene restrictions. Failure to prepare adequately for possession may result in gods or goddesses either not attending or becoming angry and disruptive during a possession. The husband of a *dya: māju* may assist in ritual procedure for his wife during and after her possession by helping to make offerings, by shifting ritual items and cleaning up. He also helps clients to converse with the deities by verbally punctuating highlights of the *dya: māju*'s words. Assistance may also be provided by a close friend or relative, who aspires to become a *dya: māju* herself one day.

Types of healing

The *dya: māju* is consulted *primarily* for infant and childhood illness, but she is also consulted in difficult pregnancies, after a miscarriage, for infertility or for healing bereaved parents over the loss of a child. Adults with other maladies may also consult her before or after consulting other specialists for an opinion or prognosis. *Dya: mājus* regularly refer clients to other specialists, including Western hospitals and clinics. These days, offering advice on dehydration is quite commonplace.

Childhood and maternity illnesses, by their nature, are rarely simple matters, though. Responsibility of the parent always looms large, whether at the edges or the centre of the illness. Clients who come to heal a child want not only relief for the physical suffering but also need reassurance and guidance in affirming the appropriateness of their actions. If the goddess can find a root of the illness to be caused by a simple oversight, then restoring confidence and hope to the parent can always help improve the chances for the child. But infant mortality fills parents with blame and remorse. It is as though the Buddhist idea of impermanence, exemplified in rebirth, becomes unfulfilled by a denial of rebirth. There is awkwardness all around. Newborn infants or stillborn babies are not yet full lineage members. In Barbara Johnson's film, *We Know How To Do These Things*, about Newar childbirth (see Chapter 2 this volume), the conversation among the women drifts on to the topic of how to dispose of the remains of such a child, and whether the hospitals can be trusted, since the spirits of dead infants can cause problems. The spirit of a dead infant may jealously keep subsequent children from being born. These spirits have to be given something too, and often feel neglected. Prenatal care involves ensuring that the spirit of the not-yet-born child is adequately fed to keep it from becoming an over-desirous person in life. Sometimes the spirit of a living infant can get lost, and has to be found and restored by a *dya: māju*.

Healing pain through removal of blame

One of the primary techniques employed by the *dya: māju* and her tutelary goddess, Ajimā, is to work together to physically and mentally *remove blame* from the victim. This is called *doṣa likāya*. Removal of guilt and self-blame from victims who have resulting physical or mental afflictions is an effective dimension of her healing techniques. When excessive physical problems are present, the *dya: māju* also refers her clients to local area hospitals. But her initial assistance to her clients' mental condition is invaluable for helping the clients overcome despair on the one hand, while aiding clients in their understanding of the injustice of their illness on the other. The client is asked to assist in her or his own healing through co-meditative ritual actions and questions and answers and dialogues.

Removal of blame is accomplished in a *pūjā* session, separate from the initial diagnosis, in which the client makes sets of seven offerings (prescribed during the diagnosis) to Hāritī and her six children. The *dya: māju* mimes consumption, enjoyment and acceptance of offerings, and the Goddess Ajimā expresses satisfaction. After this, she states where she will go to pacify certain other gods. She has multiple conversations. Usually, as each god or goddess manifests itself, the client is asked to offer obeisance, with some grains of rice.

If a former child spirit is causing problems, the *dya: māju* pacifies it with offerings, and tells it, 'You can be one of Hāritī's children. Now you will always be fed, and cared for.' If infertility is a problem, Ajimā asks additional gods who are *givers of children*, for example Nārāyaṇa or Harasiddhi, to give a prognosis for the client. Protocol also must be worked out between mutually jealous, or senior and junior, gods or goddesses.

The god might make pronouncements about good or bad deeds of the client, and project how many children the client can expect to have. The *dya: māju* tells the client: 'These future children will also become Hāritī's children, spiritually and physically protected, and carried proudly on the shoulders'. Ajimā also checks with her god sisters and finds out what possible unintentional infractions the client might have committed. This involves direct dialogue with the client, re-enacting or revisualising a past set of actions, retracing steps and being guided through to the source of a problem. When the source of the problem is found, Ajimā and her sisters, or sometimes one of her children, work with her to remove the blame or responsibility from the client. This involves reassuring recitations, elaborate mūdras, and choreography, aimed at sucking and sweeping away, and drawing the *doṣa* or blame and related physical pain *out* of the individual. By removing blame, the guilt and bad feelings are transferred away from the individual.

The ability of the *dya: māju* to remove blame ranges from individual to community at large. For a woman who has miscarried, she may help the client retrace past actions, diagnosing the client gradually and teasing out information about oversights and mistakes that the client might have made, even unknowingly. Like a good Western counsellor or crisis intervention specialist, she explains to those who are afflicted or victimised that it is not their fault and counteracts the tendency to self-blame. She then suggests ways that this can be avoided in the future and proceeds to remove the blame ritually through co-meditation. Women who were victims of physical abuse, who felt remorse or guilt, seemed to benefit from her treatments.

As already mentioned, the *dya: māju* has an ability to be possessed by any goddess or god, and she can even summon evil spirits to negotiate with them. She is not limited, restricted or assigned to a specific geographical region, pantheon or an individual deity.[19] She may speak directly with the client, telling them what to do. Her possession requires modest ritual offerings of incense and lamps, and she herself sings songs in Newari (sometimes in Sanskrit or Nepali) to assist in her possession. She makes possible a means for actual dialogue with a god or goddess through her human physical support as *dya: māju*. The *dya: māju*'s accessibility is enhanced by her not using distancing masks or costumes. The *dya: māju* is accessible throughout the year, at any time, and may perform in her home shrine or away from home. Male *pātras* differ from *dya: mājus* in each of these areas, by usually being host to only one particular god or goddess, on limited occasions, and often through hereditary or family obligation.

Figure 3.4 During a healing ritual the *dya: māju* uses *mūdras* (author's video still, 1992)

Figure 3.5 During a healing ritual the *dya: māju* holds her hands to her head like a crown to indicate her possession by the god Nārāyāṇa (author's video still, 1992)

Bedside manner and interactions with clients

A *dya: māju*'s interaction with her clients is much less predictable than the male *pātra*'s interaction with an audience. While certain mūdras, songs and stotras are memorised works, her diagnosis and healing dialogues and sequences are unique to every case. She engages the clients with physical contact, questions and co-meditative practice. She uses inclusive, friendly language with her clients, and livens the performances by mixing languages and voices in dramatic and convincing ways.

By contrast, Western-trained Nepali doctors use the lowest of familiar forms in addressing many village and Newar women patients, and display one of the most exclusionary and ill-received styles of bedside manner I have ever seen. Some Newars are so put off by Western-trained doctors they disdainfully proclaim 'they're all the same, doctor, *ḍhākka* [thief!] and dentist', and they feel the Western-trained clinicians are interested only in showing off their superiority, by inflicting additional pain and charging exorbitant fees to get rich quick. Barbara Johnson's film, *We Know How To Do These Things* (Chapter 2 this volume), also revealed some negative impressions of *nursni* mannerisms. During a visit to a hospital in Nepal, I witnessed a family standing at the bedside of a sick relative, nearly paralysed by a Western doctor who stormed in shouting to them in Nepali 'I crave blood! Give me blood!' without reference to what it was for, i.e. a transfusion for their relative. It was idiomatically spoken in the exact phrasing that a fierce goddess demanding a bloody sacrifice would have used, '*Malāi ragaṭ cāhincha! Ragaṭ dinus*' (Nepali).

Whether consulted for diagnosis of an illness or to receive a protective blessing, the *dya: māju* listens to the *nāḍī* (pulse), and checks the condition of hands and palms, discussing the overall symptoms. Then she summons the Goddess Hāritī, and presents the symptoms to her for consideration. The goddess frequently calls out the names of her six children to help search for answers, recalling also the grandmother–child idiom of the stories. Occasionally the Goddess Hāritī asks questions directly to the client through the *dya: māju*, sometimes in unusual god language, *dya: bhāy*, that the *dya: māju* has to translate to the client, occasionally with the help of her husband or designated assistant. During her consultations she is possessed first by Hāritī, and then through Hāritī by other gods and goddesses, one god at a time; negotiations with other gods are mediated through the *dya: māju* as Hāritī. Surprisingly, the *dya: māju*'s everyday closest kinship affiliations and alliances may temporarily be of no consequence when she becomes possessed and makes pronouncements. Once when her own husband consulted the *dya: māju*, Hāritī suggested that he (the *dya: māju*'s own husband) offer himself as a human sacrifice at the Bhāṭbhaṭinī temple in Kathmandu. The *dya: māju* negotiated the request on her husband's behalf so that he could donate a live goat every year to live at the temple instead.[20]

Dya: māju provides both a direct physical and visual realisation for her clients, but she also has the ability, while possessed, to instigate direct dialogues and negotiations with clients. Sometimes through unusual miming gestures, and also by spoken comments, questions, and detailed orders, a *dya: māju* informs the individual and or community of positive and negative forces. She may also mediate between rivals or opponents in families and in the community. I once witnessed her possessed by a tiger god, at a neighbourhood ceremony, where she kittenishly pawed and stroked a Vajrācāryā priest who, two weeks earlier, had been the victim of a political sectarian

Hindu–Buddhist dispute, wherein he was beaten and chased out of town. She pleaded with him not to feel offended by those past actions, and this amounted to a public apology that was accepted and respected by all. This led to the community arriving at a consensus that a new Buddhist Vihāra should be constructed in the town.

While not all *dya: mājus* may have quite the same experiences, this *dya: māju* is a primary agent for conflict resolution. Her solutions do not involve overt protest or resistance against a patriarchal system, yet the women, men and children who seek her assistance benefit from her peaceful, practical and innovative assistance. Her actions certainly do not reproduce a system of patriarchal authority since, if anything, her husband, the family and community defer to her as a human representative of the goddess. Through her mastery and performance of the orally transmitted texts, she uses mixed languages (Newari, Sanskrit and Nepali) with engaging powerful authority, and offers new ways of seeing life to those in the community who are faced with inevitable suffering in a constantly and rapidly changing world environment.

The power of a *dya: māju* is in part determined by her age, experience and identification with a senior grandmother goddess. But we should not forget the living human woman who makes all this possible. She, herself, not a male priest, successfully uses the tantric techniques of an accomplished practitioner. She is not passively receiving or reproducing symbols generated and controlled by male priests. She gives her own shape and meanings to tantric practice each time she performs, for a woman may empower herself to act independently and creatively, taking for herself the powerful symbolism of her 'tantric' culture, embodying and enlivening it in her own acts, ideas and words. If this is not subjecthood, perhaps it is what we should be thinking and talking about in place of the subject.

Conclusions

Since this volume addresses the issue of women as primary actors in health care, I would like to frame my discussion in light of current theoretical trends. What I find to be significant in the case of the *dya: māju* is that the technologies and symbols used by her in effecting her subjecthood are arguably an integral part of a cultural religious system, rather than being peripheral or isolated incidents of protests against a system. If this is an example of 'resistance', then it has reached a level of being an institution and gone beyond.

In an article about mediumship in the Kathmandu Valley, David Gellner (1994) classifies *dyaḥmā* (*dya: māju*) women healers as being peripheral to other kinds of male healers; and in another article about Hāritī and mediumship in Nepal, Brigitte Merz (1996) classifies the goddess among a category of 'wild goddesses'. Gellner (1994) argues in favour of I.M. Lewis's (1971) hypothesis, that women mediums emerge in response to women being correspondingly oppressed, but suggests that democratisation and liberalisation can have a similar effect on the increased incidence of mediumship by making it easier for people to express themselves. Gellner, with little evidence to show either way, seems to suggest that an increase in Newar women spirit mediums, such as the *dya: mājus*, constitutes a relatively recent phenomenon in Nepal, dating from the 1950s around the time of the first democratic reforms. While recognising that Newar women have greater freedom than their Brahman and Chetri Parbatiya counterparts, he nevertheless points to an overall similarity of subservient status that Newar women share with Parbatiya (Brahman and Chetris). Based on conversations with researchers of Parbatiyas, though, he notes that mediumship would be impossible for women in the Parbatiya contexts.

Given what we know about Newar women generally having more freedom to move outside the home and to start businesses than Parbatiya women, this begs the question of why Parbatiya women are not even more predisposed to mediumship than the Newar women, considering the increase in democratic reforms. Among the Tamang Bonpos, women shamanic practitioners are not as uncommon as Gellner suggests (1994: 44 n. 5), and Tamang women are in some ways culturally less restricted than their Newar counterparts. Quantifying the increases in mediumship relative to ethnicity and gender after 1950 would be a difficult task, especially since the 100 years prior to 1950 were so repressive under the Ranas that tantric Buddhists had to hide their practices, and the *dya: māju* are directly linked to instructions and initiations from tantric Buddhist priests. Accounts of spirit possession have generally not been a high priority in written *vaṃśāvali* historical manuscripts either, except in the case of Tibetan histories which refer to famous oracles. Foucher, an outside observer in the early 1900s, mentioned Hāritī worship being practised in Nepal (1972: 280).

In describing women mediums as peripheral (only one step less so than witches) and less credible than the central and 'mainstream' or accepted male practitioners, the Vajrācāryās, Gellner seems to be speaking from a high-caste Vajrācāryā-biased viewpoint. While conducting research for several years in Kathmandu Valley, including the urban centres and a farming community with a *dya: māju*, I never heard disparaging attitudes expressed *within* that community about their own *dya: māju*, even though I did hear Vajrācāryās in some communities expressing selective scepticism about certain *dya: mājus* in other locales. In fact, Vajrācāryās have a symbiotic relationship with *dya: mājus*, and since *dya: mājus* should receive training and initiation from them, the *dya: mājus* are true extensions of the same central system of Vajrayāna Buddhist practice, rather than on the fringe. The strong history of Hāritī in the Buddhist textual traditions, from the Vinaya texts to the *Lalitavistara* and other sūtras, and her iconographic continuity from Bharhut (Waddell 1912: fig. 2) to the internet,[21] indicate an ongoing popularity of this goddess in the Buddhist world that is in no way limited to Nepal, but extends to Java, Turfan and Japan. Protection of children and childbirth never goes out of style. Her popularity is only bolstered by her complementary association with her *yakṣa* husband, Pañcika, who, with his bag of jewels, is later identified with Kuvera, god of wealth.

Like Gellner's article, the recent article by Merz (1996), which situates Hāritī in a joint 'wild goddess' and 'supreme mother' category, seems automatically to assign peripheral status to the goddess, thus marginalising the status of the female divinity to subaltern. This would be like a hierarchical representation of Gellner's geo-spatial social ordering. In the case of Hāritī, she was at first good, then became an ogress and finally converted to Buddhism, where she became a protector and healer of children. In her reformed status, which is her present identity, she is not wild. Her angry, resentful emotions, which result from a miscarriage, are something any human woman would identify with and respond accordingly, although hopefully with less vengeance. The essence of her story is the Buddhist lesson about the origins of suffering and the first step to removal of suffering, which is non-attachment and the avoidance of self-blame, hatred of self and others, and of greed. But it also hints at the idea of all beings having an inherent pure Buddha Nature, which can become hidden by anger and delusion, only to reemerge spotlessly with proper care. In the story, the Buddha does not force Hāritī to convert, but rather facilitates her own realisation. In her rituals, the *dya: māju* I worked with began her possession by emphasising and enumerating the goodness, good deeds and pure qualities of her client first, before trying to find the source of temporary problems causing illness. The status of 'mother of us all' for Hāritī, suggested by Merz's title, 'Wild Goddess and Mother of Us All', is more in keeping with Hāritī's identity as Ajimā, grandmother of Newar society. And fierceness or wildness is a potent but temporary attribute in her biography.

Sometimes the words we use can produce unintended outcomes in research results and scholarly writing; and such may be the case with the terms 'peripheral', 'wild' or 'subaltern' being used in reference to women, low castes and untouchables in South Asia.[22] The relegation of all women, especially South Asian women, to a peripheral or subaltern class seems to unfairly bias our judgment with respect to women, making them guilty until proven innocent. Peripheral status situates women within a system, but not central to it; while 'wild' indicates being outside the boundaries of a system. 'Subaltern' is a term derived from a rank in the British army, that of a junior officer; its synonyms include 'vassal' and 'subject', one who defers to a central or state authority, a kingdom or royalty. This is a crude irony in light of attempts to view women as subjects in the opposite sense of the term. The term 'subaltern', itself colonial, seems subjectively to weight the victims of this classification as eternally and essentially underdogs, statically situated and such victims of oppression that their own ideas about themselves could only be considered the mirror reflection of the Eurocentric viewpoint embedded in the label. Ascribed this inferior standing, they become fashioned as subjects, not in the active sense, but in the passive sense of subjects of a hegemonic discourse. Not only are they constructed as vassals of a dominant male world order, but they become objectified as a negatively evaluated group relative to superior groups.

The classification of women as subaltern is further problematised by the Western scholar's desires to see the ascribed 'universal subjugation of women' overturned through stratagems of protest and resistance. But some women we study might consider the concepts of protest and resistance to be too narrow an interpretation of what they consider themselves to be doing. The power of protest is in its effect on an intended audience. What if women's laments about men are performed only in the presence of other women? Is the power lost? Probably not, if the intended audience is other women. But until we can determine precisely whether a protest is an intentional protest or, if it is pointed, pointed at whom, then the 'for whom', and 'by whom' can be difficult to assess.

There are two fundamentally problematic aspects of our discourses related to women and women healers. The first is the projection of discourses constructed out of Western experience on to women in other cultures, implying an analytical equivalence that may hold true in some respects, but can never be absolute because of local differences. As Arjun Appadurai reminds us in his article 'Putting Hierarchy in its Place' (1988), transplanted analytic concepts and categories can introduce complex distortions and colourations under the guise of analytic universality. Second, the particular discourses we have considered here – wild, peripheral and subaltern – all have markedly negative connotations, and thus frame any subject to which they are applied in fundamentally negative terms. The explicit or implied opposition of 'wild' to 'tamed' or 'domesticated', relies on a metaphor of implicit bestiality to distinguish two objects requiring different means of subordination and control. 'Wild' in such usage corresponds to the original meaning of 'savage' in early ethnographic literature; and, as Ter Ellingson reminds us in *The Myth of the Noble Savage* (2001), the use of 'wild' and 'savage' in anthropological discourse is fraught with racist overtones, which not only dehumanise but debase the recipients of such labels. 'Peripheral' seems to trivialise whatever it refers to, identifying it with something less important. For some kinds of sociocultural analysis, centre–periphery models may be appropriate, but there is a danger that when the group forming the subject of the study is designated as the lower of two hierarchically contrasted categories, then for the purpose of that study the subject becomes irrevocably marginalised, because the marginalisation is inherent in the fundamental terminological framing itself. And, as already noted, 'subaltern' frames the subject of enquiry, in this case women, in a hierarchically static lower social position, one constructed not only in the terminology of colonial discourse, but more explicitly framed in terms of the extreme stratification of military ranking.

The idioms of contestation, protest and resistance, viewed as positive, empowering and liberating from the Western scholar's perspective could, from the perspective of the women being analysed, be too forcefully identified with such negative forces as disruption of community or corruption of moral power and wisdom. Ultimately, we need to clarify the cultural range and boundaries of understandings about protest for the protesters themselves before we can label something protest for ourselves. Likewise, to associate resistance with subaltern status seems to deflate the power that resistance has as a part of living, changing cultures. If cultures are changing and fluid, rather than monolithic unchanging essences or organisms, then the dualism of rigid, dominant power and authority and an essentially separate, subjugated and antithetical resistance should also be questioned.

In challenging the identification of women healers as peripheral or wild, and women in general as a subaltern group, I do not wish to imply that real oppression and subjugation of women is non-existent, or that protest and resistance are not present and necessary. There is much evidence to suggest otherwise. However, extending the perceived reality and discourse of our own situation to the situations of others should be recognised as a subjective exercise. If we instead attempt to see women as women see themselves, describe what they do and what they say, and work outwards from the subject of enquiry, rather than trying to overinterpret their actions or arrange them as part of a hierarchical system, we can begin to at least solicit data that is less the product of external discourses, and more the voice of an experienced grandmother.

Notes

1   This paper was originally presented at the Association of Asian Studies Meetings in Washington, DC, in April 1995 under the title, 'Knowing all the Gods: Grandmothers, God families, and Women Healers in Nepal', for the panel on *Birth in South Asia: Midwives and Female Healers*. My choice of spelling for Hāritī (rather than Hāratī or Hārītī) is based on pre-existing preference for this spelling in numerous publications. The Sanskrit derivation is from *hārin*, meaning one who 'removes, steals, or carries away'.
2   See for example Lynn Bennett's work (1983).
3   For further discussion of Āju Ajimā, see Juju and Shrestha 1985 and Slusser 1982.
4   See Misra 1979: 73.
5   Getty (1928: 84–7), followed by Misra (1979: 73), has a thorough discussion of Buddhist textual origins of Hāritī, based on the earlier research of Foucher, Peri and Waddell, and citing references to Hāritī in *Samyuktavastu*, *Vinaya Piṭaka* of Mulasarvastivāda School, and the Chinese texts *Samyukta Ratna Sūtra*, *Sūtra Piṭaka* (Hinayana) as well as in Ch. XV of *Lalitavistara*. The conversion of Hāritī is also mentioned in *Mahāvaṃsa*, XII, 21 (Geiger 1964: 83). In describing the first conversions done by the Buddha, 'a *yakkha* named Paṇḍaka with (his wife) the *yakkhini*, Hāritī, and his five hundred sons obtained the first fruit (of sanctification *sotāpatti phala*)' from the Buddha. The *Suvarṇa[pra]bhāsottamasūtra*, Sutra

of the Golden Light, verse 162 (Emmerick 1970: 68), states that 'Hārītī, mother of the Bhūtas, with her five hundred sons, will give them [the hearers of this *sūtra*] protection whether they are sleeping, sitting or standing' (Emmerick 1970: 68). See also Peri 1917 for a complete exploration of Indian, Chinese and Japanese Buddhist texts relating to Hārītī.

6 This image, painted on cloth, is in the Museum für Indische Kunst in Berlin, item MIK III, 6302. See also Pl. 147 in Härtel and Yaldiz 1982: 207. Foucher (1910, 1972) describes the children as playing hockey and hitting balls with bats.

7 The translation of Koyasu Kannon might better be parsed as Goddess of Childbirth, since Koyasu-jizo is another Buddhist deity in Japan worshipped for easy childbirth. Mizuko Jizo is also worshipped by mothers for care of the spirits of miscarried babies and aborted fetuses.

8 For references to later archaeological evidence on this, see Misra 1979: 76–7.

9 Some Buddhist iconographers suggest possible influences of early Hārītī iconography on Chinese and Japanese Bodhisattva imagery of female protectors of children. I-tsing refers to the goddess-mother of demon sons as Kwei-tsu-mu-chen (Chinese), and Ki-si-mo-jin (Japanese) is the name given to Hārītī in Japan (Misra 1979: 76–7 n. 1, cf. Foucher 1972: 286ff, Pls XLIX 1–2 and L 1,2). See also Zimmer 1960: vol. II, Pl. 154–5 for a seventh-century image of Hārītī at Ājanta, and an eighth-century image of Hārītī at Caṇḍi Mendut, Java (Pl. 473).

10 Since Vajrācāryās are the equivalent of monks in Newar tantric Buddhism, they continue their responsibility for feeding Hārītī and her family by making classic tantric offerings that include cooked meat, fish and wine (or symbolic substitutes). The Sanskrit text describing the tantric offerings (especially line 2) for this ritual is as follows:

> 1) The Goddess Hārītī, together with her 500 sons, resides on the west side of Śri Swayambhū [*stūpa*] facing south.
> 2) People should make pūjās with the five-fold offering, with poured alcohols, and *bali* [sacrifice] offerings of meats and fish.
> 3) Because of the merit derived from the blessed leftovers (*prasāda*), of the licked, sipped, fed and drunk portions of offerings made, suffering will be prevented from arising.
> 4) Wise people know that always honouring or worshipping [Hārītī] in this way results in the attainment of a life free of illness.
> 5) Beings born of this and other worlds, whether followers of Śiva or Buddha, always happily make *pūjā* offerings to the Yakṣiṇī.
> 6) Because once the demon-born Hārītī worshipped the Buddha, [she] became happily respected as a good Goddess.
> 7) Now [she] resides next to Buddhist monastic residences (*vihāra*). With the wisdom of the Buddha, she protects against evil obstacles.
> 8) In this way, the self-born powerful Goddess Hārītī indeed protects all beings (even demons and *kinnara*).
>
> (my English translation of the Sanskrit verse from *Svayambhū Purāṇa*, folio 428, cf. Shakya 1978: 526)

For a more complete description of the *chāhāykegu pūjā*, which involves the clients pouring liquor or beer over a meat offering, see Vaidya 1986: 147–54.

11 Senior Tibetan monks and Tibetans in Nepal mentioned this practice to me.

12 In his exhaustive study, *Svayambhū Mahācaitya*, NS 1098 (Shakya 1978: 524–8), Hemrāj Shākya notes the stories of her origins at this site from the *Svayambhū Purana*. He mentions the names of Hārītī's five children, Dhanabhāju,

Dhanamayju, Vāsiṃbhāju, Vāsiṃmayju, Jilaṃbhaju (also called Lātābhāju). He also identifies eight names for Hāritī: Hāratī Māju, Ajimā Dyaḥ, Mayjudeva, Hāratī Mahāyakṣiṇī, Hāratī Vajrayakṣiṇī, Śītala Māju, Svayambhū Saṃrakṣitkā Dharmapālī, and Dhākwasikwamā Macāpyāsi (the one with babies clinging all over). The Hāritī shrine at Svayambhū, located to the west of the stūpa and facing south, is also referred to as Ratna Piṭhā, or Ratnapur because she protects the birthplace of Svayambhū. This is recalled in this verse from the *chāhāykegu pūjā* ritual text:

> Ratnapīṭhasthitā devīṃ gauravarṇasahaprabhāṃ
> Isadvaśīta vadanāgni namāmi jagatmohinīm
> Pañcānāṃ śataputrāṇāṃ parivāramaotsavām
> Buddhaśāsana sthithā devīṃ Hāratīṃ praṇamāmyaham

> I offer obeisance to the Goddess at Ratnapīṭha,
> Supreme enchantress, who shines with golden colour, of fire-like brilliance
> With her family of celebrated five hundred sons
> I bow to the Goddess Hāratī follower of the path of the Buddha

He also notes that in oral tradition concerning her devotion to Swayambhū, Hāritī claims to care for children of 12 years old and younger.

13 See oral tradition versions of story in Coon 1989, Dougherty 1986, and Merz 1996: 345–6.

14 Coon 1989, Dougherty 1986, Gellner 1994, and Merz 1996 all mention spiritual illness prior to becoming a medium. This is not something that my primary informant claimed to have experienced as part of her pre-initiation experience.

15 Gellner 1994 mentions the existence of Vajrācārya healers, *vaidyas*, who primarily practice Ayurveda and do some tantric healing with mantras, mūdras, and *jhār-phukne* (blowing on and sweeping the patient). But interactive possession is not mentioned as part of this practice by Gellner, nor did I observe possession with Vajrācāryā *vaidyas* whom I observed doing healing rituals of this kind.

16 *Pātra* can also refer to a skull cup drinking bowl used in tantric rituals.

17 The same term, *dubina* may be used to describe the possession of a person by a witch, a condition that is clearly distinguished from going insane/crazy (*uī cāla*). Also in literature, I have seen this term used to describe a god disappearing or changing to a transformed state. For further discussion of mediums, witches and possession in Kathmandu Valley with respect to Hāritī, see Gellner 1994.

18 During my research on women and religion and ritual dance dramas, I conducted interviews with this informant periodically during three field trips, 1981–83, 1987/8 and 1992. This included videotaping a complete diagnosis ritual and corresponding healing ritual for miscarriage problems (field tapes 92–4, 92–5) and additional video of a *dya: māju* possession during a Satyanārāyāna ritual.

19 In my own unsolicited experience of being diagnosed for causes of infertility by a *dya: māju*, she claimed that she had 'flown' to my backyard with a large tree, and that there was something evil near there. (I surmised that this was my old-growth cedar tree and the dry cleaners behind it.)

20 Donations of live goats, as protected temple goats, not intended for sacrifice, is common at Buddhist temples in Kathmandu Valley and around Nepal. When one such goat died in Sankhu from a rock thrown by a careless child, a funeral procession and cremation for it involved nearly the whole town. The *dya: māju* makes monthly visits to both the Hāritī and Bhāṭbhaṭinī shrines. Bhāṭbhaṭinī is considered

to be the sister of Hārītī and has a related connection to her as being another child-eating demoness, converted by Lord Viṣṇu to be a protector, through trickery and stealing of her own child, as in the story of the Buddha and Hārītī (see Regmi 1966: 603–4).

21 Over 200 websites came up on a search for Hārītī. One purely devotional site is: *Shri Ma Harati Ma Sarana*, at http: //www.bridgeport.edu/~bibhoo/holy.html. Hārītī also appeared on a website listing of names for female babies marked 'not recommended!'

22 For an example of this use of the term 'subaltern', see O'Hanlon 1988.

References

Appadurai, A. 1988. Putting hierarchy in its place. *Cultural Anthropology* 3: 36–49. Reprinted in *Rereading Cultural Anthropology*, edited by G.E. Marcus. Durham, NJ: Duke University Press, 1992.

Bennett, L. 1983. *Dangerous Wives and Sacred Sisters: Social and Symbolic Roles of High-Caste Women in Nepal.* New York: Columbia University Press.

Coon, E. 1989. Possessing power: Ajima and her medium. *Himalayan Research Bulletin* 9 (1): 1–9.

Dasgupta, S. 1969. *Obscure Religious Cults.* Third edition. Calcutta: Firma KLM Private Ltd. Reprinted 1976.

Dougherty, L. 1986. Sita and the goddess: a case study of a woman healer in Nepal. *Contributions to Nepalese Studies* 14 (1): 25–36.

Ellingson, T. 2001. *The Myth of the Noble Savage.* Berkeley: University of California Press.

Emmerick, R.E. (trans.). 1970. *The Sūtra of Golden Light.* London: Luzac and Company.

Foucher, A. 1901. *Notes on the Ancient Geography of Gandhara: A Commentary on a Chapter of Hiuan Tsang.* Translated by H. Hargreaves. Archeological Survey of India. Reprinted Varanasi: Bharatiya Publishing House, 1974.

—— 1910. La madone bouddhique. In *Commission de la Fondation Eugène Piot, Monuments et Memoires publiés par l'Académie des Inscriptions et Belles-Lettres.* Paris: E. Leroux, Vol. XXII, fasc. II. (Translated in Foucher 1972 as 'The Buddhist Madonna'.)

—— 1972. *The Beginnings of Buddhist Art and Other Essays in Indian and Central-Asian Art.* Translated by L.A. Thomas et al. Delhi: Indological Book House (items originally published in 1910 and 1914).

Geiger, W. (trans.). 1964. *The Mahāvaṃsa.* London: Pali Text Society.

Gellner, D. 1994. Priests, healers, mediums and witches: the context of possession in the Kathmandu valley, Nepal. *Man* (NS) 29 (1): 27–48.

Getty, A. 1928. *The Gods of Northern Buddhism: Their History and Iconography.* Oxford: Clarendon Press. Reprinted New York: Dover, 1988.

Härtel, H. and M. Yaldiz. 1982. *Along the Ancient Silk Routes: Central Asian Art from the West Berlin State Museums.* New York: Metropolitan Museum of Art.

Juju, B. and S.M. Shrestha. 1985. *Nepā: yā tāntrika dya: wa tāntrika pūjā.* Kathmandu: Hisi Press.

Lewis, I.M. 1971. *Ecstatic Religion: An Anthropological Study of Spirit Possession and Shamanism.* Harmondsworth: Penguin.

Merz, B. 1996. Wild goddess and mother of us all: some preliminary remarks on the cult of the goddess Hāratī in Nepal. In *Wild Goddesses in India and Nepal*, edited by A. Michaels, C. Vögelsanger and A. Wilke. Berlin: Peter Lang.

Misra, R.N. 1979. *Yaksha Cult and Iconography*. New Delhi: Munshiram Manoharlal Publishers.

O'Hanlon, R. 1988. Recovering the subject subaltern studies and the histories of resistance in colonial South Asia. *Modern Asian Studies* 22 (1): 189–224.

Peri, N. 1917. Hāritī, la mère-de-démons. *Bulletin de l'École française d'Extrême-Orient* 17 (3): 1–102.

Regmi, D.R. 1966. *Medieval Nepal*. Calcutta: Firma K.L. Mukhopadhyay.

Shakya, H. 1978. *Śrī Svayambhū Mahācaitya*. Kathmandu: Swayambhu Vikas Mandala.

Slusser, M.S. 1982. *Nepal Mandala*. Princeton, NJ: Princeton University Press.

Toffin, G. 1984. *Société et religion chez les Newar du Népal*. Paris: Editions du Centre National de la Recherche Scientifique.

—— 1986. Dieux souverains et rois dévots dans l'ancienne royauté de la vallée du Népal. *L'Homme* 99, XXVI/3 (July–September 1986): 71–95.

Vaidya, K. 1986. *Buddhist Traditions and Culture of the Kathmandu Valley (Nepal)*. Kathmandu: Sajha.

Waddell, L.A. 1912. Evolution of the Buddhist cult, its gods, images, and art: a study in Buddhist Iconography, with reference to the Guardian Gods of the World and Hariti, 'the Buddhist Madonna'. *The Imperial and Asiatic Quarterly Review* XXXIII (nos 65 and 66): 105–60.

Zimmer, H. 1960. *The Art of Indian Asia*. Princeton, NJ: Princeton University Press.

Chapter 4

Contaminating states
Midwifery, childbearing and the state in rural North India

Patricia Jeffery, Roger Jeffery and Andrew Lyon

Introductory note by Patricia Jeffery, August 2000

Several issues were crucial when we were preparing for our first piece of research in rural Bijnor (from which this chapter derives). The 1970s had seen the development of a body of literature (to which contributions are still being made, of course) critiquing the medicalisation of childbirth in the 'developed world' and advocating (a return to) a rather romanticised and ultimately illusory 'natural childbirth'. Much of this literature made reference to childbirth in non-medicalised 'traditional' or 'premodern' settings, either in earlier times in the North or in contemporary 'developing' countries. Assertions about non-intervention and especially about the low use of technology, about high levels of social support and about the roles of traditional birth attendants (TBAs) in birthing experiences were often juxtaposed to accounts of (and complaints about) the opposite as the supposedly typical birthing experience in today's developed world.

At much the same time, concerns about high rates of maternal and infant mortality, as well as of fertility, were reflected in such organisations as the World Health Organisation (WHO) that proposed global training programmes directed at TBAs. Their advocacy rested on several assumptions: for instance, that TBAs could be trained in 'better' and more hygienic obstetric techniques; that they were respected members of their communities and could put this training into practice; and that their position in local communities meant that they could also be a conduit through which child health and family planning messages could be disseminated more effectively and cheaply than through the formal health and family planning services.

The ethnographic basis for this kind of policy initiative depended, however, on just a few reports derived from fieldwork in small-scale and relatively egalitarian societies, in which birth attendants were valued, trusted and respected members of their communities. Unfortunately, many writers extrapolated from these excellent reports, but such a limited ethnographic repertoire was a poor basis for developing a global policy approach to maternal and child health problems. The WHO's position had a marked tendency to universalise birthing, in effect to treat it as a basically biological or natural phenomenon. To the extent that it was seen as socially organised, the 'social' tended to be assumed to be similar across the globe. Yet, like any other human activity, childbirth is culturally variable and socially organised. In other words, we should not expect that a policy that 'works' in one place would necessarily work in another. Global programmes for training traditional birth attendants, then, were resting on very problematic foundations.

We had already been alerted to the need to interrogate such programmes by Roger's research on health policy in India in the colonial and postcolonial eras. Two issues are particularly salient here. First, his work had unearthed several references to training programmes for *dais* (traditional birth attendants), dating from the 1860s. The records justifying such programmes smacked of an unrelenting and orientalist hostility. The writers were often male medical doctors who portrayed village *dais* as dirty and ignorant old hags, and certainly not as laudable experts in the business of birthing. Laments about rural women's poor health echoed in the pages of the archives and the blame for obstetric mishaps was laid on the village *dai*. For anyone wishing to excavate the history of *dais* the problems were immense: the normal processes of marginalisation of oral traditions obscured women's knowledge and practices, while the sources that were available had been written from patently biased and professionally interested and hostile positions.

Second, one of the overt intentions behind the introduction of *dai* training programmes had been to make obstetric and other health services more accessible to women in the rural areas. These *dai* training programmes aroused our curiosity not least because they seemed to have been quite short-lived and unsuccessful (as defined by their own aims) and yet were repeatedly introduced as if *de novo*, a classic instance of bureaucratic amnesia that was on the brink of being enacted once more in the 1980s (for more on this, see P. Jeffery et al. 1985).

In our Bijnor research, then, we wanted both to retrieve the expertise of local *dais* and of their orally transmitted knowledge about women's bodies and birthing practices and to assess how the new *dai* training programmes might benefit local women. One of our primary concerns was to locate childbearing and the *dais* (who were the main non-family members present at births) in the wider, changing social, cultural, political and economic environment. Perhaps by the turn of the millennium and with the impact of postmodernism and deconstruction on the social sciences, the need to emphasise the specific and the local is more likely to be heeded than when we were first working on these topics. In *Labour Pains and Labour Power* (where we focus on young married women as the bearers of children and as workers), and in this chapter and other papers that focus on *dais*, our arguments rest on our understanding of childbearing as a socially organised, and thus a locally specific, experience. For instance, during pregnancy and even more so in the post-partum period, local medical ideas and gender politics come into play in the regulation of the mobility and diet of the childbearing woman, or her access to social support from her natal kin.

In our accounts of childbearing in Bijnor, then, we have taken our lead from interviews and informal conversations with local people, especially with young married women, their mothers-in-law, other relatives and the village *dais* who attended births. Patricia also attended several births that enabled her to observe village *dais* at work as well as how their clients interacted with them. Perhaps Patricia's own overly medicalised birthing experience had allowed us to be somewhat enticed by images of non-medicalised and women-friendly birthing practices. If anything, we had gone into the field hoping to find a vibrant and respected *dai* tradition with which to counter the negative stereotypes that stalked the historical record (see also Jeffery and Jeffery 1993).

Certainly, village births in Bijnor could hardly be described as medicalised. While the *dais* and other women intervene in various ways in the progress of a birthing woman's labour, their interventions do not generally involve complex technology (except when the *dais* summon a male medical practitioner or pharmacist to inject the labouring woman with synthetic oxytocin). But it does not follow from this that village *dais* are highly respected female healers. Indeed, many spontaneous comments stopped us in our tracks and revealed a rather different (and frankly depressing) picture. For instance, on all fronts, there was amazement at Patricia's interest in birthing practices and her wish to meet village *dais*: as an educated woman, people would comment, she had no need to get involved with such 'dirty matters'.

Some strands of feminism, particularly radical feminism, have been concerned to demonstrate women's sameness to one another (and difference from men) and the unity of women by virtue of their childbearing capacities has been a central theme. By contrast, our view of childbearing as socially organised was already pointing to cross-cultural variations in birthing practices. But it is also clear that women should not be homogenised even within one 'culture'. In Bijnor villages, there are numerous fracture lines between women, between mothers-in-law and their daughters-in-law, among the women married to brothers, between women in different economic positions or members of different religious communities, as well as between birthing women and the *dais* who attend them. Outside the delivery and the immediate post-partum period, most women had no contact with the *dai*. Women talked about village *dais* in disdainful terms, often denying that they had any skills beyond cutting the umbilical cord and describing them as just 'cord cutters' (*naal khatney-wali*). Female kin attending a birth would often argue with the *dai* about what should be done and the *dai* who delivered a girl was likely to be verbally abused (and paid less than one who delivered a boy). As far as village women were concerned, the *dai*'s primary function was to perform defiling tasks (cutting the cord, dealing with the placenta, bathing the newborn and the new mother) that the birthing woman's kin would not wish to do. Conversations about childbirth would be peppered with local notions of shame (*sharm*), impurity and dirty work (*ganda kaam*). From the *dais* came denials of lengthy induction into the role, whether formal training or informal apprenticeships with the mother or mother-in-law. Most village *dais* presented themselves as reluctant recruits to the role, being pressed to attend a delivery when no one else was available, being thereafter required to continue delivering babies when people summoned them. Most were elderly and impoverished women who said that they did the job out of necessity (*majboori main*) only because it provided them with income for 'one–two pieces of bread'. A few Muslim *dais* claimed that the work of a *dai* is valued in heaven (if not on earth) but the general tenor was of distancing from the job.

All this makes uncomfortable reading for those who would prefer to see woman-friendly birthing practices and respected female healers. Yet while historical accounts of *dais* were undoubtedly often offensive and critical, there are also dangers in the kind of anti-colonial rhetoric that tends towards an uncritical romanticism about 'traditional India'. Indeed, recent revisionist accounts of British colonialism in India increasingly recognise that the British did not invent the caste system or notions of pollution, or the views about women connected with them, even though British policies in many realms of Indian life certainly altered the forms that they took. We find it implausible that the views of local people in Bijnor on childbirth pollution and the role of the village *dai* can be blamed on British incursions. At any rate, it would certainly be hard to find convincing direct evidence that that is the case. In many respects, though, that archaeology is not the salient issue. No matter where these images and ideas originate, the crucial point is the common-sense character that they currently have for people in Bijnor, whether birthing women and their relatives or village *dais* themselves.

In other words, our description of *dais* as 'low-status menials' is our academic glossing of local views that were reflected in people's dealings with *dais* during and after deliveries and in the *dais'* own distancing from their work. Our intention was not to pass judgements about village *dais* and their skills, but to engage with how local people view the work of the *dai* and to understand childbearing in the local social and economic context of Bijnor. It would, in any case, be hard for us to comment on the *dais'* skills without being entrapped by the (current) canonical fashions of cosmopolitan medicine. If required to do so, though, we could point (on the positive side) to having birthing women (sometimes) squat rather than lie flat during labour or to cutting the cord after the placenta is delivered and pressing the cord to return blood to the baby, for example. On the negative side, though, are the *dais'* denials that they wash their hands before delivery, our own observations that *dais* use old razor blades or pieces of old bamboo extracted from the roof thatch and shaved with a knife (all unsterilised) to cut the cord, or the role *dais* play in decisions to administer labour accelerating injections. While we have been appalled by the treatment meted out to women in hospitals, we cannot wholeheartedly advocate the typical 'home delivery' in local non-medicalised settings.

In brief, our work is neither an endorsement of the WHO training programmes for traditional birth attendants nor of the romanticism of the critics
of medicalised childbirth about the supposedly woman-friendly birthing
practices in developing countries. But nor should our work be viewed as a
latter-day version of the orientalism of nineteenth-century writers, combin-
ing praise for cosmopolitan medicine with critique of the village *dai*. Rather,
our purpose is to locate village *dais* in a wider social and economic context
and thereby to raise questions about the role of *dai* training programmes in
improving maternal and child health in the villages of north India. While
such top-down programmes almost certainly harbour organisational limitations, we should not ignore the impact of local views about women's bodies
and of birthing (despite the high value placed on having the products of such
processes, the children) on the success of such schemes. Crucially, local
people's negative appraisals of the village *dai*, combined with local responses
to the family planning programme, lead us to question how effective *dai*
training could be in fulfilling the WHO agenda.

Introduction (1987)[1]

Childbearing can only be fully understood within the specific social and economic context in which it occurs. In rural India, the pregnant woman and the
newly delivered mother are simultaneously workers and the bearers of the
next generation of workers.[2] The high levels of maternal and infant mortality current in North India result in part from the high price paid by Indian
village women, as the day-to-day requirements for their labour power often
run counter to longer-term considerations for their own, or their babies',
health. Moreover, piecemeal maternal and child health programmes will
founder if they are based on an inadequate understanding of women's position in society and local evaluations of it.

Most international health agencies now take the view that TBAs are a
valuable medical resource, socially close to their clients, and an important
source of assistance towards the goal of 'Health For All by the Year 2000'
(WHO 1978; World Bank 1980; see also Cosminsky 1976: 229–49; Kakar
1980; Greer 1984: 15–19). Indian mortality statistics certainly indicate that
there is plenty of room for improvement in maternal and child health: in
rural Uttar Pradesh, for instance, the mortality rate for women in the childbearing years was four to five times that for men during the 1970s and
neonatal mortality was fairly stable at over ninety deaths in the first month
of life for every 1000 live births (Government of India 1980, 1983: 701).
Such considerations have recently led the Indian government to opt for the
training of TBAs (Jeffery 1981, 1986). But childbirth and women's relationships to the state are not such that a single style of state intervention will
have universal benefits in maternal and child health (Velimirovic and
Velimirovic 1978). We address this issue here by considering the role of the

dai (traditional birth attendant) in rural North India, and state-sponsored attempts to raise the standards of midwifery through *dai* training schemes. We consider that such programmes are unlikely to be successful there, for three main reasons. First, North Indian birth attendants work in a context in which the physiological processes entailed in childbirth are associated with degrading views of midwifery. Second, the acceptability of trained midwives is limited because of their connection with a state whose legitimacy was seriously undermined by the sterilisation programme (especially as experienced during the Emergency of 1975–77). Finally, directed attempts to improve maternal and child health in India may well be counteracted by the effects of secular changes on women.

This chapter arises from our fieldwork in Bijnor District, Uttar Pradesh, in 1982/3. We were based in two adjacent villages (one totally Hindu and one Muslim) for over a year. The material used here comes from our intensive study of forty-one women who were pregnant or had recently given birth when the research began, and our survey of 301 new mothers in eleven randomly selected villages in Bijnor District. We interviewed the *dais* (TBAs) mentioned by these women (twenty-five in all), covering such topics as their career histories, obstetric practices and other types of expertise. This material was supplemented through discussions with the *dais'* clients (especially those in the base villages) about their views of *dais*, the management of childbirth, contacts with the *dai* at times other than delivery, and so forth. In addition, several births were attended in the base villages. Our research was initially hampered by our informants' fears that we were sterilisation workers. Gradually, their anxieties receded and we were, instead, regaled with memories of the Emergency, on which we have also drawn.

Midwifery and childbirth in North India

Childbearing in human society is socially organised and, consequently, inter-related with wider aspects of gender relationships and social organisation in general. Different societies are likely to be associated with distinctive medical systems, in which midwifery and the TBA have characteristic places. In India, 'elite medicine' (Ayurvedic and Unani medicine) is highly sophisticated, but the classical texts pay little attention to obstetric and gynaecological issues (Jeffery, Jeffery and Lyon 1983; for more general accounts, see Leslie 1976). 'High-culture' medical practitioners are all male, and local medical arrangements for women are rarely well developed. Women's access to medical services is generally less than that of their menfolk, because they have limited mobility in public, restricted access to funds, and their complaints may be considered inappropriate to take to male practitioners, especially if they pertain to 'embarrassing matters' (*sharm ki baat*) such as menstruation and childbirth. This must be appreciated when trying to understand the role of the TBA in North India.

In what follows, we focus on local understandings of childbirth and the *dai*'s role in Bijnor District, Uttar Pradesh. We want to show that the role of village *dais* in Bijnor is virtually limited to the removal of childbirth pollution; and *dais* themselves are in a structurally poor position to remedy this. The *dais* we interviewed can be divided into three groups: the village, *desi* or *gaon-ki-dai* (who were nineteen of the twenty-five); five 'intelligent' or *hoshi-yar dai*; and one woman probably better described as an apprentice medical practitioner. Here we shall concentrate on the *desi dai*. Of these, eleven are Muslim, and eight are *Harijan* (Untouchable), normally *Chamar*. They are illiterate and very poor; most are widows aged 45 or over.

First, we want to highlight the *dai*'s role in the management of pregnancy and childbirth. There is rarely any contact between a pregnant woman and a *dai* before the delivery. Many of our informants said that their *dai* would not even have known of their pregnancy, while *dais* say that few women seek their advice. Women normally give birth in their husband's family home, which seems unusual in North India and possibly has some implications for maternal and child health.[3] Once in labour, a woman is generally surrounded by women from closely related households. She will probably be attended by a *dai*, usually untrained, but she may be in labour for some hours before the *dai* is summoned. Generally, her mother-in-law determines which *dai* to call and when.

Once the *dai* arrives, it is evident that she is not considered an expert whose advice should be taken without question. The *dai* usually squats on the foot of the bed and offers her opinion; some *dais* also perform internal examinations to assess cervical dilation, but none possesses special equipment to aid or monitor the delivery. Indeed, rather than the *dai* alone, the labouring woman's female affinal kin – especially the mother-in-law and other elderly women – pass judgement on the management of the labour. If progress seems slow, they may suggest remedies – all well known to the women present – to 'heat up' (accelerate) the woman's contractions. These include giving her warm milk with almonds or tea with semi-refined sugar ('hot' items to counteract the 'cooling' of the contractions); opening locks on grain stores and loosening the woman's plait; circling a sieve containing wheat and one and a quarter rupees round her head and placing it under the bed head; and changing the woman's position from lying on her bed to squatting on a pair of bricks. Some women these days are given labour accelerating injections of oxytocic drugs administered by private or government-employed male medical practitioners.[4] Here again, the decision to give an injection does not rest with the *dai* alone. She does not possess the wherewithal to give injections and, while she may suggest an injection, her advice is rarely accepted readily and immediately. The issue is debated (often lengthily) and the practitioner who gives the injection is fetched only once the women present agree. Since the *dai* remains at her post, the timing of an injection is not under her control.

Shame and pollution are dominant features of childbirth in rural Bijnor. Shame (*sharm*) means that a woman should deliver in silence, to avoid attracting attention; she gives birth fully clothed, usually lying under a quilt on an old string bed, in the dim light of her hut. The new mother is considered impure (*a-sudh* or *na-paak*) until she has taken a purifying bath some days after delivery. The baby also causes feelings of disgust until it has been properly cleaned. Cutting the umbilical cord, burying the placenta and washing clothing and rags soiled (made *ganda*) by the mother and the baby are regarded as *ganda kaam* (dirty work), in which the *dai* plays a central role.

Once the baby is born, the *dai* delivers the placenta, massaging the woman's abdomen or pulling from inside if this is at all delayed. Then the *dai* places rags against the woman's vulva which she presses in with her heel; she has no means of stitching a woman who tears during delivery and does not examine a woman after giving birth. Then she cuts and ties the umbilical cord using instruments and thread provided by her client's household. She usually applies some medication which they also provide. Next she moulds the baby's nose, 'opens' its throat and anus by inserting her finger, and clears up the placenta, the baby's faeces, and the blood spilt during delivery. The mud floor is chipped or scraped clean, and the placenta is buried in the hut or in the dung pit. The *dai* repairs the floor with new mud, and bathes the baby either immediately or sometime later, depending on the time of delivery.

Childbirth, then, is considered an extremely polluting occurrence. Much of the pollution is dealt with by the *dai*, whose position is analogous to the *Bhangan* or Sweeper, who removes night soil and is permanently degraded by the work. Indeed, some of the Harijan *dais* are also Sweepers. Performing the 'dirty work' associated with childbirth contaminates the *dai*, and our Hindu informants in particular consider that the new mother should not be touched by the *dai* after the purifying bath, for fear of becoming polluted again. Generally, the *dai* and her client are unlikely to be in contact apart from the delivery and shortly afterwards. The exceptions are *Chamar* (Untouchable) women who are closely related to their *dai*. The management of the labour is not demonstrably in the hands of the *dai* and she is not seen as an expert. Indeed, the obscenities directed at a *dai* when she makes what are considered outrageous demands for payments, and the arguments about how much to pay her (which were observed after all the deliveries attended) suggest that the *dai* is viewed as an inferior menial by her clients – and not as an expert, superior both in knowledge and social status.

Why, then, do *dais* do this work? Only about half of the *dais* reported 'training' received by accompanying a female relative (usually their mother or mother-in-law). Several were drawn into midwifery somewhat by chance, or even against their will. There is certainly a rhetoric that the work is undesirable. But *dais* say that they lack marketable skills and that employment opportunities are scarce. Several do have other sources of income – the *dai* for the village where we lived is a goatherd, and others cut fodder, weave baskets or work as Sweepers – but none of these provides a comfortable living. They say that they deliver babies *majboori main* – out of necessity – and that they can hardly think too badly of work which keeps them alive.

Most village *dais* took up the work after a domestic crisis (generally the death or serious illness of their husband or marital breakdown). Many reported considerable pressure from kin not to do the work. Two women (one a Muslim *Nai* or Barber) said that their own brothers began to refuse to eat food they had cooked. Several *dais* had been prevented from doing midwifery by their husbands, but they had to take it up when they were widowed. If a *dai*'s sons try to stop her, she tells them they should support her properly instead, as she is only working to 'fill her stomach'. Most *dais* say they deliver babies wherever they are called, though a small number of Muslim *dais* deny that they deal with the birth pollution of Untouchables. The veracity of these statements is less significant than the rhetoric employed, which reflects the ethos of shame which permeates midwifery.

Village *dais* say they generally carry out two or three deliveries a month. Incomes from midwifery are impossible to estimate accurately, since there is no fixed fee. The *dai* gets nothing if the baby is stillborn or is delivered in hospital. Otherwise, fees are negotiated according to the wealth of the family and the 'happiness' caused by the birth. Most *dais* say they are paid more for a boy than for a girl and more for a first delivery than for later ones. Payments rarely exceed Rs 25 for a boy's birth. Generally, the *dai* also receives one or two kilos of grain (usually wheat, with a market price of about Rs 2.50 a kilo) and occasionally some cloth (usually old clothing, very rarely some new cotton for a sari). Several *dais* say that poor clients often fail to pay them anything. Only delivering the first son of a wealthy landowning family could provide the *dai* with a surplus to see her through until she delivers another baby. Unfortunately for the *dais*, these are precisely the customers who are beginning to look to the towns for clinic deliveries.

In other words, midwifery provides an income for desperately poor women – often quite elderly widows – with few marketable skills. The work is seen as undesirable and dirty and is generally not eagerly taken up.

The routine involvement of medical practitioners in antenatal and obstetric care is considered unnecessary. None the less, childbirth is considered a potentially life-threatening event: a woman may haemorrhage, the labour may be obstructed or the baby might die *in utero*. The *dais* themselves are painfully aware of their own limitations. They say they can deal only with normal deliveries. When asked about maternal or infant deaths, they give a stock response, 'I have never lost a mother or a baby'; but we soon discovered that they withdraw from cases they consider beyond their capacity. A *dai* might be *present*, then, at a death for which she bears no *responsibility*. One woman reported that she had four *dais* present when she gave birth: the first three had refused to deal with her, but stayed on to watch. Generally, *dais* say that difficult cases should be taken to a hospital or health centre. Thus, a vital part of the *dai*'s diagnostic skill is the ability to assess bad risks, which they basically do by external and internal examinations to assess whether the presentation is normal, the baby's head is engaging on the cervix and cervical dilation is proceeding efficiently. They have no instruments to assess the baby's condition, but if the mother's abdomen becomes 'cold' during labour they take this as a sign that the baby has died *in utero*. Village *dais* are preoccupied with avoiding dangerous cases, for they have their reputations, their incomes – and maybe even their lives – to protect.

Most village *dais* play little part in more general gynaecological work. None admits to knowledge of medicines to treat infertility, to prevent miscarriages, or for *seh palat* (creating a boy *in utero*). They all deny performing abortions.[5] Clearly, *dais* might wish to conceal their practices (perhaps particularly abortions), and they might be secretive about medicines they prescribe. We feel justified in asserting this limited role of the village *dai* only when we juxtapose their denials with comments from village women, who probably have less reason to conceal the *dais*' activities. Our informants deny that village *dais* have any expertise beyond delivering babies, they say they do not consult *dais* for their complaints – they go instead to male practitioners or else have no treatment at all – and, further, few village *dais* are reputed to perform abortions.

We should briefly note that five of the *dais* we interviewed did claim involvement in some treatment, although they often rely on male medical practitioners to provide the remedies which they administer. The most obviously differentiating characteristic of these 'intelligent' (*hoshiyar*) village *dais* is their greater wealth and self-assurance. Two Muslim women, for instance, both with living husbands, say that several women in their families worked as *dais* and taught them the work; they consider that midwifery should be highly regarded among Muslims because the Prophet treated his mother's midwife so respectfully. Their clientele is spread through several nearby villages, and they claim higher rates of pay and more deliveries than the ordinary village *dais*. A sixth woman – a Sikh from Punjab and the only literate woman among them – is developing a medical practice with her husband. She provides a range of treatments, including labour-accelerating injections, postnatal tetanus injections, injections to prevent miscarriages and early abortions using pills or injections.

There are also urban 'intelligent' *dais*, usually in the larger towns, who hold clinics and have widespread reputations. We did not meet these women, but we have material from women in the base villages who had consulted them. These urban 'intelligent' *dais* seem to offer a wide range of remedies: for infertility, for women who have frequent miscarriages or a succession of daughters, or for those wanting abortions or contraceptive treatments. They are apparently the only *dais* locally who act as healers with a wide range of expertise, though we are unsure if their skills are diagnostic only or involve pharmacological knowledge too. However, these women have no base in a specific community, for their clients come from miles around for what are generally one-off consultations. Moreover, it is our impression that these *dais* are not (at least now) birth attendants (Crooke 1921: 25). They are unlikely to have much enthusiasm for the outreach entailed in health education work, given their already busy and lucrative practices.

These few exceptional *dais* should not, in any case, distract us from the salient characteristics of the ordinary *dais* who serve the villages we studied. Our data suggest that the typical North Indian *dai* is illiterate (Young 1983: 1205–11). She therefore has little chance of access to 'elite' medical knowledge, though illiteracy *per se* need not reduce her ability to accumulate 'folk' knowledge, which may be quite complex and sophisticated. She may have had little midwifery instruction and there is no institutionalised means of collecting, sharing and preserving knowledge. *Dais* are relatively isolated from other practitioners because of their immobility (though they are less tied to domestic responsibilities than most other women) and they compete with their fellows, the younger *dais* waiting to poach the clients of elderly ones who fall sick or die. They tend to explain problems in childbirth or the postpartum period as the working of evil spirits, or 'God's will'. They are thus difficult to persuade to use modern methods, and unlikely to perceive the possibility of control over childbirth. In any case, a trained *dai* would face problems in implementing her training if opposed by the labouring woman's female affinal kin. The dynamics of recruitment are also significant, for village *dais* distance themselves from their work, employ a rhetoric of involuntary recruitment brought about by poverty, have negative images of their work and generally come to it late (so training will not have long-term benefits). They would probably give the work up if they could. Their clients employ *dais* to remove pollution, do not see *dais* as repositories of knowledge and are resentful when *dais* patrol their village to drum up custom. For them, contact with *dais* should be limited. If the expert *dais* are respected and designated *hoshiyar* (intelligent) by their clients, the village *dais* are written off as mere *naal khatney-wali* (cord-cutters).

We have concentrated on the village *dais* at whom the training schemes have been directed because their characteristics provide some reasons why these schemes are unlikely to work. The village *dai* is socially distant from her clients – an inferior menial to be kept at arm's length, and not someone from whom villagers are likely to accept maternal and child health education or family planning advice. Local understandings of childbirth are only part of the story, however. In the next section we consider the uneasy relationship between the populace and government personnel and the role of the state in providing maternal and child health services.

Women's health and the state

In India, there have been numerous legislative reforms apparently intended to produce profound changes in the position of women (see for example Everett

1981; Minattur 1975; Pappu 1975). However, women have remained largely under the control of domestic authorities (males and elderly females) and subjected neither to the direct control nor the protection of the Indian state. Entrenched ideas and interests have rarely been seriously challenged and the direct impact of the state on women has, in practice, been slight (ICSSR 1975). One area which is no exception to this is maternal and child health.

Before 1947, several Viceroys' wives (sometimes in collaboration with missionary societies), rather than the state, seemed to feel duty-bound to raise funds for medical programmes to ameliorate the position of women in India. But these early schemes were restricted in their impact. The limited numbers of female medical staff (doctors and also, by the 1920s, health visitors) who were trained hampered the expansion of medical facilities for women. Only relatively wealthy urban women could benefit from plans to enable female doctors to visit *parda-nashin* (secluded) women in their homes; while poor urban women could attend the general dispensaries, or the female dispensaries staffed by women, which began to be established in North India in the 1890s (Balfour and Young 1929).

For rural women, there were merely the attempts to train the *dais* or local midwives. *Dai* training schemes in India are an interesting case of bureaucratic amnesia. Efforts to improve the conditions in which women bear and rear children have been made for over a century, and a common component has been the attempt to draw on traditional birth attendants or *dais*. The earliest example we have found from North India is a course held in Amritsar from 1866, still in operation in the early 1880s. Such schemes have been repeatedly re-invented since then.

Several points should be made about maternal and child health facilities in the rural areas. The scale of *dai* training ebbed and flowed and the impetus came from private funds raised by leading British women, not from the state apparatus, although the state helped with funding these schemes. Furthermore, the infrastructure of health services directed specifically at women – female dispensaries, in most district headquarter towns, and the female nurses working in clinics in other sizeable towns – strikingly demonstrate the urban bias of the provision. By 1947, then, there had been no concerted effort to improve the availability of medical services for rural women. Attempts to train *dais* were sporadic, urban-biased and had little noticeable impact on obstetric practice in most of the country.

After 1947, *dai* training courses were somewhat expanded and more trained *dais* were employed, some of whom are still working in rural subcentres and clinics. The post-1947 expansion of medical provision for women, though, has largely depended on a new cadre of personnel – the auxiliary nurse midwife or ANM, whose training was introduced after 1956, following proposals in the Second Plan (1956–61). Prospective ANMs are required to have at least eight years of schooling; they are, thus, mainly from urban literate backgrounds (often from Kerala in Southern India). This in itself sets a barrier between them and their village clients. But the ANM, moreover, has always worked primarily as a motivator for contraception, in spite of a training schedule which covers basic medical care. Indeed, only the urgency provided by the perceived 'threat' of a rapidly growing population made the government give ANM training any priority. This same urgency has all but deprived the ANM of the time or incentive to deal with more broadly based maternal and child health work. The population programme, then, contrasts with many other aspects of overt state action, for it has a high profile with people at the 'grassroots'.

Initially, family planning services were effectively restricted to urban clinics and the programme had little impact. The 1961 Census showed that the Indian population was growing much faster than had been believed (Cassen 1980: 145–8). In 1963 a review of the population programme led to a new emphasis on 'extension' – taking services to the clients by using ANMs based at Primary Health Centres, and employing mass education and propaganda techniques to increase knowledge of contraception and persuade people of the attractions of small families (Banerji 1974). At first, the preferred contraception was the IUCD, first introduced in 1966/7 when 900,000 were inserted; but its side-effects soon destroyed its credibility with the populace (Cassen 1980: 149–60). After that, sterilisation (initially vasectomy) was favoured and 'incentives' were introduced for 'acceptors' and 'targets' for family planning workers. But the number of 'cases' declined during the late 1960s – probably (as Cassen argues) because the programme still only reached people near the hospitals and clinics where operations were performed (1980: 161). Numbers only rose again, briefly, in the early 1970s with the introduction of 'mass camps' which created temporary operation facilities in the countryside. But popular resistance to sterilisation led to renewed emphasis on spacing children rather than on ending a couple's childbearing altogether.

However, the Emergency of 1975–1977 brought a new attempt to reduce the birth rate (Vicziany 1982/3). It was, indeed, this facet of the Emergency which met with most widespread hostility. Sterilisation was again the favoured technique, but there were some novel components in the programme: the wider range of official personnel given 'targets', the strong political support (especially from Sanjay Gandhi) for those who met or surpassed their targets, and the use of the police by some officials desperately attempting to meet them. People approaching government personnel for whatever reason experienced efforts to 'motivate' them for sterilisation. 'Family limitation' achieved a salience for the mass of the Indian population, and the state was forcefully felt through state employees, who often depended on motivating enough 'cases' to be paid or promoted. In 1976/7, there were about eight million 'cases', over six million of them men (Government of India 1977: 82–3).

Our informants' views on the Emergency revolve around the intrusion of state agencies into 'private' matters, an intervention which is virtually unparalleled in India. Public debate was generated about issues which, until then, would rarely have been discussed even in private by married couples. Many of our informants are outraged by the shamelessness of the Delhi government. But a more significant recurrent theme for people in Bijnor is resentment at the state's audacious attempt to *compel* people to limit their families by *irreversible* means. Infant and child death is part of 'normal' existence in rural North India and this lies behind many people's objections to sterilisation. The household is the basic unit through which the elderly are cared for and labour power is recruited – and the need for at least one son to survive to adulthood is paramount. This was recognised somewhat, for the requirement to be sterilised was waived for couples with no sons. But we heard of couples (no doubt many apocryphal, but none the less important) who had been forcibly sterilised and whose sons or even all of whose children had subsequently died. For rural people, the disjunction between the state's population programme and the conditions in which they and their children live and die was all too painfully obvious during the Emergency.

After the 1977 elections, the new Janata government pledged to return to voluntarism in family planning matters; proposals pending since 1975 were implemented, introducing Community Health Workers (CHWs) and expanding the *dai* training programme. The ANM is now to spend more time and effort on maternal and child health services, to recruit and help to train *dais* and to maintain a referral network with them for abnormal presentations and antenatal care. But the population programme revived somewhat in 1978/9 and again in 1980 when Mrs Gandhi returned to power, though vasectomy was no longer the main method being offered: the present emphasis is on tubectomies and on IUCDs (Vicziany 1982/3; Gwatkin 1979; Brown 1984).

The *dai* training scheme has almost reached its target of providing one *dai* for every 500 people. However, we doubt that it will have significantly reduced maternal and perinatal morbidity and mortality in much of North India. Only four of the *dais* we interviewed had taken government training, all in the recent past. Two Hindu *dais* are employed as part-time helpers for the local ANM – and they say this reduces their income, since they attend fewer births now. Two others (both Muslims) are ambivalent about their training, saying they are being undercut by untrained *dais* who accept lower payments; but they do register pregnancies with their ANM, ostensibly so that tetanus injections can be given. Several other *dais* fear that training would make their clients view them as government employees who no longer need to be paid. And, crucially, ANMs are still under great pressure to produce 'cases' for sterilisation. Most *dais* are wary of close involvement with the ANM, in case they are pressed to motivate 'cases' themselves: indeed, several had adamantly refused training, fearing that their clientele would decline.

An ANM visiting a village is assumed to have a 'case', because similar willingness to come for maternal or child health purposes is rare. Motivating 'cases' is believed to be the ANM's major concern and villagers are unwilling to avail themselves of her antenatal care. The ANM for our base villages talks of 'all I have done for these villages' (tetanus injections or helping women needing admission to the government hospital in Bijnor) 'but they haven't given me any cases'. From the other side, we have accusations that she visits daily before a 'case' goes to hospital, but shows no interest once the sterilisation has been performed. Indeed, villagers view maternal and child health services as mere sweeteners, which enable ANMs to pressurise people into being sterilised. Consequently, ANMs are rarely called to attend births. Trained *dais* do not replenish their delivery kits or consistently refer women for care, and the ANM cannot provide continuing training, or be sure that her lessons are being applied.[6]

Briefly, Indian villagers display a shrewd and not misplaced cynicism about the motives of government health workers – exacerbated by the sterilisation drive during the Emergency – and they and the village *dais* maintain a distance from them. This, then, is a further reason why the recent *dai* training scheme is unlikely to ameliorate maternal and child health in rural North India.

Midwifery in a wider context

Now we want to broaden our perspective, for changes in midwifery and maternal and child health provisions *alone* cannot, in any case, be a panacea for Indian women's obstetric ills (let alone all the others from which they suffer). Exclusive concentration on legislation or on other purposeful state action is not very enlightening: we must also consider the impact of the state through the secular changes which ensue from policies which are not overtly related to women. State programmes in all spheres, not just in health, can have an impact on maternity and infancy, by affecting gender relationships in society at large. Clearly, rural Indian women are virtually 'hidden from history' so anything we say must be very tentative. However, viewing midwifery in a wider context adds a further – and necessary – dimension to our assessment of *dai* training programmes.

Many writers have suggested that 'development' has differential effects on males and females (for example Ahmed 1985; Beneria 1982; Boserup 1970; Mukhopadhyay 1984; Rogers 1979; Young, Wolkowitz and McCullagh 1981). Evidence, though, is often patchy; moreover, women in a stratified system are not uniformly affected by social change. None the less, many of our informants in Bijnor consider that the Green Revolution has fuelled both the escalation of dowry demands and the associated devaluation of daughters, especially among the relatively wealthy and the newly rich. Certainly, demographic records indicate a very marked gender differential in the improvements in life expectancy since 1901. Infant mortality rates for boys and girls in rural Uttar Pradesh have declined in this period, but female rates remained about 16 per cent higher than those for males throughout the 1970s. The adverse sex ratio in Bijnor has been steadily deteriorating to the 1981 level of 850 females per 1000 males (Government of India 1980; Government of India 1981; Government of India 1983: 701). These figures are not out of step with the general picture in North India (Miller 1981).

Our comments on the effects of secular changes on village *dais* must be even more circumspect. There is virtually no plausible historical material against which to set our own data. Official documents from the latter part of the nineteenth century onward portray *dais* as illiterate, usually middle-aged or old, with experience their only qualification, and predominantly drawn from Untouchable castes. British doctors were adamant that *dais* endangered their clients because of their lack of intelligence, their dirty habits and their incapability of learning new methods (for example Balfour and Young 1929; Mistry 1936). But we cannot legitimately generalise from comments such as these and we simply cannot know if village *dais* offered additional services, such as abortions, treatments for menstrual problems, or massage.

However, three possible scenarios can be outlined. One is that women's knowledge and referral systems elude male historical enquiry, yet an oral tradition can develop valuable skills and methods of initiating novices. Alternatively, some expertise would surely have survived, if it ever existed; but *dais* came from such disadvantaged castes, regarded midwifery as dirty, probably took it up unwillingly, and were thus incapable of effectively transmitting skills to new practitioners. However, in a hierarchical system, a more plausible view is that any category of workers is internally differentiated, which raises the question of how secular changes might affect this.

In Bijnor, women at the bottom of the economic hierarchy (perhaps especially those in female-headed households) seem to have been relatively pauperised by the Green Revolution, as various means of supplementing household incomes have become more unattainable. This might propel more women into midwifery, which may now be more dominated than before by women without links to family traditions of midwifery and with skills limited to cord-cutting. 'Intelligent' *dais* are probably not a new phenomenon, but they are now suffering competition from medical practitioners, usually male. Since 1947, increased rural wealth has created a market for medical services and there has been a dramatic influx of practitioners – private and government employees, trained and untrained – who provide allopathic, Ayurvedic and Unani treatments.

Such developments may have brought some benefits, perhaps especially in the mass programmes to control malaria and smallpox. But optimism needs to be tempered by an awareness of the implications of male-dominated systems of medicine for women. In the realm of childbearing alone, powerful labour-accelerating drugs – available on the open market and administered by men unable to examine their clients properly – will probably worsen the conditions of childbirth rather than enhance them.[7] Similarly, we cannot be sanguine about amniocentesis services to detect female foetuses and abort them (Jeffery and Jeffery 1984). 'Modern' medicine is not an unqualified good for women. Its impact is no less permeated by gender inequalities than are general processes of social change.

Midwifery must be socially located: the lowly village *dai* is symptomatic of other features of social organisation. To be successful, maternal and child health programmes would also require a dramatic shift in women's favour in the gender- and age-based power relations typical of the Bijnor village household. This might (among other things) improve the access of women in their childbearing years to food and to health facilities, and re-orientate women's views of the physiological processes involved in childbirth. Put in these terms, the task is monumental.

If our interpretation is correct, though, secular changes are not clearly working to the relative benefit of women. Thus, ideas about childbirth pollution and midwifery are unlikely to be subjected to much challenge. Certainly, too, *dai* training schemes are undermined by people's lack of trust in the state, and by the state's own lack of commitment to their value in their own right, rather than as a carrot for population control programmes. But equally surely, trained *dais* cannot combat maternal and child health problems in the face of often countervailing trends, many of which, indeed, have been generated through government action. In a different social context, of course, traditional birth attendants could be important agents in state attempts to improve maternal and child health. But we cannot be optimistic about the prospects in rural North India.

Notes

1 This chapter, first published in Afshar 1987, is a revised and abridged version of an Indian Social Institute monograph (Jeffery, Jeffery and Lyon 1985). The research reported here was funded by the Economic and Social Research Council, to whom we are grateful. Thanks to the generosity of the late Dr Alfred D'Souza we were Visiting Research Fellows at the Indian Social Institute, New Delhi, while we were in India. Kunwar Satya Vira and Dr K.K. Khanna were immensely helpful during our stay in Bijnor, and we should also like to thank our research assistants, Swaleha Begum, Radha Rani Sharma and Savita Pandey. Many people have helped with comments on earlier versions of this paper: our particular thanks go to Haleh Afshar, Jocelyn Kynch and Carol Wolkowitz.

2 We do not restrict our understanding of 'work' to Census categories (which show very few of these women as workers) nor to views which belittle the considerable efforts expended by women. See further Beneria 1982.

3 See Jeffery, Jeffery and Lyon 1984 and Jeffery, Jeffery and Lyon 1988. Contrast this with Gideon 1982.

4 We also interviewed twenty of these practitioners; most were men who had education to tenth grade and then worked in a hospital or for a private pharmacist for a few years before setting up in independent practice.

5 We attempted a number of indirect approaches to ask about abortions (such as asking if the *dai* was ever asked to do abortions and if so how she responded) but we cannot be sure that alternative methods might not have produced different answers.

6 Gandhi and Sapru 1980 gives supporting evidence from Meerut District, Uttar Pradesh.
7 For an account from Britain, see Cartwright 1979.

References

Afshar, H. (ed.) 1987. *Women, State and Ideology: Studies from Africa and Asia.* London: Macmillan.

Ahmed, I. (ed.) 1985. *Technology and Rural Women: Conceptual and Empirical Issues.* London: Allen and Unwin.

Balfour, M.I. and R. Young. 1929. *The Work of Medical Women in India.* London and New York: Oxford University Press.

Banerji, D. 1974. *Family Planning in India.* New Delhi: Progress.

Beneria, L. (ed.) 1982. *Women and Development: The Sexual Division of Labour in Rural Societies.* London: Praeger.

Boserup, E. 1970. *Woman's Role in Economic Development.* London: Allen and Unwin.

Brown, C.H. 1984. The forced sterilization programme under the Indian Emergency: results in one settlement. *Human Organization* 43 (1): 49–53.

Cartwright, A. 1979. *The Dignity of Labour? A Study of Childbearing and Induction.* London: Tavistock.

Cassen, R. 1980. *India: Population, Economy, Society.* London: Macmillan.

Cosminsky, S. 1976. Cross-cultural perspectives on midwifery. In *Medical Anthropology*, edited by F.-X. Grollig and H.B. Haley. The Hague: Mouton.

Crooke, W. (ed.) 1921. *Islam in India.* Oxford: Oxford University Press.

Everett, J.M. 1981. *Women and Social Change in India.* New Delhi: Heritage.

Gandhi, H.S. and R. Sapru. 1980. *Dais as Partners in Maternal Health.* Mimeo. New Delhi: National Institute of Health and Family Welfare.

Gideon, H. 1982. A baby is born in Punjab. *American Anthropologist* 64: 1220–34.

Government of India. 1977. *Family Welfare Programme in India Yearbook 1976–77.* New Delhi: Ministry of Health and Family Welfare.

—— 1980. *Sample Registration Scheme 1970–75.* New Delhi: Office of the Registrar-General.

—— 1981. *Census of India 1981.* Series-22, Uttar Pradesh, Paper 1 (Provisional Population Totals). Lucknow.

—— 1983. *Survey on Infant and Child Mortality 1979.* New Delhi: Office of the Registrar-General.

Greer, G. 1984. *Sex and Destiny.* London: Secker and Warburg.

Gwatkin, D.R. 1979. Political will and family planning. *Population and Development Review* 5 (1): 29–59.

ICSSR. 1975. *Status of Women in India: A Synopsis of the Report of the National Committee on the Status of Women.* New Delhi: Indian Council of Social Science Research.

Jeffery, P., R. Jeffery and A. Lyon. 1985. *Contaminating States and Women's Status: Midwifery, Childbearing and the State in Rural North India.* New Delhi: Indian Social Institute. (Monograph Series, no. 22.)

—— 1988. When did you last see your mother? Aspects of female autonomy in North India. In *Micro-approaches to Demographic Research*, edited by J.C. Caldwell, A.G. Hill and V.J. Hull, pp. 321–33. New York and London: Kegan Paul International.

—— 1989. *Labour Pains and Labour Power: Women and Childbearing in India.* London and New Jersey: Zed Books; New Delhi: Manohar.

Jeffery, R. 1981. Medical policy-making: out of dependency? In *Asie du Sud*, edited by M. Gaborieau and A. Thorner. Paris: Mouton.

—— 1986. New patterns in health sector aid to India. *International Journal of Health Services* 16 (1): 121–39.

Jeffery, R. and P. Jeffery. 1984. Female infanticide and amniocentesis. *Social Science and Medicine* 19 (11): 1207–12.

—— 1993. Traditional Birth Attendants in Rural North India: the social organisation of childbearing. In *Knowledge, Power and Practice in Medicine and Everyday Life*, edited by S. Lindenbaum and M. Lock. Berkeley and London: University of California Press.

Jeffery, R., P. Jeffery and A. Lyon. 1983. The medicalisation of female illness in North India. Paper given at the IXth European Conference on Modern South Asian Studies, Sweden, July 1983

—— 1984. Only cord-cutters? Midwifery in rural north India. *Social Action* 34 (3): 229–50.

Kakar, D.N. 1980. *Dais: The Traditional Birth Attendants in Village India.* Delhi: New Asia Publishers.

Leslie, C. (ed.) 1976. *Asian Medical Systems.* Stanford: California University Press.

Miller, B.D. 1981. *The Endangered Sex: Neglect of Female Children in Rural North India.* Ithaca, NY: Cornell University Press.

Minattur, J. 1975. Women and the law: constitutional rights and continuing inequalities. In *Women in Contemporary India*, edited by A. de Souza. New Delhi: Manohar Book Service.

Mistry, J.E. 1936. My experience of the harm wrought by Indian dais. Extracted in V. Anstey *The Economic Development of India*, pp. 489–91. London: Longman Green.

Mukhopadhyay, M. 1984. *Silver Shackles: Women and Development in India.* Oxford: Oxfam.

Pappu, S. 1975. Legal provisions – an assessment. In *Indian Women*, edited by D. Jain. Publications Division, Ministry of Information and Broadcasting, Government of India.

Rogers, B. 1979. *The Domestication of Women: Discrimination in Developing Societies.* London: Kogan Page.

Velimirovic, H. and B. Velimirovic. 1978. The role of traditional birth attendants in health services. *Curare* 1 (2): 85–96.

Vicziany, M. 1982/3. Coercion in a soft state. *Pacific Affairs* 55 (3) (Fall 1982): 373–402 and 55 (4) (Winter 1982/3): 557–92.

WHO. 1978. Declaration of the Alma-Ata conference on primary health care, September 1978. Geneva: World Health Organisation.

World Bank. 1980. *Health Sector Policy Paper.* New York: World Bank.

Young, A. 1983. The relevance of traditional medical cultures to modern primary health care. *Social Science and Medicine* 17 (16): 1205–11.

Young, K., C. Wolkowitz and R. McCullagh (eds) 1981. *Of Marriage and the Market: Women's Subordination in International Perspective.* London: C.S.E. Books.

Chapter 5

Midwives among others

Knowledges of healing and the politics of emotions in Rajasthan, Northwest India[1]

Maya Unnithan-Kumar

Introduction

Childbirth in a number of cultures is usually considered an arena exclusive to women and this is certainly the case in rural Rajasthan. In this chapter, I am concerned with the politics between women surrounding childbirth and more generally relating to healing associated with reproduction. In particular, I am concerned with the extent to which knowledges of healing (specialist vs. 'common', 'indigenous' vs. biomedical) separate out women (as midwives, mothers, kin) and men (kinsmen, religious healers), and the role that such emotions as friendship, desire and fear play in structuring the relations between women in their attitudes to reproduction and related health care. The chapter shows the importance of a range of women and their relationships (supportive, contested, hierarchical, emotional, financial) in determining the outcome of the birthing event. This perspective allows me to see women as agents in their own and in other women's reproductive lives and to under-stand the intentions, motivations, desires and influences that lie behind their decisions to seek out specific healers (both 'traditional' and biomedical). It also allows me to question the somewhat romantic notions attached to birthing at home.

On the basis of ethnographic observations, I make three main points in this chapter.

1   Building on recent work on childbirth and authoritative knowledge (Davis-Floyd and Sargent 1997), I suggest that there are different types and levels of 'indigenous' knowledge concerned with the processes of reproduction which are spread among different categories of women and men. It is perhaps due to the diffusion of the knowledge related to birthing and healing and its consideration as 'common' knowledge that little power and status is gained through association with it. Although 'traditional' birth specialists are a separate category, and it is acknowl-edged that not everybody can manage a delivery, the expertise of these specialists is devalued, not only by the biomedical community but more

so by the women who have experienced childbirth in their own communities. The recent development emphasis on the empowerment of community midwives as a means of enhancing safe delivery practices may therefore be misplaced. Given the socially diffuse nature of birthing knowledge, its undue privileging through development programmes may be locally unacceptable, not least because of the restructuring of social relationships which it implies.[2]

2   I propose that it is insightful to study healing and reproduction in terms of women's agency, their desires and motivations, and in terms of the differences between what women say they do, what they actually do and what they desire to do. I find that a focus on emotions as stressed in the recent perspectives on culture and emotions (Shweder and Levine 1984; Lutz and Abu-Lughod 1990; Scheper-Hughes 1992, for example) leads me into a study of agency and motivations, which goes deeper into explanations for social action than, for instance, discourses on kinship and gender. This helps to explain why, for example, there are some kin with whom one shares more intimate information than others, some kin who have more influence than others and why, in general, healers who help overcome grief and anxiety are more sought after than other healers. Following Lutz and Abu-Lughod, I see emotions not as 'natural' (essentialised) states, but rather as connected with issues of sociability and power (1990: 1).

3   Taking into account the hardship, physical danger and lack of personalised attention faced by birthing rural women in Rajasthan, I argue against the somewhat romantic perspective which suggests that women in rural India either desire to give birth to children at home or are better off doing so. I suggest that resort to home births is more a result of helplessness and an inability to command the resources (finances, transport, company) which would be needed to birth in clinics and hospitals. Moreover, the state's inability to provide public delivery facilities which are small scale, efficient, inexpensive and convenient to access in terms of distance and opening times reinforces women's dependence on their own resources (women's networks and local knowledges). Poor women seem to be caught in a bind between the power and hegemony of medicalised institutions which are prone to alienate women from their bodily and social experiences, on the one hand, and the often oppressive nature of kinship institutions and the requirements of the domestic economy which serve to devalue the work and emotions associated with reproduction, on the other hand.

The observations in the chapter relate to Nagori Sunni Muslim women and lower-caste Hindu women in the villages in Sanganer on the outskirts of Jaipur city. There is very little on the ethnography of health among rural communities in Rajasthan (Patel 1994 and 1999 are exceptions). Especially lacking is material on rural Muslims. Most of the work on health among Muslims is on urban groups; see for example the recent NFHS survey (Government of India 1995). The study by Jeffery, Jeffery and Lyon in Uttar Pradesh is an exception (1989 and Chapter 4 this volume). Both Nagori Sunni women and lower-caste Hindu women resort to the services of public and private health personnel for various reproductive ailments, but in matters of childbirth they routinely consult with local midwives, kinswomen and spiritual healers. While class (occupation, standard of living) and regional culture (including that of healing) make for many similarities in Muslim and Hindu experiences of childbirth, far fewer differences emerge as a result of religious beliefs and practices. In this section I predominantly draw upon Nagori Sunni women's experiences, referring to lower-caste Hindu women for purposes of comparison only.

The birthing context

According to the National Family Health Survey (NFHS) findings, only 7 per cent of urban births and 3 per cent of rural births in Rajasthan take place in an institutionalised (public or private) setting (Government of India 1995: 155). In rural Rajasthan 42 per cent of all births are attended to by traditional birth attendants (henceforth TBAs) and 38.9 per cent only by 'relatives and others', with these two categories accounting for over 80 per cent of the births. The NFHS fails to define TBAs or to give further details about the category 'relatives and others', presuming the two to be distinct sets of health service providers. As I show for the Nagori Sunnis, traditionally it is often relatives who are birth attendants, blurring the distinction between the two. Nagori Sunni births are usually attended by two kinds of 'midwives'[3] – midwives who are kin, and lower-caste Hindu midwives. The former are referred to by their kin connection as 'aunts', *bua* (father's sister) or *jethani* (husband's elder brother's wife), while the latter are referred to by their caste with the suffix of *dai* attached (for example, Raigarin *dai*).

While both kinds of midwives are experienced in delivering children, there is usually a division of labour between them. When both are present, the 'kin-midwife' usually provides emotional and physical support to the mother and advises the lower-caste midwife when to check for dilation of the cervix and for progress of the baby in the birth canal. The lower-caste midwife, when present, usually assists the mother in the descent and delivery of the baby. In the delivery this means assisting the baby out of the birth canal, handling the umbilical cord and delivering the placenta. Once the placenta has been expelled, the lower-caste midwife is free to take her small remuneration and leave. Sometimes the whole process is carried out by the kin-midwife herself. The number and combination of insider/outsider midwives present at a birth is not so much a function of the number of children (for example, fewer midwives the more births a woman has had) but more to do with the relative difficulty and danger associated with birthing as estimated by the mother[4] and her kin.

Jetoon's delivery

In March 1998, Jetoon, who was 35 years old, delivered her ninth child (she had six live children, one previous miscarriage and a child who had died at a year and a half). The women present at her delivery were Samina, the kin-midwife (she was Jetoon's father's brother's son's wife), Mehmuda, the well-regarded elderly Pathan midwife of the minority Muslim community in the village, Dhanni, the Raigarin midwife, and myself. I arrived to find Jetoon in the designated 'delivery hut' having contractions every three to five minutes. In one corner was a rope bed (*charpai*) with some thin cotton covers in a heap. The ground was covered in loose sand and in the middle lay a jute sack (*bori*). At the other end there were a few bricks. Jetoon had her *kurta* (shirt) on but had removed her *salwar* (pants). She was holding on to Dhanni, the Raigarin. As the contractions increased she lay on the jute sack clasping her legs to her sides. She would get up every five minutes, usually for a contraction and get on to two bricks, one set under each foot, facing the Raigarin. She kept moaning '*bai, bai, baiyon*' (literally: woman, woman, women). After every couple of contractions, Dhanni would pour a teaspoonful of sesame seed oil in Jetoon's vaginal opening and vigorously massage and stretch it. At one point Jetoon asked to be cut at the opening but Mehmuda, the Pathan midwife, said that they never do that and that it was up to Allah to make the opening big enough.

Samina and Mehmuda mainly rubbed Jetoon's back at intervals and then during a contraction they vigorously pushed her stomach downwards (seemingly unaware of the risk of rupture to her uterus). Dhanni, on the other hand, sat all the time watching with intermittent attempts to further widen Jetoon's vaginal opening. Before she inserted her fingers (the nails of which were long and dirty), she would wipe them with a scrap of cloth taken from a small bundle placed next to the jute sack. Mehmuda helped with lifting Jetoon and easing her down, and along with Dhanni and Samina inserted her fingers into Jetoon's vagina at regular intervals to check the position of the baby's head. Mehmuda proclaimed the baby's head was a whole finger away from the opening and said that it was only when it came to the top third of the finger (*choodi*) that any injection should be used to speed the delivery. We had all been told that Maulana, the Unani doctor from the nearby village, had been summoned by Jetoon's husband. Despite Mehmuda's instruction to the contrary, Maulana immediately entered the hut, eyes cast on the ground, and injected Jetoon with oxytocin in her thigh.

Few other women entered the hut. Jetoon's mother did not come into the hut although she prepared the hot water, provided the bucket and all else that was requested. This was, I was told because of embarrassment (*sharam*) and also because mothers could not watch their daughters under-going any pain and suffering. Jetoon's *nanad* (husband's younger brother's wife[5]) went to and fro, bringing whatever the midwives requested and bear-ing advice and information to people on both sides of the door of the hut. Mehmuda requested a small iron stool which was brought from Samina's house. Mehmuda circled this seven times over Jetoon. She then asked for a 5-rupee coin which she also swept around Jetoon seven times saying 'Respected old man of the valley, give us your favour for a child is to be born in your neighbourhood' (*ghati vale baba, ahsaan karo, aapke mohalle mein bacchha hone vala hai*). Mehmuda said she needed to placate the spirit of the Baba as Jetoon was in such pain, as she was at the time of each of her births. She said they should have given Jetoon castor oil to drink with her milk and the baby would not have had such difficulty moving (*arundi ke tel se bachha ghoom jaata hai*). Samina spoke less than Mehmuda and when she did, it was usually to confer with her and Dhanni about the passage of time. Dhanni only ever said anything when she enquired about the time. The rest of the time she either stretched Jetoon's vaginal opening, provided physical support when Jetoon was helped on to the bricks by Mehmuda and Samina or lit herself a local cigarette (*bidi*). She said the cigarette helped her mark time.

Both Mehmuda and Samina were anxious to leave as soon as possible. Mehmuda said her husband was unwell and Samina complained that her household chores were left undone. Meanwhile Maulana dashed in to give Jetoon a second injection. Approximately two and a half hours after I arrived, Jetoon proclaimed, 'a big one is coming' and two contractions later a large part of the head of the baby emerged. Dhanni put her hand in and removed the cord (*bachhe ki nalli*) from around the emerging baby's neck and then helped him out, but she did not touch the baby once it lay on the sandy floor of the hut. The baby was covered in white skin and both Mehmuda and Samina said this was because of the buttermilk that Jetoon had probably drunk. Dhanni then slowly pulled at the umbilical cord and brought the placenta (*olnaal*) out. Both the baby and the placenta were very small (the latter fitted in the palm of the hand and the baby could not have been more than a kilogram). Dhanni then rolled the remaining scraps of cloth into a ball and inserted this into Jetoon's cervix after which Dhanni got up to wash her hands. Her work was over. Mehmuda left to go back to her husband.

Samina took over where Dhanni had left, and massaged the umbilical cord (with attached placenta) towards the baby. Jetoon was made to sit up. A reed and thread were passed in through the door. Samina tied the yellow and deep orange thread tightly around the cord and then Jetoon cut it with the sharp-ened reed. Jetoon was then helped on to the rope bed and Samina took hold of the baby. She asked for hot water. When this was brought a couple of min-utes later, she asked me to add this to the bucket of cold water. Both the bucket and the *parat* (a slightly deepened iron vessel used for agricultural and domestic tasks) were brought to her. Samina then balanced the baby on her feet in the *parat* and vigorously washed it with soap and water and then wrapped it in a clean old shirt. Samina held the baby for a short while and massaged the bridge of his nose. He was then further wrapped in another small piece of cloth and placed on the left side of Jetoon.

Jetoon's mother and sister-in-law brought some mud to cover the placenta and the excreta and blood which lay in the hut and removed these in the *parat*. They returned after throwing the placenta in the nearest rubbish heap to put fresh sand on the floor and recoat it. They then gave Jetoon a cup of tea. Samina had a quick cup of tea and rushed back home to tend her buffaloes. Jetoon's children then came in and surrounded their mother. Several other women neighbours also entered and joked with the children about the qualities of the newborn. Samina said the baby should be named Akib. After this Akib was brought outside to an elderly *maulavi* (a person knowledgeable about the Koran) who had arrived to give him the *ajaan* (blessing of Allah in his ears). Only after this ritual, which is called *roza kholna*, was he allowed to ingest food or drink.

What is clear from the example of Jetoon's birthing experience is the complementarity of a range of women perceived to be knowledgeable about birthing (which is referred to as the work of the midwife, *dai ka kaam*). Samina, the kin-midwife, Mehmuda, who was also a Muslim midwife but not of the Nagori Sunni community, and Dhanni, the low-caste Hindu midwife, have all assisted births in their own capacity as midwives, yet each performed only specific tasks during Jetoon's delivery. Clearly, Samina, the kin-midwife was the most authoritative. (She has delivered approximately 200 babies in her three to six years' work as a midwife.) She supervised only the last stages of labour but took over the actual handling of the baby when it came to cutting the cord and bathing. In reality, then, only the kin-midwife handled the baby after birth. Samina's social and emotional proximity to Jetoon was I think exemplified in her providing a name for the child. Samina lived close by and had closely followed Jetoon's pregnancy.

Mehmuda seemed to deal only with the religious aspects of the birth. She was by far the most dominant presence in the room and the most vociferous, but she did not always achieve the control she wanted over events. Dhanni did not touch the child once it had emerged, but then neither did she remove the afterbirth or clean the area. So although Dhanni is regarded as impure as she belongs to the Raigar community, who are perceived by Hindu and Muslims alike as being one of the polluting and polluted castes in the area because of their historical association with dead flesh, she did not see her role as dealing with polluted (*napak*) material such as the afterbirth. Her main incentive would seem to be the remuneration in cash which she received for her attendance at a birth. This was Rs 51/- (a little over US$1) in Jetoon's case, but if the child is a first-born and male it can be several hundred rupees. Neither

Mehmuda nor Samina received any material remuneration, although they are believed to have gained the community's goodwill.

In terms of the attitudes of the three midwives during the birth, as with the other women present, there was little sense of the momentousness of the occasion. Mehmuda and Samina were constantly proclaiming that their presence was needed elsewhere. Jetoon's *nanad* (sister-in-law) also displayed some annoyance at the added burden of tasks the birth meant for her. Even Shahnaz, Samina's husband's younger brother's wife, came in the hut for a few minutes to assess the situation before her domestic duties claimed her. None of these women really consoled Jetoon or appreciated her efforts. Jetoon too did not obviously seem to need any emotional support. I got the impression that Mehmuda and Samina were also fearful of being associated with the possibility of a problem with the birth. In fact, one of the reasons for the mother herself to cut the cord is the recent widespread awareness of the risks associated with this stage in the birth.

Samina says she delivers children only when there are no birth complications. She usually delays the cutting of the umbilical cord of the child until the placenta is out so that if there are any problems with the child or mother, then the newborn can be sent, still attached to the cord, to the hospital. In any case, according to Samina, if the cord is cut before the placenta is out, the placenta may ascend and stick to the upper side of the uterus causing danger to the mother's life. When there are difficulties, usually in cases where Samina feels the head of the baby is not descending through the birth canal even though the cervix is fully dilated or when the foetus is in breech position, she calls Nurse Parvati. Parvati works as a nurse in the state-run hospital in Ramganj, approximately 12 km away. She charges around Rs 500/- (about US$12) for her services, which include any medicines given, two injections which make women deliver speedily, and her transport charges.

Finally, Jetoon's birth was, by her own admission and as predicted by Samina, a difficult one. What happened in cases where the birth was considered to be relatively easy? I talked to Rashida, who was 29 years old and expecting her fifth child, about her plans for the birth. For the delivery, she said, she would only call Samina, who was her father's sister's husband's son's wife (FZHSW), and also perhaps her husband's elder brother's wife (*jethani*). In case the latter was busy, she would call her father's sister (*bua*). Samina was important because she knew the 'work of a midwife' (*dai ka kaam*) and her *jethani* was necessary as she could heat the water, milk, make tea and massage Rashida when she had pain. According to Rashida, one or two women are usually sufficient if a woman does not have a history of birthing problems. One woman can put pressure on the stomach while the other sits in front and delivers the baby (*parshani nahi ho tho ek ya do bahut hain – ek peth ko dabaane aur doosri aage bethne ke liye*).

There was no mention in either case of postnatal care. I was, however, not surprised to find that both Jetoon and her son developed high fever the following day. Since she was unable to walk due to her weakness, it was fortunate that we were able to bring the doctor to Jetoon.

Women's bodily processes and healing: specialist knowledge and 'common' knowledge

Cultural beliefs and curative medicine

There are strong beliefs about bodily fluids and processes, particularly those involved in reproduction, which affect the way women experience and manage related health or illness. These beliefs are both widespread and entrenched. They range from prescriptions about the nutrition of pregnant women, new mothers and children, including breastfeeding, and specific notions about menstrual blood and its management, to wider concepts of privacy, purity and hygiene, urination and defecation. Among women who have given birth to children, it is particularly middle-aged women in the community who have the most knowledge and experience of birthing coupled with the ability to influence other women. A woman's kin-peer group is, however, the most influential when it comes to decisions about whom to consult for reproductive ailments. It is because most of the sharing of information and experiences takes place among kin-peers when they perform their morning ablutions or when they work on menial tasks together. In particular, there is a tendency for close emotional relationships to develop betweeen women and their sisters-in-law.[6]

Outside the birthing event, midwives were usually consulted mainly for when there were pains in the stomach, in the 'tubes' or *nalli* (associated with menstruation or suspected miscarriage), at times for vaginal discharge (*safed pani*) but seldom for uterine, rectal or bladder prolapse (*shareer nikalna*). Local specialists (biomedical, religious healers, unani and Ayurvedic practitioners) were consulted either in conjunction with or independently of midwives, depending on what was recommended by the kin-peer group (in particular by sisters and sisters-in-law[7]). Most consultation takes place initially among kinswomen of the same age with whom one feels an intimacy or solidarity.

In this section, I mainly concentrate on cures sought for menstrual disorders, pelvic inflammation (locally referred to as pain in the 'tubes', which could mean an infection of the fallopian tubes, ovaries, uterus, including the cervix) and the inability to conceive (usually, secondary sterility) which are the main reproductive complaints recognised by the women themselves. Anaemia, nutritional deficiency, vaginal discharge and uteral, rectal or bladder prolapse are so widely prevalent that they are regarded as normal experiences. The endemic nature of low blood counts and the extremely high incidence of infected vaginal discharge contribute significantly to the high levels of reproductive morbidity (see for example, Gupta et al. 1992; Bang and Bang 1992; Unnithan 1999).

Menstruation, conception and miscarriages: the range of specialists

Kinswomen, midwives, religious healers, and private women gynaecologists (discussed on pp. 122–3) are key agents in advising and providing assistance with health care. Locally, women refer to menstruation as *maheena* or *mahwari* (meaning 'month') or as 'MC', short for the English term 'monthly cycle' (a term used as a result of contact with nurses or government health workers). Most of the information on menarche, its onset and management is shared between friends and sisters or procured from brothers' wives or husband's brothers' wives. Surprisingly little talk on menstruation takes place between mothers and daughters in the region generally. Among Sunni Muslims and Hindus alike, it is believed that menstruation is connected to the well-being of the woman. Zahida and Kamlesh both agreed that the blood of women who do not have periods turns to water and their eyes become weak, making sight difficult. It was also widely believed that the more blood one has in one's body, the greater the blood flow during a menstrual period. In general, menstruation is regarded as the flow of waste or dirt (*kachra/gandagi*), which is why there is a ban on sexual intercourse of approximately seven to eight days for a three-day menstrual period. According to Zahida, the 'dirt' and 'heat' is contagious and as a result men can have itching and pain in passing urine.

The majority of reproductive ailments in rural Rajasthan have to do with menstrual problems. This was borne out by my observations at a rural voluntary health centre in Sanganer. The scarcity of water and of privacy to wash oneself, and the cloth used as menstrual protection, are likely to contribute to reproductive tract infections, although the connection between hygiene and menstrual problems is not made by the women themselves.[8]

Most of the Nagori and Hindu caste women I met consulted either midwives or religious healers for menstrual disorders (*maheena/mahwari ki pareshani*). This is because menstrual problems are considered to result from the *kachra/gandagi* (waste) left in the body after childbirth and because menstruating women are considered particularly susceptible to the force of 'ill-winds' (*hawa ka jor*). Often the problem is presented in terms of *dard/dukhna* or general pain, or more specifically a problem with 'the tubes'. While lower-caste or kin-midwives are consulted to ascertain the physical nature of the problem, invariably the cure is seen to lie with the religious healer. However, if the problem of bleeding arises during pregnancy, then it is very often the case that a cleansing (*safai*) is resorted to for which private women gynaecologists are consulted (see p. 122).

The religious cures are always considered effective and, even if combined with the use of biomedical or herbal cures, are considered the primary source of well-being. They are perhaps the least expensive of all the cures and also deal most with the mental state of the women. Most religious healers are men, either kinsmen or from the lower Hindu castes. Miraim, who is married to Zahida's husband's elder brother, was pregnant and Samina had diagnosed that the foetus was in breech position. When Miraim was in labour, her father-in-law (husband's father), recited *mantra* (chants) in order to facilitate the birth. He is known to get possessed by the spirit of 'Shukker Baba'.

During her pregnancy, as with previous pregnancies, Miraim had also consulted Pooran, the lower-caste Hindu healer. Pooran is referred to by his caste as *bhangi*, rather than by his role as a religious healer (*jhad phoonk waala*). Pooran works mainly by becoming possessed himself by 'Baba'.[9] He then transfers the power of the counter-spirit into saffron and red threads with which he 'ties' the affliction. The threads are wound around different parts of the body but particularly around the waist for reproductive ailments. Pooran also prescribes that lemons and cloves be ingested or tied with the sacred thread at different places in the house or on furniture. One pregnant woman consulting Pooran in my presence was asked to eat a lemon, place another at a crossroads, tie two cloves to her left upper arm and tie two more cloves to the head of her bed. Previous to this a red and yellow thread was measured to her length. Then, between four and seven knots were placed in the thread before the pregnant woman was asked to tie this around her waist. Pooran was usually paid in the form of a couple of rupees, a coconut and bundles of local cigarettes, with no total payment exceeding Rs 25/- in value.

Zahida had first visited Pooran with Miraim almost eight years ago. This was because she had problems with her second conception. For seven years after her first child she was unable to conceive. Her fertility was so much in doubt that her in-laws advised their son to divorce her (*talaq de do*). Her husband sent her back to her natal home. She then sought out Pooran's help. She also went to see a private gynaecologist who was an expert on infertility. She took whatever medicines the doctor prescribed. She became pregnant but the doctor found the foetus was not growing. In the village the women said it was because *unpar ka hai* ('there was something of the above'). She first saw a man from the Meena caste who got possessed with the spirit of Bhairu. He gave her an amulet to wear. She had also got a thread made by Pooran. When she could afford them, she also took the medicines the doctor had prescribed. She became better and delivered a son.

As is clear from Zahida's case, women do not limit themselves to one kind of healer but consult with a range of specialists for a single complaint simultaneously, believing in the effectiveness of combined treatment. Nevertheless, it is the religious healers who are likely to be consulted in every case, whether or not medical doctors are consulted.

The religious healer clearly emerges as the dominant healer in rural Rajasthan compared to the kin- and non-kin-midwives. This is both in terms of the numbers of clients and the range of curative measures, both physical and mental, he (most often male) is able to provide. His range of expertise is seen to derive from his efficacy in treating the spirit (variously conceived as wind, looks, feeling, heat) especially when there is no outward physical manifestation of an ailment.[10] Anxieties about infertility, infant mortality or suspected foetal disorders are of this nature.

Emotionally, one of the most difficult birth-related events which Nagori and other rural women in the area face is the death of their infants before the first birthday. Of the Nagori Sunni women I got to know, 48 per cent reported deaths of their children (as distinct from miscarriages or abortions), with over 84 per cent of these taking place under the age of one year.[11] Neither midwives nor medical personnel were consulted when children died, primarily because it was believed they had little to offer. Paradoxically, midwives and medical personnel could contribute significantly to preventing the deaths through supporting nutrition, hygiene and immunisation delivery to antenatal and postnatal women.

Kinswomen seldom have the time or knowledge to assess the health needs of the infant following the delivery, and this contributes to the neglect and often death of newly born infants. Most of these deaths are put down to the 'evil winds' or witchcraft (*unpar ki bimari*, 'illness from above'; *kissi ne kuchh kar diya*, 'someone did something'; *dakan kaleja nikaal kar le gai*, 'a witch took her heart out'). It is the religious healer again to whom the women turn in order to exorcise the evil which has entered them or surrounds them. Thus, it is religious healers who attend to the mental states of grief and anxiety which follow both the death of children but also birthing more generally.

Lactation and breastfeeding

Usually kinswomen who are of the same generation advise on breas (*boba dena*) of the newborn through a sharing of their experience: would be either sisters, if the woman is visiting her natal village at the is married into her own village, or sisters-in-law if she is in the husbai lage.[12] The first breastfeed among the Sunni Nagoris depends availability of a suitable person to perform the *ajaan* after which inges food may commence (see the description of Jetoon's delivery). As a quence of this ritual, a Sunni mother has less control over this perioc women in the lower Hindu castes. But, as I observed, among Sunni N   ɪs as well as among the Raigar, Dhanka Hindus and the Mina (who are ɔn-sidered 'tribal'), infants are usually first put to the breast within 48 hours of birth. In the case of the rural Hindu women (including women of the Mina community), there are other cultural notions that work to delay the first breastfeed. For example, among the Khateek and Mina women, if the child is born during the day, then the first breastfeed is preferred to be given the same night or the next day. Among both Muslims and Hindus, newborn infants received some drops of water with sugar/molasses (*gola/gutka*) after birth and when they cry in this period. In all cases there is the belief that colostrum (referred to as *keela* among the Nagoris and *kheench* among the lower-caste Hindus) is bad as it is 'stored' milk and therefore should be removed, In fact, the *keela* is removed by the *jethani* or husband's elder brother's wife among the Sunni Nagori women.[13]

Breast-milk itself is said to be of two main varieties: *phulna doodh* or milk that makes babies grow, and its opposite, *katna doodh*, milk that is deficient, making for weak babies. Lactating mothers are also divided accordingly, with the notion that it is thin mothers who produce the best (*phulna*) milk. In general thin women are regarded as hardworking, whereas fat women are taunted for being lazy. In rural Rajasthan, where women's labour is paramount to the success of the domestic economy, we see that such gendered notions permeate the arena of women's reproductive health. We return to the implications of such ideologies for women's nutrition in the next section.

Among both Hindu and Muslim women in the region, infants are breast-fed until the next conception, which, given the lack of contraceptive use, is usually between seventeen and twenty-four months.

Only Nagori mothers claim to breastfeed girls for twenty-seven months and boys for twenty-one months as stipulated in the Koran. According to Mehmuda, girls are breastfed for six months longer than boys because they have a greater right over their mother (*ladkiyon ka maa ke unpar zyada huq hai*) and in any case girls always take from their natal kin as they please. In practice, I found there to be a great deal of variation, and on average the tendency is for girls and boys to be breastfed until the age of eighteen months or so. The connection between these practices and the onset of the menstrual cycle was not made by the women themselves, but was one I observed. The mothers told me, much to their surprise, that they became pregnant while breastfeeding infants of around eleven months.

Breastfeeding after birth is not only important for the infant's health but also for the mother's health, especially with regard to the contraction of her uterus. Neither midwives nor elderly women seemed to have much control over this aspect of infant and mother care. Moreover, there seemed to be a generational difference in approaches to breastfeeding. While most of the older Nagori women (40 to 55 years) stressed the need exclusively to breast-feed the infants, the younger generations of mothers (20 to 40 years) were more enamoured by bottle-feeding, seeing it as a sign of being progressive. In most cases the infant is bottle-fed with a mixture of goat's milk and water, from as early as four to five days onwards.

The younger mothers had different ways of explaining to me their inability to breastfeed. Jetoon, for example, says she has never had much milk for any of her children.[14] Zahida, told me that her left breast never had any milk and that when she had twins for her sixth delivery, she would take turns to feed them from her right breast. Munni, Zahida's sister-in law, however, claimed that her children did not drink milk from her right breast and would scream when placed on that side. I also met a woman from the Raigar caste who insisted that her milk was poisonous, that an ant had died drinking it, and hence she did not breastfeed her child.

The older women, on the other hand, took pride in their ability to breastfeed. Most of the older women I met claimed to have enough breast-milk to raise their infants. Zahida's mother for example, said she did not use any *unpar ka doodh* (literally; 'milk on top') referring to goat or cow's milk for her babies. Many of the older women also ascribed their inability to provide the 'right' nutrition for their children (biscuits, tinned milk, bottles, etc.) to their poverty.

In relation to breastfeeding and the process of lactation generally, midwives have little additional knowledge apart from that which comes from the fact of their being mothers themselves. The same is true for knowledge relating to nutrition and its connection with the processes of reproduction, which I describe in the next section.

Nutrition and reproduction

With regard to the nutrition of mothers, it is common knowledge among mothers that special foods are eaten not before but after childbirth, and then only for fifteen to twenty days. There is a belief across castes that women should eat less, drink less and that 'thin mothers make for fat babies' through better breastmilk, as implied in the differences between *phulna* and *katna* milk mentioned earlier. Women themselves did not consider it important to change the type or quantities of foods during pregnancy or lactation. A number of women said they were incapable of ingesting much food under normal circumstances as well. This may very well be the case, as in anaemic conditions there tends to be a loss of appetite, due to a reduced oxidation of the body. Also, women ate less because they were afraid of being called fat, especially by other women, as this would imply they were not working hard enough. It is also important to note that a new mother (*jacchha*) is prohibited from touching the hearth and water pots due to pollution arising from child-birth which can be active for up to forty days. She is thus dependent on other women feeding her.

Mothers, mothers-in-law and elder sisters-in-law[15] give advice on which and what quantities of special foods are to be eaten in the eighth month of pregnancy. These include, for example, coconut, sesame seed oil and castor oil because of their lubricating properties, which help the foetus move easily within the womb to ensure a smooth delivery. Only women who are grand-mothers or who have pregnant daughters are aware of the ingredients of the special sweetmeat (*ladoo*), compulsory for women to ingest after the birth. Jetoon told me her mother put thirty-two different items in it but could name only a few. Kamlesh said normally thirty to forty of such sweetmeat balls are made, one for every day after the birth until normal food was resumed. Jetoon said she never ate hers because she did not like the taste, so in fact they were all eaten by her children instead.

Therefore, in reality, women continued to drink a few cups of sweetened tea and after a week or so of eating semi-solid food (usually broken-wheat porridge or rice if they could afford it), returned to their regular diet of *roti* (unleavened bread) accompanied by a small portion of *subzi* (fried vegetable), chillies/onions or, for the more affluent among them, buttermilk/lentil soup.

Preventive medicine and women's desires: encountering biomedical expertise

The services of private women gynaecologists were very much in demand among Nagori and other rural women in the area. Most of the Nagori women and Hindu caste women were so severely anaemic or physically exhausted from previous pregnancies or hard physical labour with little nutritious intake that they usually suffered tremendous weakness during their pregnancy. With any sign of bleeding during pregnancy all women readily sought the services of these women doctors, despite the hefty fee. The outcome of such bleeding was routinely to carry out a *safai* (literally, 'cleansing', referring to a medical termination of pregnancy or MTP) and 'sonography' (or the ultrasound scan) with fees ranging from around Rs 400/- for women who were two to three months pregnant, to Rs 800/- for later pregnancies. Thus, when we include transportation costs, medicines and bed charges, women spend between Rs 500/- to 1500/- for a medical termination of pregnancy.

Nagori and other rural women in the area differentiated between *safai* (an induced abortion) and *girna* (literally 'to fall', referring to miscarriage or spontaneous abortion). While some midwives provided medicines to abort the foetus, there was a general feeling that this was a risky procedure. Samina, the Nagori kin-midwife, said it was relatively easy to abort a foetus, as all that was needed was to pierce the sac (*bachhadani*) with a cloth-tipped stick dipped in a particular solution. Usually the foetus was aborted between half an hour and two hours after this. In some cases it could take up to twelve hours. She said she never performed abortions as they were dangerous and there would be retribution from the community.

However, Zarina, a Muslim midwife who lived in the city, had performed abortions for women such as Gathro and Zahida's sister. Both Zahida and Gathro warned me of the suffering (*pareshani*) and great heat of the medicine (*garmi*), which entered the head to cause dizziness (*chukker*) and nausea (*ulti*). Such medicine was dangerous (*khatarnak*) and it was best to get *safai* performed in a hospital. I found that Nagori women, having assessed the risks attached to undergoing abortions from local healers, were, in fact, resorting to the medical termination of pregnancy (MTP) in high numbers. The religious sanctions against 'unnatural' interference in childbirth did little to stop Nagori women from undergoing an MTP. In fact, both Nagori and indeed other Hindu women in the area resorted to the MTP almost as a means of spacing children in lieu of using contraceptive devices.

The high incidence of *safai* then leads me to suggest that it is regarded as the easiest means of spacing children over which women have control. The women complained of pain, bleeding and weakness when using the pill or intra-uterine devices. As well as the physical harm they cause, they are little understood and culturally unacceptable. Moreover, women seem to be able to mobilise their networks of kin, natal and affinal, effectively to lend them money for necessary consultations to secure their reproductive ability.

For their MTP, Zahida and most other women from the Nagori village would visit 'Neetu', a female gynaecologist who worked in a privately funded hospital. There are a growing number of such hospitals because of the inability of state-run hospitals to cater to the demands of their women patients, both because of the sheer numbers and because of their reputation for providing shoddy services, even if they are free. Private women doctors were seen to have both the knowledge and the means to treat women's reproductive ailments effectively. Most women of the same community, whether in one or more villages, tend to use these services for two main reasons. Since they can refer to a kinswoman who has previously been treated, the women expect to get a sympathetic consultation. They also feel that, if the need arises, the doctor may be more able to accept delays in payment from known as opposed to unknown persons. These are some of the feelings and thoughts which motivate most women in Jetoon, Samina and Zahida's village to consult with 'Neetu', for example.

Despite expressing an interest in contraceptives, few Nagori women used them. The Nagori Sunni hesitation to use modern contraceptives was perhaps wise as the contraceptive options presented to women were, in general, neither proven safe (for example Nirodh, the brand of condoms distributed through the public health system) nor physically tolerable by weak-bodied women, since intra-uterine devices such as the Copper T and contraceptive pills can cause excessive bleeding in weak and anaemic women. When it came to contraceptives, and intra-uterine devices and condoms in particular, kin-midwives and married women generally had similar ideas. According to Samina, the kin-midwife, the Copper T sticks right up in the women's vagina and gets full of 'meat' or it comes right down to the mouth of the vagina and causes discomfort. She was keen to see a specimen as she had heard about them from other women and also from the television.

Zahida, the only woman among fifty-five Nagoris who used the Copper T, which had been fitted for her during her last MTP, claimed her husband complained of physical irritation during intercourse. She said, however, she was afraid to remove the Copper T as she knew she would become pregnant again. She did not want any more children as she had conceived six times already and her last pregnancy had resulted in twins. In a more recent communication with her I learnt that she had removed the IUD and was pregnant again. In effect, Zahida had chosen to undergo yet another pregnancy as it would enable her to meet the sexual demands of her husband. At the same time, she had been convinced by her conversations with other women, in particular with Samina, the kin-midwife, that the Copper T was undesirable.

Shahnaz, who is in her early twenties, was among the younger Nagori mothers I got to know. Unlike Zahida, Samina, Jetoon and scores of other women in their thirties in the village, Shahnaz had had a secondary education. She was also the only woman I met who used condoms. Yet she was as ignorant of them as Samina. She and Samina asked me if condoms (Nirodh) were safe, saying that they had heard that they were unreliable and could fill up and burst (*phatna*) inside the woman. Shahnaz also asked me if it was true that men and women stuck to each other during intercourse if they used condoms. I said that I also used condoms and thought that, with correct use, they are effective. They have an added value because they prevent the spread of disease. Then Shahnaz said I probably bought the expensive ones rather than using the government ones which were distributed free of cost. I agreed that this was indeed the case and that I did not have any experience of the safety of the Nirodh condoms. Shahnaz said she used condoms only because her husband, who worked in the export factory nearby, had got all kinds of progressive ideas from his workplace. They had to hide them from his parents, whom they stayed with, since they would have disapproved. They had only recently started using condoms and Shahnaz wanted to continue, at least until her young daughter was 2 or 3 years old.

Shahnaz's use of condoms and Zahida's use of the Copper T reflects the influence of kinswomen and men, as well as their own initiatives and predisposition, rather than the effects of education (in Shahnaz's case) or the effective outreach of health services (for Zahida).

None of the Nagori women consulted with the Auxiliary Nurse Midwife (ANM, the primary public health worker in the area) on the issue of contraception. This is despite the fact that among the ANMs' main duties is the promotion of contraceptives as a means of spacing children. They are provided with hormonal pills, condoms and IUDs (Unnithan 1998). ANMs are also trained to be midwives but the ANM in the area was not involved in a single Nagori delivery. In fact, Jetoon said she had never seen an ANM in all her thirty-five years in the village. The Nagori village was barely 12 kilometres from Jaipur city (the state capital).

As others writing on midwifery in South Asia have observed (Jeffery, Jeffery and Lyon 1989 and Chapter 4 this volume; Rozario 1998), ANMs have little success because they are recruited from non-kin communities, put in charge of large populations of women, and underresourced in terms of medicines, facilities and transport. Moreover, their work continues to be determined by demographically driven goals, making 'family planning' their main objective. Despite the state's protestations to the contrary, ANMs as well as community health doctors continue to be promised promotions if they increase their 'targets' (figures relating to numbers of women/men

sterilised), although this is based on a discreet understanding between officials rather than official policy.[16] Among health personnel it is widely believed
that the wave of ill-feeling towards the government resulting from the forced
sterilisations which were part of the family planning campaigns of the late
1970s still influences rural people's views of public health services.

Ironically, however, the greatest desire of the Sunni Nagori women I met
was for sterilisation (locally referred to as the 'operation'). In particular, the
desire to terminate fertility once and for all was expressed when the ideal mix
of girl and boy children was attained (four to five children, with equal numbers or more boys than girls, as with other communities in Rajasthan, see
Patel 1994). I therefore found that, in contrast to the public health authorities'
views on the subject, the idea of sterilisation had taken root amongst Nagori
and Hindu caste men and women as an effective means of coping with otherwise unregulated fertility. It was also noteworthy that the demand for
sterilisations were made equally by both Muslims and Hindus, once again
belying the notions of local health workers that the Muslim community in the
area had no use for reproductive services.

While the government overtly promotes contraceptives and the training of
midwives (ANMs as well as selected traditional birth attendants), there is a
demand among the villagers for sterilisations at a particular point in the
reproductive life-cycle and for experienced, inexpensive yet socially familiar
birthing agents. It is unlikely that the more recent, well-intentioned, government schemes to empower midwives in the community will be successful in
changing women's experiences of birthing. This is in part because of the
socially diffuse nature of birthing knowledge, on the one hand, and the control which kinsmen and older women can exert over the processes of
conception and reproduction, maintained through various cultural beliefs
concerning bodily processes, on the other hand.

The point about the ineffectiveness of midwife training schemes has also
been made by Jeffery, Jeffery and Lyon (Chapter 4 this volume) for North
India, and more recently by Rozario for Bangladesh (1998). Jeffery, Jeffery
and Lyon believe that midwife training programmes will not work because of
the association of trained midwives with a state whose legitimacy was undermined by the sterilisation programme, because of the inability of the
midwives to ward off competition from the untrained village midwives and,
finally, because of the views of the midwives themselves of their work as
degrading and lowly (see Chapter 4). Rozario suggests that the midwives
actually have serious deficiencies in terms of delivering effective health care,
both in their knowledge and capabilities as well as by being compromised by
the cultural and material situation in which they work (1998: 144). This reinforces my own observations of Nagori birthing and healing practices.

Given the particular social, cultural and economic context in which the
Nagoris and other rural Rajasthani women in the area live, perhaps one of
the ways to assure a drop in maternal morbidity and infant mortality would

then be not so much to emphasise midwives as the crucial agents of health-care delivery in themselves, but to examine their strengths and provide an extension of delivery facilities and antenatal and postnatal care at the level of the primary health centre. Here the gynaecologists could work with local kin- and non-kin-midwives to be socially connected with their patients at the same time providing inexpensive, yet expert services. The experience of NGOs (for example, Search in Maharashtra), has proven that such an initiative is possible, practical and effective (see Mavlankar, Bang and Bang 1998).

Conclusions

In this chapter I have shown that the knowledge of healing in relation to birth and reproductive processes in general is diffused among the community of women and some men in rural Rajasthan. In this context women who are midwives, although possessing some expertise in the physical management of childbirth and related processes, are not the sole repositories of healing related to reproduction. They work along with different categories of kinswomen, kinsmen, and men and women from other communities, to meet the physical and psycho-social needs of birthing women. Midwives, both those who belong to the community and those from outside, are in large part unable to treat the main reproductive disorders, especially those relating to menstruation, without addressing income, diet and nutrition. Their low social status, as I suggest in the chapter, is a result of their incomplete knowledge and skills, evident in the fact that their care is regularly supplemented by access to gynaecological expertise and/or religious healing, together with the diffusion of reproductive knowledge among other women in the community, making reproductive experiences 'common', 'natural' and normal.

While the chapter has focused on women's knowledge of reproductive processes and the associated politics between women, the intention has not been to exclude men from the analysis of women's reproductive health. In fact, as the ethnographic material has shown, most religious healers, the dominant category of local healers, are in fact men (kinsmen and lower-caste Hindu men). Furthermore, kinsmen (as husbands, brothers-in-law, fathers, fathers-in-law) often provide both financial and emotional support facilitating the processes of healing. They can both enable or block women's access to biomedical health services, as, for example, in cases of the medical termination of pregnancy (by providing or withholding money) or in the case of sterilisation (by providing or withholding their consent).

Intimacy, friendship and social solidarity within one's kin group are important dimensions to consider in understanding the motivations underlying women's health-related actions. They explain why, for example, certain sisters-in-law rather than others become important in their influence over women's decisions regarding the health care they choose. Because of their marriage patterns, Nagori Sunni women often remain geographically close to their natal kin. As a consequence, and unlike the majority of Hindu caste women, they are able to draw on natal networks of support and a group of familiar, local healers, resulting in more confident interactions when they seek health care. Natal kinship networks, however, need not always work to support women. These networks have to be regarded in terms of the shifting politics among members of the natal kin household and between the natal and marital homes. Often, if a woman's natal kin live under difficult economic circumstances relative to her affinal kin, she can expect little support from them. There is also the 'politics' between women married into the natal kin households and those married out. So the amount of emotional and material support the Nagori women are able to draw on for birthing, or for other occasions when they face reproductive vulnerability, is a complex function of the numbers and economic and emotional disposition of their relatives.

Furthermore, the expectations of conforming to the social hierarchy, wherein young wives have little control over their bodies, along with the cultural codes related to birthing and reproductive healing (the impurity related to birthing and menstruation, for example) in general are most rigorously, if not oppressively, enforced by these very same kinspeople, notwithstanding the possible detriment to the woman's reproductive health. Fear and anxiety are other emotions which underlie women's choices of specific healers (for example, religious healers to explain and/or cure the causes of infant deaths; or seeking abortions from medical doctors rather than midwives) or of certain methods (for example, the decision to undergo sterilisation rather than use contraceptives is very much shaped by the husband's perspective).

Given the uncertain nature of women's kinship connections, the low use made of the Auxiliary Nurse Midwives or of trained traditional birth attendants, and the insufficient competence of village (kin and non-kin) midwives to deal with reproductive disorders, it becomes imperative to redesign the delivery of reproductive health services in rural Rajasthan. One of the possible ways in which this may be achieved is to have a number of strategic, small-scale, inexpensive, reproductive health units which offer delivery services and antenatal and postnatal care, advice on fertility and sexuality, support for nutrition and hygiene, and which at the same time draw on and mobilise local expertise and support.

Notes

1   The information presented in this chapter is the result of close collaboration over five years with the Khejri Sarvodaya Health Centre, a small, rural, charitable organisation, and backed up by fourteen years of work on rural Rajasthan. I received crucial support from members of the health centre; residents of the Jagatpura area, and Zahida Bano, Vipula Joshi and Mohan Singh. In turn, I was happy to be able to contribute to a strengthening of the effectiveness of the health-care delivery of the centre. The field research was supported by the Wellcome Foundation for Medical Research, UK. I am also grateful to Sonya Leff and

Heather Frost of the Sussex NHS Trust for their comments. For further material on this study, see Unnithan 2001 and forthcoming.
2 Sillitoe 1998 makes a similar observation in relation to the analysis of indigenous knowledge on farming systems
3 Throughout this chapter I use the term 'midwives' to refer to all women who deliver babies, and in the context of rural Rajasthan these are usually traditional birth attendants. Some of these women may have received 'training', information or basic medical supplies as part of the public health outreach programme.
4 Wherever I use the term 'mother', I refer to the woman whose delivery is in question.
5 The term *nanad* is used locally to refer to husband's younger brother's wife as well as to the husband's sister.
6 Especially the husband's younger sister, husband's younger brother's wife and brother's wife.
7 That is, brothers' wives, husband's sisters and husband's brothers' wives.
8 Rozario makes a similar point when she suggests that pollution associated with reproduction is not associated with unhygienic practices among the Bangladeshi familes of her study (1998: 153).
9 This could be either Ramdeo Baba of the lower castes, Guru Nanak of the Sikhs, or the spirit of a Muslim pir.
10 These healers also deal, however, with snake, scorpion and other insect bites.
11 The significantly low rate of medical attendance during delivery as well as in the antenatal period is shown by the NFHS to have a significant impact on infant mortality figures (maternal mortality figures are unrecorded) with infant mortality rates at 76 per 1,000 births with no care, 71 per 1,000 births with either antenatal or delivery care, and 45 per 1000 births where the woman had both antenatal and delivery care (Government of India 1995: 157). Figures based on fieldwork substantiate the very high infant mortality rates as well as extremely high levels of maternal morbidity, especially with regard to reproductive tract infections.
12 Brothers' wives, husband's sisters and husband's brothers' wives.
13 In reality two to five drops are removed and so the child does ingest some colostrum. This observation is contrary to that made by the recent NFHS, which suggests that no benefits accruing from ingestion of colostrum are available to babies born in rural areas (Government of India 1995).
14 While generally suckling the breasts should stimulate milk production, in weak and malnourished mothers this may not be the case (Dr Banerjee, personal communication).
15 Brothers' wives, husband's sisters and husband's brothers' wives.
16 This comment is based on personal communication with both ANMs and government doctors.

References

Bang, R. and A. Bang. 1992. Why women hide them: rural women's viewpoints on reproductive tract infections. *Manushi* 69 (March/April): 27–30.
Davis-Floyd, R. E. and C. Sargent (eds). 1997. *Childbirth and Authoritative Knowledge: Cross-cultural Perspectives.* Berkeley and Los Angeles: University of California Press.
Government of India. 1995. *National Family Health Survey 1992–93: Rajasthan.* Udaipur: Population Research Centre; Bombay: International Institute for Population Sciences.

Gupta, N., P. Pal, M. Bhargava and M. Daga. 1992. Health of women and children in Rajasthan. *Economic and Political Weekly* 17 October: 2323–30.

Jeffery, P., R. Jeffery and A. Lyon. 1989. *Labour Pains and Labour Power: Women and Childbearing in India.* London: Zed Books.

Lutz, C., and L. Abu-Lughod, eds. 1990. *Language and the Politics of Emotion.* Cambridge: Cambridge University Press.

Mavlankar, D., A. Bang and R. Bang. 1998. *Quality of Reproductive Health Services in India: The Search Experience.* Selangor, Malaysia: International Council on Management of Population Programmes. (Series on upscaling innovations in reproductive health in Asia, no. 2.)

Patel, T. 1994. *Fertility Behaviour: Population and Society in Rajasthan.* Oxford: Oxford University Press.

—— 1999. Popular culture and childbirth: perceptions and practices in rural Rajasthan. In *Communication Processes*, vol. 2 *Defiance and Dominance*, edited by B. Bel, B. Das and G. Poitevin, forthcoming. Preliminary version available as e-text at http://www.iias.leidenuniv.nl/host/ccrss/cp/cp2/cp2-Popular.html (accessed April 10, 2001).

Rozario, S. 1998. The dai and the doctor: discourses on women's reproductive health in rural Bangladesh. In *Maternities and Modernities: Colonial and Postcolonial Experiences in Asia and the Pacific*, edited by K. Ram and M. Jolly. Cambridge: Cambridge University Press.

Scheper-Hughes, N. 1992. *Death without Weeping: The Violence of Everyday Life in Brazil.* Berkeley: University of California Press.

Shweder, R. and R. Levine. 1984. *Culture Theory: Essays on Mind, Self and Emotion.* Cambridge: Cambridge University Press.

Sillitoe, P. 1998. The development of indigenous knowledge: a new applied anthropology. *Current Anthropology* 39: 223–52.

Unnithan (Unnithan-Kumar), M. 1998. *Of Households and Beyond: Rural Muslim Women's Access to Reproductive Health Care in Jaipur District, Rajasthan.* Jaipur: Institute of Development Studies. (Working Paper No. 103.)

—— 1999. Households, kinship and access to reproductive health care among rural Muslim Women in Jaipur. *Economic and Political Weekly* 34, 10–11 (March 6–13): 621–30.

—— 2001. Emotion, agency and access to healthcare: women's experiences of reproduction in Jaipur. In *Managing Reproductive Life: Cross-cultural Themes in Fertility and Sexuality*, edited by S. Tremayne. Oxford: Berghahn.

—— Forthcoming. On the empowerment of midwives in Rajasthan: implications for healthcare policy. *Economic and Political Weekly.*

Chapter 6

The healer on the margins
The *dai* in rural Bangladesh

Santi Rozario

Introduction

I have explored aspects of childbirth in rural Bangladesh in several recent
publications (Rozario 1995a, 1995b, 1998). Broadly speaking, as discussed
below, my findings were close to those of researchers such as Thérèse
Blanchet (1984), also working in rural Bangladesh, and Patricia Jeffery, Roger
Jeffery and Andrew Lyon, working in Uttar Pradesh in North India (Jeffery,
Jeffery and Lyon 1989; see also Chapter 4 this volume). I found that birth was
strongly associated with shame and pollution. Most births took place at
home, with the assistance of traditional birth attendants, called *dais* (sometimes *dhatri* or *dhoruni*). These *dais* were elderly women from low-status
backgrounds. Their expertise was routinely devalued and their authority
given little recognition. They received little or no payment for their services.

This was the pattern both in the village in Dhaka district ('Doria') where I carried out my initial research on childbirth in late 1991 and early 1992 (Rozario
1995a, 1998) and in a village in Noakhali district where I did further research in
late 1994 and early 1995 (Rozario 1995b, see Figures 6.1, 6.2 and 6.3).

My initial aim in this research had been to examine the impact of modern
medicine and contraception, and the significance of local concepts of purity,
on women's reproductive health. My data included interviews with family
planning workers, folk healers (*kabiraj*), biomedical (allopathic) and homeopathic doctors, pregnant women, and mothers with small children as well as
with the *dais* themselves. In making sense of my findings, I developed ideas
from my earlier work, especially from the study of gender relations and communal boundaries in Doria which I undertook for my Ph.D. (published as
Rozario 1992).

My previous publications on childbirth (1995a, 1995b, 1998) have been
mainly about the birthing families, the choices they made and the moral uni-
verse within which these choices were made. The present chapter, by contrast,
looks at the experience of the *dais* themselves, and asks how they cope with
their marginalised and devalued position. It was first written in 1993, so it is
based primarily on the 1991/2 Doria research.[1]

Figure 6.1 Gaynoda, a *dai* from a village in Dhaka District, Bangladesh
(photo by Santi Rozario)

Doria is a village in the Rupganj subdistrict, two to three hours by road
from the city of Dhaka. It is a large village with a population divided relatively evenly between Muslims, Hindus and Christians (Rozario 1992). When
I started to work on childbirth in Doria, I had already been back to the village several times since my initial research in 1983/4, and I knew many of the
villagers quite well. My own family, who are Christians, come from a nearby
village. This chapter is based mainly on conversations with three *dais* who
worked in or near Doria, one Hindu woman (Gaynoda) and two Christians
(Teri and Pishima). I also spoke to a number of other *dais* in the area more
briefly.

Gaynoda, the Hindu *dai* (Figure 6.1), was in her mid-forties. Her husband
had left her and her two small children some years before, and she was in very
difficult financial circumstances. She had learned some *kabiraji* (folk healing)
from her mother and another woman. However, she claimed to be self-taught
as far as her work as a *dai* was concerned. By 1991, she had been practising
for about six years. She said that she carried out about six or seven childbirths
a year.

Teri, who was about 50 years of age, was living with her aged mother, who had also practised as a *dai*. Her husband had died some years before and the family was again very poor. Teri's mother had been trained as a midwife at a Catholic mission in the region many years earlier, at a time when the missionaries had a *dai* training campaign. Teri herself had learned from watching her mother. Unlike the other two, she had some formal schooling. She claimed to be very popular and to carry out many births, perhaps ten to twelve a year.

Pishima, who was 62 in 1991, again lived in a very poor household. She claimed to have been practising for twenty-five to thirty years. She said that she began to work as a *dai* soon after she had her own first baby, and that she had learned from the experience of giving birth herself. She claimed to do two to five deliveries a month. Pishima has a special relationship with a *pari*, a benevolent female spirit, who aids her in her *kabiraji* and her work as a *dai* (see p. 142). In 1991 she had attended a three-day government *dai* training programme, but when I interviewed her in 1992 she was still waiting to receive her delivery kit from the government.

In the following sections I begin with a general discussion of childbirth, and then look at the ways in which the *dais* deal with the negative valuation Bangladeshi society places on their work.

The pollution of childbirth and the marginal status of the *dai*

To understand the marginal status of the *dai*, we need to begin with the most central and most problematic aspect of her role: the *dai*'s involvement with the pollution of childbirth. In the North Indian context, Jeffery et al. (1989) argue that the *dai*'s function is centrally concerned with the removal of pollution:

> [I]t is inappropriate to regard the *dai* as an expert midwife in the contemporary Western sense. Even in the absence of medically trained personnel, the *dai* does not have an overriding control over the management of deliveries. Nor is she a sisterly and supportive equal. Rather, she is a low status menial necessary for removing defilement.
>
> (Jeffery, Jeffery and Lyon 1989: 108)

They also note that '[c]hildbirth pollution is the most severe pollution of all, far greater than menstruation, sexual intercourse, defaecation or death. Consequently, touching the amniotic sac, placenta and umbilical cord . . . and delivering the baby, cutting the cord and cleaning up the blood are considered the most disgusting of tasks' (106).

I would argue that these ideas are very much present in Bangladesh as well, and that the removal of pollution is at least one of the major functions of Bangladeshi *dais* (cf. Rozario 1995a, 1998). The emphasis on pollution is found in most other recent writings on birth in Bangladesh, including the numerous studies carried out by researchers at the International Centre for Diarrhoeal Disease Research, Bangladesh (ICDDR, B). Thus, Katy Gardner, who did extensive anthropological fieldwork in Talukpur (Sylhet district), notes that 'a woman who has given birth is seen as dangerously polluted in rural Bangladesh. If her dirt or blood contaminates the place where the family wash or clean their food . . ., great sickness is thought to ensue' (Gardner 1991: 26). Frances McConville, in a general article on birth attendants in Bangladesh, also mentions childbirth pollution and its consequences for the status of the *dais* (McConville 1989). Naseem Hussain, working in a village close to the Dhaka metropolitan region, again mentions childbirth pollution (Hussain 1992). In the writings of ICDDR, B researchers (e.g. Bhatia, Chakraborty and Faruque 1980, Fauveau and Chakraborty 1988), of Blanchet (1984) and others, it is evident that the women in the childbirths they describe were concerned about the *dai*'s absence not because they needed her expertise, but because none of them were willing to take on the pollution involved in delivering the baby. All this is despite the high value placed on the birth of children (particularly sons) in rural Bangladesh, as in South Asia generally.

Gaynoda, Teri and Pishima are typical of the *dais* in Rupganj, who are usually very poor, elderly, with little or no formal education or training, and often widowed. While some middle-class women may engage in the task of delivering babies, they do this only for their close relatives and do not leave their household or hamlet to deliver babies for other women. The poor background and low status of *dais* are also emphasised in the work of Blanchet (1984) and Gardner (1991), working elsewhere in Bangladesh. Although she does not explicitly say so, it is also clear from Shamima Islam's (1989) accounts of Bangladeshi birth attendants that they are always from the lower classes and may or may not receive a cash payment for their services.

In the Hindu-dominated society of North India, *dais* are almost always from low-status, normally 'untouchable', castes. Louis Dumont's model of caste, with its emphasis on the underlying ideology of purity and pollution, has only a limited relevance in the predominantly Muslim society of Bangladesh (Dumont 1972).[2] Bangladeshi village society is not, at least from the Muslim or Christian perspectives, divided into named endogamous groups ranked according to criteria of purity and separated by explicit restrictions on the sharing of food. However, notions similar to the purity–pollution ideology of caste are undoubtedly present at a covert level. Commensality, let alone intermarriage, between low- and high-status groups is rare, and physical contact with low-status groups is undoubtedly seen by high-status groups as inappropriate and to be avoided. The *dais*, it should be noted, virtually all belong to these low-status groups.

Strategies used by *dais* to counter their low status

We can see that the *dais* in Bangladesh, as in North India, are generally regarded as people of low status, who are engaged in a 'dirty' and polluting occupation. But how do the *dais* see themselves and their role? In the following pages I show how the *dais* attempt in various ways to counter their low status and the pollution associated with their task of delivering babies, and to give meaning to and legitimise their role. For the sake of convenience, I will classify the strategies used by the *dais* to counter their devalued status under four headings:

- seeing their work as characterised by the possession of significant professional skills, particularly in comparison with doctors and other medical personnel;
- taking pride in their individual skills in comparison with other *dais*;
- seeing themselves as engaged in the performance of charitable work;
- claiming spiritual or religious sanction for their work.

I shall discuss these one by one, but there is often significant overlap between them.

The dai *as possessor of significant professional skills*

In my interviews, the *dais* often made it clear that they were proud of their skills and went on to elaborate on the various methods they employ in different problem situations. The *dais* take pride in the special knowledge they gained from more experienced *dais* on how to deal with difficult labour. Thus, Gaynoda explained how she could judge whether or not a baby was due by pulling out a certain plant. 'If the plant comes up with the root then the baby is ready to be delivered, if the plant breaks somewhere in-between then the baby is not due.' By following this method Gaynoda had been able to predict in one case that the pain felt by the birthing mother was not labour pain. She said, 'I delivered that baby after eight days'.

Gaynoda uses various other techniques in dealing with difficult labour. For example, she explains that

> to bring on labour pains I tie the root of a particular tree to the woman's left thigh, and take it off as soon as she delivers. Otherwise the whole of the mother's inside will come out with the baby. This is because the root is so very potent.

Another *dai* told me that the woman in labour is sometimes given basil leaves to sniff or the root of a young tamarind tree is placed in her mouth in order to bring on her labour pains. Gaynoda also told me that she uses the root of a plant to correct the position of the baby inside the mother's womb. If the delivery looks like a really difficult one, the *dai* looks for a rare plant, the root of which has to be collected when she is absolutely naked. These practices are common among most of the *dais* in Rupganj as well as in other parts of Bangladesh as reported by Blanchet (1984).

The *dais* also compared their skills and integrity of their work with the village doctors or city hospitals. Even though the families give higher status and higher value to doctors, it is interesting to see the way *dais* compare their work to that of the doctors.

Although it is a common custom that a family give a sari to a *dai* after she has delivered a baby, the *dais* claim that they do not necessarily attend a birth for this reason. They cite examples of performing difficult deliveries and yet not receiving any form of remuneration. On the other hand, they describe the enormous amount of money that the family have to pay to a village doctor if he is called. The costs involved in sending a birthing woman to a city hospital are far higher again. Thus, when I asked *dais* why they thought that the families called them instead of a doctor, the reply usually was because doctors are very expensive: 'A *dai* is merely given a sari, if anything, and maybe a meal of chicken curry.'

There is a clear distinction between the way a family treats a doctor on the one hand and a *dai* on the other. This is so despite the fact that the *dais*, who are accorded low status, are recognised as experienced women, whose presence is desirable at a birth. Within the limited options available to rural families, it is not surprising that a *dai* is often perceived as the only person who can help. After all, unless there are complications, delivering babies is a relatively simple task for *dais* who have sufficient knowledge of female anatomy.

However, when complications arise, a *dai* will usually advise the family to call a doctor or to take the birthing woman to a hospital. She does this (i) because she feels unable to tackle the situation, and perhaps more importantly (ii) because she does not want to be responsible for any mishap or to ruin her reputation by being involved in a problem delivery which may lead to the death of the birthing mother and/or the baby. In such a situation, if a family can afford it, a doctor (usually uncertified) will generally be called. Usually, he simply gives an injection or administers a packet of saline and waits outside. Sometimes, he simply watches the *dai* deliver the baby without making any physical contact with the birthing mother or the baby. At other times, the baby may be killed as a result of the doctor's attempts to deliver it by force. Whatever the case, and even if the mother or the baby dies, the doctor, who is almost always male, has to be paid a very substantial amount.

While for some health problems the family may have the utmost faith in doctors as compared to *dais*, the *dais*' perception of the doctors' knowledge is not as positive. The following stories help illustrating the conflicting interests of the *dais* and the doctors. But more significantly, we see the emphasis *dais* place upon their knowledge and expertise in delivering babies.

Gaynoda related to me one case in which she believed the doctor was responsible for the death of the baby. In this case, when she was called by the birthing woman's guardians she felt the woman's pain was not linked to labour but to something she had eaten the day before. Gaynoda said,

> I told the guardians that it was a false alarm. They didn't listen to me but called a doctor. The doctor came and immediately gave an injection to increase the labour pains. The mother was in great pain but there was no sign of the baby. Finally, with great difficulty the baby was delivered, but it died straight away.

In Gaynoda's opinion the baby was not due for some time yet but the doctor forced the baby out, and so caused its death.

In another case Gaynoda attended, the birthing mother had been in labour for three days, but the doctor said the baby was not due for another week. Apparently two other elderly *dais* also said that the baby was not due for some time yet. But Gaynoda said that she delivered the baby in two hours. 'The mother's head was hot and I knew the baby was due.'

Gaynoda says that so far she has had no major problems when delivering babies. The first delivery she attended as a *dai*, though, was a breech delivery, and the mother was her younger brother's wife. On this occasion she was assisting an elderly Muslim *dai*:

> The baby's legs were down and head up. With great difficulty I together with Niat Ali's mother delivered the baby, but it died almost instantly. The mother and the baby were both very dry.

Although it is difficult to make any conclusive judgement about Gaynoda's expertise, it is clear that she has considerable experience with delivering babies and that she is generally successful. I could not help feeling that she took on a fair number of risks which had the potential to result in disaster. However, neither Gaynoda, nor other *dais* I have interviewed, saw their involvement in breech deliveries as necessarily risky. Many *dais* boasted to me that they had also done breech deliveries despite their difficulty, and would cite some examples. Thus, Teri often said, 'If the mother has courage I can do anything.' When questioned what they do in complicated cases, many *dais* said that they tried to take care of the situation themselves. Teri commented that she had only ever referred one case to the hospital, and the baby had died anyway.

The *dais* are of the opinion that on the whole doctors have little under-standing of women's problems. For example, a Muslim *dai* said to me,

Figure 6.2 A *dhatri* from Noakhali, Bangladesh (photo by Santi Rozario)

'Doctors do not understand women's problems – where the pain is, why the pain, what the position of the baby is.'

A number of *dais* also related stories about doctors who were called in emergency cases but were unable to save the situation. Often the story took the form of the doctor coming to the birth and asking the woman's guardian, 'Do you want the tree or the fruit?' Usually the guardians agree to save 'the tree', meaning the mother. The doctor then proceeds to save the mother by 'bringing the baby out bit by bit'.

Another *dai* told me of a case where a local doctor was called and tried to deliver the baby by force, with the result that the mother died. Apparently the umbilical cord was torn.

It is clear that the *dais* have reservations about both the local untrained doctors as well as the city hospitals. Teri commented that these days many women are taken to the city (Dhaka) for delivery. She added:

I do not know why, but these days women appear to suffer more during delivery. In the olden days women did not suffer this much. Yet, when they go to the hospital in the city they still suffer – maybe the mother dies, or the baby dies, or some such trouble. For this reason many women are afraid to go to the hospital.

Teri also commented that birthing women are not given immediate attention when they are taken to the city hospitals. She gave the example of a birthing mother who was referred to the Medical Hospital because of a breech delivery. Her baby was 'too big' and she was small in build. Apparently she had to wait for three days before a Caesarean was performed on her. By then, it was too late, and the baby was dead.

All these examples of *dais*' impressions of local untrained doctors and the city hospitals reveal that *dais* see their role as indispensable for rural birthing women. What is more, they are convinced that, all in all, they provide a better service than the local or national medical system. This does not, of course, mean that they are not at the same time aware of the limitations of their expertise. Almost all *dais* said that they refer the really difficult cases to doctors or hospitals. They also said that they like to maintain their reputation and hence refrain from taking on unnecessary risks.

The dai *as superior to other* dais

While in the above accounts we see the *dais* being concerned about the validity of their profession *vis-à-vis* other medical professionals, and the community of *dais* is presented as a united front, in this section we see that the *dais* are also at the same time anxious to preserve their individual professional reputation *vis-à-vis* other *dais*. Thus, when I asked Teri what she does in difficult deliveries, she said:

> It has never happened that I could not deliver the baby – yes, once I had to call the sister [the midwife-nun from the Catholic dispensary] who gave a saline to the birthing mother . . . In *my hands* nothing happens to babies, there is no trouble . . . People do not call the *dai* in whose hands babies have died or the birthing mother had haemorrhage. With God's blessing no baby died in *my hands*, and no woman experienced haemorrhage in *my hands*. This is why people call me all the time. People do not call other *dais* because they do not know about haemorrhage, when it happens, how or why it happens they do not understand.

Then she continued to explain why a woman may haemorrhage. Note the emphasis placed on 'my hands' signifying the importance of her expertise, and implying that it is not necessarily characteristic of other *dais*.[3]

Two further stories from Teri and her mother reinforce this emphasis on individual professionalism. In the first, Teri was called to attend a delivery case which was already being attended to by a nurse. By the time Teri arrived on the scene the nurse had apparently administered a douche to the birthing mother and made her lie down. Teri told the nurse (with whom she enjoyed a joking relationship), '*Kiyer baler nurse tumi?* [What sort of a nurse are you?] It is more than time for the delivery. You had better get out of here.' Then Teri locked herself inside the room with the birthing mother.

> I helped her get up and holding her by her waist shook her up. At that moment the birthing mother said, 'I can feel the baby coming forward'. Then I delivered the baby.

Teri reported to me with evident pride that after the delivery the nurse said, 'Oh, Teri is the one with the degree, I am really embarrassed.' The incident helped to build up Teri's own reputation. She reported the father of the new-born baby as saying, 'If we hadn't brought Teri today, but had sent the baby's mother to a hospital, we would be in for a Tk. 4000 bill [about US$80 at 2001 rates]'.

Teri was obviously enjoying telling me this story and went on to narrate another incident: Malati was taken to the hospital by her husband to deliver. Malati watched how the women's legs were tied up to poles. She got frightened and ran away from the hospital, leaving her husband behind. Teri said, 'This baby was then delivered in *my hands.*' According to Teri, the dispensary-trained midwives are amazed at her courage. One dispensary nun told her, '*Hai hai*, how do you handle such big cases? Even the doctors get scared, so how do you manage?' Teri added that the Medical Hospital staff often do not know how to handle the kind of cases she deals with.

Teri's elderly mother chimed in: 'You need courage. The one delivering needs the courage as well as the birthing woman.' She then told me of a case in which the husband of a birthing woman came to call her: 'He touched my feet and said, "You are my godsister, save me."' Another birthing woman she attended was apparently in labour for fourteen days, but Teri's mother did not have any trouble delivering the baby.

These stories clearly reveal the individual *dai*'s concern about their reputations. The popular *dais* are the ones who enjoy a good reputation for their skill when compared with other *dais*. The competitive attitude of the *dai* is understandable given that most *dais* engage in this task for some material gain.

The dai *as engaged in public service or charitable work*

In Rupganj the *dais* often said things like, 'I cannot say "no" when people call, so I go', or 'What can I do? I know the job, they call me'. None of the *dais* whom I interviewed explicitly described their role in helping the birthing

Figure 6.3 Another *dhatri* from Noakhali, Bangladesh (photo by Santi Rozario)

woman as being primarily a source of income. It is true that almost all the *dais* were from poor families, but they did not focus on the material gain from their involvement in childbirth. Instead they related their involvement in childbirth in terms such as 'So-and-so came to call me in the middle of the night' or 'He was desperate, his wife had been in labour for three days'.

This way of describing their work makes the question of payment seem irrelevant. It is often an emergency, people are desperate, there are no alternatives, especially for poor families. Thus, one gains the impression that the *dai*'s prime motive is to save the situation, to save the mother from her terrible pain by delivering the baby. A Bengali phrase commonly used by *dais* to refer to the delivery is *khalash kora*, literally meaning 'to relieve' or 'release' the mother from her burden. *Dais* will often relate instances in which a member of the family of the birthing woman came and 'fell upon their feet'. After that, what choice could they have but to accompany the suppliant to the scene of delivery? This seems to give the *dai* a sense of power, a self-worth, which she is denied otherwise as a poor woman and a member of the despised lower class.

Pishima, whom I mentioned earlier, was from a very poor background and said that her first delivery was an illegitimate child. Because the whole community had turned against the mother of the illegitimate child, no *dai* dared to come near the woman. She, however, came forward and delivered the baby, although it died after six days.

Thus, while the pollution associated with childbirth keeps wealthy women away from this occupation, a poor woman, who has no worries about having to protect her and her family's 'pure' status, is able to gain, if not explicitly recognised high status, at least a certain degree of respect for her role by seeing it as a kind of social or charitable work for the good of the community.

The dais' work as receiving spiritual or religious sanction

The *dais*' view of themselves as carrying out a kind of charitable work for the community is frequently extended through claiming some kind of spiritual or religious sanction for that role. Thus, *dais* often pointed out the religious merit gained from helping out women in need. After all, the material gain is not substantial, and no *dai* relies on this occupation as the only source of her livelihood. In Rupganj, the *dais* often complained that they were paid only very nominal fees. Often families would promise to present them with a sari, but it would never come. Elsewhere in Bangladesh, Shamima Islam (1989: 239) reports how some *dais* refrained from taking any remuneration as they believed that 'the road to heaven is a straight way to a person who helps delivering 101 babies without taking any remuneration'. However, in Shamima Islam's accounts these *dais* too were often presented with saris upon successful completion of deliveries. Thus, if the *dai* does not take any remuneration, it is perhaps not her choice, but because *there is no remuneration* for this task except sometimes in the form of a sari or other fabric.

Nevertheless, the point is that the poorly paid *dais* define their predicament in terms of being interested not so much in the monetary gain as in the spiritual prosperity. The *dais* and villagers I spoke to in Noakhali used the Islamic term *sawab*, 'spiritual reward'.[4] Blanchet also notes that 'those who do not receive payment often stress the religious merit of their work. They believe Allah will give special blessings to the *dai*' (1984: 143). Blanchet also came across the statements from a *dai* that 'to deliver 101 women equals a pilgrimage to Mecca'. Another said to her that 'after attending 39 deliveries, she is sure of a place in Heaven' (1984: 143).

Both in Rupganj, and in Jamalpur where Blanchet did her fieldwork, the *dais* also practice some *kabiraji*, that is, herbal medicine. I have already discussed some of the methods, such as pulling out roots of plants, which the *dais* use to deal with difficult births. They also employ preventive measures, such as scattering mustard seeds around the delivery hut or drawing a line around the outside of the hut with a bent knife, to deter the evil spirits (*bhut*) from entering and harming the birthing mother and the newborn baby. However, once a particular illness like eclampsia or tetanus is identified as caused by *bhut*, the patient is referred to the established male *kabiraj* who are believed to be able to tackle the *bhut* more directly. Blanchet's analysis of this state of affairs is that the *dais* are prevented from dealing with spiritual agencies because they come in contact with pollution by their physical contact with the birthing woman during childbirth. She points out that *kabiraj* and *fakir*, who are believed to have the power to expel *bhut*, do not touch their patients (1984: 128–9).

Yet on closer examination it would seem that the reasons why the *dais* do not deal with *bhut* are more complicated than Blanchet's pollution argument. From both Blanchet's and my findings, while the *dai* may not tackle the *bhut* directly, they nevertheless engage in healing practices which are certainly linked to spiritual agencies of some kind. For example, all *dais* appear to have some secret knowledge of herbal cure, which they claim to have found in their dreams. In any case the potency of the various plants and their roots which are used in difficult deliveries must be explained by some spiritual connection.

Pishima's case is especially revealing in this instance. Pishima not only practises as a *dai,* she also practised as an abortionist until very recently. Pishima said that she learnt how to perform abortions in a dream. She said

> My own monthly period had stopped for a while when I had a dream about how I could regularise my period. I administered this treatment upon myself and within half an hour it worked. Since then I started to carry out abortions.

Pishima says that she gave up carrying out abortions after she became involved with the Charismatic Movement among Christians in Bangladesh, who warned her that it was a sin to kill.

Pishima is also a well-known *kabiraj*. She claims to be confident she can cure any of the illnesses or problems for which villagers come to see her. When I asked how she acquired her abilities, she said that she received her power almost twenty-five years ago from a *pari* (a female benevolent spirit), whom she can call upon whenever there is a danger. Pishima deals with *sutika* (postnatal diarrhoea), stillbirth and abortion problems, but many of her clients come to see her for other reasons as well. For example, a cook/bearer working in an expatriate's household might have been facing problems with the employer, or someone might have been unsuccessful in finding a job, or someone else might want to know whether her husband has arrived safely in Kuwait or Bahrain. Pishima said she even has overseas clients. Their relatives in the village take the medicine from her and send it by post or through personal couriers.

However, it is interesting to note that she emphasises that for all of these problems she uses roots and plants to offer help and never uses *jharfuk* (exorcism of evil spirits). It seems that she is anxious to dissociate herself from the *bhut* and align herself with her *pari*, a benevolent spirit. She said she is possessed by this *pari* every now and then, and when she is possessed she prays, sings religious songs and goes to the Church. In other words, her religious activities take priority.

In these examples we have seen a variety of ways in which *dais* claim that their work has some kind of spiritual or religious sanction, again countering their low status and polluting occupation.

Discussion and conclusion

The *dai* (midwife) occupies a precarious position in rural Bangladesh. She is vital to the system because birth cannot take place without a *dai*. However, she is at the point of maximum conflict and contradiction. For example, fertility is of utmost importance, and a Bengali woman is anomalous until she is married and bears children. Yet at the same time childbirth is associated with the worst pollution. As one main function of *dais* is to remove the birth pollution, it is not surprising that she is accorded low status in Bengali society. This is true both for Hindus and Muslims (Blanchet 1984).

The ways in which *dais* deal with their low status and lack of respectability have analogues elsewhere in South Asian societies. For one significant analogy, I turn to the work of Margaret Egnor (Margaret Trawick). In an article on the concept of *sakti* among Tamil women (Egnor 1980), Egnor describes *sakti* as a kind of power separate from the formal status of the caste hierarchy and in some ways countervailing to it. *Sakti* is explicitly associated with women, who are by definition structurally subordinate in Tamil (as in Bangladeshi) society. *Sakti* in Tamil society is also associated with suffering, servitude and self-sacrifice.

While these values are perhaps less explicit in the Muslim context of Bangladeshi society than in the Hindu society of Tamil Nadu, I would see them as very much present in Bangladesh as well. Several of Egnor's case-studies have points of similarity to my own material. Thus, the stories of Valliammae, who worked for many years as an Ayurvedic doctor, and of Sarasvati, a priestess and medium of the smallpox goddess Mariyamman, both stress themes of suffering, of service and of spiritual power (Egnor 1980: 7–9, 11–13). Egnor says of these two women, along with a third, Lakshmi, that all three have 'a kind of spiritual power that clearly falls into the category of *sakti*'. All three have 'suffered more severely than most the painful consequences of their subordinate status as females' and yet none sees a contradiction between their subordinate status and their spiritual power.

> On the contrary, for each woman the possession of extraordinary *sakti* came as a consequence of her subordinate status, or more accurately, as a consequence of the suffering that that subordination entailed.
>
> (Egnor 1980: 14)

Sakti represents a kind of recognition that purity is not the only source of power or status in Brahmanical society, and it may be linked to the value of 'auspiciousness' which some writers have identified as an alternative dimension of value in Indian society, to be contrasted with the strictly Brahmanical axis of purity and pollution (Carman and Marglin 1985; Das 1987; see also Samuel 1997). It is striking that the carriers of 'auspiciousness' in modern South Asian society are often people, such as the *devadasi* (girls married to a temple deity) or the *hijra* (eunuchs), whose identity is in other respects compromised or marginal (see Marglin 1985, Srinivasan 1988, Assayag 1990 for *devadasi*; Nanda 1990, Jaffrey 1997 for *hijra*).[5]

Ravindra Khare's writing on the importance of the ideology of asceticism and of the values of world-renunciation among untouchables (specifically Lucknow Chamars, see Khare 1984) also has points of contact with my material. In his material, as in the discourse of the *dais*, poverty and low status is to some degree given positive value by linking it with ideas of spiritual renunciation of conventional society. Similar themes are explored on a larger scale in Ashis Nandy's discussion of the South Asian reaction to the colonial predicament (Nandy 1983). Nandy emphasises how deeply this has marked the self-understanding of modern South Asians. We could compare, for example, Mahatma Gandhi's self-presentation as a poor ascetic, and the enormous resonance which this had among the Indian population, with the *dais'* attempts to construct their role as one of spiritually sanctioned public service.

These studies suggest that, particularly in seeing their role as one of public service and as having religious sanction, the *dais* are developing themes which have considerable presence and depth within South Asian societies. The role of the ascetic or renunciate has a long history in South Asia of being used as a way of giving a positive value to the subjectivities of those whom society as a whole devalues or marginalises. While these ideas of public service and religious sanction may not be taken as seriously by the villagers for whom they work as by the *dais* themselves, they at least provide ways in which *dais* can understand their difficult, demanding and necessary work as something of real value, rather than as merely a despised occupation which relegates them to the status of social outcastes. Perhaps I can end with the words of another *dai*, Viramma, a Tamil woman from an 'untouchable' caste (Viramma, Racine and Racine 1997: 73):

> I know that the way to the resting place of Vishnu is open for us midwives and marked out in full. If I die today or if I die an old woman, Yama or his guards won't be there to stop me and tell me my sentence. Isvaran won't sentence us midwives to hell. We see too much suffering with our own eyes! The blood that we see flowing! The blood that we collect in our hands! The pain! That's why there won't be any obstacles for us. The sixteen gates will be flung wide open and we'll go straight through and shut ourselves away in the residence of Yama. He won't send us to be reborn! No, not this damnation of rebirth.

Notes

1 An earlier version of this chapter was presented at the Women in Asia conference, University of Melbourne, 1993. About half of the 1993 version was published under a different title, in a garbled form and without the author's participation, in

the volume *Representations of Gender, Democracy and Identity Politics in Relation to South Asia* (Delhi: Sri Satguru Publications, 1996). The present version supersedes this earlier publication.

2 I do not enter here into the controversy on how fully Dumontian analysis applies to Hindu caste society in India (e.g. Appadurai 1986; Madan 1971; Marglin 1977; Quigley 1993; Reichle 1985; Searle-Chatterjee and Sharma 1994).

3 Cf. Egnor (1980: 9) on the idea of the healing power in the hands of some doctors (the Tamil term is *kai raci*).

4 See Rozario 1995b. The term *sawab* (Arabic *thawab*, reward, recompense) refers to the Qur'ān, Sura 3, v. 195: 'I shall forgive them their sins and admit them to gardens watered by running streams as a reward' (David Waines, personal communication).

5 One of the main occasions on which *hijra* visit families to demand money in South Asia is that of the birth of a male son, where their ambivalent presence, both welcome and unwelcome, has a structural similarity to that of the *dai* herself.

References

Appadurai, A. 1986. Review article: Is homo hierarchicus? *American Ethnologist* 13: 745–61.

Assayag, J. 1990. Modern devadasis: devotees of goddess Yellamma in Karnataka. In *Rites and Beliefs in Modern India*, edited by G.E. Ferro-Luzzi. Delhi: Manohar.

Bhatia, S., J. Chakraborty, A.S.G. Faruque. 1980. *Indigenous Birth Practices in Rural Bangladesh and Their Implications for a Maternal and Child Health Programme.* Dhaka: International Centre for Diarrhoeal Disease Research, Bangladesh.

Blanchet, T. 1984. *Women, Pollution and Marginality: Meanings and Rituals of Birth in Rural Bangladesh.* Dhaka: University Press.

Carman, J.B. and F.A. Marglin. 1985. *Purity and Auspiciousness in Indian Society.* Leiden: E.J. Brill.

Das, V. 1987. *Structure and Cognition: Aspects of Hindu Caste and Ritual.* 2nd edn. Delhi: Oxford University Press.

Dumont, L. 1972. *Homo Hierarchicus: The Caste System and its Implications.* London: Paladin.

Egnor, M. (M. Trawick.) 1980. On the meaning of Sakti to women in Tamil Nadu. In *The Powers of Tamil Women*, edited by S.S. Wadley. Syracuse, NY: Maxwell School of Citizenship and Public Affairs.

Fauveau, V. and J. Chakraborty. 1988. *Maternity Care in Matlab: Present Status and Possible Interventions.* (Matlab MCH-FP Project.) Dhaka: International Centre for Diarrhoeal Disease Research, Bangladesh.

Gardner, K. 1991. *Songs at the River's Edge: Stories from a Bangladeshi Village.* Calcutta/Bombay/Delhi: Rupa & Co.

Hussain, N. 1992. Women in a Bangladesh village: sources of female autonomy. Ph.D. dissertation, Department of Anthropology, Macquarie University.

Islam, S. 1989. The socio-cultural context of childbirth in rural Bangladesh. In *Gender and the Household Domain: Social and Cultural Dimensions*, edited by M. Krishnaraj and K. Chanana. New Delhi/London: Sage.

Jaffrey, Z. 1997. *The Invisibles: A Tale of the Eunuchs of India.* London: Weidenfeld and Nicolson.

Jeffery, P., R. Jeffery and A. Lyon. 1989. *Labour Pains and Labour Power: Women and Childbearing in India.* London and New Jersey: Zed Books Ltd.

Khare, R.S. 1984. *The Untouchable as Himself: Ideology, Identity and Pragmatism among the Lucknow Chamars.* Cambridge and New York: Cambridge University Press.

Madan, T.N. (ed.) 1971. A review symposium on Louis Dumont's *Homo Hierarchicus*: on the nature of caste in India. *Contributions to Indian Sociology* (NS) 5: 1–81.

Marglin, F.A. 1977. Power, purity and pollution: aspects of the caste system reconsidered. *Contributions to Indian Sociology* (NS) 11 (2): 245–70.

—— 1985. *Wives of the God-king: The Rituals of the Devadasis of Puri.* Delhi: Oxford University Press.

McConville, F. 1989. The birth attendant in Bangladesh. In *The Midwife Challenge*, edited by S. Kitzinger. London: Pandora.

Nanda, S. 1990. *Neither Man nor Woman: The Hijras of India.* Belmont, CA: Wadsworth.

Nandy, A. 1983. *The Intimate Enemy: Loss and Recovery of Self under Colonialism.* Delhi: Oxford University Press.

Quigley, D. 1993. *The Interpretation of Caste.* Oxford: Clarendon Press; New York: Oxford University Press.

Reichle, V. 1985. Holism versus individualism: Dumont's concepts of hierarchy and egalitarianism as structural principles. *Contributions to Indian Sociology* (NS) 19 (2): 331–40.

Rozario, S. 1992. *Purity and Communal Boundaries: Women and Social Change in a Bangladeshi Village.* Sydney: Allen and Unwin.

—— 1995a. TBAs (Traditional Birth Attendants) and birth in Bangladeshi villages: cultural and sociological factors. *International Journal of Gynaecology and Obstetrics* 50 (supplement no. 2): 145–52.

—— 1995b. Dai and midwives: The renegotiation of the status of birth attendants in contemporary Bangladesh. In *The Female Client and the Health-care Provider*, edited by J. Hatcher and C. Vlassoff. Ottawa: International Development Research Centre (IDRC) Books. Also available as e-text at: http://www.idrc.ca/ books/focus/773/rozario.html

—— 1998. The dai and the doctor: discourses on women's reproductive health in rural Bangladesh. In *Modernities and Maternities: Colonial and Postcolonial Experiences in Asia and the Pacific*, edited by K. Ram and M. Jolly. Cambridge: Cambridge University Press.

Samuel, G. 1997. Women, goddesses and auspiciousness in South Asia. *Journal of Interdisciplinary Gender Studies* 2 (2): 1–23.

Searle-Chatterjee, M. and U. Sharma. (eds) 1994. *Contextualising Caste: Post-Dumontian Approaches.* Oxford and Cambridge, MA: Blackwell Publishers/The Sociological Review.

Srinivasan, A. 1988. Reform or conformity? Temple 'prostitution' and the community in the Madras Presidency. In *Structures of Patriarchy: Sate, Community and Household in Modernising Asia*, edited by B. Agarwal. New Delhi: Kali for Women.

Viramma, J. Racine and J.-L. Racine. 1997. *Viramma: Life of an Untouchable.* Translated by W. Hobson. London and New York: Verso; Paris: UNESCO.

Chapter 7

Hawa, gola and mother-in-law's big toe

On understanding *dais'* imagery of the female body

Janet Chawla

All over the world women rise to their daily work, care for their families and participate in community life. Too often, women must face these challenges while struggling against illness – lacking even basic information about their health.

(Advertisement for *Where Women Have No Doctor*, a health guide for women)

. . . I believe that by subjugated knowledges one should understand something else [. . .], namely, a whole set of knowledges that have been disqualified as inadequate to their task or insufficiently elaborated: naïve knowledges, located low down on the hierarchy, beneath the required level of cognition or scientificity.

(Foucault 1980: 82)

Locating *dais*: a context for understanding *dais'* imagery of the female body

I choose to begin this chapter with the above quotes because they foreground the issue of what we might label the subaltern[1] or subjugated knowledges of traditional Indian midwives, *dais* – and the exclusion of that knowledge, and of those who hold that knowledge, from such forums as the Indian Institute of Advanced Study seminar for which this chapter was first written.[2] The first quotation represents the dominant discourse on women's health in India today and includes the presupposition that the majority of women (read poor, non-literate, non-English speaking) in such 'underdeveloped' countries as India lack even basic health knowledge. Also included in this assertion is another presupposition – that allopathic medicine is the source of all health information. The 'doctor' referred to is not a nurse-midwife or an ANM (auxiliary nurse midwife), a homeopathic practitioner, a *vaidya* or *unnani* doctor, an *oja* or ritual specialist, a masseuse, a herbalist or a *dai*, nor even an elderly family member who has imbibed, over the years, her family and community healing modalities. No, the assumption is that 'basic information about health' is available through doctors – that is, Western biomedically trained doctors.

These commonly held assumptions disturb me and belie much of what I have learned in my twenty years of living, learning and working in India. MATRIKA (Motherhood and Traditional Resources, Information, Knowledge, and Action) is a three-year research project I have initiated in order to generate less biomedically biased data. We have interacted with mid-wives and non-government organisations in three parts of North India: Bokaro District, Bihar; Lunkaransar in Bikaner District, Rajasthan; and slum areas of Delhi. In our workshops we have attempted to document, understand and reclaim indigenous women's ethno-medical knowledge, practice and religio-cultural body imagery. This chapter emerges from the MATRIKA effort.

My contentions are as follows:

- Health and body knowledge systems about the female body which are internally coherent, empirical and culturally embedded, exist within indigenously oriented (as opposed to cosmopolitan and globalised) communities. Indian women generally, and midwives in particular, have been the inheritors of rich and varied health information and body knowledges.
- *Dais* can be seen as indigenous specialists in women's well-being and cultural repositories of such body knowledge/practice. These knowledges are decentralised and collectively held; non-textual and orally transmitted; usually acquired by apprenticeship with an older relative and often caste based.
- Dominant, urban, English-educated elites, as well as global establishments have had considerable difficulties accessing, understanding and appreciating indigenous body knowledge and its holders, *dais*, because of macro-level historical forces and also because of epistemological (i.e. grounds of knowing) problems.
- The historical forces (poverty, colonialism, Brahmanism and casteism, modernisation and development, social and intellectual neglect) have also eroded the quality of care offered by the midwives as well as their confidence in their own knowledge and customs. *Dais*, in their project of caring for parturient women, also cope with problems of ecological devastation (making access to food, water and healing herbs more difficult) and gender biases (spousal abuse, familial pressures for male offspring, female infanticide, etc.).
- Inadequate food, hunger and starvation of women and their families must be named as the crucial problem it is. It is absurd to tout Safe Motherhood and critique the ignorance of *dais* when the women they serve eat rice and salt for the nine months of pregnancy. (I was told about one woman who died immediately post-partum in Bihar. When investigating the circumstances of this death I learned this had been her usual diet.)

- The reclamation, decoding and 'rehabilitation' (because in our research we have seen much which needs rehabilitating) of indigenous knowledge and practice is not only important for poor and marginalised women. It is also relevant, however, to women's health initiatives at all levels in India, as well as other 'developed' and 'developing' nations.
- Accessing and interpreting women's body knowledges involves acceptance of blurred boundaries between categories sometimes considered mutually exclusive: mind/body; medicine/religion; sexuality/spirituality; woman-as-mother/woman-as-sexual being; purity/pollution; *swarg* (heaven)/*narak* (hell, demonic, underworld). Thus, our reclamation involves an epistemologically challenging task.
- An empathetic understanding of body imagery requires a step outside of biomedical anatomy and physiology and an entrée into a radically dif ferent 'poetics' of bodies.

In most cultures birth has been handled primarily by women. The biomedical model of childbirth began to rely on technology (forceps and chloroform for Queen Victoria) rather than touch (massage and female support). Likewise, this European ethno-medical approach to pregnancy and birth pathologised the female body, viewing it as a potential site of disease. European knowledge of anatomy was attained through the dissection of cadavers, hardly the best way to learn about life and life-bearing bodies. Simultaneously women were eased out of their roles as caregivers and definitive knowers of their own bodies. Cosmopolitan obstetrics and technology can provide powerful, life-saving interventions, but it is currently functioning to contaminate what is essentially a normal, natural life event (constructed differently in different cultures), not a medical one.

In many parts of India midwifery was a part of the feudal *jajmani* system where *dais*, along with other artisans and service providers, were affiliated to a patron family.[3] In this context *dais* were compensated by gifts (grain, saris, etc.), not by money. Traditionally, *dai* work is women's work – an extension of household work and not given monetary value. Many traditional *dais* find negotiating commercial exchange networks difficult, if not impossible. Today this lack of skill and tradition is further complicated by the extreme poverty of those women they serve. Many of the older and more 'traditional' *dais* say that their work is done with the feeling of service. One *dai* asked, 'How can I refuse to help a woman in labour just because she has no money and is poor – so has nothing to pay?' Three elderly and very experienced Rajasthani *dais* with whom we interacted had worked for years breaking stones for road building because the earnings of their traditional occupation could not sustain them.

The undervaluation of the contribution of the *dais* was a part of British colonial devaluation of indigenous health practitioners generally. Midwives were negatively impacted by two ideological thrusts of imperial rule: the

Figure 7.1 Aasibai, the *dai* (seated on the bed) conversing with the mother after the birth. In the foreground the mother-in-law is holding the infant. From Bikaner District, Rajasthan (photo by Sameera Jain)

superiority of Western notions of health and the backwardness of women's status. Vast armies of 'lady health visitors' were loosed on the countryside to clean up and educate ignorant, 'backward' women and the *dais* who served them. Surely the bleak picture of traditional midwives we have today has come, in part, from that very successful colonial enterprise which rescued Indian women from their 'barbaric and superstitious' body knowledge and traditions.[4] At the same time obstetric biomedicine, a model of childbirth now being contested and negotiated by many in the West, was promoted as modern, hygienic and safe.

Who is a *dai*?

Approximately one million women work as traditional midwives in India and attend 60 per cent of births (in poor and rural areas, as many as 90 per cent). *Dais* share the cultural and ethno-medical orientations of the women they serve. *Dais* are also often the only affordable and accessible practitioners available to poor urban and rural women.

However, we encounter many problems when attempting to speak about traditional midwifery. The first one is who is a *dai*? And what is *dai* work?

About five years ago the head of UNICEF in Delhi told me that they had cut back on funds for *dai* training because their anthropological studies showed that nobody could identify, precisely, who was (and who was not) a *dai*. He went on to say that UNICEF was thus funding efforts to educate pregnant women as to the danger signs of childbirth – because she was the only person they were absolutely certain would be present at the time of the birth! I felt this was a terrible decision for many reasons.

- Mothers who are haemorrhaging do not have the capacity to influence decisions regarding their care;
- not being able anthropologically to describe indigenous, ethno-medical support systems does not mean that they do not exist;
- modern institutions which bypass indigenous practitioners' support and knowledge serve to undermine and replace them, often with *sui-goli* (injections and pills) medicine dispensed by 'quacks'. Such quacks are compounders, RMPs (Rural Medical Practitioners), traditional *vaidyas* (who sometimes dispense allopathic drugs as well as Ayurvedic remedies).

It should not surprise us that modern institutions and their representatives have been confounded by the phenomenon of traditional midwifery. Especially when we consider Sukumari Bhattacharji, Sanskrit scholar and historian, on the *dai*:

> The *dai* is a substitute priest working between two worlds (like the priest's intermediacy between the sacred and the mundane). She mediates the prenatal, foetal, and the parturition/postnatal. And, like the priest, or more like the shaman, she discharges her function through control of the spirit world. This is because there are demons which seek to delay, prevent or muck up the birth (causing a defective or stillborn babe or the post-partum diseases or death of the mother). Birth means the advent of a departed soul in a new incarnation, a fact which has cosmic significance, hence other hostile souls/spirits/persons seek to prevent it.
>
> The *dai*'s unique position is equivalent of a shamaness's. She pre-empts male intervention in a literal *rite de passage*. She was allowed this privilege possibly because the whole process is 'dirty'. The Asvins, the divine physicians, were deprived of the *soma* drink in the later Vedic-Epic literature because as physicians they had to touch uncleanness connected with disease. Later Indian literature lays down that doctors may not be ritual guests.
>
> The role of the initiating priest, the *acarya*, in the Upanayana (sacred thread) ceremony, is similar to the *dai*. The sacred thread is a replica of the umbilical cord in reverse: the *dai* removes it, the *acarya* winds it on the ritually newborn.
>
> The birth rite is the only wholly female rite where male presence is precluded; yet it is solemn, awesome and throbbing with tension. Birth rites

uniquely empower the female assistant and are the only rites where a new life enters the earthly plane. The dai is symbolic of mother earth. Whereas the earth gives birth unaided, in a human birth she symbolically splits herself in two: the mother and the *dai*. This is because human mothers, unlike the *prima dea*, are not self-procreative and are also exposed to dangers from the spirit world.[5]

Locating the *dai* is a bit like the story of the men touching the elephant and each feeling a different part!

Imagery: *Hawa*, *Gola* and mother-in-law's big toe

During the workshop phase of our MATRIKA research I visited a respected Ayurvedic physician in order to discuss our initial findings. He opened the conversation by stating that *dais'* and Ayurvedic knowledge and practice were similar. I have learned much from *dais* about the female body and birth which is not in the Ayurvedic texts (at least the English translations available to me) and which seems quite different from the practice of the *vaidyas*. So I stated that there were major differences between the textual and the folk streams of indigenous body knowledge and I gave an example. In a workshop in Gomia, Bihar, we were told that if a woman's labour was not progressing she was made to drink a glass of water in which her mother-in-law's big toe had been dipped. Of course this ritual facilitation of labour had pushed both our hygiene and feminist buttons. How dirty! How demeaning! But none the less we noted it down and it is this rite which came to my mind as an example of something *dais* might do, but surely would have no place in dignified Ayurvedic practice.

It is always a good thing for a researcher to have her hypotheses challenged. And that's exactly what happened. The respected *vaidya*, when he heard the above folk facilitation, immediately noted that in Ayurveda the *nadi* for *pran vayu* (which is understood to be a carrier of knowledge and experience) exits the body via the big toes. Thus, the custom of touching elders' feet allows for the transmission of their knowledge to those of lesser knowledge-experience. It is logical to assume, thus, that the mapping of the body implicit in the mother-in-law's big toe ritual is similar to the mapping in Ayurvedic understanding. The social hierarchy of mother-in-law/daughter-in-law is perhaps encoded in this rite, transmitting the respected female elder's permission for the birth to proceed – granting the status of maternity to the *bahu* (daughter-in-law), but at the same time asserting her authority and primacy. Certainly the folk understanding of the inner terrain of the body is closer to that of Ayurveda than it is to the anatomy and physiology of allopathic medicine.

During another interview with a *dai* in Bihar she said, 'If labour is getting delayed then I make her wash the toe of the person with whom she had fought during her pregnancy. She drinks this water.' It appears that conflict resolution, in order to facilitate the labour, is also affected through the toe-water ritual! I have also learned from a scholar of Tantra that *sadhus* are loath to have their feet touched, perhaps fearing this transmission and the diminishing of their powers.[6]

Hawa-gola *as energy, not anatomy or physiology*

In our very first workshops we began hearing some unfamiliar terms such as *hawa*, which is loosely translated as wind, but more specifically in Ayurveda means movement or motion. Colloquially *hawa* can refer to the activities of spirit forces, usually with negative associations, as in *burra hawa*, a bad wind.

We initially understood another term *gola*, meaning ball or something round, as a clot, but now think of it as matter associated with force or energy. It was, and still is, difficult to ferret out what the meanings of *hawa-gola* are, but one thing was perfectly clear. The *dais* emphasised that *hawa-gola* are threats to the woman's well-being post-partum as they are some kind of matter, force or energy which must come *out* of the body (through the vagina or birth canal), and which must in no way go *up* into the upper part of the body.

I was not totally unfamiliar with the concept of things going up in the body. As a natural childbirth instructor I had interacted with a few traditionally oriented mothers and mothers-in-law of pregnant women who used to talk of the uterus moving up into the chest during labour. It occurred to me that these women were not speaking of the literal organ, the womb, shifting position upward, but of a bodily energy, which was supposed to be in the belly, being in the chest. This was not a strange idea because childbirth educators, and those experienced in helping women give birth, are familiar with mothers' bearing-down efforts being misplaced, and the need to help women direct their efforts toward the abdominal area rather than the throat or chest. I have also heard many doctors scoff at 'ignorant' women's references to 'the uterus moving up' thinking they were simply unfamiliar with their bodies. They were not aware that women were using an anatomical term to refer to a process-oriented phenomenon. This seems to be a key in understanding some of *dais'* language which refers to a life *energy* rather than anatomy.

Notions of *direction* are important in body mapping in Indian spiritual traditions as the male is counselled to conserve his semen so the reservoir of energy, called *kundalini*, can be directed upwards, towards the crown *chakra* and enlightenment, rather than downwards in the service of sexual pleasure and procreation. That this mapping is hardly confined to *yogis* and *sadhus* is displayed by the popularity of traditional sex clinics, which treat impotence. Young males, it seems, are often fraught with conflicts and insecurities, I would suggest, relating to this battleground of mappings involving the meanings and valuations of sexual bodily fluids and 'directionality'.

In our first Delhi workshop Ram Pyari, a *dai* of around 70 from Rajasthan who had lived and practised in a resettlement colony of Delhi for many years, said:

> In the hospital no one is allowed to accompany the pregnant woman. If the labour is very long they make a cut. This can get infected. Hospitals cause a lot of infections. The woman can get swellings and golas. If there are golas we should give hot fomentation to clear the tubes.

Ram Pyari names a crucial need of the labouring woman by its absence in the hospital context – that of someone to *accompany* the woman during the process of the labour. All *dais* emphasise that empathetic, knowledgeable women are needed to support the *jachcha* (literally she who births) physically and psychologically, and also to negotiate the dangers which threaten the process. This negotiation often involves diagnostics and ritual interventions which we moderns label 'superstitious'.

Bhagwania, an experienced and confident *dai* from Gomia, Bihar, in our second Bihar workshop claimed:

> After the placenta is out we try to get out the dirty blood by pressing her stomach with our hands and even using the head. Two clots of blood come out – *gangi* and *jamuni*. The woman gets a lot of relief from this.

As long as we discussed and tried to understand these terms in our own, basically biomedical, framework, our MATRIKA team made little progress. Instead, we just kept questioning and searching for possible linkages with our world – as well as simply listening and trying to enter theirs. At this second Bihar workshop we also gathered information about a maternal death, which occurred within a few hours after birth. This investigation, funded by UNFPA, led to a report, *Saroj's Death: Multiple Perspectives on One Maternal Death*, in which we probed possible meanings of post-partum embolism and thrombosis – obstetrical diagnostics. We followed an interpretative path that *gola* might be equivalent to a blood clot; and *hawa*, a pulmonary embolism – both of which can be fatal.

Bhagwania used the nomenclature *gangi-jamuni* for these 'clots' of blood. This language shows a correlation between energy or blood pathways in the body and the two great rivers of the Gangetic plain, Ganga and Yamuna. This way of speaking, and diagnosing, reveals the *dais'* ethno-medical tendency to hold knowledge in terms of correspondences between natural processes. Here, the cleansing and circulatory functions of the female body and the earth body are rendered as analogous.

Both *dais'* ethno-medicine and obstetrics advocate the mother's physical movement immediately post-partum. Obstetrical rationale is that because of the increased venous activity, extra blood in the uterine, vaginal and thigh area, the circulatory system needs to be stimulated in order to prevent thrombosis and embolism formation. The *dais* explain that 'stagnant', 'bad' or *kala* blood needs to move and be expelled so that *golas* will not move upwards in the body and cause problems for the new mother. (It is fascinating to hypothesise, but impossible to prove, that the original impulse behind so-called 'pollution taboos' is this conceptualisation that the blood of menstruation and childbirth are cleansing functions of the female body. According to this logic this blood is 'bad' because it is no longer needed by the body and, if retained, is dangerous to the woman.)

We learned more about *gola* in our first workshop in Rajasthan, Bikaner District. Here the *dais* were particularly homogeneous in their practice and culture. The following is a discussion from that workshop in which they are trying to help us understand what *gola* is and how they handle it:

Manori: After the birth of the baby the woman has pains in the *gola*. Because when the baby is in the womb then *gola* is the protector of the baby. *Gola* is located beside the baby. After birth *gola* is left alone so it looks for the baby in the womb. And this gives pain to the new mother. Therefore we immediately give warm *halwa* to the mother to eat and this foments the *gola*. A warm pot is placed on the abdomen for fomentation. This eases her pain.

Guddi: This is a *gola* of *jama hua khoon* [stagnant or clotted blood]. It bleeds out in three days and the abdomen is cured.

Manori: *Gola* can be felt on touching the abdomen. After delivery the woman is made to stand and the *dai* puts her head against the woman's abdomen. She takes out all the collected blood (*jama hua khoon*). This is called *kala khoon* [black blood]. Later we make the woman sit and put our heel on her *shareer* [here perineum is meant]. By this her *shareer* does not come out [i.e., uterine prolapse is avoided].

Shifting meanings, nuances of goal are apparent here. *Gola*, on one hand, seems to be the womb – the 'pains in the *gola*' we recognise as contractions. *Gola* seems to be both womb and womb energy – and consequences derived from that gestational power.

In our second Delhi workshop we also had discussions on post-partum and *gola*:

Praveen: *Gola* is not blood. *Gola* is the *rakhwala*, the protector of the baby. When the baby comes out, it [*gola*] searches for the baby, it goes around in the womb. Therefore there is pain. When it does not find the baby then it gets tired and defeated and settles.

Pushpa:	Also, by eating this space gets filled up and slowly the pain goes away. By having food in the stomach pressure is applied and the space gets filled. This way the pain goes away.
Vidya Devi:	Yes, by eating, drinking things like *ghee, ajwain* – whatever is the custom – the distension goes away.
Praveen:	Amongst us, alongside the head of the woman a *gola* [i.e. something round], a coconut, is broken. This makes the pain go away. A small piece of coconut is given to the *jachcha* and the rest is distributed among other people.
Kamala:	Gola is the baby's home. When the house becomes empty, only *ganda khoon* is left. When blood will come out then there will be pain. *Ajwain, saunth, pipar* – this is ground and mixed in boiling water with jaggery. If this is given to drink then the belly clears up.
Dhapo:	Even when it moves a little it is like *pran nikal jata hai* [the life force goes out of you, like death]. The *dai* presses the place from where it moves. Then it stays on the side of the lower portion of the abdomen.

On one hand this *gola*, in obstetric physiological terms, is related to the contracting uterus. As a muscular organ the womb, which has stretched to accommodate the growing baby, begins to contract after the birth – involution as it is called. Especially when women have many children (the womb having been stretched many times) post-partum contractions can be very painful. And yet this *gola* signifies in many more realms than simple anatomical functioning. I think it is important to note that:

- There is an active notion of the space the baby has occupied. The *gola* is 'the baby's home'. It 'searches for the baby' after birth.
- Pain is understood to be caused by this 'search' for the baby.
- 'Heating' – fomentation and hot foods and drinks are therapeutic interventions to deal with *gola*.
- Massage to expel the 'bad blood' is also a post-partum therapy to manipulate the space and control it.

At our last Delhi workshop we also got the following information:

Dhappo:	Bhagwan puts *gola* along with the *bacha*. This *gola* roams around.
Deepti:	Is this *anwal* [placenta]?
Tara:	This is *gola*. This roams around and by this, it is said that mother's *mamta* [maternal love] increases. It is looking for the baby.
Naseem:	After the birth of the baby, in the womb *gabelan* [*gola* or fire] arises. This searches for the baby.
Tara:	It is for six days.

Pushpa: It reduces by eating.
Rani: There are four terms for it – *gabelan, gola, aag* and *mamta*.

Above I have noted that one *dai* used the terminology of *gangi-jamni* to describe the 'clots' which needed to be expelled by the body after the birth. This way of naming phenomena and processes in terms of correspondences utilises microcosm–macrocosm analogues. In Ayurvedic understanding the theory of the *panch mahabhuta* (earth, air, fire, water and 'ether') explains how internal bodily forces and external cosmic forces are linked together. What is inside the body has its correlates externally in the natural world. The health of the body is represented as a balance of the *panch mahabhuta* which actually are viewed as forces rather than substances. Likewise, all physiological processes involve delicate balancing acts between these forces. The *dais'* descriptions of post-partum *hawa-gola* and also *aag* (fire) seem to use similar mapping of bodily forces which need to be kept in balance during labour and birth for the health of the mother.

In Ayurvedic thought the *panch mahabhuta* condense to the three doshas: *vata, pitta* and *kapha* which are, effectively, air, fire and water respectively.

Interestingly one Ayurvedic scholar writes: 'In the mind *vata* retrieves previous data from memory for comparison with new data. *Pitta* processes the new data and draws conclusions, which *vata* then stores as new memories' (Svoboda 1996: 36). Certainly the female bodily shift from pregnant to not-pregnant is one of the most profound normative changes the human body could undergo! It seems that the *dais* are describing this shift in indigenous ethno-medical terminology – and this involves notions of fire, wind and energy.

The now-empty womb is also a potential problem because the space must be filled (by food and drink, warm fomentation, massage). Excessive empty space in the body with insufficient power of movement can result in stasis (*gola*?) with adverse implications for health.

In all the areas in which we have worked – Rajasthan, Delhi, Punjab, and Bihar – as well as in reports from South India, *dais* do not cut the umbilical cord until after the placenta is delivered. They use the placenta, still connected to the baby, as a resuscitation device if the child is not breathing – stimulating it by heating. It is important for us to notice that these ethno-medical practitioners have extensive knowledge of, and use interventions based on, bodily parts considered highly 'polluting' in the Brahmanic texts and the high-caste Hindu mind. One Delhi *dai*, Kamala, stated that if the *naal* (cord) is cut then there is the danger of the placenta climbing up. Furthermore she stated that:

We never throw away the placenta. The way the child is dear to us, so is the *anwal* also precious. For nine months it has protected and sustained the child, so how can we just throw it away?

A feminist hermeneutics demands that we consider carefully this valuation of the flesh-and-blood bonds between maternal and child bodies and not simply turn away in civilised distaste.

Furthermore it seems that in these representations the womb is rendered as a sensate, perceptive organ. This is a radical departure from Western anatomical understanding of the uterus which considers the organ incapable of sensation – the pain of childbirth is considered to be caused by pull and pressure on other surrounding body parts. The *dais'* imagery attributes to the womb a capacity to sense and to know (of course the womb is not dislocated from the person of the mother, as in Western anatomy).

For our purposes, the representation of space and womb as being active attributes to them a kind of agency lacking in biomedical obstetrics, and is congruent with hands-on, non-invasive and woman-centred post-birth care. The womb, or *gola*, is depicted as searching for the baby, thus the use of the word *mamta* – motherly love – attachment, literally.

These mappings of the body are holistic or non-dualistic. Finally the *gola* is the *rakhwala* of the baby – its keeper, responsible for it. I would interpret this *gola* energy to be the life force sustaining and growing the foetus. And it is precisely that same energy which has the potential to turn against the mother and harm her if it stays in the body and moves upward. This *gola* energy must be released by the maternal body and go down and out – with the help of the *dais*. And it is related to the bad blood (*kala khoon, ganda khoon*) which signifies that no-longer-needed channel for the life force energy.

Narak ka samay: priestly defined impurity or dais' ethno-medical terrain?

Dais use terms such as *narak ka samay* (hellish or demonic time or time of the netherworld) and *nau mahenae ka narak kund* (nine months hellish/underworld pond) to speak of the post-partum period. Strictly speaking, from the time of the cutting of the umbilical cord to *chatti* or the post-birth ritual (time differing among different castes and communities) the woman, baby, *dai* and woman's family are unclean or untouchable. We moderns view these 'superstitions' through lenses constructed by Brahmanism, colonialism and orientalism. Our MATRIKA project is attempting to explore this ritual construction of time and mapping of the female body in non-value-laden terms (i.e. devoid of their negative caste and gender associations). We are attending to the *dais'* words within their own context in order to understand them as purely descriptive language for female life-body events. My own emerging working hypothesis is that ritual uncleanness is the language of Brahmanic sacerdotal and textual tradition and that women's work of birth involves different forms of sacrality and ethno-medical rite and practice.

Repeatedly *dais* use the word *narak* to describe the birth time. They also use *narak* in relation to the lower part of the body – including reproductive organs. In Bihar, at least, women were clear that that the mundane, ordinary world is equivalent to the midsection (chest, arms and back) and the heavenly realm to the head. We recognise a similar division found in the Rig Vedic *Purush*, the cosmic man divided up, considered to be prototype for caste delineations.

During our second Bihar workshop we learned:

> On *chhati* day the *narak* time ends. The *dai* checks if the umbilical cord of the baby has fallen. Then she bathes the baby and beats a *thaali* and gives the baby to *chaachi* who does *namaskar* to Bhagwan and gives the baby to *jethani*. The *jachcha* is bathed and she wears new clothes. The *dai* cleans the room where the delivery took place and the woman was kept separately for six days. She washes the dirty clothes of mother and child and then is herself given soap and oil for bathing. Then the woman's *sasural* [husband's home] people go and invite *maike* [wife's natal home] people. They come and are welcomed by sprinkling of water and being embraced.
>
> The woman's mother brings new clothes for her son-in-law and *samdhis* [other in-laws]. The new mother is dressed up, puts on *sindur* [red paste worn in the part of the hair signifying a married woman] and *kaajal* [kohl lining the eyes]. Different types of food are cooked – from today she can eat everything. Next day the *dai* takes leave. The *saas* [mother-in-law of the birthing woman] puts *sindoor* and *kaajal* for her. The *dai* is given a new *sari*, rice and sometimes money. On the third day after the *chhati puja* they have simple *kuan puja* [well worship]. The new mother puts *tika* [sacred mark] on a well or pond.

Ritual, birth time, and women's bodily knowledge and practice are interwoven with concepts of *narak*. From an interview with Saubatia, a Bihari *dai*:

> We do not give any medicines for swellings. We give hot fomentation with arandi oil. The placenta and cord are buried near the *chula* [hearth]. We see that during pregnancy water is retained in a woman's body. Food is only given on the second day after delivery. The two days of fast is called *narak upwaas* [again, hellish or underworld fast]. Food is only given after all the dirty blood comes out. If she has delivered in the morning, then in the evening tea, bread and *gur-haldi* [jaggery-turmeric] sweet is given. Nothing is given at night. She only drinks warm or hot water. The stomach bloats if one drinks cold water.

Although often translated as hellish or demonic place, *narak* can be understood as the site/energy of the unseen inner world – of the earth and of the body (see Khare 1993). *Narak* has the connotation 'filth' but also signifies the fertility or fruitful potential of the earth and the female body. So called 'pollution taboos' are related to *narak*, so radically separating the idea of the sacred from the reproductive potential of the female body. During menstruation and post birth women are 'unclean'. However, the *dai* speaks about *narak* with a very different voice than the pundit. To her the placenta, the ultimate polluting substance in the *shastras* (Hindu scriptures), is spoken of reverently. It is no coincidence that *dais* are mainly from low- and outcaste communities. Both caste and gender are involved in concepts of *narak* (Ayurvedic and naturopathic practitioners often employ low-caste people to apply the hands-on therapies which they prescribe).

The concept of *narak* is a foundational idea which also allows for a host of therapeutic interventions. *Narak* seems to signify the inner world of the body, which is invisible to the eye – particularly the mysterious procreative power of the female body. This concept then provides a mode of understanding which allows practitioners and therapeutics which can negotiate and affect the inner body without violating the integrity of the skin/body/life force. And indeed the *dais'* health modalities are high-touch (massage, pressure, manipulation), use natural resources (mud, baths and fomentation, herbs), application of 'hot and cold' (in food and drink, fomentation, etc.) and isolation and protection (from household work and maternal and sexual obligations).

And repeatedly we heard how integral the notion of uncleanness is to the *dai's* management of a mother's post-partum care. From our last Delhi workshop:

Kamala: According to me, the baby is born. Then *gola* roams around. This *gola* took care of the baby. Warm fomentation is done and *gola* finishes – this is *maila* [dirt], it gets cleaned and the *gandh* [filth] comes out.

Kaushalya: My thing is that whether you say *gola* or you call it *lothara* [lump] or call it anything, it is inside the *bachadani* [womb, literally holder of the baby]. The *gandigi* [filth] is blocked because of this reason. It roams around everywhere and then the pain comes – with this the *gandigi* comes out. This cleans the whole womb.

I would suggest that *gandigi* and *narak* in this context are diagnostic nomenclature in the language of midwives. They do not partake of the pejorative caste- and gender-laden meanings given to these terms by the twice born.

The *dais'* imagery of the female body involves analogies and correspondences. Thus, the placenta is analogous with the *kund* or spring-fed pond. *Narak* emerges as meaning unseen source, of water and of human life. This underworld is demonic or hellish only in that it is the nether, chthonic world of the body of the earth/woman – both fertile and finally outside of patriarchal control.

In concluding I would like to distance myself and our work from two popular misconceptions about women such as *dais*. The first is that they are individual 'wise women' who suddenly seem to appear out of nowhere. Such women are represented as being extremely intuitive and devoid of any 'learning' or cultural context. The *dais'* knowledge and practice is embedded in a shared, collectively held religio-cultural context. *Dais*, although they may rely on ways of knowing we might label intuition, have *learned* their skills through experience and/or apprenticeship. For this reason it is very important to refer to indigenous knowledge traditions.

The second misconception is that somehow lower-class and poor women are simply closer to nature and thus birth easily. Although there may be a modicum of truth in this, humans have a tremendous capacity for learned behaviour, which will override 'nature'. We must not confuse a culture of birth and of the body (which may be more congruent with 'nature') with primitivism and doing things *au naturel*.

These myths demean the sophistication and complexity of the *dais'* knowledge and body imagery – which I hope I have demonstrated above.

Notes

1 Ranajit Guha, in his *Subaltern Studies* series (Guha 1982, 1983 etc), presents a historiography of the region which exposes power relations. 'Subaltern' is his term for women or other marginalised groups whose views go unrecorded in conventional history.

2 The original context of this presentation was the Seminar on Images and Self-images: Indian Women in History, Myth and Fiction, held at the Indian Institute of Advanced Study, Rashtrapati Nivas, Shimla, 5–7 November 1999.

3 Sociologist Amrit Srinivasan organised a panel discussion on 'Caste Out Knowledge, Outcaste Communities' at the Congress on Traditional Sciences and Technologies in Chennai at Anna Malai University, December 1995. Her theme notes are available in the Congress Abstracts. She made the important point that agriculturalists of necessity were brought into the colonial enterprise – people had to be fed. But the artisan communities were marginalised – their products were not needed. Artisan knowledge and skills, like that of the *dais*, were eclipsed by modernity.

4 I am grateful to Dr Janet Price of Liverpool School of Tropical Medicine for providing me with archival material such as 'The Countess of Dufferin's Fund, 1885–1935' and Report of the Dais Improvement Scheme for 1925, Headquarters, Hyderabad, Sind. The Dufferin Fund article exemplifies the nexus between ideology and the rescuer mentality: 'In 1903, Lady Curzon appealed for funds for a memorial to Queen Victoria and devoted the proceeds to the organization of a scheme for improving the indigenous dais of India whose ignorance is responsible for so much suffering.'

5 Sukumari Bhattacharji, Sanskritist and historian, personal communication, 8 August 1993.

6 Madhu Khanna, co-author of Mookerjee and Khanna 1996. This book is valuable in its rendering of Tantric body mapping and microcosm–macrocosm connections.

References

Foucault, M. 1980. *Power/Knowledge: Selected Interviews and Other Writings, 1972–1977*. Edited and translated by C. Gordon. New York and Brighton, Sussex: Harvester.

Guha, R. (ed.) 1982. *Subaltern Studies I: Writings on South Asian History and Society*. Delhi and Oxford: Oxford University Press.

—— 1983. *Subaltern Studies II: Writings on South Asian History and Society*. Delhi and Oxford: Oxford University Press.

Khare, R.S. 1993. The seen and the unseen: Hindu distinctions, experiences and cultural reasoning. *Contributions to Indian Sociology* (NS) 27: 191–212.

Mookerjee, A. and M. Khanna.1996. *The Tantric Way: Art–Science–Ritual*. London: Thames & Hudson.

Svoboda, R.E. 1996. *Prakruti: Your Ayurvedic Constitution*. Delhi: Motilal Banarsidass.

Chapter 8

'Baby-friendly' hospitals and bad mothers

Manoeuvring development in the post-partum period in Tamil Nadu, South India[1]

Cecilia Van Hollen

> This is a Baby-friendly Hospital, you see. So we are insisting that these women give mother's milk as soon as the baby is born. And we force them to eat some nutritious food right away. The women who come here are mostly illiterates, you see. So they don't know what is best for them. They have very superstitious beliefs and will starve the mother and baby for three days after the delivery. Women will do what they are told while they are here on the board.[2] It is after they go home that the problems begin.
>
> (Medical Officer, World Bank funded IPP-V Hospital, Madras;
> original quote in English)

The words of this doctor are testimony to the fact that in the South Indian state of Tamil Nadu the post-partum period is a key site within which discourses of development are manoeuvred. I use the expression 'manoeuvring development' in two senses. First, it refers to the ways in which development apparatuses manoeuvre individuals and groups to adopt new sets of ideas and practices in an attempt to fashion modern subjects. Second, it refers to the ways in which the people who are the 'targets' of development manoeuvre within and around the discourse in ways which collude with, resist, or alter the discourse.

As the anthropologist Arturo Escobar has argued, the transnational discourse of development has been a central element in the modernising process and in the construction of social and cultural difference in the post-Second World War era (Escobar 1995). James Ferguson has argued that the term 'development' is to this era as 'civilisation' was to the nineteenth century (Ferguson 1994: xiii). Both are discourses of evolutionary progress which serve to reify and legitimise differential positions of power between and within nations or empires. Although at its inception the agenda for international development emphasised economic transformation of so-called 'less developed' or 'Third World' nations by replicating the Western model of industrialisation and urbanisation,[3] by the 1970s the agenda shifted to a broader goal of providing 'basic human needs' or 'minimum needs' to improve the 'quality of life' for those living in the Third World.

Within this new framework the provision of biomedical maternal and child health (MCH) care has become a central component of the development process and a key indicator for determining levels of development. Based on this criterion in combination with such demographic statistics as birth rates and maternal and infant mortality rates, Tamil Nadu is considered to be one of the more developed states in India. For example, in 1994 60.6 per cent of all reported deliveries in Tamil Nadu took place in biomedical institutions,[4] whereas at the national level no more than 20 per cent of all deliveries took place in hospitals (Jejeebhoy and Rao 1995: 125). The maternal mortality rate (MMR) in Tamil Nadu in 1991 was 130 per 100,000 live births whereas the national MMR was 500 per 100,000.[5] And Tamil Nadu's infant mortality rate (IMR) in 1991 was 57 per 1,000 live births while the national IMR was 80 per 1,000.[6]

Despite the state's relative 'developed' status, the development apparatus in the area of MCH care in Tamil Nadu is still highly active and lower-class women are the object of its projects. Governmental and NGO workers in the field of MCH care in Tamil Nadu, working both within hospitals and as out-reach workers connected to hospitals, continue to construct lower-class women as 'less developed' and attempt to reform their minds and transform their bodily practices.

Escobar has proposed that development is first and foremost a discourse, a coherent system of representation that creates the 'reality' of its objects and exerts control over them. This Foucaultian approach accomplishes a radical relativisation of development discourse by showing it to be a distinctively modern and Western formulation. It suggests, as well, that the logic of development discourse is fundamentally cohesive. Ethnographic research, however, highlights the gaps in what appears to be a totalising development discourse. The perspectives and experiences of both the people who are constituted as the 'objects' of development as well as the people in the institutions that implement development locally point to a much messier and often contra-dictory experience of development. Akhil Gupta describes this as the 'complex border zone of hybridity and impurity' (Gupta 1998: 6). In short, we cannot assume that the logic of development discourse produced in offi-cial reports, studies and programmatic statements necessarily structures the way these categories will be used and experienced at the local level. In my analysis I want to focus on the contradictions which permeate development discourses in *practice* and on the ways in which the discourses become localised.[7]

I do this through an analysis of the discursive interactions between MCH workers and the women who are their 'targets' as the health workers attempt to transform women's post-partum practices. In particular I will examine discourses on the diet of the new mother and of the baby. My findings are based on ethnographic research conducted in Tamil Nadu during the full year of 1995 and for one month in both 1993 and 1997.[8] I conducted research both in Madras (now Chennai) and in the semi-rural town of Kaanathur-Reddikuppam, south of Madras, which was going through rapid socioeconomic transformation.

New mother's diet

The first three days

Most of the women I met believe that for the first three days following delivery, the new mother should not eat much at all. Many will only take coffee or tea and bread or *roti* for those three days. Several types of explanations are given in support of this initial dietary taboo. One woman explained why they don't eat food for the first three days:

> When we are in the hospital we bleed. So in order to ensure that the 'blood' will come out, we won't give rice. After delivery the *vayiru* [see below] will have small wounds (*poon*) all over it. When we give rice to the woman who has just delivered she will not be able to take it because of all these wounds in the *vayiru*. So as far as possible, she should not be given rice until three days have passed and the wounds have begun to heal.[9]

Three important notions are revealed in this passage. The first is that the part of the body evoked here is the *vayiru*, which is usually translated as 'stomach'. Here, however, the term describes a body part which is both stomach and uterus in its functions. Second, there is a concern that eating rice, a viscous food, will inhibit the flow of blood from the *vayiru*. A steady flow of post-partum blood is critical to ensuring the new mother's health. Third, there is the notion that the rice will aggravate or infect the 'wounds' in the *vayiru* and thus prevent them from healing.

Another frequent explanation given for the initial three-day dietary taboo was the need to keep the new mother's body 'dry'. In particular her *vayiru* should be kept as 'dry' as possible. This refers to humoral categories of 'hot' vs. 'cold' and 'wet'/'watery' vs. 'dry' in reference to bodies and foods found throughout much of the world.[10] In Tamil Nadu post-partum bodies are generally thought to be both 'cold' and 'wet' (*neer udambu*), and both these states render the post-partum mother vulnerable to colds and fevers, whereas a 'dry' body is said to be strong and impenetrable to disease. The 'wetness' of the post-partum body is associated in part with the post-partum blood. But there is also concern that taking food at this time will cause diarrhoea, and a fear that this will render the body even more 'wet.' There are other dangers associated with diarrhoea. As one woman said: 'If we have had stitches during the delivery [from routine episiotomies done in hospitals] and we eat something on the first day which causes diarrhoea, then the stitches might come out. I am afraid of that. So that is why we don't eat for the first three days.'

If a woman delivers in a government hospital she will typically remain in the hospital for three days following a normal delivery and for five to seven days following a Caesarean. During the hospital stay there are ongoing negotiations and debates between the medical staff, the post-partum mother and the mother's family members regarding what constitutes an appropriate post-partum diet. Generally doctors and nurses in these hospitals believe that women should begin to eat regular food within a day of delivering their baby. They advocate a regular diet based on nutritional theories. Many doctors and nurses believe that one of their missions is to educate post-partum women about the value of nutrition following delivery and to convince them to take regular food.

The following comments by a nurse at a World Bank funded IPP-V public hospital in Madras elucidate the tensions, contradictions and strategies which are common to the negotiation between biomedical and non-biomedical models of health within the context of a development discourse:

> The doctors and nurses say that new mothers should eat everything right away after delivery. They try to get them to eat *idlis* – something soft – and spinach or other greens. But women don't always listen. They think if they eat food, their system will not get cleaned out of blood. They think they should keep their bodies dry (*kaay*) and if they eat food their bodies will not be dry. But nurses and doctors tell them that the 'digestive system' and 'reproductive system' are separate systems so that the food they eat will not have an effect on cleaning out the blood from the 'uterus'. They say that it is important to eat for strength. But many won't listen. Some people won't even drink water which nurses say is important for breastmilk. On the third day women will always eat *rasam* and *saatam* [*rasam* is a watery soup made with peppers and cumin; *saatam* is rice] without fail. But *rasam* has no nutritive value, only water. This problem is better now. Those people who live in the 'streets' now eat more. If some new mother eats good food in the hospital and others see, then she will serve as a 'model'. There was an Anglo-Indian woman who was eating normal food after her delivery. We pointed this out to the other women and when the others saw her they too ate. Similarly most women won't do 'abdominal exercises' but when they saw the Anglo-Indian woman doing 'exercises' others did them as well.

This passage provides insight into the discursive manoeuvrings involved in promoting a biomedical model of the post-partum body. Biomedical practitioners often conceive of the body as being composed of distinct anatomical systems; in this case the 'reproductive system' and the 'digestive system'.

These 'systems' are presented as not only distinct but wholly unrelated to one another 'so that the food they eat will not have an effect on cleaning out the blood from the "uterus"'. The irony is that in attempting to critique the post-partum dietary taboos, the nurse employs this compartmentalised view of anatomical *systems* while simultaneously promoting regular food intake by using a nutrition model which is itself based on a more holistic view of the body. Furthermore, she glides from one sentence in which she condemns the lack of water intake based on the effect that this will have on producing breastmilk to the very next sentence in which she scoffs at the nutritious inadequacy of *rasam* taken after the third day because it is 'only water' and has no nutritive value. These kinds of shifting epistemologies and differential posturing in the name of 'the scientific method' suggest that in many of these contexts the development discourse may be more concerned with construct-ing and reifying social difference than with improving individual women's health.

In this passage, class distinctions are constructed and hierarchically organ-ised on a scale of developed vs. less-developed by saying that those who live in the 'streets' now eat more food after delivery. The people living in 'the streets' here are hierarchically ranked above those living in the 'slums' made up of government housing-board complexes or clusters of huts which are connected by footpaths rather than streets (i.e., this does not have the same connotation as 'street people' as used in the US). And racial distinctions are evoked when the body of the Anglo-Indian woman, symbolising a tie to the 'civilising' process of British colonialism, stands as a 'model' for the modern body – a body which is self-consciously fortified by nutrition yet disciplined by the 'slimming' craze of the transnational beauty discourse.

Day three onwards

Pattiya saappaadu

From the third day onwards women begin selectively to introduce other foods to their diet. This diet is called *pattiya saappaadu*.[11] After the third day, the post-partum mother will eat a rice-based meal with *rasam* and a vegetable *kuzhambu* (a sauce) only once a day. Certain kinds of vegetables which are fre-quently included in normal *saappaadu* must be avoided in this *pattiya saappaadu*. For example, all vegetables which are considered to be 'watery' (such as pumpkin, snake gourd and Bangalore eggplant) should be avoided since they may cause *sitalam*[12] in both the mother and child. *Sitalam* is a con-dition of coolness and dampness and can cause one to catch colds (*sali*) and/or to get fever accompanied by fits (*juram*). *Sitalam* is not only caused by 'wetness' in the body but also by 'cold' foods producing 'cold' bodies. Whereas a preg-nant woman's body is thought to be very 'hot', a post-partum woman's body and a newborn's body are usually said to be 'cold'. Therefore, 'cold' foods

Figure 8.1 A traditional midwife (*maruttuvacci*) on the outskirts of Kaanathur-Reddikuppam bathes a baby as part of the *teeddukkazhittal* ceremony (photo by Cecilia Van Hollen)

(including such vegetables as cabbage, eggplant and cucumber as well as fruits like bananas, *sappoddaas* and jackfruit) are avoided. 'Hot' foods may be given, not only to counteract the 'cold' quality of the post-partum body but also to dry out the body. Yet I was also told that women should avoid eating some 'hot' foods, particularly fruits such as papaya and mango, during the post-partum period just as these things are avoided during pregnancy. During pregnancy 'hot' foods are avoided to prevent the risk of miscarriage. During the post-partum period some 'hot' foods are believed to cause excessive bleeding for the mother and diarrhoea for both mother and baby.

Most non-Brahmins I met also said that non-vegetarian food (*kavicci*) should not be included in the *pattiya saappaadu* until after the ceremonial day of *teeddukkazhittal* when the new mother and baby are ritually bathed and purified (see Figures 8.1 and 8.2). This is usually done on the ninth or eleventh day after delivery for Hindus and on the fortieth day for Muslims. Non-vegetarian food is considered to be very fatty and hard to digest. Furthermore, the fat which passes through the breastmilk to the baby will cause indigestion for the baby as well.[13]

International development agencies which are engaged in the promotion of biomedicine often divide 'traditional' practices into three categories according to their effects on health: 'positive', 'harmless' and 'harmful'. Ever since the

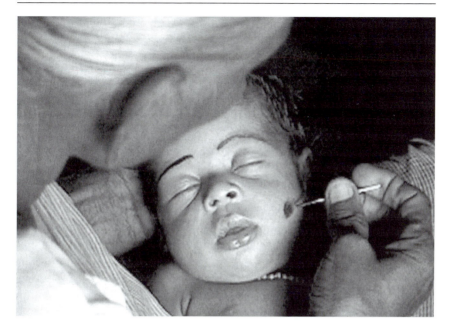

Figure 8.2 The *maruttuvacci* applies marks on the baby's face to ward off the evil eye after giving the baby its first full oil bath (photo by Cecilia Van Hollen)

first major World Health Organisation (WHO) report on Traditional Birth Attendants, 'diet restrictions' have fallen into the category of 'harmful'.[14] In Tamil Nadu MCH workers frequently complain that post-partum dietary taboos are superstitious and are depriving mothers and children of essential nutrition.

In practice, however, women in Tamil Nadu do consume many foods which fall into the various taboo categories. In her analysis of post-partum food taboos in Malaysia, Carol Laderman writes:

> The richness of ambiguity and variability of interpretation of Malay systems of food avoidance, at the practical level do not allow us the liberty of formulating a simple cause and effect relationship between traditional food beliefs and nutritional health.
>
> (Laderman 1983: 186)

In fact, she argues, there is a great deal of dietary experimentation at the individual level, and the rules restricting certain foods must be seen as models which people can draw on to explain individual problems and not necessarily as rules which dictate practice. This is precisely the way in which post-partum dietary rules in Tamil Nadu must be understood as well. This is *not* to deny that there is a serious problem of malnutrition among poor women in Tamil Nadu, particularly during their childbearing years. Rather, I simply want to argue that cultural conceptions of the post-partum body and post-partum diet are not responsible for malnutrition because they are used in a flexible way. Similar dietary taboos a_ie often evoked by women in the middle and upper classes who do not suffer from malnutrition. Rather, the problems of malnutrition stem more directly from structures of class and gender discrimination.

In an attempt to combat the problem of malnutrition during women's childbearing years the state and NGO organisations are trying to convince pregnant and lactating women to consume more *raagi* (a cereal grain). Due to a patriarchal cultural ethic of self-sacrifice among women in Tamil Nadu, poor women are not willing to take much food for themselves, even during pregnancy and the post-partum period. In particular, they refrain from taking extra rice, since rice is a highly valued food in Tamil culture. *Raagi*, on the other hand, is as nutritious as rice but is associated with low social status. By encouraging women to eat *raagi* instead of rice, women will not feel as though they are depriving their husbands and children of their share of rice. According to a doctor involved in this campaign: 'Only by working within the cultural context of the sacrifice of women to their husbands and children can you achieve better nutritional status for pregnant and lactating women' (original in English). This comment is typical of the ways in which development projects attempt to be 'culturally appropriate'. Frequently the goal of development seems to be to get people to change a practice which is perceived to be deleterious without changing the social structure which leads to that practice in the first place.

Pirasava maruntu

In addition to the *pattiya saappaadu*, many women begin to take a special medicine known as *pirasava maruntu* (delivery medicine) from the third day following delivery onwards. The ingredients will vary somewhat from family to family but always include dried ginger, asafoetida and black jaggery. The asafoetida helps to clear the blood out, and the dried ginger helps with digestion.

In my discussions with MCH workers in Tamil Nadu I found that the use of *pirasava maruntu* in the post-partum period held ambiguous and shifting positions with respect to the three categories of 'positive', 'harmless' and 'harmful'. For the most part, these medicines were relegated to the category of 'harmless'. Doctors and nurses, however, strongly opposed the use of this medicine following either a Caesarean or sterilisation because, they argued, these medicines can cause diarrhoea and thus cause complications with the stitches. Most post-partum women I met who had undergone such surgical procedures readily accepted this advice because they were already keenly aware of the dangers of diarrhoea in the post-partum period as evidenced in the explanations for many of the food taboos. What is interesting here is the

Figure 8.3 The *maruttuvacci* grinds a medicine of dried ginger, asafoetida and roasted garlic to give to a newborn baby on the thirteenth day after birth. This medicine is given to aid digestion (photo by Cecilia Van Hollen)

fact that in one context, the MCH workers discredit local concerns about diarrhoea associated with consuming certain foods in their attempt to promote a nutritional model of post-partum health. And yet they point to the potentially harmful effects of diarrhoea caused by local medicines in other contexts. In the development discourse each shifting model is presented uncritically as if it alone were right both scientifically and morally.

Nandy and Visvanathan have attributed this lack of reflexive scepticism to the methodological premise of 'modern medicine' itself, namely the 'principle of falsifiability'. As they write:

> It is possible to argue that modern medicine, which was one of the last sciences to grow out of the traditional sciences in Europe and consolidate itself as a 'proper' science in the nineteenth century, was the first major system of healing to try to do away with this element of scepticism and self-criticism. Some amount of scepticism and criticism survived in the popular culture, but it did not easily translate into philosophical doubt within the system. The Popperian principle of falsifiability, so central to the positivist self-concept of science, does not include within its scope any scepticism towards the basic philosophical assumptions or

culture of post-seventeenth-century science. Once medicine became a positivist science, it also became philosophically and culturally less self-critical.

(Nandy and Visvanathan 1990: 147)

In the context of the interactions between MCH workers and their targets, however, my sense is that the lack of self-critique has more to do with the relations of power in these person-to-person interactions and is rooted more in the discourse of development itself, rather than in the structure of 'modern medicine' *per se*.

Baby's diet

Breastmilk

Tamil women take many of the post-partum dietary precautions mentioned above because of a belief that the infant's body at this time is a *pacca udumpu*, which literally means a 'green body'. The sense here is that the body is weak and vulnerable like the tender green shoot of a plant. And just as a tender shoot is nourished by water, this *pacca udumpu* is nourished by mother's milk and is highly sensitive to fluctuations in the content of the milk.

Many women in Tamil Nadu do not put the baby to the breast to drink the colostrum, which in Tamil is called *seempaal*, immediately following delivery.[15] They fear that the *seempaal* will cause diarrhoea and nausea for the baby. A few women also told me that because the *seempaal* was thick it was too hard for the baby to suck. Furthermore, some believe that colostrum is derived from menstrual blood which ceases at conception and which has been stagnating during pregnancy (Zeitlyn and Rowshan 1997: 61). It is, therefore, viewed as 'polluting'.

Within the MCH development discourse, concern over the refusal to give newborns colostrum is part and parcel of a general anxiety over the decrease in the prevalence and length of breastfeeding throughout the world. This concern emerged as a public development issue in the early 1970s.[16] Third-World communities were thought to be particularly crippled by the shift from breastfeeding to bottle-feeding because conditions of poverty in the Third World militated against sanitary uses of bottles, and formulas were often diluted, leading to an increase in infant disease and mortality. However, rather than change the social conditions that prevent people from using formulas in a safe fashion, or that were forcing many women in the Third World into urban industrial labour that did not allow the time and space for breast-feeding, there is a tendency to fixate on the value of breastfeeding alone.

The recent UNICEF- and WHO-sponsored Baby Friendly Hospital Initiative (BFHI) to promote breastfeeding was first initiated in India in 1992 in collaboration with the Ministry of Health and Family Welfare. This was part of a global movement that was formulated at the World Summit for Children in 1990. The primary goals of the BFHI are to end the free and low-cost distribution of infant formula in maternity wards, and to encourage hospitals to follow 'Baby Friendly' practices, including the Ten Steps to Successful Breastfeeding.[17] Seventy per cent of all certified Baby Friendly hospitals nationally are in Tamil Nadu and the neighbouring state of Kerala alone.[18]

In the early months of my research I was discussing my project with a doctor who was at the centre of this Baby Friendly campaign. When she found out that I had a seven-month-old baby myself, she wanted to know if I was breastfeeding. I explained that I was but that because of the demands of my research I had begun to introduce Lactogen formula during the day. She shook her head disapprovingly and said (in English): 'You must stop the formula immediately. I will teach you how to express milk into a *paaladai*[19] so that someone can give it to your daughter while you are away. It is the Indian way. Let the research begin at home!' I went home that day feeling humbled but somehow exhilarated about the opportunity to learn some wonderfully natural 'Indian way' to combine work with breastmilk without the humiliation of the mechanistic electric breast-pump I had used back in America. It was a moment where I was swept away by the romantic rhetoric of a 'natural India'.

Several months later I watched this same doctor conducting a workshop for a group of women who were being trained to become outreach health workers. When the doctor discovered that one of the women had a five-month-old baby who was sick, she began publicly interrogating and humiliating her for giving her baby Lactogen. The trainee meekly explained that since she had started this training programme she began giving the baby formula a few times in combination with breastmilk. The doctor replied: 'In your role as a Multi-purpose Health Worker you are telling other mothers to breastfeed continuously at least up to six months. Are you so mighty that you don't have to practise what you preach?' The doctor told the woman that she would have to discontinue the course until her baby was older and she sent her off. The woman left, biting her lip to hold back her tears. It was then that I realised that the tenor and fervour of this breastfeeding campaign seemed to be at times more concerned with legitimising state and NGO development institutions' apparent commitment to a pro-child, 'Baby Friendly' approach, giving them the moral high ground, rather than providing the social and economic framework within which long-term breastfeeding is both acceptable and feasible.

Baby food

According to the MCH policy in Tamil Nadu women should give their babies mother's milk exclusively for three to four months. After that they should begin introducing foods to their children little by little for taste. Beginning in the sixth or seventh month they say that mothers should give all foods to their children with the intent of providing good nutrition. Within a year the child should have tried all types of food.

Despite the MCH recommendations, many people restrict certain foods from their children's diet during the first few years. Rather than discuss all the child dietary taboos at length, I will provide an example of the nature of the MCH development discourse as it manoeuvres to change people's practices and as it is manoeuvred by those it seeks to change. Priya[20] was a 29-year-old Brahmin woman who was nine months pregnant with her second child when I met her at a World Bank funded government hospital in Madras where she was coming for her prenatal check-ups. The following discussion took place between Priya, a nurse, myself and my research assistant. The nurse had just explained the MCH recommendations for baby food to Priya.

Priya:	We will not give banana until three years of age because it's a 'cold' food. For my daughter I didn't give banana until she was three years old. There was no problem because of it. Now she is eating everything.
Nurse:	Will you not give it for this child [*in utero*] either?
Priya:	[Shakes her head to indicate 'no.']
Nurse:	Aiyyaiyo! Will you *still* have this superstition [*mood nam-bikkai*]?
Priya:	Nothing goes wrong because of that belief does it?
Nurse:	You are doing wrong [*tappu*]. You are not giving what you *should* give for the child and yet you are saying that you are not doing anything wrong.
Priya:	After three years you can give anything. Now my daughter eats four bananas a day!
Nurse:	Then your child will never grow in those three years.
Priya:	Why won't it? It grows well.
Nurse:	The 'maximum growth' ... the 'period' when the child grows well is in those three years only.
Priya:	Instead of that we are giving lots of milk, curd ...
Nurse:	You can't get all the 'nutrients' in milk and curd.
CVH:	Do you give *daal*?
Priya:	Yes, we give *daal* from the tenth month on. We boil *daal* separately, add *ghee* and give it. There is 'health' in all those, isn't there?
Nurse:	There is ... I am not saying no. But for the 'brain development', for the 'brain cells' ... I'm saying don't restrict certain foods. Why are you restricting 'particular food-stuffs'?
Research Asst:	When will you do the *anna piraasanam*?[21]
Priya:	After one year.

Nurse:	Won't you give the child rice before one year?
Priya:	No, we won't. For my daughter I didn't give it. Not even *idli*. We will give only milk, *kanji* . . .
Nurse:	Will you not give it for this child [*in utero*] either?
Priya:	If it eats I will give.
Nurse:	It will eat. It won't say 'I won't'.
Priya:	Maybe we can look for a good day [i.e. astrologically auspicious day] in the sixth month and start giving.

Just at that moment Priya's first daughter came skipping into the room. She asked her mother who I was and when her mother explained, the daughter began to speak to me in English. 'I have put her in an "English medium" school and she is doing very well in her studies', her mother explained proudly, as if her daughter was living proof of the efficacy of the family's dietary practices.

Several interesting moves can be gleaned from this discussion. First, we hear the outrage that despite the nurse's advice regarding the proper diet for the child, Priya 'still' believes it is better not to give banana and does not intend to change her practice with the second child. For the nurse there is a sense of progress disrupted. After repeated enquiries about what she will do for 'this child' *in utero*, in the end Priya concedes and says that 'maybe' she will give rice for the second child as early as the sixth month. Priya seems to be trying to extricate herself from an uncomfortable conversation rather than being convinced of the nurse's claims.

Nowhere does the nurse explain *why* the absence of bananas or rice specifically will harm the development of the child when other foods are clearly being given. Rather, as soon as there is mention of restricting any foods and when humoral theories of 'hot' and 'cold' are evoked, a red flag goes up and people are accused of doing something wrong (*tappu*). When the 'wrong' is being done to the baby the tone of the discourse becomes saturated with a sense of criminality. The nurse accuses Priya of potentially stunting the brain development of her child, yet she does not elaborate on the effects of specific foods on brain development. It was because of the nurse's accusational tone that the daughter's stellar English performance seemed to carry such a sting of vindication.

It is important to note Priya's class and caste status here. The fact that she has placed her daughter in an 'English medium' school, requiring extra fees, reveals her middle-class status. And, as mentioned above, she is from the Brahmin caste. Yet, because she has chosen to seek maternal health care from a World Bank funded IPP-V hospital which has been established to provide services for the urban poor, she finds herself being subjected to the same kinds of developmentalist critiques as lower-class women using the same services. Unlike many other interactions I witnessed between patients and medical staff in public hospitals, however, Priya continues to defend her

post-partum practices in the face of an ongoing critique. This may be due to
her class and caste position. Most of the very poor women in these hospitals
conceded more rapidly to the medical staff's recommendations, though their
concessions were often more in speech than in practice.

This passage emphasises the degree to which the MCH development discourse in Tamil Nadu reproduces unequal power relations, constructing
mothers as not only backward, uneducated and superstitious, but also as
criminal. Elsewhere I have argued that the national and international media
attention on the contemporary practice of female infanticide which was
said to have been first 'discovered' in Tamil Nadu in the mid-1980s[22] has
contributed to the criminalisation of poor mothers in the development discourse and was partially responsible for the government of Tamil Nadu's
shift in its MCH policy from an emphasis on the mother to the child, especially the girl child in the early 1990s[23] (Van Hollen 1998). In short, the
media's attention on female infanticide in Tamil Nadu has created a localised
version of the MCH development discourse in Tamil Nadu which crimi-
nalises poor mothers by constructing them as always potential 'murderers' of
their girl babies.

It was in this context that I could understand why one health worker went
so far as to tell me that *karuppu* was a disease which 'backward' people had
fabricated to cover up acts of female infanticide. *Karuppu* (meaning blackness
or darkness) is a locally constructed disease in Tamil Nadu. Symptoms
include dark blemishes on the baby's skin and difficulty breathing. The disease is said to be potentially fatal.[24] If a mother says her girl baby has
karuppu, this health worker warned me, it is a sure indication of the mother's
criminal intent. Therefore, she explained that from now on she would make it
her mission to take any baby who reportedly dies of *karuppu* immediately to
the hospital for a post-mortem to check for poisoning. Her plan was to
deceive a mother into letting her take the dead baby by telling her that the
doctors would try to revive the baby's life. In her zealous imaginings of this
crusade it never occurred to her that this presumption of criminality could
leave parents holding on to a fragile, false sense of hope, further prolonging
their loss.

The question of 'choice'

How does the contradictory, condescending and criminalising tenor of the
MCH development discourse influence poor women's decisions about where
to seek maternal health care? This is of course a very difficult question to
answer in any quantifiable way. For poor women in Madras the options are
quite narrow. Reports indicate that 99 per cent of all deliveries in Madras are
hospital deliveries.[25] So for poor women it is a matter of choosing between
different kinds of public hospitals. In the semi-rural town of Kaanathur-
Reddikuppam outside of Madras where I also did research, slightly less than

half (twenty-nine) of the deliveries in 1995 were at home and slightly more than half (thirty-one) were in hospitals.

Many of the women from this town who had gone to the hospital explained that 'these days everyone goes to the hospital.' When I asked why everyone was going to the hospital some would say that it was because 'these days we are *naveenamayam* (modern/developed); in those days everything was *pazhakkam* (tradition/habit)'. *Naveenam* is somewhat of an erudite way of talking about being developed, of naming it as a thing. More commonly, women would refer to development as a process of coming to know. Those who are developed, therefore, are *terincirukkiravankal* (those who have come to know); those who are not developed are *teriyaatavankal* (those who do not know). This process of coming to know which makes one developed is usually associated with formal education. So some refer to people whom they consider to be developed as *padiccirukkiravankal* (those who have studied). And people speaking in English almost always use the term 'illiterates' to refer to all those people whom they consider to be undeveloped and backwards.

But for those women who remained home *one* of the reasons given for not going to the hospital was their fear of being vociferously scolded and insulted for trying to follow their family's post-partum dietary practices. This pervasive fear of the medical staff's scoldings underscores the process of infantilisation which is part and parcel of development discourses (Gupta 1998; Escobar 1995). Thus, in some cases the development discourse may backfire: rather than getting women to accept biomedical practices, it may in fact deter women from using biomedical services. Rather than development discourses inadvertently serving the interests of the state, as Ferguson has shown (Ferguson 1994), they may in fact inadvertently undermine them. This could of course compromise women's health. Women should be deciding about whether to stay at home or go to the hospital based on obstetric risks rather than based on fears of discrimination.

In her discussion on the development discourse and the construction of 'the village' in Nepal, Stacy Pigg remarks that 'Development discourse creates a paradox: It locates villages on the periphery of development, yet its ostensible aim is to make villages developed' (Pigg 1992: 511).

Although a similar construction of the urban/rural divide is also operative in the development imaginary in the Indian context, with respect to the development agenda of spreading allopathic MCH care I found that class, particularly understood in terms of levels of education, is the dominant category evoked to explain this contradictory need for, and obstacle to, national development that Pigg points out. Furthermore, because this discourse revolves around the fact of reproduction and the bodily production of new citizens (i.e., babies), the obstacle (i.e., the lower-class, 'illiterate' mother) is constructed as not only 'backwards' but as one who can potentially endanger the life of these future citizens. MCH development discourse is thus always infused with the opposition between criminal mothers and innocent babies with the state and biomedicine always allied with the innocent. The 'scientific' grounds for MCH policy at any given point in time and in any given context are always shifting, yet the balance of moral power remains the same. The irony is of course that many lower-class women in Tamil Nadu may not use government biomedical MCH care services, particularly in-hospital services, in part because of the forms of condescension, blame and discrimination they experience.

Notes

1 This material is part of a larger research project, which was funded by the US Fulbright-Hays Foundation. Special thanks are due to Annette Mathews, Haripriya Narasimhan, Rajeswari Prabhakaran and Kausalya Hart for their assistance with this research and with translations. I am particularly grateful to the women and men who participated in this research and to the Working Women's Forum for their ongoing support of this project. Additional thanks go to Lawrence Cohen, Akhil Gupta, Kathleen Erwin and Sandra Cate for their insightful comments on this chapter.
2 Here 'board' refers to the delivery table which in most of the government hospitals is a long narrow metal table which is cut out at one end to catch the baby.
3 Rostow's well-known economic theory of the stages which a Third World country must go through in order to 'take off' into the hallowed realm of the 'developed' nations is exemplary of this time (Rostow 1991 [1960]).
4 From Government of Tamil Nadu 1994a: 36. Because a number of home deliveries go unreported, these figures reflect a higher percentage of hospital deliveries than is actually the case. Nevertheless the comparisons with the national figures are dramatic.
5 From Government of Tamil Nadu 1993: 44, and 1994a: 15.
6 These are Sample Registration System (SRS) statistics taken from the *Statistical Handbook of Tamil Nadu 1994* (Government of Tamil Nadu 1994b). It is important to note that all IMR and MMR statistics are based on *registered* deaths and therefore are often lower than the actual rates.
7 I would like to thank Akhil Gupta, Stacy Pigg, Jenny Springer and Rebecca Klenk for their fruitful discussions on my theoretical engagements on this topic in our panel entitled 'Manoeuvring Development in South Asia' presented at the American Anthropological Association Annual Meeting in Washington, DC, in November 1997.
8 Funding for the research conducted in 1995 was provided by a Fulbright Doctoral Dissertation Abroad Fellowship. The research in 1993 was funded by the University of Pennsylvania Dean of Arts and Sciences Research Abroad Grant. The research in 1997 was funded by a Robert H. Lowie Grant from the Department of Anthropology at the University of California, Berkeley.
9 Unless otherwise noted, all quotes are English translations of the original Tamil speech. Words in quotations represent those words spoken in English. Original Tamil words are in italics.
10 'Hot' and 'cold' foods do not refer to the thermal temperature of the foods themselves, but rather to the effects that such foods have on a particular body once they are consumed.
11 *Pattiyam* means a prescribed diet, and *saappaadu* is a word used to mean food or meal in a general sense but only rice-based meals are considered to be real *saappaadu*.

12 This is also known as *sitala*. In many parts of North India, the goddess of small-pox is known as Sitala Devi. Since smallpox is associated with intense heat, the goddess Sitala is known as one who is desirous of cooling offerings (see Miron Winslow's *Tamil–English Dictionary*; see also Marglin 1990).

13 In addition to the various restrictions placed on the post-partum *pattiyam*, women are encouraged to eat certain kinds of foods, particularly foods which are believed to enhance the mother's milk supply. These include such things as garlic and *pazhayatu* (the previous night's rice which is reheated with warm water). Among non-vegetarian foods, soups made with chicken, mutton liver, or the chest bone of the goat, as well as particular kinds of fish (such as *kaarappodi* and *paalsuraa*) are said to enhance mother's milk.

14 See Verderese and Turnbull 1975: 38 for WHO.

15 For discussion on the widespread cross-cultural restrictions on colostrum see Baumslag and Michels 1995: 23–5.

16 See Baumslag and Michels 1995, Section III, and Raphael 1979 for more discussion on critiques of the export of formulas and baby foods to the Third World. Concerns over the decline in breastfeeding existed prior to the 1970s and were attached to different kinds of social movements. In India, for example, this concern was voiced as early as 1917 in the context of nationalist critiques of the effects of industrialisation on cultural notions of femininity (see Srinivasmurthi cited in Nandy and Visvanathan 1990: 159). The point here is that it was in the early 1970s that this concern became a part of the development agenda.

17 The 'Ten Steps' are as follows: (1) Have a written breastfeeding policy; (2) train all health staff to implement this policy; (3) inform all pregnant women about the benefits of breastfeeding; (4) help mothers initiate breastfeeding within half an hour of birth; (5) show mothers the best way to breastfeed; (6) give newborn infants no food or drink other than breastmilk, unless medically indicated; (7) practice 'rooming in' by allowing mothers and babies to remain together twenty-four hours a day; (8) encourage breastfeeding on demand; (9) give no artificial teats, pacifiers, dummies or soothers; (10) help start breastfeeding support groups and refer mothers to them.

18 Personal communication with Dr Srilata, Director of Madras UNICEF office, May 1997.

19 A *paaladai* is a small shallow metal cup which sits in the palm of the hand. It is shaped like a teardrop or like a *yoni* and is commonly used to feed small children.

20 Unless otherwise noted, all names of non-public figures are pseudonyms.

21 The *anna piraasanam* is a Vedic ceremony performed by Brahmins in which a baby is given its first solids, usually a rice-based food which is served to the baby on a silver plate or coin (for more information on this, see Stevenson 1971 [1920]: 19–20).

22 For example, see 'Born to die' (*India Today*, June 1986); 'Infant killers of Dharmapuri' (*Hindustan Times*, 29 September 1994); 'Born to die: tragedy of the doomed daughter' (*Hindu*, 20 November 1994); Usha Rai 'Where there is no place for baby girls' (*Indian Express*, 26 September 1995); Carol Aloysius, 'She's also made of flesh and blood: Why destroy the girl child?' (*Sunday Observer*, 29 June 1997). Elizabeth Bumiller's (1990) journalistic report on female infanticide in Tamil Nadu in her widely distributed book, *May You Be the Mother of a Hundred Sons*, helped to bring international attention to this story. Most reports on female infanticide in Tamil Nadu are from Dharmapuri in Salem District and Usilampatti in Madurai District.

23 As the former Chief Minister of Tamil Nadu, Jayaram Jayalalitha said in her speech inaugurating the new government of Tamil Nadu's State Plan of Action for the Child in 1993: 'The child in the Indian tradition is not viewed in isolation but

was and is considered as part of a larger matrix in which the mother–child unit is the very foundation. Measures to promote the child [sic] growth or to alleviate its distress are required to be directed towards this unit with the centre of protection shifting gradually from the mother to the child.'

24 It is of course possible that people could use the category of *karuppu* to explain the death of an infant who was in fact killed, but that is different from claiming that the disease itself was invented for this purpose. In their restudy of the status of health in the village of Thaiyur (also in Chingelput district), Djurfeldt, Lindberg, and Rajagopal translate *karuppu* as neonatal tetanus (Djurfeldt, Lindberg and Rajagopal 1997: 187). In my discussions, however, people referred to neonatal tetanus as *rana janni*, associated with severe fever and 'fits', and distinguished this from *karuppu*, which was associated with skin blemishes and listlessness.

25 From 'India and the World Bank' (*Hindu*, 23 February 1993).

References

Baumslag, N. and D.L. Michels. 1995. *Milk, Money, and Madness: The Culture and Politics of Breastfeeding*. Westport, CT: Bergin and Garvey.

Bumiller, E. 1990. *May You Be the Mother of a Hundred Sons: A Journey among the Women of India*. New Delhi: Penguin.

Djurfeldt, G., S. Lindberg and A. Rajagopal. 1997. Coming back to Thaiyur: health and medicine in a twenty-five years perspective. In *The village in Asia Revisited*, edited by J. Breman, P. Klaas and P. Saith. Delhi: Oxford University Press.

Escobar, A. 1995. *Encountering Development: The Making and Unmaking of the Third World*. Princeton, NJ: Princeton University Press.

Ferguson, J. 1994. *The Anti-politics Machine: 'Development', Depoliticization, and Bureaucratic Power in Lesotho*. Minneapolis: University of Minnesota Press.

Government of Tamil Nadu. 1993. *State Plan of Action for the Child in Tamil Nadu*.
—— 1994a. *Child Survival and Safe Motherhood in Tamil Nadu*. January 1994. Directorate of Public Health and Preventative Medicine, Madras.
—— 1994b. *Statistical Handbook of Tamil Nadu*. November 1993. Directorate of Public Health and Preventative Medicine, Madras.

Gupta, A. 1998. *Postcolonial Developments: Agriculture in the Making of Modern India*. Durham, NC: Duke University Press.

Jejeebhoy, S.J. and S.R. Rao. 1995. Unsafe motherhood: a review of reproductive health. In *Women's Health in India: Risk and Vulnerability*, edited by M.D. Gupta, L.C. Chen and T.N. Krishnan. Bombay: Oxford University Press.

Laderman, C. 1983. *Wives and Midwives: Childbirth and Nutrition in Rural Malaysia*. Berkeley: University of California Press.

Marglin, F.A. 1990. Smallpox in two systems of knowledge. In *Dominating Knowledge: Development, Culture and Resistance*, edited by F.A. Marglin and S.A. Marglin. Oxford: Clarendon Press.

Nandy, A. and S. Visvanathan. 1990. Modern medicine and its non-modern critics: a study in discourse. In *Dominating Knowledge: Development, Culture and Resistance*, edited by F.A. Marglin and S.A. Marglin. Oxford: Clarendon Press.

Pigg, S.L. 1992. Inventing social categories through place: social representations and development in Nepal. *Comparative Studies in Society and History* 34 (3): 491–513.

Raphael, D. (ed.) 1979. *Breastfeeding and Food Policy in a Hungry World*. San Francisco, CA: Academic Press.

Rostow, W.W. 1991 [1960]. *The Stages of Economic Growth: A Non-communist Manifesto*, Third Edition. New York: Cambridge University Press.

Stevenson, Mrs S. 1971 [1920]. *The Rites of the Twice Born*. New Delhi: Oriental Books Reprint Corporation.

Van Hollen, C. 1998. Criminal mothers and superstitious fathers: a shift from the mother to the child in Tamil Nadu's maternal and child health programme. Paper presented at the University of Wisconsin–Madison Annual Conference on South Asia, October 1998.

Verderese, M.D. and L.M. Turnbull (eds). 1975. *The Traditional Birth Attendant in Maternal and Child Health and Family Planning: A Guide to Her Training and Utilization*. Geneva: World Health Organisation.

Zeitlyn, S. and R. Rowshan. 1997. Privileged knowledge and mothers' 'perceptions': the case of breastfeeding and insufficient milk in Bangladesh. *Medical Anthropology Quarterly* 11 (1): 56–68.

Chapter 9

Tibetan and Indian ideas of birth pollution

Similarities and contrasts[1]

Santi Rozario and Geoffrey Samuel

Introduction

This chapter is based on field research carried out with a Tibetan community in the refugee settlement of Dalhousie in Himachal Pradesh, North India in June and July 1996. While birthing practices have obviously been affected by the situation in which this refugee population is living, we suggest that much of what we found reflects more general Tibetan attitudes to childbirth and health. We contrast the approach to childbirth among the Tibetan refugees with that found in studies of childbirth in North India and Bangladesh, in order to bring both the Tibetan childbirth practices and the characteristic North Indian–Bangladeshi approach into clearer focus.[2]

While Rozario's field research at Dalhousie was specifically on childbirth, Samuel's, carried out in conjunction with a third colleague, Linda Connor, was on a traditional Tibetan medical clinic (see Samuel 1999, 2001; Connor 1996; Connor, Monro and McIntyre 1996). There was substantial interaction between the research projects, and the present chapter results from joint reflection on the material by Rozario and Samuel.

When we first arrived in Dalhousie, we knew relatively little about Tibetan ideas regarding childbirth. However, we knew quite a lot about childbirth in Bangladesh, since Rozario had been doing research on childbirth in Bangladesh for the previous five years (see Rozario 1995a, 1995b, 1998 and Chapter 6 this volume), as well as carrying out a short study with Maithili people in southern Nepal in 1994. We had also read enough of the literature on childbirth in South Asian societies to know that what Rozario had been seeing in Bangladesh and southern Nepal was part of a widespread pattern in Bangladesh, much of North India and parts of Nepal.[3]

In the remainder of the Introduction we provide a brief description of this widespread pattern of childbirth in Bangladesh, North India and Nepal, and an initial comparison with childbirth among the Tibetan refugees. The next section situates these birth practices within the wider context of pollution concepts and practices in India, Bangladesh and Nepal. The third section considers childbirth among the Tibetan refugees and explores Tibetan pollution concepts. In the final section, the two regions and approaches are contrasted. We suggest that while concepts that might be glossed as 'pollution' are significant in both cases, there are important differences between them, and these differences have significant consequences for South Asian and Tibetan women.

As noted in Chapters 4 to 6, childbirth in Bangladesh, North India and much of Nepal, among Muslims and Christians as well as Hindus, is dominated by what is usually referred to in English by anthropologists as 'pollution'. The most usual term in formal Bengali is *oshouch*, which derives from the Sanskrit term *aśauca*. Pollution implies risk of attack by malevolent spirits (usually called *bhūt* in Bangladesh). It also implies the need for separation, since people who are polluted can transmit their state of pollution to others, placing them at risk. So people who are in a state of pollution have to be kept apart from those who are not. This is part of the logic for why men, including those of the birthing woman's immediate family, are strictly excluded from birth in Bangladesh, North India and Southern Nepal. Birth is very definitely a women's affair, and men should be kept well clear of it.

Most births even today in villages in Bangladesh and elsewhere in the region take place at home, and are attended by low-caste and low-class traditional birth attendants (usually called *dai* in Bangladesh and North India). For a woman to give birth in a public space or with men present is not only dangerous, it is shameful, and most village families are unwilling except in extreme emergency to risk the shame of exposing birthing women to the local hospital with its male medical personnel. Only a few wealthy families, generally with some exposure to urban values, would take their women to give birth in a clinic or hospital.

Birth therefore takes place at home in the vast majority of cases. Where possible, particularly among high-caste Hindus, the birth will take place in a hut outside the house itself though within the compound. While birth, especially the birth of a male child, is usually a strongly desired event, the pollution associated with childbirth is a serious matter, and is sometimes described as being, along with the pollution of death, the worst of all forms of pollution. The cutting of the umbilical cord is a matter of particular concern, and it is often left to the birthing woman herself, since no-one else is prepared to undertake the pollution and the need for consequent purification (Cameron 1998: 260; Rozario 1998; cf. also Unnithan Chapter 5 this volume).[4] The mother remains in seclusion for some days after the birth, until a ritual feast which marks the end of her period of pollution.

The *dais* or traditional birth attendants themselves generally come from an untouchable caste (such as Chamar, leather-worker, or Lohar, blacksmith) or from other low-status and impoverished groups. They rarely have any formal medical training. Indeed, it has been argued that the family of the birthing woman views their function less in terms of assisting with the birth than of dealing with the associated impurity and pollution (Jeffery, Jeffery and Lyon Chapter 4 this volume, and 1989). Some recent writers have contested this and stressed that the *dais* do have skilled knowledge about childbirth (Chawla 1994 and Chapter 7 this volume; Patel 1994). In Rozario's own research in Bangladesh, she found that while many of the *dais* she met were conscious of their skill and knowledge, it was often not recognised by the families of the birthing women, and their opinion was not necessarily listened to (see Chapter 6 this volume). Generally, it seems that older women from the birthing woman's family who have some experience of childbirth take charge of the situation, while leaving most of the physical side of delivering the child to the *dai*. This is a pattern also reported by Maya Unnithan in a recent paper on childbirth in Rajasthan (1999a) and in Chapter 5 of this volume. No doubt the extent to which the *dai*'s opinion is sought or her advice taken depends a lot on the personalities of the individuals involved in any particular case.

While there have been campaigns to train traditional birth attendants in North India and Bangladesh, as elsewhere in the Third World, these have been much less successful than in, for example, South East Asia or Central America, since the low social status of the *dais* means that even if they receive training, their opinions are not necessarily taken seriously (see Jeffery, Jeffery and Lyon Chapter 4 this volume). In addition, most *dais* are elderly and illiterate. Younger, educated women are very unwilling to do this kind of work.

All this is a well-known and familiar pattern, repeated in a range of studies from North India, Bangladesh and Nepal, including those in the present volume.

Studies of Tibetan childbirth, whether in 'traditional' or refugee communities, are far fewer, and much of what is available is normative and textual rather than ethnographically based.[5] We were thus unsure what Rozario would find when she began to investigate childbirth among the Tibetan refugees of Dalhousie.

At first sight, childbirth among the Tibetan refugees in India seemed to have many similarities to this pattern. Tibetans too have concepts which can be described as 'pollution', and they too regard birth as a dangerous and threatening situation from the supernatural as well as strictly medical point of view. Possibly, too, the fact that much of this Tibetan population had been living in India for nearly forty years, and that Rozario was a South Asian woman who might be expected to have standard South Asian attitudes, also led people to present childbirth to her in ways that more closely resembled South Asian patterns. Thus, for example, while Rozario quite soon came across cases of men, usually husbands, assisting in childbirth, an almost unthinkable situation in Bangladesh, these cases were presented to her as not being typical and as taking place only because no-one else was around to assist. In addition, the Tibetan births that took place during her fieldwork occurred in local hospitals, rather than at home, and were handled by Indian medical personnel, which meant that specifically Tibetan aspects of the birth situation were perhaps relatively muted.

Yet the closer we looked, the more it seemed to us that the Tibetan situation was in fact very different from that we knew from in Bangladesh, North India and Nepal. In particular, while the Tibetans did have a concept that could be translated into English as 'pollution' (the usual Tibetan term is *drip*), it was really quite different from the 'pollution' we were familiar with in the Bangladeshi, North Indian or Nepali contexts. To understand the differences, though, we first need to look in more detail at ideas and practices relating to 'pollution' and childbirth in the North Indian, Bangladeshi and Nepali context.

Pollution concepts and practices in India, Bangladesh and Nepal

The term 'pollution' is a very familiar one in the sociology of South Asian societies, being particularly associated with Louis Dumont's classic analysis of Hindu caste society as structured around ideas of purity and pollution, *Homo Hierarchicus* (Dumont 1972). For Dumont, Hindu society is structured around the opposition between purity and pollution. These form the poles of a linear scale along which castes (*jāti* or *jāt*) can be arranged as more or less pure, with the Brahmins, the most pure, at the top end, and the untouchables, the most polluted or impure, at the bottom. The scale was associated with traditional occupations, with the Brahmin's traditional priestly duties linked to their position at the top of the scale, and work such as sweeping, cleaning and leather-working being associated with the polluted castes at the bottom of the hierarchy. It was expressed through restrictions on marriage and the sharing of food between different castes.

Dumont held that the caste hierarchy was not merely an ideological principle. It was also the basis of Hindu caste society as a social reality. While non-Hindu societies such as the Muslims of South Asia might adopt features of caste society, they could not really have a caste system, because they could not have the central disjunction between the principle of purity, represented by the Brahmins, and the principle of political rule. There has been an extensive literature criticising and extending Dumont's work. While there is probably general agreement that Dumont provides an accurate picture of a dominant mode of discourse within Hindu society, one particularly associated with the Brahmins, there is much less agreement about how widely this ideology is shared throughout Hindu society or how useful it is as a description of social reality (see e.g. Appadurai 1986; Searle-Chatterjee and Sharma 1994).

An extended treatment of this literature would be out of place here, but there are a number of points which are important for our argument:

1   While the Brahmanical discourse of purity and pollution defines an important set of values within Hindu society, this is not the only set of values present. In particular, we would agree with those authors, such as Triloki Nath Madan (1987: 48–71), Frédérique Apffel-Marglin (1985) and Veena Das (1987), who have suggested that a distinct set of values is associated with what has come to be called 'auspiciousness'. The term 'auspiciousness' is used by these authors to refer to concerns with everyday life, human and agricultural fertility and productivity, health, good fortune and success. This whole area has its own set of ritual procedures which are not generally carried out by Brahmin priests and which have little to do with Brahmanical values.

Childbirth, in particular, may be 'polluting', but it is also generally 'auspicious'.[6] The degree of penetration of Brahmanical ideology throughout Hindu society, particularly among untouchable and other low-status groups, is variable and uneven, so there is a real question about just how important Brahmanical values were, particularly to those non-Brahmin groups who had less invested in the purity principle. We will return to this question of the relationship between auspiciousness and Brahmanical values at the end of the chapter.

2   Despite Dumont's assertion that caste and Hinduism are indissolubly linked, there have been and still are strong elements of caste or caste-like practices among Muslims, Christians, Buddhists, Sikhs, Jains and other non-Hindu groups in South Asia. These groups too were divided into ranked sub-groups, with higher groups avoiding intermarriage with lower groups and behaving in other ways similar to high Hindu castes. For Muslims, these high status groups often justified their status in terms of an ideology of descent from the Prophet Muhammad, his companions or other immigrant populations from the Islamic homelands to the west.

These groups formed part of the same social field as the Hindu castes throughout much of South Asia, with villages and wider regions typically containing both Hindu and non-Hindu groups (see e.g. Rozario 1992: 96–8; Bhattacharya 1973).

3   The relationship between the 'pollution' underlying the caste hierarchy and the 'pollution' associated with childbirth and other female biological processes such as menstruation is a complex one. There was certainly an overlap between them, in that similar ceremonies were prescribed for purifying Brahmins or other high-caste males who encountered the two types of pollution. People saw them as similar at times. Mary Cameron, for example, tells of a low-caste *dai* from the blacksmith or Lohar caste in western Nepal joking with the high-caste woman whose baby she had delivered by saying, 'Now you are a Loharni' (1998: 261) – meaning that she now shared the polluted status of the low-caste *dai*. But the pollution of childbirth or menstruation is temporary, unlike that of the untouchables. Some ideas about pollution in the context of childbirth and

menstruation seem to occur in most parts of Asia, if not throughout the world, so it may be that we need to regard pollution ideas as part of a shared body of folk religious concepts as much as derivations from Brahmanical ideology. In addition, Islam and Christianity have their own ideas of pollution, and the several centuries of Muslim rule which preceded the British in the region no doubt had some effect on popular conceptions.

Despite these various qualifications, it does seem likely that Brahmanical ideas of pollution have had a very marked effect on the whole North Indian-Bangladeshi-Nepali pattern we are describing here. Muslim groups in Bangladesh, North India and southern Nepal continue to use traditional low-caste birth attendants, where these are available, and to regard them with much the same attitudes as those found among Hindus. This is in large part because they appear to have internalised the Brahmanical logic according to which pollution has to be removed by a low-caste specialist, even while not consciously subscribing to other aspects of caste ideology. Muslim doctors and nurses in Bangladesh, just like Hindu doctors and nurses in much of North India, are unwilling even to touch birthing women if they can avoid it, and low-caste and often untrained nursing aides are usually entrusted with any work which involves actual physical contact with the patients (see Blanchet 1984; Leppard 1997; Rozario 1995a).

The significance of pollution is acted out symbolically in the ritual practices surrounding childbirth, which are found among Hindus, Muslims and Christians in North India, and no doubt among other religious groups as well. These rituals involve the woman's seclusion during the birth and for a fixed period afterwards. How long the period lasts varies from place to place and between religious communities, but there always is a period of seclusion, which is associated with the danger of attack by *bhūt* and other malevolent forces while the woman is in the polluted state following childbirth.

Whatever the number of days and the degree of rigidity, all women regardless of class and religious background practise confinement and all perform certain rituals as they leave the delivery room. In the region of Bangladesh where Rozario carried out most of her fieldwork (immediately north of Dhaka city) this room is referred to as *oshouch ghor, atur ghor* or *chodi ghor. Ghor* means room, but the three terms used to specify the room are of interest. We have already referred to *oshouch*, meaning 'pollution'; *atur* means sickness and distress. *Chodi* in village dialect appears at first sight to be simply another term for pollution or impurity; Lina Fruzzetti refers to the same term, which she spells *chutti*, as being used by the Muslim villagers of Bishnupur in West Bengal (Fruzzetti 1981). Thus, Bangladeshi village women refer to the rituals that accompany the conclusion of confinement as *chodi tula* ('removal of *chodi*'). These rituals take various forms, but most households will clean and plaster the mud floor of the hut, wash bedding and personal clothes, as well as wash the birthing mother.

However, as Sanjukta Gupta has pointed out,[7] the word has an interesting and significant derivation, since *chodi* or *chutti* in fact derives from the word for 'sixth' – *ṣaṣṭhī* in Sanskrit – which is also the name of the goddess Ṣaṣṭhī who presides over childbirth. Ṣaṣṭhī's rituals, usually called *chaṭhī* in Hindi, form an integral part of the removal of pollution after childbirth for many Hindu groups in North India. These rituals may, but are not necessarily, performed on the sixth day after the birth.

In 1994, when we did some fieldwork with Maithili families near Janakpur in southern Nepal, Rozario was able to attend a Ṣaṣṭhī ritual which marked the end of the pollution period for a Hindu Maithili family of Kayasth caste. This ritual, known as *chhatiyar*, involved the mother making an offering to an image of the goddess Chhati, another version of Ṣaṣṭhī's name, here made out of cow dung (Samuel 1997: 2–4, Figures 1 and 2). This was followed the next day by further purificatory rituals, including the washerwoman coming to wash the bedclothes, and the *dai* coming to do other cleaning of the confinement room.

Ṣaṣṭhī rituals following childbirth have been quite widely reported (Freed and Freed 1980: 373). Ṣaṣṭhī appears to have been a figure of considerable importance in rural Bengal in the early nineteenth century, with a number of village rituals in her honour each year apart from the offerings made after the birth of a child.[8] In parts of North India Ṣaṣṭhī is replaced by a figure called Bemātā (Freed and Freed 1980: 372–9), Baimātā (Chawla 1994) or Bahamātā (Minturn and Hitchcock 1966) who in Hindu mythology was the midwife of the deity Krishna.[9] Bemātā may also be worshipped in the form of a cow-dung image (Minturn and Hitchcock 1966: 103). Both Ṣaṣṭhī and Bemātā may be represented by a painting rather than a solid image (e.g. Figure 9.1; see also Grierson 1885: 390, for Maithili people in Bihar; Freed and Freed 1980: 372–3), and again cow dung seems to be a standard constituent.[10]

Ṣaṣṭhī, like Bemātā has some Sanskritic sanction, figuring as the wife of the war-god Kārttikeya or Skanda, and being represented alongside him in some Gupta-period sculptures, but neither Ṣaṣṭhī nor Bemātā in this village context are really Brahmanical deities. Ṣaṣṭhī in particular seems to have close affinities to the ambivalent goddesses such as Śītalā and Manasā who are associated with infectious illness, snakebite and other misfortunes, but who are also invoked for protection against these misfortunes.[11] These goddesses are quite important in the Hindu villages of North India and there is evidence of them from at least the sixth to seventh centuries BCE onwards.[12] The ambivalence surrounding these deities is another indication of the complex relationship between folk religion and Brahmanical values.

Cow dung is strongly associated with rituals and practices to do with 'auspiciousness' and good fortune, and its use here for the images and drawings of Ṣaṣṭhī and Bemātā is not surprising. It is particularly linked with Lakṣmī, the most important goddess associated with the whole field of 'auspiciousness'

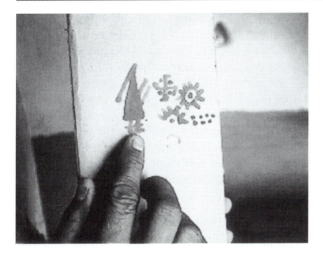

Figure 9.1 Bemātā image reproduced from drawing on the leg of a *charpoy*. From Bikaner District, Rajasthan (photo by Sameera Jain)

and 'success'. Lakṣmī's cult certainly goes back to the second or third centuries BCE,[13] and, while she has again been incorporated into the Brahmanical pantheon as the wife of the major deity Viṣṇu, she too has a complex relationship to Brahmanical values and in some respects stands quite separate from them (Samuel 1997: 9–12).

While the Bengali Muslim villagers Rozario knew in Bangladesh did not appear to know of the connection between *chodi* and the goddess Ṣaṣṭhī, the West Bengali Muslims with whom Fruzzetti worked did, perhaps because they were a minority within a Hindu population. While they did not actually worship Ṣaṣṭhī directly, they referred to the day of the purificatory ritual as Ṣaṣṭhīr Din, the Day of Ṣaṣṭhī. On this occasion a Koranic verse dedicated to Ṣaṣṭhī and known as the *Shasthir fatiha* is recited (Fruzzetti 1981: 100–1).

Closely associated with the Ṣaṣṭhī/Bemātā rituals is the idea that a deity or spirit comes to write down the child's future that night. The Bangladeshi Muslims with whom Rozario worked referred to this night as *haturar rat,* and believed that spirits called *feresta* ('angels') would come and write the child's *bhāggho* (future or luck) on its forehead. These days many families among both Muslims and Christians keep a pen and an exercise book near the baby or touch the baby's forehead with these items, and they also keep a lamp burning all night. This is so that the baby will obtain a good education and have a good future. Rozario was told that in the olden days people would touch a baby boy's forehead with a plough on this night as a way of enhancing the chances of the baby boy becoming a good worker in the field. Fruzzetti describes the Bishnupur Muslims as placing a bamboo pen, ink and paper or leaf in the corner of the room, keeping an oil lamp burning and waiting 'in a semi-purified state' for the coming of Bidata Purush (Bidhātā Puruṣa, God) to write down the child's fate. Bidata Purush 'is the giver of life whereas Ṣaṣṭhī (referred to as his consort) is the protectress of children's life' (Fruzzetti 1981: 101). Bidata is also frequently referred to in accounts of childbirth among Bengali Hindus (e.g. Day 1906: 37–8; Dimock 1963).

Other purificatory rituals may follow at various times after the birth,[14] and Muslim women, in accordance with Islamic law, are not regarded as fully purified until forty days after the birth, at which time they may say their prayers (*namaj*) and undertake religious fasts. Enough has perhaps been said to indicate the close connection between pollution, its cleansing and the rituals for protection and welfare of child and mother.

Pollution concepts and practices among Tibetans

'Pollution' is an issue among Tibetans as well, but by North Indian or Bangladeshi standards, Tibetan notions of birth pollution and the associated rules appear relatively mild. The term used to refer to childbirth pollution is *kyedrip* [skye grib]. *Kye* means birth, whereas *drip* [grib] is a generic term, usually translated as 'pollution', 'defilement' or 'contamination', and used to refer to numerous other conditions or situations. Its most basic meaning is perhaps 'shadow'.

> *Drib* is the prime cause of misfortune in everyday life, and has to be remedied by appropriate ritual action to the gods. In addition, *drib* makes the individual vulnerable to attack by malevolent spirits of various kinds. Some degree of *drib* is almost unavoidable in everyday life and the attacks of offended deities and of malevolent spirits have to be ritually combatted on a regular basis.
>
> (Samuel 1993: 161)[15]

Pilgrimage to sacred Buddhist sites is one of the prime means of cleansing *drip* in general. There are long discussions of *drip* in Christine Daniels' doctoral thesis on the pilgrimage site of Bodhnath (Boudha) in Nepal (Daniels 1994: 27–42) and in Toni Huber's book on the major mountain pilgrimage site of Tsari in Southeast Tibet (Huber 1999: 16–18). In an Appendix to her doctoral thesis, Daniels lists twenty-two named varieties of *drip*, of which *kyedrip* is the seventh (Daniels 1994: 286–90). Her discussion, however, is mainly from the point of view of the risk the birthing woman and child pose to others:

> The custom of abstaining for at least one week from visiting a place of childbirth was in decline in Boudha. However, certain persons were warned, for example, those susceptible to birth pollution or likely to be particularly inconvenienced by illness, such as students about to take

exams or women with much work awaiting them in the household. To visit in order to help in the household was a virtuous act but: 'They say you shouldn't handle the baby straight after the birth because it's dirty with childbirth and should be taken only by those helping with the birth. But most people don't bother to purify themselves afterwards. The mother and baby are given *trü* [holy or consecrated water, a standard purifying substance] and that's enough.'

(Daniels 1994: 287)[16]

Rozario, who had not previously worked with Tibetans, first encountered the term *drip* on the second day of her fieldwork in the Tibetan refugee community of Dalhousie in Northern India. She was talking to Jigme, a Tibetan woman who was the Community Health Worker and ran a small dispensary in the main refugee settlement, about whether birth or birthing substances were perceived as a problem. Jigme commented that birth and its associated substances were 'dirty' (Tibetan *tsokpa*) and that they cause sickness, including conjunctivitis and *drip*. During our fieldwork in Dalhousie, the term *drip* came up regularly when people were discussing their various health problems, not necessarily only to do with birth.

Rozario asked our interpreter Jampa, a trained nurse and midwife who was employed at the school clinic, about *drip* associated with birth and birthing substance. Jampa explained that those who attend and handle birth are affected by *drip*. As an example, she said that her grandfather had delivered all the babies of one of his own daughters (Jampa's aunt), as well as cleaning up afterwards. When he has burning or irritation in his eyes even today, many years later, he says that this is *drip*, because he handled all those deliveries. Similarly Tsamcho, a middle-aged woman who was one of our main informants, told Rozario that her husband, who had done all the cleaning after her deliveries, had also been subjected to *drip*. He had problems with his eyes, and felt shivery and tired in the evenings. To counter these problems, he used holy water blessed by the Rinpoch'e, the main Tibetan lama in the community, to sprinkle over his head, shoulders and wash his face, and also drank some of it. He also took *jinden*, consecrated pills and other substances obtained from lamas which are used generally for purificatory and protective purposes.

In order to avoid health problems caused by *drip*, Rozario was told that people should not enter the delivery room for three days if it is a boy, or four days if it is a girl. On the third or fourth day, whichever is applicable, the birthing woman's family will do various purification rituals, after which they can receive visitors.

In fact, protective and purificatory rituals begin immediately after the birth. In the case of Lendzom, a woman from the settlement who gave birth at the District Hospital at Chamba, some three hours by bus from Dalhousie, during our stay in Dalhousie, the rituals began when her husband Samdup's

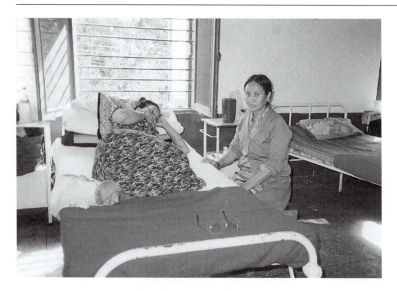

Figure 9.2 Lendzom and Samdrup's mother in Maternity Ward, Chamba
Hospital (photo by Santi Rozario)

mother was allowed into the delivery ward immediately after the delivery.
Samdup's mother used Tibetan incense (*pö*, referred to in Hindi as *dhūp*) in
which she also burned a little cloth from a lama.[17] Its smoke was spread
around the newborn baby, around its mother, around an Indian woman who
had given birth at the same time, around the Indian woman's baby, and
around the two nurses who delivered the babies. After Lendzom was moved
back to her own bed (Figure 9.2), Samdup's mother repeated the ritual in
Lendzom's ward, taking the *dhūp* to all the women in the ward.

Here the incense was being used not only as a purifying agent, but also to
protect the newborn and its mother from *nopa*, a condition caused by the
envy of other people. *Nopa* is similar to the North Indian concept of *nazar*,
often translated as the 'evil eye'. In this particular case, two of the other
women in the ward had been in the hospital for a considerably longer period
than Lendzom, but neither had yet given birth, and it is possible that
Samdup's mother thought they might be envious of Lendzom and her baby,
though at least one of the Indian women had in fact asked Samdup's
mother if she had any of the lama's cloth or incense left over so that she
could use it herself.

Before they left the hospital on the second day after the birth Samdup's
family did a *sang* ritual, an offering of incense and prayers to the deities.[18] As
soon as they arrived home at Dalhousie they all sprinkled consecrated water
on their eyes and faces and all over their bodies in order to rid themselves of
all impurities (Hindi *gandā*) from the hospital. The water had been brought

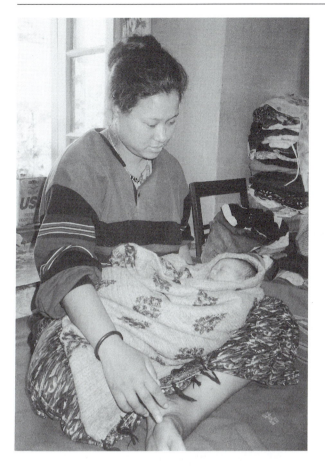

Figure 9.3 Lendzom with baby (photo by Santi Rozario)

from Dharamsala, the seat of the Tibetan refugee administration and location of several important monasteries. They had not taken it to the hospital
because it would itself have become *gandā* (impure).

Rozario went to see Lendzom and the baby that afternoon, and found that
except for one of Samdup's aunts no other members of his family or any
friends were to visit them until after the third day of the delivery. She was told
that this precaution was taken to avoid people getting *drip* by being exposed
to the mother and the baby and their clothes before the purification ritual was
carried out. The purification ritual involved washing all the clothes and cleaning the household in general as well as using *pö* mixed with other empowered
substances and sprinkling holy water everywhere in the house. Apparently in
the larger Tibetan settlements, for example those in South India, most people
also arrange for a puja to be conducted by a lama at this time.

On the whole, beside the husband, mother-in-law, mother or whoever else may be assisting at birth, such as a married sister or perhaps a neighbour, other people avoid coming in contact with the delivery room. In practice, because most people have only one or two rooms per family, the children of the birthing family cannot avoid going near the delivery area even during the first three or four days. Whoever comes in contact with the birthing mother, the baby and the birthing substance, for example through washing their clothes, performs purification rituals using *pö* and holy water.

Despite the purification rituals carried out after they have completed the 'dirty' work, the Tibetans we spoke to told us that the persons who help during and after delivery are routinely subjected to *drip*. The usual symptoms of *drip* associated with birth are burning or irritation of eyes, tiredness and general body ache. Most people are able to deal with these problems by doing more purification rituals. However, *drip* can lead to serious problems, in particular blindness.

Often the main person who does all the work in relation to the delivery is the husband, as a mother or mother-in-law may not be around to help. That husbands clean up the mess after the delivery, and indeed often deliver babies themselves when nobody else is around, came up many times in talking to other young and middle-aged and older women. They all said that it is usually the husbands who clean up. A number of women said to Rozario that all their babies were delivered by their husbands, explaining that this was either because there was no one else around, or (as Jampa put it) because 'a husband is the closest person to the birthing woman'. This was a significant contrast to the North Indian and Bangladeshi situation where men will stay away from the birthing scene almost at any cost for as long as possible. Moreover, with the Tibetans, even when a non-relative assists, she is usually a neighbour. There is no equivalent to the low-status *dai* (traditional birth attendant) of North India and Bangladesh.

The Dalhousie Tibetans told Rozario that the husband's involvement at birth or after birth was contrary to Tibetan tradition. Samdup (Figure 9.4) commented that it was not good for men to go in to the delivery room. His mother did not want him to go near the delivery, but he said, 'I do not follow this. But your mother keeps telling you, then you begin to take some of these seriously . . . My uncle helped his wife with the delivery. But if you ask him he will not admit it.' Samdup said his father went inside the delivery room to clean up after most of the deliveries. He said when there are four or five women present, then husbands do not go in during delivery. It was particularly important for the men to avoid coming in contact with the placenta. Samdup also commented that 'women are always in *drip*', to which his uncle added 'women are always handling *gandā* (dirty) things anyway' as if to imply going into the delivery room does not affect women in the same way as men.[19]

The husband of the second woman whose birth Rozario was able to follow up also told her that men were not supposed to go in the delivery room, but

Figure 9.4 Samdrup with baby (photo by Santi Rozario)

that when where is no-one else, they have to go in. His wife (speaking in English) said 'my mother is not here, sister is not here.' Then she added, 'if baby is dying in tummy, or mother is in trouble, we ignore *drip*.' They both said that men, not only husbands but also brothers and fathers, go in during delivery quite often.

Jampa, the school nurse who was also our interpreter, said that pregnant women should not go near dead people as this will cause *drip* to the unborn baby. She added that indeed dead bodies and graveyards are avoided by all women. She mentioned how her mother was opposed to her training to be a nurse/midwife as this would mean that she would have to handle dead bodies, pus, blood and birthing substance, all of which may cause *drip*. That dead bodies do not only pose a problem for women but also for men became clear in the case of one man who linked a chronic arthritic problem in his knees to an incident that took place some ten years earlier, when he and a friend had seen a dead body floating in a lake. He had gone very close to the body as he felt that he 'needed to do something for it'. This same man's wife had been subjected to *drip* from looking after small children and cleaning after them, all 'dirty' work, at a nursery many years ago. When asked about redness in her eyes, she put it down to *drip* resulting from her work with small children. Thus, *drip* is a widespread concept going well beyond just explaining contamination from coming in contact with birth.

Hildegard Diemberger (1993) and Christian Schicklgruber (1992), who worked together in the 1980s in the Tibetan community of Khumbo in Northeast Nepal, have both written at some length on *drip*, and Diemberger has also provided one of the few substantial discussions of childbirth for Tibetan society. Khumbo was not a refugee community, but a fairly remote settlement in an area of Northeastern Nepal which had long been ethnically Tibetan, so their account can perhaps be taken as giving a more 'traditional' picture than our Dalhousie fieldwork.

Diemberger says of *drip* (*dip*, in her spelling) that it

> originally means 'shadow', and, in an extended sense, everything which darkens or interrupts a relationship – man and gods, man and man, man with himself. In a derived sense, it is applied to everything which lies beyond or is against the social order . . . Each event or behaviour considered to be *dip* evokes shame, *ngotsha* . . . and if not properly dealt with means a loss of *uphang* [prestige] and, in the most serious cases, social marginalization.
>
> (Diemberger 1993: 105–6)

Diemberger says of birth among the Khumbo Tibetans:

> Birth takes place outside the house lest the deities dwelling there would be defiled . . . As a consequence, they would withdraw their protection and this would invite hail and diseases. Birth usually takes place in the pasturage huts . . . The father is usually the one who helps at birth . . . Once the baby is born onto a clean cloth laid in front of the mother, he cuts the umbilical cord . . . with a knife sterilized in fire. He buries the placenta . . . in the forest. Then he offers a special *chang* (*menchang* [sman-chang]),[20] prepared for the occasion in advance, to the mother and prepares a chicken soup in order to help her produce milk.
>
> For three days the whole family is in a condition of defilement (*dip*) and is cut off from every social contact. The people of the village whisper the news of the event to each other and avoid going to the '*min ma taba* [min[g] ma btags-pa]', 'the not name-bound'. The mother especially cannot share the cup with anybody, nor can she serve food. She is outside the rules of commensality.
>
> The baby is not yet born socially. If it dies at this point, no burial is performed; it is simply buried in the forest in a hole filled with flowers.

The baby is still part of the mother earth and returns whence it came. After three days (or at any propitious day after that), the baby is brought to the house and a name-giving ceremony eliminates the *dip*.

With the *mindachang* [min[g]-gdag-chang] 'the name-binding *chang*', mother, child and family return to the community. The name marks the entrance of the new human being into society. Since natural birth is *dip* and lies outside the symbolic border of society, there has to be a ceremony to remove the baby, its parents and the whole family from this state. It is a social birth in which the child is presented to the clan and mountain deities as their child and as the continuation of their 'human root' (*mi tsa* [mi-rtsa]).

(Diemberger 1993: 115–16)

We notice that while birth for North Indian and Bangladeshi villagers takes place within the household, if sometimes in a special hut outside the main building, birth in Khumbo takes place outside the household, in the pasturage huts, physically and symbolically in the 'wild', and the family make a kind of temporary exit from human society while the birth takes place. During this period they are in a state of *dip*.

Dip thus represents a state outside the social order guaranteed by the protective deities of household, clan and mountain. Schicklgruber, referring to the same community, notes that

[a]t his birth the newborn child does not yet bear a clan name. He or she is still outside of society in a state of *dip*. In the name giving ceremony the newborn child is 'introduced' to the clan deities in a speech and they are asked for protection.

(Schicklgruber 1992: 729)

Diemberger suggests that for the Khumbo Tibetans,

life moves between shadow on the one hand and the order granted by household, clan and mountain deities on the other. A Khumbo enters this order at the name-giving ceremony and comes into *dip* whenever he or she has contact with death, birth or conflicts, with moral sins (in a Buddhist perspective) and with any *dip*-carrying thing or person.

(Diemberger 1993: 106)

We notice that, among the Khumbo Tibetans, the husband is not only *allowed* to be present, he is the most usual person to help. In fact, despite the ambivalence shown by our Dalhousie informants, it seems clear that this was frequently the case with them too, particularly in the past. Here there is a strong contrast with North Indian and Bangladeshi village childbirth, where husbands do not go anywhere near delivery huts, and in fact often do not even see the baby until after the purification ritual. The cutting of the umbilical cord, which among the Khumbo Tibetans is performed by the husband, is, as we saw earlier, perceived by Indians and Bangladeshis to be so dangerous that it is often left to the birthing mother herself, to avoid the risk of pollution to others. It would be inconceivable for the father to be involved.

In part, this goes along with the much greater emphasis on male–female difference among North Indians or Bangladeshis in comparison with Tibetans. While in ordinary life Tibetan men and women have different spheres of responsibility within the household, there are very few tasks that cannot be performed by either should the need arise. The concept of *pardā* or seclusion of women, which is central in Bangladeshi society and important in many parts of North India and Nepal, is totally absent from Tibetan society, where women are very much part of the public sphere. However, there is perhaps more to the contrast than this, and we will return to this point later.

It is hardly surprising that Tibetan childbirth practices in Dalhousie, a North Indian Tibetan refugee settlement, differed in many respects from the picture drawn by Diemberger and Schicklgruber. Most of the older members of the community had been refugees in India for up to thirty-five years, and the majority of the community had been born in India or had come in early childhood.[21] They had been extensively exposed to Western biomedicine (locally known as *gyagar men*, 'Indian medicine'), both through local public hospitals and private clinics and through the Tibetan refugee administration's own health-care system (Samuel 1999, 2001). Unlike many of the larger settlements, such as that at Bir, the Dalhousie settlement did not have a Tibetan health clinic with a biomedically trained midwife, and local medical facilities were limited in some respects. The norm, however, was for births to take place in clinics or hospital.

However, while the Dalhousie Tibetans gave birth in hospital, not in the pasturage huts, there is some structural similarity, since in both cases the birthing family go completely outside their household, are separated from their ordinary social context, and are in a state of *drip* until the purificatory ceremonies after their return. Possibly, the willingness of Dalhousie Tibetans to use hospital facilities is linked in part to this congruence with established Tibetan cultural patterns.

In addition, as we have seen, ideas of *drip* were still very much alive among the Dalhousie community. In fact, Rozario has suggested elsewhere that the marginal position of the Tibetan refugees in India made them feel, if anything, more vulnerable to attacks of *drip* (Rozario 1996). *Drip*, in other words, became an idiom for talking about their relationship to a social, cultural and political environment which was in many ways alien and outside their control. Much of this *drip*, of course, was not related with childbirth, but with encounters with risky situations such as the common winter occupation of sweater-selling on the streets of Indian cities, exposed to the dirt, the fumes of passing traffic and to attacks by local police and ruffians (Rozario 1996). *Drip* was still very much a feature of concerns about childbirth, however, as we have seen.

Two myths and a conclusion

In the final section of this chapter, we want to try to sketch the wider complex of ideas within which the North Indian-Bangladeshi and Tibetan ideas about childbirth are embedded. We hope that this will help show the ways in which the 'pollution' ideas in the two situations are both alike, and different.

As a way to approach this comparison, we will consider two myths about the origin of pollution, one Tibetan, the other Indian. The Tibetan myth comes from the Khumbo Tibetans of Northeastern Nepal and is told by Christian Schicklgruber:

> In the beginning of time there lived a dog-son and dog-mother. The dog did not say mother and did not say sister [in other words, it did not know the proper rules of kin relationships]. In this state the dog-son went to the dog-mother and made love to her. The human-mother who saw this said the dog commits 'dip'. The human-son, too, saw the dog going to his mother to copulate with her. He, too, said the dog commits 'dip' with his mother. Whereupon he went to his mother too, and demanded to do the same. At that his mother said: 'I see in you the love of defilement, you sprang from me and now you want to repenetrate where you have come from'. Then she pronounced this curse: 'At birth the earth, the stones and the beams of the house will break for you. At your death the earth, the stones and the beams of the house will break for you. At birth [Sashi Ama, the Earth Goddess] will burst open in the very place that you will return to later, your face wrapped in a shroud.' Then, before the son made love with his mother, she demanded that he shrouds [sic] his face with a white cloth. Then he penetrated her. Since that day, at a human's birth from his mother's womb the earth bursts open in the very place that he will return to after his death, wrapped in a white shroud. This birth and death are defilement, birth- and death-'dip' . . . are the same, birth-, death- and conflict-'dip' are the same, there is no 'dip' but for these three.
>
> (Schicklgruber 1992: 723–3)

Schicklgruber, who analyses this myth at some length (Schicklgruber 1992: 724–34), and Diemberger, who refers to it in the article on kinship and gender relations among the Khumbo from which we quoted above (1993: 105) both argue that this myth associates *drip* with what lies outside the social world of order, name and regulation – with incest, namelessness, birth, death and conflict. *Drip* is unavoidable in human life (Schicklgruber 1992: 734), yet it is a shadow or affliction from outside the social world. Consequently, it makes sense that Tibetans have as little as possible to do with *drip* and that, when *drip* is unavoidable, as with birth, they involve as few people as possible, and remove the whole situation outside the realm of Tibetan human and divine order, into the wild where such things belong.

The Indian myth to which we now turn is a literary rather than a folk myth, but it also deals with the origins of pollution, and it contrasts in interesting ways to the Khumbo Tibetan story. This is the myth of the killing of a Brahmin by Indra, chief of the Vedic gods, and Indra's subsequent purification. This story is told in many versions in early Brahmanical texts, including the *Taittirīyasaṃhitā, Mahābhārata, Rāmāyaṇa* and *Skanda Purāṇa*. This quote is from Julia Leslie, who begins with one of the earliest versions, that of the *Taittirīyasaṃhitā*:

> When the universe is threatened by [the demon] Viśvarūpa, Indra destroys him. But Viśvarūpa is a brahmin and Indra is condemned as a brahmin-killer. To escape the consequences of this particularly dreadful crime, Indra persuades the earth, the trees and women to assume one-third of his guilt each. In return, he grants each a wish: the earth, when dug, will heal within a year; trees, when cut, will grow again; and women, unlike all other creatures, will enjoy sexual intercourse at any time, even in advanced pregnancy. In several variations on this theme in other texts, Indra distributes his brahminicide in four parts: among rivers, mountains, earth and women in one text (Mbh. 5.10.13); among fire, trees, cows and women in another (Mbh. 12.329.28–41); among trees, earth, water and women in a third (*Bhāgavatapurāṇa* 6.9.6–10). In all versions, however, one recipient is constant: women. In some texts, Indra's sin causes the recipients to become impure; in others, the recipients are already impure . . . In this somewhat confused context, the issue of which came first – the impurity of women or the assumption of Indra's guilt – is blurred.
>
> Either way, the mark of Indra's guilt has two crucial implications: a cyclical fertility and a recurrent power to pollute. In the case of the earth, Indra's guilt takes the form of fissures in the ground during the dry season, the sign of an infertile (and hence inauspicious) land prior to the release of the monsoon rain. During this time, the earth should not be 'ploughed', an obvious metaphor for sexual intercourse[22] . . . In the case of rivers, the swirling mud-red waters of the rainy season are described in terms of a symbolic menstruation: they are *rajasvalāḥ*, 'full of dirt' or 'full of passion', a word also applied (in both senses) to menstruating women. Such waters should not be entered for fear of pollution: a ruling that applies equally to muddy monsoon rivers and menstruating women.
>
> In women, Indra's guilt takes the form of menstrual blood. Menstruation is thus the sign of a woman's participation in brahmin-murder. It marks her innate impurity, her cyclical fecundity, her

uncontrollable sexuality, and, by extension, the inescapable wickedness of her female nature.

(Leslie 1996: 90–1)

While childbirth pollution is not mentioned directly here, it is pretty clear that it belongs within the same overall constellation of ideas, in which fertility and pollution are the positive and negative poles of woman's nature, as of the earth herself.

Here we can see a clear contrast with the Tibetan story. For Hindu India (and the same is essentially true for Muslim India and Bangladesh as well), impurity is not something at the edge of society, outside the social order, but something which is right at its centre, in the intrinsic identity of women, their polluted and fertile nature, without which human life could not continue. There is no point in trying to banish this situation to the wild country outside, since pollution and impurity are essential to the ongoing processes of human life. Instead they have to be dealt with, as in the wider contexts of Hindu and South Asian social life, by a complex series of rituals and ritual practitioners who transfer, cleanse and remove impurity so that human beings, especially high-caste men, can be as pure as possible as much as possible of the time.

This is a Brahmanical story, and the sin of Indra, a Vedic god who has much more to do with success and getting things done than with purity and holiness, was the killing of a Brahmin. This is not accidental, because the essential corollary to the impurity of women, untouchables, childbirth and traditional female birth attendants is the purity and high status of Brahmins. As Dumont rightly noted, the logic of Brahmanical thought demands that the purity of Brahmins has to be matched by the impurity and low status of the untouchables. The Brahmins (and by extension, other high castes whose high status is supported by the Brahmanical system) are thus the beneficiaries of the downgrading of women and of the natural world within the system and their essential linkage with impurity.

Consequently 'pollution' in the Indian context – including the pollution associated with childbirth – is integrally tied in with the social and gender hierarchy. Pollution is part of how society works, it marks the superiority of men to women and of high castes to low castes, and the low-caste birth attendant removing the pollution of the high-caste mother is a central feature. The same system of ideas also involves the downgrading of the rituals of everyday life, the rituals of 'auspiciousness', in comparison to the Brahmanical rituals, which are essentially to do with the maintenance of status and the superiority of the high castes (Samuel 1997).

By contrast, the pollution associated with childbirth in Tibet does not entail or reinforce the social and gender hierarchies in the way that the pollution rules of Indian childbirth do. Ideally, as few people as possible should be exposed to *drip*, but if someone apart from the birthing woman must be, then the husband, who is the closest person to her, is the obvious choice.

But what about the Muslims of Bangladesh and North India? We suggest that there has been a kind of tacit conflation here of two vocabularies of purity. Islam took over from its Judaeo-Christian background a rather similar complex of ideas, in which menstruation is linked to women's innate impurity, which is of course itself related in the Judaeo-Christian tradition to the story of Eve's original sin. For Indian Muslims, purity is represented by the mosque, the Quran and the *hadith*, with their own associated rituals of washing and the removal of impurity, and these could easily provide an alternative logic to support the intrinsic impurity of women. Yet the inner logic of Islam does not in fact involve such a radical ambivalence towards female fertility, and elsewhere in the Islamic world, for example in Muslim Malaysia, Islam appears to have been able to coexist with a much more positive attitude towards women, childbirth, birth attendants and the whole process of human procreation (e.g. Laderman 1983).

To close, it may be worth thinking about the consequences of these different sets of pollution ideas for how childbirth takes place. As we have seen, it has been relatively easy for Tibetans to adopt hospital births and biomedical approaches to childbirth, in part, perhaps, for the somewhat ironic reason that childbirth was already something 'outside' the normal processes of social life. Leaving the community to give birth in the hospital in fact mirrors traditional practices of giving birth away from the village quite well. In addition, childbirth seems to have received little cultural elaboration in Tibetan societies in the past. There were no traditional birth attendants or midwives, at any rate for non-elite families, and not much in the way of ritual surrounding childbirth, so hospital birth does not conflict with any particular demands for how birth should be handled.

For rural families in North India and Bangladesh, the practices and rituals surrounding childbirth were much more significant and culturally elaborated, and the move to biomedical approaches has been much more limited. This is not because modernity and biomedicine as such are unwelcome. The popularity of oxytocin injections to speed up childbirth is enough to show that this is not the case. Nor is hospital or clinic birth as such necessarily rejected. In the urban context, women from middle-class families today routinely give birth in private clinics (e.g. Donner 2001 for Calcutta). For poorer rural families, however, private clinics are unaffordable, and the conditions in public hospitals combine with the complex of ideas regarding childbirth, pollution, and shame combine to make hospital birth more or less unavailable (e.g. Rozario 1995a, 1998). Consequently, women are taken to these hospitals as a last resort, when there are serious complications that the *dai* cannot handle.

Given the conditions in many of these hospitals, a properly managed home birth, with appropriate biomedical backup, would probably be a better option for most village families. However, whether or not one takes the biomedical critique of *dais* at face value, it is clear that *dais* vary very considerably in their level of expertise, and that the low status of the job prevents many younger and better-educated women from taking it on. In addition, the *dai* often has little authority in the birthing situation in relation to family members, so she cannot make effective use of the knowledge she has.

Thus, the potentiality for effective midwifery care in the home situation is limited by the low social status of traditional birth attendants, itself a product of the specific form of North Indian and Bangladeshi pollution concerns. Where affordable midwifery services have been made available in a culturally acceptable form at the local level, rural families have been quite willing to use them, as Rozario has pointed out elsewhere in relation to the Catholic mission clinics in Bangladesh (Rozario 1995a). However, the provision of rural mother-and-child care has in practice, family planning aside, received relatively low priority in recent years in both India and Bangladesh. Rural families continue to be caught between the problems of traditional birthing and the lack of any real alternative.

Notes

1 This chapter was first delivered as a seminar paper to the Centre for Cross-cultural Research on Women, Oxford, in June 1999. A revised version was presented to the Department of Sociology and Anthropology, University of Newcastle, NSW in October 1999. We would like to thank members of both audiences, and in particular Sanjukta Gupta and Andrew Lattas, for their helpful comments.
2 As discussed in Chapter 1 of this volume, the situation in southern India and Sri Lanka is somewhat different, and it should not be assumed that our account applies to these areas. In particular, while Brahmanical pollution concepts are evidently present in southern India, they may in practice have been less thoroughly internalised by the population as a whole.
3 See for example the work of Patricia and Roger Jeffery and Andrew Lyon (Jeffery, Jeffery and Lyon 1989, and Chapter 4 this volume), Maya Unnithan (1999a, 1999b, and Chapter 5 this volume) and Janet Chawla (1994 and Chapter 7 this volume) for India, Thérèse Blanchet (Blanchet 1984) and Margaret Leppard (Leppard 1997) for Bangladesh, and Mary Cameron (Cameron 1998) for Western Nepal.
4 Freed and Freed (1980) report that in the village they studied, just outside Delhi, upper-caste Hindu women did cut the cord for women giving birth in their own families. As they note, this is quite unusual.
5 Maiden and Farwell (1997) and Pinto (1999) both discuss Tibetan birth practices, but their accounts, deriving from refugee sources, are overgeneralised and appear to conflate normative and textual concepts with actual practice. Norberg-Hodge and Russell's account of birth and child rearing in Zanskar (Ladakh, Western Tibet), though containing useful material on childrearing, relies entirely on textual sources for childbirth (1994: 521). Kirat (1980) gives a sketchy and not entirely consistent account of childbirth among Rolwaling Sherpas (another culturally Tibetan group in Northern Nepal), while Sagaster gives a brief description of childbirth among the Muslim Tibetans of Baltistan (Sagaster 1989: 36–40). A recent Ph.D. thesis by a student at the University of Newcastle, Australia, discusses childbirth in another North Indian refugee settlement (Monro, 1999). The work of Hildegard Diemberger (1993) is discussed in the text below.

6 As Madan has pointed out, there are circumstances in which childbirth can be 'inauspicious', for example when it occurs at an inappropriate time in astrological terms (1987: 55).

7 Personal communication, Oxford, May 1999.

8 William Ward 1863: 110–12; the same passage occurred in the first edition, published in Bengal in 1812–15. The principal festival was in the month of Jyaistha. See also Lál Behári Day's *Bengal Peasant Life* (Day 1906, first published 1872), though Day's account is so similar as to suggest some borrowing from Ward.

9 Freed and Freed suggest that Ṣaṣṭhī, who is associated with Śiva through her husband Skanda, son of Śiva, is found in areas where the worship of Śiva and related deities dominates, as in Bengal. In areas where Krishna worship is more important, she is replaced by Bemātā (1998: 122–3).

10 Figure 9.1, p. 189.

11 For Manasā see e.g. Sen 1953, Dimock 1963; for Śītalā see Auboyer and de Mallmann 1950; Dimock 1961, 1986. Freed and Freed (1998: 122–36) have an extensive discussion of the festival of Śītalā and of the seven sister goddesses, of whom she is one, associated with infectious diseases in Shanti Nagar. In relation to Ṣaṣṭhī, they note that '[t]etanus and puerperal fever, both diseases related to childbirth and common in India, occur during the first six days after birth and are blamed on the will of [Ṣaṣṭhī]' (1998: 123). In Shanti Nagar, where Ṣaṣṭhī has been replaced by the benevolent figure of Bemātā, Śītalā has a significant role in relation to causing and preventing illness in small children (1998: 122–3).

12 As with the cult of Hāritī, who is reported by Xuanzang in the seventh century and whose iconographic representations are found from a considerably earlier period again (see Chapter 1). On Ṣaṣṭhī see also Gadon 1997. Fruzzetti cites Ahmad: 'The *Chhatti*, or the celebration of the sixth day after the birth of the child, when the mother takes the bath of purification, actually represents deliverance from the dread of a Hindu godling, *Chhatti*, who personifies the septicaemia which often follows childbirth in unhygienic conditions' (Ahmad 1969: 47, in Fruzzetti 1981: 101). The *Agni Purana* gives a list of female demons attacking children at various times after birth; it seems that Ṣaṣṭhī is listed as a demon attacking on the sixth day in at least one version (Agnipurāṇa 1967, vol. 2 p. 1105ff), although in another edition her place is taken by Phaṭkārī (Agnipurāṇa 1984–7, vol. 3 pp. 820ff).

13 Note the Gajalakṣmī carvings on the second century BCE stupas at Bharhut and Sanchi.

14 See Khare, referring to a village in Lucknow in Uttar Pradesh, for another example of rituals after the *chatti* on the sixth day (1976: 162–4).

15 Toni Huber likewise sees *drib* 'as a form of both physical and social pollution that is associated with various substances and proscribed practices and relations, as well as with deities inhabiting both the body and the external world' (Huber 1999: 16).

16 The quotation at the end comes from a 21-year old woman yak herder from Chamdo in East Tibet.

17 Tibetans often burn fragments of cloth from the clothes of lamas, especially deceased lamas with whom they have had a personal connection, at times of particular danger or seriousness, as a way of calling upon the lama's power.

18 *Sang* is primarily directed towards local deities, asking for their protection and positive influences, although the *sang* texts now used generally also include reference to Buddhist Tantric deities. See e.g. Samuel 1993: 183.

19 This same uncle of Samdup said: 'It is good for a husband to be by his wife's side during birth.' On another occasion, however, he said that men usually go in after

delivery, but because they only have one room in Dalhousie they do not follow these rules.

20 *Chang* is beer, usually brewed from barley or rice. *Men* = 'medicine', so this *chang* is meant to be medicinal. *Chang* also forms a part of virtually all Tibetan folk ritual. Alternative spellings in square brackets are Wylie transcriptions.

21 Dalhousie was one of the first refugee settlements, though many of the original settlers had moved on elsewhere. Further settlement had been discouraged by the Indian authorities, in part apparently because of its sensitive position close to the Pakistani border, so a high proportion of residents had been there since the first years of exile.

22 This recalls the idea, widespread in Bengal, Orissa and Assam, of an annual festival celebrating the Goddess's menstruation, during which the earth may not be ploughed (Samanta 1992; Apffel-Marglin 1994). Frédérique Apffel-Marglin, who discusses this festival in the Orissan context, stresses the positive aspects of menstruation and fertility, both human and divine, in the Hindu context, but as the present myth reminds us, there is also a very real down side to the situation for human women.

References

Agnipurāṇa. 1967. *Agni Puranam*, second edition. Translated by Manmatha Nath Dutt. Varanasi Chowkhamba Sanskrit Series Office (Chowkhamba Sanskrit studies v. 54).

—— 1984–87. *The Agni Purana*. Translated by Natesa Gangadharan. 4 vols. Delhi: Narendra Prakash Jain (English Puranas, 27, 28, 29, 30).

Ahmad, A. 1969. *An Intellectual History of Islam in India*. Edinburgh: Edinburgh University Press.

Apffel-Marglin, F. (F.A. Marglin.) 1985. Introduction. In *Purity and Auspiciousness in Indian Society*, edited by J.B. Carman and F. Apffel-Marglin. Leiden: E.J. Brill.

—— 1994. The sacred groves: menstruation rituals in rural Orissa. *Manushi* 82 (May–June 1994): 22–32.

Appadurai, A. 1986. Review article: is homo hierarchicus? *American Ethnologist* 13: 745–61.

Auboyer, J. and M.-T. de Mallmann. 1950. Śītalā-la-froide: déesse indienne de la petite vérole. *Artibus Asiae* 13: 207–27.

Bhattacharya, R.K. 1973. The concept and ideology of caste among the Muslims of rural West Bengal. In *Caste and Social Stratification Among Muslims in India*, edited by Imtiaz Ahmed. Delhi: Manohar Book Service.

Blanchet, T. 1984. *Women, Pollution and Marginality: Meanings and Rituals of Birth in Rural Bangladesh*. Dhaka: University Press.

Cameron, M.M. 1998. *On the Edge of the Auspicious: Gender and Caste in Nepal*. Urbana and Chicago: University of Illinois Press.

Chawla, J. 1994. *Child-bearing and Culture, Women Centered Revisioning of the Traditional Midwife: The Dai as a Ritual Practitioner*. New Delhi: Indian Social Institute.

Connor, L. 1996. Underdetermining the empirical ground of therapy regimens among Tibetan refugee patients. Paper for the international research workshop on Healing Powers and Modernity in Asian Societies. Faculty of Arts and Social Science, University of Newcastle, Australia, December 1996.

Connor, L., K. Monro and E. McIntyre. 1996. Healing resources in Tibetan settlements in North India. *Asian Studies Review* 20 (1): 108–18.

Daniels, C.M. 1994. Defilement and purification: Tibetan Buddhist pilgrims at Bodhnath, Nepal. D.Phil. thesis, University of Oxford. Faculty of Anthropology and Geography.

Das, V. 1987. *Structure and Cognition: Aspects of Hindu Caste and Ritual*, second edition. Delhi: Oxford University Press.

Day, The Rev. L.B. 1906. *Bengal Peasant Life.* London: Macmillan.

Diemberger, H. 1993. Blood, sperm, soul and the mountain: gender relations, kinship and cosmovision among the Khumbo (N. E. Nepal). In *Gendered Anthropology*, edited by T. del Valle. London and New York: Routledge.

Dimock, E.C., Jr. 1961. The goddess of snakes in medieval Bengali literature. *History of Religions* 1: 307–21. (Reprinted in E.C. Dimock, Jr., *The Sound of Silent Guns and Other Essays.* Delhi: Oxford University Press, 1989.)

—— 1963. *The Thief of Love: Bengali Tales from Court and Village.* Chicago: University of Chicago Press.

—— 1986. A theology of the repulsive: the myth of the goddess Śītalā. In *The Divine Consort: Rādhā and the Goddesses of India*, edited by J.S. Hawley and D.M. Wulff. Boston: Beacon Press. (Reprinted in E.C. Dimock, Jr., *The Sound of Silent Guns and Other Essays.* Delhi: Oxford University Press, 1989.)

Donner, H. 2001. The place of birth: pregnancy, childbearing and kinship in Calcutta middle-class families. Unpublished paper.

Dumont, L. 1972. *Homo Hierarchicus: The Caste System and its Implications.* London: Paladin.

Freed, R. and S.A. Freed. 1980. *Rites of Passage in Shanti Nagar.* Volume 56: Part 3, New York: Anthropological Papers of The American Museum of Natural History.

—— 1998. *Hindu Festivals in a North Indian Village.* No. 81, New York: Anthropological Papers of the American Museum of Natural History.

Fruzzetti, L.M. 1981. Muslim rituals: household rites vs. public festivals in rural India. In *Ritual and Religion Among Muslims in India*, edited by I. Ahmed. Delhi: Manohar.

Gadon, E.W. 1997. The Hindu goddess Shasthi: protector of women and children. In *From the Realm of the Ancestors: An Anthology in Honor of Marija Gimbutas*, edited by J. Marler. Manchester, CT: Knowledge, Ideas and Trends, Inc.

Grierson, G.A. (ed.). 1885. *Bihār Peasant Life.* Calcutta: Bengal Secretariat.

Huber, T. 1999. *The Cult of Pure Crystal Mountain: Popular Pilgrimage and Visionary Landscape in Southeast Tibet.* New York: Oxford University Press.

Jeffery, P., R. Jeffery and A. Lyon. 1989. *Labour Pains and Labour Power: Women and Childbearing in India.* London and New Jersey: Zed Books Ltd.

Khare, R.S. 1976. *The Hindu Hearth and Home.* New Delhi: Vikas Publishing House.

Kirat, J. 1980. The Sherpas. In *Traditional and Prevailing Child-rearing Practices among Different Communities in Nepal*, edited by S. Paneru. Kirtipur, Nepal: Centre for Nepal and Asian Studies, Tribhuvan University.

Laderman, C. 1983. *Wives and Midwives: Childbirth and Nutrition in Rural Malaysia.* Berkeley: University of California Press.

Leppard, M. 1997. Embodied understanding: birthing in a Bangladeshi district hospital. Paper for the South Asian Anthropologists' Group Meeting, London, September 1997.

Leslie, J. 1996. Menstruation myths. In *Myth and Mythmaking*, edited by J. Leslie. London: Curzon.

Madan, T.N. 1987. *Non-renunciation: Themes and Interpretations of Hindu Culture.* Delhi: Oxford University Press.

Maiden, A.H. and E. Farwell. 1997. *The Tibetan Art of Parenting: From Before Conception through Early Childhood.* Boston, MA: Wisdom Publications.

Minturn, L. and Hitchcock, J.T. 1966. *The Rajputs of Khalapur, India.* New York, London and Sydney: John Wiley and Sons.

Monro, K.S. 1999. Tibetan mothers in India: medical pluralism and cultural identity. Ph.D. thesis, Department of Sociology and Anthropology, University of Newcastle, New South Wales.

Norberg-Hodge, H., with H. Russell. 1994. Birth and child rearing in Zangskar. In *Himalayan Buddhist Villages: Environment, Resources, Society and Religious Life in Zangskar, Ladakh*, edited by J. Crook and H. Osmaston. Bristol: University of Bristol.

Patel, T. 1994. *Fertility Behaviour: Population and Society in a Rajasthan Village.* Delhi: Oxford University Press.

Pinto, S. 1999. Pregnancy and childbirth in Tibetan culture. In *Buddhist Women across Cultures*, edited by K.L. Tsomo. Albany: State University of New York.

Rozario, S. 1992. *Purity and Communal Boundaries: Women and Social Change in a Bangladeshi Village.* London: Zed Books; Sydney: Allen and Unwin.

—— 1995a. Dai and midwives: the renegotiation of the status of birth attendants in contemporary Bangladesh. In *The Female Client and the Health-care Provider*, edited by J. Hatcher and C. Vlassoff. Ottawa: International Development Research Centre (IDRC) Books.

—— 1995b. TBAs (Traditional Birth Attendants) and birth in Bangladeshi villages: cultural and sociological factors. *International Journal of Gynaecology and Obstetrics* 50 (Supp. No. 2): 145–52.

—— 1996. Indian medicine, *drib*, and the politics of identity in a Tibetan refugee settlement in North India. Presented at the International Workshop on Healing Powers and Modernity in Asia, held at Newcastle University. Revised Version at Australian Anthropological Society Conference, October 1998.

—— 1998. The Dai and the doctor: discourses on women's reproductive health in rural Bangladesh. In *Modernities and Maternities: Colonial and Postcolonial Experiences in Asia and the Pacific*, edited by K. Ram and M. Jolly. Cambridge, Cambridge University Press.

Sagaster, U. 1989. *Die Baltis: ein Bergvolk im Norden Pakistans.* Frankfurt am Main, Museum für Völkerkunde.

Samanta, S. 1992. *Maṅgalmayīmā, sumaṅgalā, maṅgal:* Bengali perceptions of the divine feminine, motherhood and 'auspiciousness'. *Contributions to Indian Sociology* (NS) 26: 51–75.

Samuel, G. 1993. *Civilized Shamans: Buddhism in Tibetan Societies.* Smithsonian Institution Press, Washington, DC.

—— 1997. Women, goddesses and auspiciousness in South Asia. *Journal of Interdisciplinary Gender Studies* 4 (November 1997): 1–23.

—— 1999. Religion, health and suffering among contemporary Tibetans. In *Religion, Health and Suffering*, edited by J.R. Hinnells and R. Porter. London and New York: Kegan Paul International.

—— 2001. Tibetan medicine in contemporary India: theory and practice. In *Healing Powers and Modernity*, edited by L.H. Connor and G. Samuel. New York: Greenwood Press.

Schicklgruber, C. 1992. Grib: on the significance of the term in a socio-religious context. In *Tibetan Studies: Proceedings of the 5th International Association of Tibetan Studies Seminar*, vol. 2, edited by S. Ihara and Z. Yamaguchi. Narita, Japan: Naritasan Institute for Buddhist Studies.

Searle-Chatterjee, M. and U. Sharma (eds). 1994. *Contextualising Caste: Post-Dumontian Approaches*. Oxford and Cambridge, MA: Blackwells. (Sociological Review Monograph Series, 41.)

Sen, S. 1953. *Vipradāsa's Manasā-Vijaya*. A fifteenth-century Bengali text edited with a summarised translation, notes and glossary and with an introduction on the literature, myth and cults relating to Manasā. Calcutta: Asiatic Society.

Unnithan (Unnithan-Kumar), M. 1999a. Women's agency and reproductive health in Jaipur District, Rajasthan. Paper for Fertility and Reproduction Seminar, Institute of Social and Cultural Anthropology, University of Oxford, May 1999.

—— 1999b. Households, kinship and access to reproductive healthcare among rural Muslim women in Jaipur. *Economic and Political Weekly* 6–13 March, Bombay: Hitkari House.

Ward, The Rev. W. 1863. *A View of the History, Literature, and Religion of the Hindoos: Including a Minute Description of their Manners and Customs . . .*, fifth edition. Madras: J. Higginbotham.

Part 2

Southeast Asia

Chapter 10

The demise of birth attendants in Northeast Thailand

Embodying tradition in modern times

Andrea Whittaker

Grandmother Yim sits rocking two children she helped deliver, laughing as she plays with them. She is a popular woman in the village, always adorned with flowers behind her ears and a betel-stained smile. She is a *mor tam yae*, a traditional midwife. She is 64 years old and has been helping women give birth since she was 40. When she was young, she would go to the houses of women giving birth to watch and learn and says she was not scared: 'that was how I learned'. When she was 52, the nurse at the village health station chose her and four other women to be 'trained' about birthing at the district public health office. I ask her about what she learned in her 'training':

> I learned to use a razor to cut the cord, in the old days we used to use a snail shell, we would put the cord on top of charcoal and then cut through. When I was trained we learned that if a woman is having a difficult delivery to send them to the health station.

Grandmother Yim is one of only two traditional midwives who has helped women give birth in the past twelve months in Baan Srisaket. In the past she would attend five or six births a month, 'but now people are only having two children and so I only see about two or one a month'.

This chapter explores the demise of traditional midwives in rural villages such as Baan Srisaket in Northeast Thailand. It takes as its starting point the simple observation that most women in this village give birth in hospital and do not use the services of traditional midwives nor those of the local health station nurse/midwife. As an anthropologist undertaking long-term fieldwork studying women's health, I was disappointed to discover that births at home in the village were rare events, despite the existence of a number of women described by villagers as *mor tam yae*. This chapter is an attempt to understand the multiple reasons for the demise of traditional midwifery practices in Baan Srisaket. The account is not a simplistic one in which tradition succumbs to the overwhelming force of modernity. Rather, the picture is far more complex.

First, I argue that government policies to 'train' traditional midwives in the 1970s contributed to a de-skilling and delegitimation of local midwives. In general, local women who had been practising these skills were not chosen and validated to practise their skills. They were replaced by women deemed more suitable for training. Thus, this chapter is in part a case study of the effects of abstract primary health care policies regarding birthing as they are translated into practice in a rural village.

Second, as hospital services and nurse/midwifery services became more widely available to villages across Thailand they were promoted as 'safer' and more 'modern' ways to give birth. Birth has always been represented as a dangerous event for Isaan women, and representations of hospital births as safer appeal to them. As more women gave birth in health stations and hospitals, local midwives had fewer opportunities to practise their skills, reinforcing an image of them as less capable. The midwives themselves lost confidence in their abilities and only two in Baan Srisaket continue to practise at all. The result is that today, despite the apparent presence of a range of options for women giving birth, including local traditional midwives, health station nurse/midwives and hospital births, the majority of women choose hospital births and only a few give birth at home. This is despite their negative experiences of hospital births.

Finally, I argue that despite the ubiquity of hospital births, the importance of post-partum rituals remain. Although not encouraged nor even acknowledged by biomedical staff, who represent post-partum rites as another set of practices which is 'dying out', they retain important meaning for women as a marker of maturity. Traditional midwives retain important roles in these rites.

My use of the terms 'tradition' and modernity' is not accidental nor a remnant of romanticised nostalgia for lost authenticity. They are used in this chapter not as academic dichotomies, but to gloss common categorisations of knowledge and practice in Thai and Isaan between *samai korn/samai kau* (past times/old times) and *than samai* (in step with the times), or *samai mai* (new times). These terms are not only used to describe health practices but are widely used in state rhetoric and by the popular media to contrast the objects, ideas and values of the past and present (Mills 1995) and carry a sense of the inevitable movement of modernity and progress (see also Hunter Chapter 13 this volume).

With reference to medical institutions, traditional practices are referred to as *phaen boraan* (ancient types [of practice]) and practitioners as a group, including *mor tam yae*, are described as *mor boraan* (ancient doctors). These terms in English, Thai and Lao imply a temporal relationship: tradition is something past, being replaced by modernity, something of the present and future. Yet, as evident from this chapter, forms of both 'traditional' and 'modern' practices are contemporaneous. Rather, this temporal metaphor used by speakers signals a differential power relation. As will be seen in this chapter, although birthing in hospitals has become the dominant way to give birth in Baan Srisaket, it has not erased other alternative representations of the body and process of birth and the post-partum period. Nor are there always firm boundaries between 'modern' biomedicine and 'traditional' therapies, despite the linguistic divisions made between them. Indeed, many of the 'traditional' practices described to me by midwives may represent techniques acquired through their 'training' by public health staff, or 'reinvented traditions'. Likewise, many 'modern' practices in hospital would not be described as conforming to current best practice standards of obstetric care.

The aim of this chapter, however, is not to engage in a debate about what constitutes 'authentic' birthing for women in Baan Srisaket, nor to explore whether the techniques of one group of practitioners are superior to another group's for the management of birth. What I am interested in is the question of the differential power relations between 'traditional' and 'modern' forms of knowledge and practice, embodied in the traditional midwives. These power relations are most evident in the representations of hospital births as clean, hygienic, modern and safe, in contrast to birth in the care of traditional midwives. Such representations are neither fixed nor uncontested. As is obvious in this chapter, traditional midwives see themselves and are still appreciated by many villagers as skilled practitioners, albeit with few opportunities to practise and maintain those skills.

I also wish to draw attention to the fact that far from being passive recipients of the 'modern' birthing in hospitals and biomedical hegemony, women are actively making choices to give birth in hospital. However, their decisions do not involve a simple exercise of choice, but rather involve movement between different forms of knowledge and practice existing in an unequal relation of power (Ram 1998).

This chapter thus offers an account of processes through which biomedical authority has come to dominate the childbirth experience (Jordan 1993 [1978]; see also Steinberg 1996). In doing so I draw upon Jordan's concept of 'authoritative knowledge'. She suggests that when more than one knowledge system exists in a given domain, one form of knowledge is afforded ascendancy and social legitimacy, 'authoritative knowledge'. People actively engage in the production and reproduction of authoritative knowledge, constantly reinforcing its validity until it comes to appear natural, reasonable and shared (Sargent and Bascope 1996: 213). As Sargent and Bascope note, the basis for authoritative knowledge lies not only in the control of technologies of birthing as suggested by Jordan, but may also 'reflect the distribution of power within a social group' (1996: 232). They suggest that in the three communities they studied, the social status and cultural authority of biomedicine maintained its ideological dominance, even in the absence of high technology (232). Authoritative knowledge thus involves differential power relations between differing knowledge systems and different groups in society. In other terms, authoritative knowledge is a form of what Bourdieu termed 'cultural capital', which is distributed unevenly within a society and allows the holders to address a certain audience in a relationship of subordination (Bourdieu 1977; Bourdieu and Passeron 1977). This chapter explores how biomedical knowledge and practice has come to be constructed as the authoritative knowledge of birthing in Baan Srisaket. Further, I am interested in the ways in which women transcend the differences between these forms of knowledge everyday in actuality as they move between practices in the hospital and practices in the village. In particular, I argue that practices surrounding post-partum remain a field in which the local knowledge and practice embodied in the traditional midwives predominates.

Methods

This chapter is based upon eighteen months' ethnographic research in the rural community of Baan Srisaket, Roi Et province, during 1992/3. Baan Srisaket has 740 households and a population of 3926 people. Like much of the northeast of Thailand, Baan Srisaket is poor. The economy is based upon the production of glutinous rice for consumption and sale, and some limited dry-season cash crops. As the income from these sources is usually insufficient to meet their needs, households in Baan Srisaket rely upon migra-tory labour for their incomes.

This chapter forms part of a broad anthropological study investigating women's health. My aim in the study was to document the rich knowledge women have concerning their bodies and health. Further, I was interested in the ways in which these knowledges are positioned within pluralistic Thai health systems and the effects of class and ethnicity. It involved participant observation, focus-group discussions, semi-structured and informal inter-views and household surveys. These were supplemented by hospital and clinic observations concentrating on gynaecological, obstetric and family planning services (Whittaker 2000). In particular, this chapter is based on in-depth interviews with six traditional birth attendants, the nurse-midwife at the local primary health station and district hospital staff. In addition, sixty-seven women of various ages participated in a semi-structured interview survey to ascertain changing birthing practices across time. The interviews were con-ducted by myself in the local dialect, which is closely related to Lao. I asked women about their antenatal care, place of birth, reasons for their choices, birth experiences and post-partum care for each birth they had experienced. A second interview survey of all fifty-seven women who gave birth in 1992 documented the experience of birthing as it is now. These women were iden-tified from district birth records and traced within the village. These interviews were supplemented with other in-depth interviews conducted with another thirty-six mothers regarding their reproductive health, birth experi-ences and practices, breastfeeding, child care and their opinions of the quality of services. Eleven births were observed at provincial and district hospitals, and in-depth interviews were conducted with obstetric staff at both of these hospitals.

In writing this chapter, I reduce to a few paragraphs the long time spent sitting and chatting with women, the lessons taught by elderly midwives, the frustrations of fieldwork and the giggles of village children. Although this chapter separates out a discussion of midwifery, it cannot be isolated from the broader context of women's lives and the massive social transformations that have occurred in the past fifty years in Thai society as it has shifted from a largely subsistence agricultural economy to an industrial and cash-crop economy.

The Thai public health system

Any discussion of birthing requires an understanding of the public health infrastructure in Thailand. Thai government health services are organised at several levels under the administration of both the Ministry of Public Health and the Ministry of Interior. As a result of policies promulgated in several National Health Development Plans, health care facilities and services have been set up in almost all rural districts and subdistricts. The public health system is based upon the principles of primary health care (PHC) promulgated by the WHO (Kachondham and Chunharas 1993). The policy to implement PHC began in the 1960s and became a national programme in 1980. Its principles included: integrated rural development, orientation of PHC to local community needs and popular participation, the utilisation of local resources and the extensive use of locally trained personnel (Cohen 1989: 116).

At the local level, village health stations (*sathaanii anaamai*) provide primary health care to each *tambon* or subdistrict consisting of three to ten villages. In 1991, there were 8040 health stations in Thailand (JICA 1992). These are usually staffed by an auxiliary midwife and a junior sanitarian or technical nurse. The health station at Baan Srisaket is staffed by one technical nurse, an administrative officer/sanitarian and a technical nurse/midwife.[1]

Such centres are responsible for antenatal, delivery and postnatal care, immunisation, nutrition and family planning services, water supply and sanitation activities. They also provide treatment for minor illnesses and emergencies, and provide referrals to district or provincial hospitals for complicated cases. According to health policy, the local health station is supposed to provide the setting for the majority of births, in the presence of the government nurse/midwife.

District community hospitals represent the next level in the government health system. At the time of this research in 1991 there were 572 such hospitals throughout Thailand. These hospitals, typically with ten to thirty beds, provide outpatient facilities and a limited range of inpatient care, including maternity services (Alpha Research Co. 1994: 82). In addition, they provide preventative and promotional health services such as family planning and immunisation services. The local district hospital for Baan Srisaket has ten beds and is staffed by one medical doctor and nine nursing staff. Most women in Baan Srisaket travel to give birth at this hospital. At the time of my research it had no blood available for obstetric emergencies nor facilities for Caesarean sections. In such cases women are referred to another district hospital, 27 km away, which does have facilities for transfusions, or to the provincial hospital in Roi Et, 60 km away.

Provincial-level general hospitals have between 150 and 500 beds. In 1991 there were sixty-nine such hospitals in Thailand providing specialist services and referrals to the seventeen specialist regional teaching hospitals such as Srinagarind Hospital at Khon Kaen University and the large hospitals of Bangkok (Alpha Research Co. 1994: 82). These regional hospitals represent the highest level of the government health system and are the most prestigious hospitals, providing specialist services, research and teaching facilities.

Changing patterns of birth in Baan Srisaket

The birthing experience has changed dramatically in the space of a single generation within Baan Srisaket. Before the extension of government health services, all women in Baan Srisaket gave birth at home either alone or in the company of their husband, kin or traditional midwife. Although some women continue to give birth at home, the majority now give birth in hospitals. This placed the women of Baan Srisaket in accord with the Seventh National Development Plan, current at the time of this research, which sought to have 75 per cent of women give birth in hospital (Government of Thailand 1992).

Within most families it is possible to trace the changes. I go, for example, to visit Faa, a 22-year-old woman who has just given birth to her first child, a boy. During my visit I talk with the members of the household about giving birth and women compare their experiences. Faa's grandmother tells me that she had nine pregnancies, and gave birth to four sons and four daughters, six of whom survived. Faa's grandmother gave birth at home, on some occasions by herself, sometimes in the company of a elderly *mor tam yae*. Faa's mother gave birth to five children at home with her own mother and a traditional midwife present. When contraceptive services became available Faa's mother had a tubal ligation and so limited her family size. Faa gave birth to her son at a local district hospital. Before the birth she attended antenatal care at the local *sathaanii anaamai* (health station). Faa and her husband plan on having only two children (fieldnotes 1992).

The same pattern is reflected in the surveys I conducted with women of a variety of ages. I have grouped the women together into two broad groups. The first includes women of ages up to 35 who have given birth since the

Table 10.1 Women in Baan Srisaket who give birth at home for their first child
and for their second child, by age group

Age of mothers interviewed	First birth at home			Second birth at home		
	Births at home	Total births	% at home	Births at home	Total births	% at home
More than 35 years of age	35	36	97	32	33	97
Up to 35 years of age	18	31	58	7	21	33

Source: Birthing Survey 1992.

introduction of government health services in the village health stations
about fifteen years earlier. The second group includes women over 35 who
gave birth before the introduction of government health services. In Baan
Srisaket, 97 per cent of women surveyed over the age of 35 had given birth to
their first child at home. This pattern continued for their second children,
with 97 per cent giving birth at home (see Table 10.1). Women younger than
35 have had more choices as to the place of birth since the development of
government health services in the 1970s. Of the women in this age group 58
per cent gave birth to their first child at home. However, only 33 per cent of
the same group did so for their second child. They explained that it is
common to give birth to second children at the hospital so that they can
have a tubal ligation immediately afterwards.

The survey of all women who gave birth in 1992 in Baan Srisaket confirms
the demise of home birthing. Only six (10 per cent) of the fifty-seven women
who gave birth during 1992 did so at home. Five of these women gave birth
at home to their first child and indicated that they would attend hospital for
their next birth for a tubal ligation. Seventeen women (29 per cent) gave birth
at the local district hospital, while eight (14 per cent) and four (7 per cent)
gave birth at two other district hospitals further away from the village.
Thirteen (22 per cent) gave birth in the provincial hospital, over sixty kilometres away. Three (5 per cent) chose to give birth at private hospitals, also
over 60 km away. Two women gave birth while living temporarily in other
provinces. Two other women were not traceable.

Only one woman gave birth at the local primary health station under the
care of the nurse/midwife. She did so because she was in labour and was
unable to get transport to the hospital. In Baan Srisaket, the midwife advises
all her antenatal clients to give birth at the local district hospital. She said to
me frankly that despite assisting in births for her first six years at the station,
she 'doesn't like delivering babies', as she is 'too scared of the responsibility'
were something to go wrong. Her feelings are known by local district hospital staff, who said that other government midwives do deliver babies at their
health stations. For women in Baan Srisaket, however, the choice about where

Figure 10.1 Grandmother Sow (right) is a traditional birth attendant (*mor tam yae*). She is pictured here with Grandmother Dii and her grandchildren. Grandmother Sow helped deliver the grandchildren (photo by Andrea Whittaker)

to give birth usually refers to which hospital they will attend. As seen from these figures above, only a few women now choose to give birth under the care of traditional midwives.

Traditional midwives in Baan Srisaket: *mor tam yae*

Mor tam yae (Figure 10.1) are traditional specialists in the rules, rites and remedies associated with pregnancy, birthing, the post-partum period and care of the infant, some are also skilled in massaging out unwanted pregnancies. In 1978, WHO suggested the promotion of the training of traditional practitioners such as *mor tam yae*, along with other traditional healers and medicines for incorporation into the primary health care system (Le Grand and Sri-ngernyuang 1989). In Thailand, attempts were made to train and incorporate traditional midwives into the primary health care system with the goal of ensuring that all women give birth in the company of a trained attendant so as to reduce maternal and infant mortality (see also Newland Chapter 12 this volume). At the time, the public health care system was developing, and unable to provide access to trained nurse/midwives.

The WHO first discussed the training of traditional birth attendants in 1966 in recognition that the health needs of women and children in many countries were not being met. An implicit assumption of the superiority of Western obstetrics was embedded in the early calls for the training and 'incorporation' or 'articulation' of TBAs into biomedical health systems by the WHO. Traditional birthing practices were selectively incorporated into the Thai government health system through a system of training and exclusion which legitimised only some practices and subordinated traditional knowledge to biomedical knowledge. An aim of the training was to modify 'harmful' practices, replacing them with approved techniques, while retaining 'beneficial' and 'harmless' TBA practices (Verderese and Turnbull 1975: 38).

In Baan Srisaket, this process of exclusion and subordination of local knowledge was enacted by choosing women for training who were not necessarily those who were practising as *mor tam yae* at the time of selection. Many of the women who were practising as traditional midwives were considered by the district health authorities as 'too old' to be trained, were no longer encouraged to practise and younger women were selected. Women who gave birth ten to twenty years ago provided the names of eighteen women considered to be *mor tam yae*, apart from the grandmothers and aunts who helped women birth but were not considered *mor tam yae*. After training, only the six selected 'trained' women were allowed to continue their practice.

Of these six women, only two continue to attend births. Grandmother Yim, whose story is related at the beginning of this chapter, practised before her 'training'. Grandmother Say also continues to practise and is also over 60 years old. All the other women have retired.

Grandmother Huwat, a mother of six, had never practised as a midwife but was selected to be trained for five days in 1977 by a public health doctor from Roi Et. In 1991 she attended five births but in 1992 she did not attend any as her eyesight has deteriorated. Now she simply refers women on to the nurse midwife at the health station. However, women still come to her when they are seven or eight months pregnant for her to massage their womb and ascertain if the child will be male or female according to the shape and position of the foetus. She also continues to be called to lead women to sit by the fire after birth and visits each day for the first few days to check that the mother and child are well.

Grandmother Wandii has had fifteen pregnancies with two miscarriages and nine surviving children. She also trained in 1977 when she was 53 years old. She only attended births for three years. As with Grandmother Huwat, women continue to come to her for her to check their pregnancies, for assistance with prolapses and to oversee the rituals of staying by the fire during the post-partum period.

Grandmother Saa, now in her late sixties, also had been trained at the district public health office to be a midwife but has long since retired. Finally, Grandmother Bay is 60 years old. She has had six pregnancies and five surviving children. She learned from the old women how to be a *mor tam yae* and had helped deliver many children in the past but also no longer practises.

In addition to these women, there is one woman who has practised as a midwife in the past but has not been officially 'trained'. Grandmother Sen, 60 years old, is a *mor sen* (massage doctor). She is called upon by many people everyday to manipulate and massage sore muscles. She has practised for over twenty years and her skills are largely self-taught. She attended a massage doctor in Mahasarakham in her younger days and learned through observing and experiencing his massage, and then by manipulating her own body and by observing results. In addition to her massage services, she is called upon to assist with prolapses and sometimes asked to assist with abortions (although she denies involvement in this). She has attended births since 1972. She has not been 'trained' but learned through watching her mother and elder sister who were *mor tam yae*. Although she did not attend a birth in 1992, she states that she is available to do so if called upon.

Birth with traditional midwives and birth in hospital

How do the experiences of birthing at home in the company of a traditional midwife and birthing at hospital differ? The services of a *mor tam yae* encompass the antenatal care of the women, care at the birth and post-partum care and advice. Before birth they monitor the progress of pregnancies, offering massage services, advice to pregnant women regarding the avoidance of humorally hot foods, and in some cases, predicting the sex of the child. After birth they visit the new mother and child regularly, with advice concerning breastfeeding, weaning and illness, and for the chance to cuddle the newborn. They have always been respected in the community for their knowledge and for the services they provide for little remuneration. They convey and embody the discourses which link women with their home, community and spirit world throughout the birth of their children.

The position for giving birth at home is kneeling or sitting. The woman in labour holds the shoulders of her husband, or in his absence, pulls on a *khaen phaa* (cloth) tied over a roof rafter or post. The midwife employs massage, moral support and a variety of prayers and spells to assist the labouring woman. She presses a cloth against the woman's perineum as the baby's head crowns to minimise tearing. No episiotomies are performed. In the past, after the placenta had been delivered, the umbilical cord was cut against a root of turmeric (*Curcuma domestica*), a stalk of lemon grass or piece of charcoal with a sliver of fresh bamboo or an oyster shell. Since 'training', traditional midwives use pre-boiled scissors, knives or razors, or the blade supplied by the government. Ordinary cotton thread is used to tie and sew the cord. The navel of the baby is commonly treated with alcohol and *phong piseet*, a sulphur-based powder bought at the local village store. In the past, I was told, the powdered nest of a mud-wasp, or the fine dust from underneath a woven floor mat was used to aid in the drying out of the navel.

The treatment of the placenta is important in traditional birthing practice. It affects the personality and health of the new child. When a woman has given birth at home, the *mor tam yae* or the husband carefully cleans the placenta in warm water and then salt is applied to it. Salt is added, 'because the old people told us to put it in, to make it healthy or happy or something' (Grandmother Yim). The placenta is then wrapped and placed into a bamboo container and buried by the husband or the midwife in a place determined by the sex of the baby.[2]

The services of traditional midwives are provided in return for a token payment. For each birth Grandmother Yim attends she receives 100 to 200 baht (US$2.50 to $5):

> It varies, some people have no money. In the old days people gave me water, rice and cloth in a basket, but now they give money instead. Some of the children I have delivered come at Songkran and pour water over my hands and pay respect to me as I am *bun khun* [a person to whom they have a special obligation]. You make a lot of Buddhist merit by helping someone give birth.

A traditional midwife such as Grandmother Yim enjoys respect from villagers for her skills and her preparedness to help others. She is regarded as a *thau kae* (elderly member of the community) with the seniority and respect that comes with age and skill. In describing her choice to give birth at home, Mother Uan explained to me:

> We called Grandmother Yim and she came and she helped me to hang on to a rope and helped me push. She washed the baby and my husband buried the placenta underneath the window. My husband got the water and wood for the fire and he helped by washing the clothes and boiling water. I decided to give birth at home because I saw that Grandmother Yim [a TBA] did lots of births and was a good woman who speaks well. She is very skilled at births so I thought I would give birth at home.
>
> (fieldnotes 1992)

In hospital, childbirth is a medical event controlled by doctors and nurses (see discussion in Muecke 1976: 381). Once labour pains begin, women from Baan Srisaket travel to their choice of hospital. In most cases, it is the closest district hospital, 23 km away. In the district and provincial hospitals I observed, birthing follows a Thai form of Western obstetric practice. Many of the practices I witnessed are no longer commonly followed in the West and would no longer be considered acceptable. The woman is dressed in a hospital gown, marking her status as a patient. She is examined, and if there is time, shaved and cleaned. She gives birth attended by nurse/midwives in one of the operating theatres. No relatives are allowed to accompany the mother. The lithotomy position using stirrups was used in all the hospital births I observed and women were never encouraged to change positions or move around during labour. Birthing in hospital involves a high likelihood of interventions such as augmentation and episiotomy. Of 199 births at the district hospital in 1992, 120 episiotomies were performed, representing 60.3 per cent of all births. Thirty-three women (16.6 per cent) were reported to have first- or second-degree tears (district hospital records, 1992).

Women cannot see the baby when it emerges, nor see what the midwives are doing. The baby is weighed and given injections (BCG and in some cases Hepatitis B) and silver nitrate is applied to the eyes. The placenta is delivered and then inspected. The new mothers are cleaned and accompanied back to the ward and then get to see and nurse their babies for the first time. After a short rest, relatives are permitted to see the mother and child. After a few hours rest, the mother is examined and allowed to return to the village. If the mother desires a tubal ligation, that will take place shortly after the birth.

In most hospital births, the placenta receives no special treatment after it is examined and weighed. In Baan Srisaket, women believed that staff at the nearby district hospital throw away the placentas and one woman suggested they were used by the nurses to feed fish in a nearby pond. Their comments recognise that hospital staff are dismissive of local practices and knowledge deemed 'traditional' and treat with disdain the desires of villagers to follow 'old' customs. Dissatisfaction about the local district hospital's practice regarding the placenta was the reason many women cited for their decision to attend a neighbouring district hospital further away. That hospital was prepared to give women the placenta to take home to bury according to custom. However, this was the only hospital I observed which allowed this (Whittaker 2000).

Women are critical of the care they receive in hospitals. As Aunt Wii disgustedly stated, 'the nurses just sat and watched the television while I was in the ward, in labour. I was in pain and they didn't care or even look at me.' Phan avoided giving birth at the local district hospital because when she was sick previously, 'the staff there weren't interested in me or in the other patients'. Phan gave birth to her child at Roi Et hospital rather than at home because she feared a difficult birth. Yet she found that 'the doctors at Roi Et weren't interested in me because I had antenatal care at the other district hospital'. These criticisms of the care and service received in hospitals centres around the hospital staff's failure to provide the nurturing relationship that is culturally expected of healers. In hospital, births are routine medical events, and attention through labour is reduced to occasional checks on the progress of labour and monitoring dilation, with greater attention concentrated upon the final stage of labour and the newborn child. Hospital staff provide only minimal necessary care to patients and do not perform the many significant acts of nurturing expected of traditional midwives. They do not acknowledge the suffering of women in labour or assist through massages or moral support, and do not help wash patients nor supply food to them after the birth.

Figure 10.2 Like most younger women, Nang Sen had a wider variety of choices as to where to give birth than in the past. She gave birth to Pui in the local hospital (photo by Andrea Whittaker)

Dangerous births

Why then do so many women decide to give birth at hospitals (Figure 10.2), despite the fact that many dislike the way in which they are treated? An important motivation for giving birth in hospital is the belief that it is a dangerous and vulnerable time for both mother and child, and the perception that hospitals offer safer births. The danger of childbirth is well described in Isaan lore. The woman giving birth is especially vulnerable to a number of *phii* (malevolent spirits). *Phii phaai* spirits are attracted by blood, especially the blood of parturition. If a woman loses consciousness or has uncontrollable bleeding, these are signs that a *phii phaai* has possessed her and is sucking her body dry.[3] *Phii porp* are malevolent spirits that will invade the bodies of the weak and are also attracted to blood. In turn, a woman who dies in labour becomes a most dangerous spirit.[4] Women in Baan Srisaket cite the past deaths of sisters, daughters and cousins. Their experiences remain part of the current construction of the danger of childbirth and influence their decisions:

The child of Ii Joi was eaten by a *phii porp* which came and ate her blood. [If eaten by a *phii porp*] a woman won't have any strength, [she will be] tired. No blood or anything comes out. They just die.

(Grandmother Thee)

There never used to be any hospital doctors in the old days. My daughter died when she gave birth to her first child. We couldn't get the child out. It was a very long time and we couldn't get the child out. Grandmother Dii was called. She was a *mor tam yae*. Then we went to Baan Don Ling and called the *mor nuat* (the massage doctor) to come and help. My daughter was 29. Both she and the baby died.

(Grandmother Yai)

As Grandmother Sow stated, '*Samai korn* [in the past], many women died in childbirth. There were no doctors.' Whatever the factual status of this statement, the demise of *mor tam yae* and birthing in the village reflects not only the extension of state health services and the hegemony of biomedical control over women's bodies and reproduction, but also the real risks of childbearing as perceived by women. Women choose to give birth at hospitals to ensure a safe birth for themselves and their children. They are willing to endure the loneliness of birthing with strangers for the perceived safety that modern medical technology provides.

The traditional midwives in Baan Srisaket acknowledge the dangers of birthing and all described difficult births they had attended, although none admitted to ever attending births where either mother or child had died. When I asked about possible problems in labour, in local terms they described the dangers of obstructed labour (a failure of the pushing winds or a blockage due to the placenta) and haemorrhage (the action of *phii*, usually fatal). Breech presentations and twins are recognised as potentially dangerous. They were also proud of the assistance they had given to women with difficult births. In one case of breech presentation, Grandmother Yim described, 'the legs came first so I moved my hands in and held around the body and the head of the child as he came out so his head wouldn't get stuck'. In the case of a retained placenta, midwives described how betel nut leaves could be forced down the mother's throat to make her vomit to assist in the expulsion of the placenta, and the mother hit on the back with a cushion. In one such case, Grandmother Yim recalled a woman she feared would die:

There was one woman, Ii Noi. Although she gave birth already the placenta couldn't come out. She stopped pushing and so we cut the cord and looked. It was a very long time. She was dizzy, faint and she was never strong. It was more than an hour, so we called the doctor and the doctor clamped it and took her to the district hospital. At the district hospital the doctor wouldn't let her sleep or lie down as they were scared that the placenta would get stuck inside and they got it out.

(Grandmother Yim)

All traditional midwives I interviewed stated that they now advise women to give birth in hospital if they have any indication that they will have a difficult birth. Signs such as a large belly indicating a large baby, small hips or poor health and weakness are all considered indications of potential difficulties. Grandmother Yim said that when pregnant women come to see her for antenatal massages she encourages all of them, except those who are very strong, to give birth at the hospital.

> Pregnant women come to see me to find out how they are. They come to have me push their stomachs and massage them and tell them the truth . . . 'Young daughter, you aren't well. Go to see the doctor and have them give you some medicine to take and an injection. Nourish yourself well.' I say, 'You are not strong, my child'. If they are weak, not strong, I tell them, 'Go to the doctor'.
>
> (Grandmother Yim)

Local understandings of the danger of childbirth are reinforced by the attitudes of health staff who admonish women to give birth in hospital when they come for antenatal visits to receive a tetanus injection. Medical staff construct home births and the practices of traditional midwives as invariably risky (see Harris Chapter 11 this volume; Rozario 1998). In discussions with medical staff about birthing they frequently recounted 'horror stories' of the dirty hands and cutting utensils used by the traditional midwives, their lack of education and ignorance of basic sanitation. These representations exist despite the fact that most traditional midwives have had 'training' and are supposed to be a recognised part of primary health care. Health staff's representations of *mor tam yae* as dangerous and uneducated form part of a broader discourse in which attachment to 'tradition', to local practices and rituals is constructed as an obstacle to change and responsible for the continuation of ignorance (Hobart 1993). It forms part of a discursive continuum linking 'modernity' with the Central Thai, urban, educated, wealthy elite and 'tradition' with ethnic Isaan/Lao, rural, uneducated, poor peasants. The power relations inherent in biomedicine's acceptance as authoritative knowledge are informed by relations of power inherent in Thai society.

Role of TBAs during the post-partum period

Although fewer births are taking place in the village, as described earlier traditional midwives do retain important roles in the supervision of the post-partum confinement called *yuu kam* (or *yuu fai* in Central Thai). Apart

Figure 10.3 Nang Twi stays by the fire after giving birth in 1992. In front of her
lies her newborn son on a *kradong*, a basket with pencils and books
at his head to ensure he does well at school when he grows up
(photo by Andrea Whittaker)

from the health benefits it is believed to impart, staying by the fire is a rite of
passage which affirms their ethnic and female identity.[5] The continuation of
post-partum practices in Baan Srisaket despite the ubiquity of hospital births
requires explanation. In the survey I conducted in 1992, 83 per cent of women
of 15 to 24 years old reported staying by the fire for their first birth regardless of where they gave birth. This percentage showed little change across
time, 88 per cent of women over 45 years reported staying by the fire for their
first birth.[6] As the post-partum period is a time relatively ignored by biomedical models of birth, it remains a space in which traditional knowledge
remains ascendant and authoritative. According to the postnatal records of
the village health station and hospital interviews, only a few village women
ever visit for post-partum examinations. For most women, the next contact
they are likely to have with medical staff is when they bring their child to the

local primary health clinic for its first immunisation. The relative lack of biomedical supervision and surveillance of women during this time creates a space for the reassertion of local practices and knowledge.

The post-partum period is considered to be a time of great vulnerability and danger for both mother and child. Villagers state that during this stage a woman is vulnerable to spirit attack and it is dangerous to draw attention to the presence of a parturient mother and newborn. Women's vulnerability to threats from outside forces, such as spirits, is because the boundaries of her body are open through the action of the heat from the fire, which forces her body to expel the decaying blood products after birth. Menstrual blood and products of childbirth emanate dangerous pollution, heat and power, capable of draining the physical and spiritual potency of men (Davis 1984: 66; Irvine 1982: 259).[7] Thus, the deliberately induced state of openness also threatens others, in particular the potency of men because of the expelling of hot magically charged blood. For this reason she is both protected from disturbing spiritual and natural influences during her confinement and is confined and sexually abstinent to protect men from the destructive body products (Irvine 1982: 273).

The practice of *yuu kam* (Figure 10.3) involves a period of lying close to a constantly burning fire for a period that varies from five to eleven days (see descriptions in Irvine 1982; Mougne 1978; Poulsen 1983). The longer one can stay by the fire the more efficacious it is said to be. Staying by the fire, combined with drinking herbal tonics, cleanses the womb of the accumulated 'bad blood', lochia and waste fluids that have built up in the body throughout the pregnancy. If these fluids are not expelled, they will stay within the body and cause weakness and chills. Combined with massage, staying by the fire is said to help women to produce an ample supply of breastmilk as it makes the woman's body *suk* (ripe) and her breasts ripe and full of milk. It is also said to flatten the belly of the newly parturient mother, help remove stretch marks, heal perineal tears and give a woman clean, clear skin.

Post-partum practices also involve dietary restrictions. Consumption of particular foods and avoidance of others is a prophylactic measure observed throughout the post-partum period (Whittaker 2000). Some foods are considered to be *phit* (harmful, poisonous) for a woman after childbirth. Eating, touching or smelling such foods might cause vomiting, diarrhoea, madness and possible death for both mother and child. Such a condition is termed *lom phit* (afflicting wind) due to the disruption of the wind element in women's bodies.

It is usually the TBA or another elder woman who leads a woman to the fire and conducts a ritual to ensure the fire is not too hot (*paap fai*). She or another elder conducts a ritual to chase away the spirits (*phii*) that may come and harm the mother and child. She is also the one to 'call the spirits' to inform them of the birth of the child and to claim it as a human child, not a child of the spirits. She gives advice as to which foods should be restricted to avoid a wind illness, how to breastfeed and how to treat sore breasts. She conducts a therapy called *ang k'ua* where salt is thrown over hot charcoal as the woman sits over it with their head covered by a blanket so as to inhale the fumes. This is said to ensure that women do not have trouble with their eyes as the smoke from staying by the fire is said to cause cataracts in old age. She also conducts the ritual for leaving the fire (*sia thit fai*) where leaves of the *phork fai* (smother the fire) plant are dipped in water and sprinkled over the mother and fire 'to reduce the fire's heat'. After the woman leaves the fire, the traditional midwife remains available for advice regarding infant care.

Staying by the fire is not encouraged by government health staff who speak of it as a potentially dangerous and unhelpful practice which tires and dehydrates women, causes hypotension and contributes to accidental burns. They focus upon the dietary restrictions, stating that they cause anaemia and affect the production of breastmilk. Despite their warnings, the continuation of post-partum practices draws attention to the contestation of power involved in the relationships between 'traditional' and 'modern' knowledge and practices. As this chapter has shown, while women appreciate the safer motherhood said to be provided through the extension of biomedical services, they also assert the importance of post-partum traditions in defiance of biomedical advice. In doing so they resist the total subordination of traditional practice. Within the spatial confines of the village, healing rituals and practices are not only practical health behaviours, but an assertion of female cultural identity and meanings not accessible through biomedical practices. The continuation of these practices depends in part upon the continued existence of women knowledgeable in these rites.

Conclusions

Changes in reproduction (Figure 10.4) reflect broader social changes. Communities such as Baan Srisaket have been exposed to urban values and practices through the state education system, mass media and migration. In addition, work patterns, family economies and gender relations are undergoing change. State-sponsored family planning provides a means of limiting family size. A consequence of this is that pregnancy and birthing are experienced only once or twice by most women, rather than being normal states of being as in their mothers' and grandmothers' time. With fewer births taking place in villages, there are also fewer opportunities for traditional midwives to practise their skills. In addition, as this chapter shows, there has been little government support for the continuance of local traditions (see also Newman 1981). The combination of lack of support for the continuation of traditional midwives' practice, along with the demographic reality of fewer births, means that the existing traditional midwives are becoming deskilled. As Grandmother Yim noted, she only gets to attend one or two births a year now and wishes she had more opportunity to practise her skills. This further undermines confidence in her ability to provide safe home births.

Figure 10.4 In their day, Grandmother Yim and Grandmother Kham gave birth at home either alone or in the company of kin and a *mor tam yae*. Here they are pictured playing with their grandchildren who were all born in hospitals (photo by Andrea Whittaker)

Within the West the dominance and control of reproduction by the medical profession is increasingly the object of criticism for the conversion of birth from a natural process into a medical problem (Oakley 1975). Proponents of the more recent 'natural birth' movement have challenged control of birthing by the medical profession and emphasised the rights of a woman to active control over how and where she will give birth (Treichler 1990). Thus, giving birth 'naturally' has become for many Western women a prestigious goal (Crouch and Manderson 1993: 58–68). In Thailand there is little public debate over the increased medicalisation of birth, which is still unquestioningly perceived and justified in terms of the provision of good health care and a safe birth. For many of the urban middle class, birthing in hospital, with pain relief, biomedical technology and the option of voluntary Caesarean section, is the modern, progressive and socially prestigious way of 'doing' birth (Van Esterik 1982: 64). Within Baan Srisaket, birthing in hospital is now the norm for women and this is strongly encouraged by the local nurse (and by her refusal to offer an option of birthing at the health station), by the provision of free tubal ligations, and by the diminishing number of skilled *mor tam yae*. For wealthier village families, even birthing at private hospitals is an option, the prestige proportional to the expense involved.

Although at a policy level, the Thai government supports the incorporation of TBA/traditional midwives' practice within the public health system, in reality there is little support given to maintain traditional midwives' skills, and in turn there is less and less demand for their services. The roles of these women are changing. Traditional knowledge, embodied in the elderly traditional midwife conflicts with the 'modern' scientific knowledge legitimised by the state. Traditional midwives do retain important roles in the supervision of post-partum confinement but their authority on matters of birth is being steadily undermined.

The case study presented here of Baan Srisaket reveals the consequences of the unequal relations of power between the institutionalised biomedical state health system and local practices and knowledge. The authoritative knowledge of birthing is no longer embodied within the local traditional midwives, but rather, is created through discourse and embodied in the uniformed nurses and doctors of the hospitals and health stations. It has become the norm for women to give birth in hospitals despite their misgivings about the quality of their experiences there. The power relations underlying the organisation of health care in Thailand shape the choices women make and the meanings of their actions. The women of Baan Srisaket make considered choices about where they give birth, but these choices take place within complex relationships influencing the meanings of knowledge and practice.

Notes

1 Nurse Silaa is a nurse/midwife who completed tenth grade at school and then underwent an eighteen-month course in midwifery training. Nurse Thong is a technical nurse who has undergone a two-year post secondary school certificate. It is possible for technical nurses to complete a further two and a half years of training to become professional nurses. See Muecke and Srisuphan 1989 regarding nursing in Thailand.
2 In 1992 the women who gave birth at home, or were given the placenta by hospital staff buried the placentas of male children under a window, under stairs, under the eaves of the house and under the eaves of the *horng phra* (room in which the images of the Lord Buddha were kept). The placentas of female babies were buried under a window of the house.
3 See Davis 1984; Halpern 1963; Irvine 1982: 266–7; and Poulsen 1983 for further description of the dangers of these spirits.
4 *Phii taai thang kom* is the name given to the spirit that arises from a death in childbirth when both mother and child die. Irvine suggests that this word is also

associated with a similar word for circle and thus signifies the binding of the mother and child in a circle of life and death (1982: 266). In such cases the bodies of mother and child are separated and buried immediately to ensure that the aggrieved souls cannot leave the corpses and remain amongst the living. After a period of time, three to five years, the remains will be disinterred and given a Buddhist cremation.

5 Similar warming practices exist throughout Asia. See Manderson 1981; Laderman 1987; Harris's description of Iban *bekindu'* (Chapter 11 this volume). There has been little recognition of the significance of this rite for women in Thailand. Only Hanks (1963: 71) suggests that in Central Thailand, it was 'one of the series of rites of the life-cycle which marked the course of an individual from birth to death', through which a woman attains full maturity. See Whittaker (2002) for a comparison between this rite and male ordination ceremonies.

6 Fewer women observe post-partum practices after second births. Women stated that doctors warn women who have had tubal ligations (the most popular form of contraception in Thailand) against staying by the fire because it will make the surgery scar *akseep* (infected) through the heat of the fire and the sutures may dissolve. Such a notion is consistent with humoral notions of the action of the fire, as in the local Lao language the term *akseep* implies a notion of inflammation and overheating. Staying by the fire is also said to be unnecessary after a tubal ligation, as there is no further need to dry out the womb and delay the next birth.

7 This potentially destructive power of female sexuality even extends to contact with the undergarments or skirts of women. Women are careful to hang these items below waist level and in a discrete location to avoid men accidentally walking underneath the washing line. Hanks suggests that the power of women's menstrual blood may even corrupt Buddhist power or men's protective amulets (Hanks 1963: 28–9).

References

Alpha Research Co. 1994. *Pocket Thailand Public Health 1995*. Bangkok: Alpha Research Co. Ltd (Manager Information Services).

Bourdieu, P. 1977. *Outline of a Theory of Practice*. Translated by Richard Nice. Cambridge: Cambridge University Press.

Bourdieu, P. and J.-C. Passeron. 1977. *Reproduction in Education, Society and Culture*. London: Routledge & Kegan Paul.

Cohen, P.T. 1989. The politics of primary health care in Thailand, with special reference to non-government organizations. In *The Political Economy of Primary Health Care in Southeast Asia*, edited by P.T. Cohen and J. Purcal. Canberra: ASEAN Training Centre for Primary Health Care Development.

Crouch, M. and L. Manderson. 1993. *New Motherhood: Cultural and Personal Transitions in the 1980s*. Camberwell: Gordon & Breach.

Davis, R. 1984. *Muang Metaphysics: A Study of Northern Thai Myth and Ritual*. Bangkok: Pandora Press.

Government of Thailand. 1992. *The Seventh National Economic and Social Development Plan (1992–1996)*. Bangkok: National Economic and Social Development Board (NESDB), Office of the Prime Minister.

Halpern, J.M. 1963. Traditional medicine and the role of the Phii in Laos. *Eastern Anthropologist* 16: 191–200.

Hanks, J.R. 1963. *Maternity and its Rituals in Bang Chan*. Ithaca, NY: Cornell Thailand Project, Cornell University.

Hobart, M. 1993. Introduction: the growth of ignorance? In *An Anthropological Critique of Development: The Growth of Ignorance*, edited by M. Hobart. London: Routledge.

Irvine, W. 1982. The Thai-Yuan 'madman' and the 'modernising', developing Thai nation as bounded entities under threat: a study in the replication of a single image. Ph.D. Thesis School of Oriental and African Studies, University of London.

JICA. 1992. *Public Health Service System Development Project at the District Level, Khon Kaen Province*. Khon Kaen: Provincial Health Office, JICA Project, Khon Kaen.

Jordan, B. 1993 [1978]. *Birth in Four Cultures: A Cross-cultural Investigation of Childbirth in Yucatan, Holland, Sweden and the United States*, fourth edition. Prospect Heights, IL: Waveland Press.

Kachondham, Y. and S. Chunharas. 1993. At the crossroards: challenges for Thailand's health development. *Health Policy and Planning* 8 (3): 208–16.

Laderman, C. 1987. Destructive heat and cooling prayer: Malay humoralism in pregnancy, childbirth and the post-partum period. *Social Science and Medicine* 25 (4): 357–65.

Le Grand, A. and L. Sri-ngernyuang. 1989. *Herbal Drugs in Primary Health Care. Thailand: The Impact of Promotional Activities on Drug Consumption, Drug Provision and Self-reliance*. Bangkok: Mahidol University.

Manderson, L. 1981. Roasting, smoking and dieting in response to birth: Malay confinement in cross-cultural perspective. *Social Science and Medicine* 15B: 509–20.

Mills, M.B. 1995. Attack of the widow ghosts: gender, death, and modernity in Northeast Thailand. In *Bewitching Women, Pious Men: Gender and Body Politics in Southeast Asia*, edited by A. Ong and M.G. Peletz. Berkeley: University of California Press.

Mougne, C. 1978. An ethnography of reproduction: changing patterns of fertility in a Northern Thai village. In *Nature and Man in South East Asia*, edited by P.A. Stott. London: SOAS, University of London.

Muecke, M. 1976. Health care systems as socialising agents: childbearing the Northern Thai and western ways. *Social Science and Medicine* 10: 377–83.

Muecke, M. and W. Srisuphan. 1989. Born female: the development of nursing in Thailand. *Social Science and Medicine* 29 (5): 643–52.

Newman, L F. 1981. Midwives and modernization. *Medical Anthropology* 5(1): 1–12.

Oakley, A. 1975. Wisewoman and medicine man: changes in the management of childbirth. In *The Rights and Wrongs of Women*, edited by J. Mitchell and A. Oakley. Harmondsworth: Penguin.

Poulsen, A. 1983. *Pregnancy and Childbirth: Its Customs and Rites in a North-eastern Thai Village*. Copenhagen: Danish International Development Agency.

Ram, K. 1998. Epilogue: maternal experience and feminist body politics: Asian and Pacific perspectives. In *Maternity and Modernities: Colonial and Postcolonial Experiences in Asia and the Pacific*, edited by K. Ram and M. Jolly. Cambridge: Cambridge University Press.

Rozario, S. 1998. The dai and the doctor: discourses on women's reproductive health in rural Bangladesh. In *Maternity and Modernities: Colonial and Postcolonial Experiences in Asia and the Pacific*, edited by K. Ram and M. Jolly. Cambridge: Cambridge University Press.

Sargent, C. and G. Bascope. 1996. Ways of knowing about birth in three cultures. *Medical Anthropology Quarterly,* 10 (2): 213–36.

Steinberg, S. 1996. Childbearing research: a transcultural review. *Social Science and Medicine,* 43 (12): 1765–84.

Treichler, P. 1990. Feminism, medicine, and the meaning of childbirth. In *Body/ Politics: Women and the Discourses of Science,* edited by In M. Jacobs, E. Fox Keller and S. Shuttleworth. New York: Routledge.

Van Esterik, P. 1982. Infant feeding options for Bangkok professional women. In *The Decline of the Breast: An Examination of its Impact on Fertility and Health and its Relation to Socioeconomic Status,* edited by M.C. Latham. Ithaca, NY: Cornell University.

Verderese, M. and L. Turnbull. 1975. *The Traditional Birth Attendant in Maternal and Child Health and Family Planning.* Geneva: WHO.

Whittaker, A. 2000. *Intimate Knowledge: Women and their Health in Northeast Thailand.* Sydney: Allen and Unwin.

—— 2002. Water serpents and staying by the fire: markers of maturity in a Northeast Thai village. In *Coming of Age: Youth in Asian Societies,* edited by L. Manderson and P. Liamputtong Rice. London: Curzon.

Chapter 11

Beranak and *bekindu'*

Discourses of risk and strength in childbirth and post-partum practice among Iban communities of Pakan

Amanda Harris

Introduction

An important dimension of socio-economic change in the lives of rural Iban women in Sarawak is their connection with the biomedically based state health-care system by virtue of their role as childbearers and mothers. The way these medical services are experienced, utilised and critiqued by women seems significantly determined by other dimensions of their lives relating to government approaches to the development of rural longhouse communities. These processes of modernity also produce transformations in the ways Iban women come to perceive themselves in relation to Iban women of the past, and Iban men and women of other ethnicities. This chapter examines the relationship between these domains of experience for rural Iban women, focusing on transformations in childbirth and post-partum practices.

There is also a particular need to conduct research with rural Iban women in Sarawak, not only because this is an area which has been largely neglected by researchers in more recent years (with the notable exception of Kedit 1993, Mashman 1993 and Sutlive 1993), but because a focus on gender relations in Iban society has been overshadowed by arguments that, to varying degrees, continue to support notions of egalitarianism. As noted also by Sutlive and Appell (1993), an enduring discourse in Bornean research in which Iban society has been represented as egalitarian has been extended uncritically to gender relations. Yet rejoinders to this discourse have, I argue, fallen short of a thorough-going critique (see Harris 1998) and the extent to which the experiences of social, economic and political transformation among rural women differ from those of Iban men has not been adequately recognised. Thus, what it means to be a woman in contemporary rural Iban society has not, I suggest, received the attention it requires.[1]

The Iban people of Sarawak constitute the largest non-Malay indigenous group in the state, comprising, in 1990, 29.5 per cent (493,000) of the population.[2] Since the incorporation of Sarawak into the Federation of Malaysia in 1963, the Iban have experienced significant transformations in their political, economic and social status. While contemporary Iban people can be

described as an indigenous minority with significant political power compared with other indigenous groups, it is also the case that as a consequence
of several factors – historical, political and geographical – many rural Iban
people in particular remain marginal to the broader economic and social
realities of Malaysian life.[3] In terms of health status and access to healthcare,
generally the eastern states of Sabah and Sarawak 'continue to lag behind the
peninsula, with higher malnutrition among children and higher incidences of
the "diseases of underdevelopment", poorer access to medical care, as well as
shortage of health personnel and relevant facilities, such as piped water and
sanitation' (Wee Chong Hui 1995: 143).[4] While some excellent and detailed
contributions have been made to issues pertaining to poverty, agricultural
development, occupational distribution and education in relation to Iban
people (for example see Jawan 1994, Kedit 1993, King and Jawan 1996,
Padoch 1978), the areas of health and health care, examined in the context of
socio-economic and political change, have remained peripheral to most
Bornean scholarship.

This chapter is based on research conducted among several Iban longhouse communities in the Pakan subdistrict, part of the Sarikei Division in
Sarawak, over a twelve-month period from February 1995. The region is
criss-crossed by a network of rivers, which, over the years, have become pro-
gressively depleted of fish and other food sources and impractical as routes of
transport due to logs and silt washed down from upriver. The road system is
minimal and only significant around the several small townships. Travelling
along forest paths and the occasional road between longhouses means passing by numerous farms of hill rice, the traditional staple for Iban people,
interspersed with corn, pepper gardens, rubber trees, vegetable gardens and
areas of secondary growth forest. Most longhouses are located along river
banks, but increasingly communities (approximately 50 to 250 individuals
each) are choosing to relocate beside a road and access the many benefits,
economic and otherwise, this provides. In 1995 Pakan township had a population of 375 and the subdistrict had a population of 15,489. While in 1990
Iban people constituted 29.5 per cent (493,000) of the state's population,
over 95 per cent of the Pakan subdistrict is Iban. Most of these people reside
in 140 longhouse communities outside Pakan and other smaller townships
that dot the region. The material presented in this chapter is drawn from
several of these communities.

Pakan women engage each other in vehement debate about the changes
they are experiencing and the ways they negotiate and experience themselves
in relation to these changes. The most striking division that emerges in the
discourses, however, is between women who have experienced greater economic security and material well-being in their lives and those for whom the
rhetoric of development has not translated into such favourable circumstances. This emerges as the discussion below attends to the contrasting views
and perceptions of women residing in a state-designated 'model longhouse',

who are therefore the beneficiaries of considerable assistance through small rural development schemes, and those in less well-endowed communities.

Beranak (childbirth): locating risk and being nakal

Maternal and Child Health Services were initiated in Sarawak in the 1950s, and in the 1960s came under the jurisdiction of local councils which injected them with much-needed managerial and organisational improvement. A decade later these facilities were gradually absorbed into the Sarawak Department of Health with the introduction of an integrated medical and health service. Current policy in Sarawak is to encourage women to give birth in rural clinics and hospitals with the ultimate aim of removing childbirth from the longhouse and from the care of TBAs.[5] The subdistrict of Pakan is served by one government Health Centre and two Rural Clinics. Residents of Pakan township and surrounding longhouse communities are provided with primary healthcare services through the larger Health Centre, or *Pusat Kesihatan*, known locally as the 'clinic'. In Pakan township the maternity section of the clinic has been in operation since the 1970s. In 1995 it had three government-trained midwives. Some years prior to this, maternal care was available through Sarikei hospital. Although Sarikei is now linked to Pakan via road, accessing this service for many longhouses still requires several hours' or days' travel on foot or by river contingent upon weather conditions. Laderman (1983) reports that in Trengganu in Peninsular Malaysia, government midwives would attend births in the homes of women. In Sarawak, however, this does not seem to have been the case in the geographically remote and inaccessible areas such as Pakan.

As elsewhere in the world (Gifford 1986, Kaufert and O'Neil 1993, Lane 1995), arguments of reducing risk to mother and child inform and serve to legitimise Department of Health policies in Sarawak. According to Pakan clinic annual reports, infant mortality had decreased over the entire Sarikei district from fifteen deaths per 1000 live births in 1994 to twelve deaths per 1000 live births in 1995.[6] Over the two years only one *en route* birth occurred. According to state government reports, infant, perinatal and maternal mortality rates continue to fall. Pakan rates, however, remain slightly higher than state averages (Kuching General Hospital 1994).

Government records categorise deliveries into three broad groupings: 'Institutional', 'Home' and 'Safe' deliveries. This last category includes deliveries in the presence of government- or privately trained personnel, which occurs in more accessible populations. By virtue of their exclusion from this category, deliveries by 'untrained *bidans*', that is, traditional Iban midwives, which come under 'Home' deliveries, are defined as unsafe. The *1994 Maternal and Child Health Service Report* states: 'Untrained midwives and traditional birth attendants conducted 2724 deliveries representing 5.5% of reported births. This percentage is steadily decreasing as more mothers opt for "safe" deliveries by trained personnel' (Kuching General Hospital 1994: 5).

Epidemiological evidence is central to the arguments of physicians, government midwives and other health workers, and defines established Iban birthing practices and the longhouse as a high-risk environment for childbirth. Although midwives at Pakan clinic report a significant reduction in mortality rates over its years of operation, it has been argued by some that 'all perinatal and neonatal mortality rates are artefacts . . . their meaning is ambiguous, contingent on the context in which they are used, changing with shift in the wording of a definition' (Armstrong 1986 and Wright 1988 cited in Kaufert and O'Neil 1993: 45).

Other researchers have similarly been critical of statistics generated from crude perinatal mortality rates used to establish delivery outside the hospital/clinic context as higher risk (e.g. Campbell and McFarlane 1987 and Tew 1990, cited in Lane 1995: 58). In Sarawak, it is difficult to compare mortality rates by place of birth as there has never been a rigorous, statistically valid study of longhouse births. As Kaufert and O'Neil note, 'The language in which people spoke about risk [in childbirth] . . . reflected who was speaking, to whom they were speaking, and the historical and political context of what they were saying' (1993: 43). Without exception, government employed medical staff at the clinic and hospital staff, many of whom at the local level are Iban, are fully supportive of government policies of a complete shift in the location of childbirth. One of the three midwives that staff the maternity section of the Pakan clinic explained:

> The policy now is to encourage women to give birth in the hospital and clinic. We encourage people by giving education. We also give incentives such as towels, soap and powder. Some women may still want to give birth in the longhouse if they have a family problem, or if they do not have time to come to the clinic, they give birth on the way. If this happens they must come to the clinic with the baby. Maybe they will have a problem such as the placenta has not yet come out. In such cases we never go to the longhouse, they must come here. Better for them to come here because maybe before we arrive the mother will have collapsed. Also there is not enough staff.

The only explanation for those women who may still want to give birth in the longhouse is that they are experiencing 'family problems'. Absent from this scenario are women who simply prefer birth in the longhouse over clinics and hospitals. In terms of the pragmatics of staffing shortages and inaccessibility, the validity of the explanations the midwife offers for requiring the expectant mother to come to the medical facility instead of providing a midwifery service to the longhouse is obvious. Yet informing her argument is a definition of the longhouse as a high risk environment and birth as requiring medical intervention. To further enforce Department of Health policies, the incentives scheme extends beyond soaps, towels and powder to include birth certificates. Birth in the clinic or hospital ensures that parents will be able to secure a birth certificate for their child. This is an essential document for all Malaysian citizens, since without it an identity card cannot be obtained, and this document enables a person to enrol at school, gain employment and obtain a passport. Another midwife in Pakan explains:

Midwife: Actually, the birth certificate is one of the incentives. So if they deliver in the clinic, we provide them with that one. If they deliver at home we cannot issue it because we do not encourage home delivery. Also because babies from other countries come in. People can cheat. So we have to be careful.
AH: What if a woman gave birth early or was unable to get from the farm to the clinic?
Midwife: They've got an excuse. But they must come and have a check. We check the mother.
AH: Do they have to come within three days?
Midwife: Yes, because we want to immunise the baby. Administer a BCG.

If a women does come within this time period for a check-up with the child, she can, in theory, obtain an application form for the birth certificate. Although this seems to have been the case for some women, a number of women report encountering extended difficulties. The factuality of their claims is difficult to verify, but this is of less importance than recognising the emotive critique of this government policy from rural Iban women. The response from medical staff to women's negative perceptions of delivery in clinics and hospital is to increase the coercive means of deterring longhouse births. However, this exclusive aim of removing birth from longhouses also increases the risk to women who are forced to travel over long and difficult distances. Although the clinic tallies only one *en route* birth for the previous two years, if the type of risk argument that is central to medical models were to be applied to this practice, then this must be deemed one of the most risk-laden. It is certainly one of the most protested factors among women in longhouses not conveniently situated alongside a road and it is the cause of much stress, anxiety, anger and fear in mothers. As Lane states, 'fear is one of the most decisive elements in the erosion of safety and ease during delivery' (1995: 65).

For the birth of their first child and after their fifth, Pakan women are advised by clinic staff to go to the better-equipped and better-staffed hospital in Sarikei. For the second through fifth they are encouraged to make use of the local clinic facilities, provided there are no complications. Childbirth in the alternatives of clinic or hospital forms a major focus for debate amongst women. Although figures suggest a trend away from the hospital and into the clinic, in conversations among women the hospital generally emerges as the more favoured option.[7] Other than reportedly routine episiotomies, a common complaint directed at the clinic is the lack of privacy, being 'looked at' by the staff, and feeling humiliation and shame (*malu*) at having to use one's own sarong during labour and wash it afterwards. Afterbirth is considered particularly unclean and bad smelling by Iban women and men and following a birth in the longhouse the placenta is wrapped securely in cloth and either buried underground or hung in a small woven basket (*raga*) high in a tree. Both practices are also intended to prevent the placenta being devoured by certain *antu*, or spirits, thereby inflicting harm on the newborn.

The midwives in Pakan report that women coming in to give birth say very little, ask for little and raise no complaint. In contrast to this site of passive compliance and acquiescence the longhouse *ruai* is a location of vigorous discussion and debate. Topics include changes in recent years that have occurred in childbirth practices, the forces effecting these changes, and women's experiences of parturition in clinic, hospital and longhouse, or somewhere in between. In providing some space for these voices that become muted in the medical setting, this material also represents a move away from the emphasis on 'the midwife' that has tended to dominate studies of childbirth.

There is no unitary 'Iban discourse' on childbirth. For some women the effect of health education initiatives has been that a former fear of giving birth outside the longhouse is replaced by a fear of giving birth in the longhouse. To these women, the longhouse is transformed into a dangerous and potentially fatal place to be. These women experience greater feelings of vulnerability in the longhouse context and tend to relinquish notions of the longhouse as a site most supportive of one's good health and speedy recovery. Yet this view is opposed by other women who argue in favour of childbirth in the longhouse, at least for uncomplicated cases. Others take a more hardline view and argue for childbirth in the longhouses in all instances, and still others remain undecided. However, discernible within this heteroglossia of voices are two dominant positions, and the most striking difference between these two groups of women is the material, economic and political conditions of their lives. In other words, a marked contrast is evident between the views of women who reside at Rumah Nari, a state designated 'model longhouse', and those who live in less well-endowed communities. This latter group is also the site of least consensus and greatest debate.

Among the women of Rumah Nari, the language of risk is drawn significantly from the discourse of the physician, the government midwife and health worker and various health education resources. Childbirth in the longhouse is regarded as a practice of the past, an unfortunate practice that women endured out of lack of choice. However, once outside this community, the tone of dialogue about childbirth takes on a more critical and disparate character. For many of these women childbirth in the longhouse is perceived as a less risky practice than anything requiring entry into a hospital or clinic. To many of these women, birth is something that occurs naturally in the course of everyday life. Neither is it unusual for woman to give birth alone, or in the company of one or two others if present. Only if there is difficulty with the birth are further individuals called – possibly a *bidan*, or a *manang* to perform a *pelian*,[8] or a man to assist in applying pressure upon the diaphragm, a practice known as *tekan* – but their presence seems to have been the exception rather than the norm. To these women the longhouse is perceived as an environment conducive to vitality, strength and the greatest chances of a rapid recovery from the strains of childbirth, and the hospital as the more risk-laden option. In other words, women's experiences in a wider social and material context significantly shape their experiences of biomedical intervention and the ways in which their perceptions of self emerge out of this interaction.

For women who prefer birth in the longhouse, forms of intervention in the hospital or clinic, such as episiotomies or the use of forceps or injections to stimulate uterine contractions are often raised as reasons for not wanting to give birth in these facilities. These views inform the words of women at Rumah Lium:

W1 (60)[9]:   I have twelve children. I've never given birth at the hospital. I've remained in the longhouse [every time]. I don't want to give birth in the hospital because of the pain of the injection they give! [Others laugh.] People there cut us women, but I don't want that. I prefer to stay in the longhouse and give birth alone!

W2 (58):   Because it's more comfortable (*nyamai*) in the longhouse if the birth is easy.

W1 (60):   It's better at the longhouse, they don't cut you here. We don't get sick. Not really sick. Those of us who go to the hospital are really sick for a long time, siiiick! Problems with urinating, problems with defecating, eeeh! In the longhouse, we already know that we don't get sick. There is no other disturbance (*nadai ngacau agi'*). When we give birth at the longhouse, we are not really sick like that. In Sarikei, ooh, they ignore those who want to give birth in the longhouse.

W2 (58):   There they cut you. There's none of that here.

For W1, the hospital, as well as the medicine received there in the form of the injection, was perceived as a place where the risk of falling ill was increased, whereas the longhouse was associated with resilience and the ability to withstand discomfort or pain (*nakal*), with individuals who are stronger, more resilient and self-healing: 'we already know that we don't get sick.' To her, the locational shift in birthing practices is seen as potentially

debilitating and undermining of women's strength and the means implemented to enforce these changes, particularly the withholding of birth
certificates, and the lack of infrastructure that would enable women to travel
to these locations, receive sharp criticism. To the women in the above dialogue the hospital is perceived as a place where women are 'disturbed'
(*ngacau*) by others (presumably the medical or nursing staff), and in the
words of W1 this disturbance and illness are practically conflated. In a
sense, the medical staff are construed as a source of debility. In contrast, the
longhouse stands as a context where women retain their power and autonomy, their health and strength.

The shift of childbirth location also deprives Iban women of the opportunity to learn the skills and pass on the knowledge of the *bidan*. Women's
vulnerability is thus increased through their increasing dependency on the
medical profession. As Kaufert and O'Neil comment, 'To be without knowledge is to be at risk; to be dependent on others is to be at risk' (1993: 49).
According to Lane, Beck (1992) argues that the medical profession – through
successful professionalisation and an absence of any separation of powers –
'has been able to convince the public that it is conceptually "uninformed" and
that it lags hopelessly behind medical innovation and medical knowledge'
(Lane 1995: 54). However, Iban women resist a redefinition of themselves as
'uninformed' through the assertion of superior birthing practices. One well-
respected *bidan* of the Pakan area, who has attended births for over twenty
years, argues for the use of hands, as opposed to scissors and forceps in delivery. She draws a comparison between the '*adat* (practice, knowledge,
tradition) of the longhouse' and that of the clinic and hospital:

Bidan (50):   The *adat* of the longhouse is that we use these [she holds up her
                hands] only. I only use my hands, to turn the baby, to the right,
                it is then on the right, slowly, thus, with the hand, like this . . . If
                the birth is not progressing, people fetch those of us who know
                how to use our hands. Or if the woman cannot push we'll be
                fetched . . . According to Iban *adat*, scissors cannot be used.
AH: And if the placenta has not come out?
Bidan (50):   Get it using the hand, pull, carefully. The placenta is then placed
                in a basket . . . and the umbilical cord is tied with a piece of
                thread.

One of the most powerful constructions of risk invoked by medical staff for
legitimising the shift of women into clinic or hospital births is a long-estab-
lished practice among Iban people of providing *tekan*, that is pressure on the
diaphragm of the parturient woman. *Tekan* is often cited by medical staff as
one of the most dangerous of traditional practices that needs to be abolished.
It was described vividly by a physician during my initial weeks in Pakan. If it
is used when the cervix is not sufficiently dilated it can, he explained, cause

rupturing of the uterus. He illustrated his point by describing a case that had occurred several years earlier resulting in the death of both mother and child. Apparently, this particular birth, which had taken place in a longhouse, had not been progressing and the people had deemed *tekan* the most appropriate action to take. According to this physician, the violence of the force exerted on her caused severe haemorrhaging and tissue rupture. By the time the woman had been taken to hospital her external physiology was impossible to distinguish and both mother and child died shortly afterward.[10] Many, although by no means all, Iban women hold quite different perceptions of *tekan*.

According to some, pressure would be applied to the diaphragm of the parturient woman every three or four contractions by those seated around her head. Several women also said that a man was called if additional strength was required and the availability of men for this purpose was one reason given by some for preferring to give birth in the longhouse. Many older Iban women relate the use of this method successfully in childbirth. The presence of kin associated with the practice of *tekan* was also important to them. Having to give birth 'alone' (*kediri'*), associated with the hospital or clinic, was viewed as a highly undesirable event. Even in cases where the woman had unavoidably given birth alone – such as one elderly woman who gave birth to one child in her longboat – Iban women report pushing down with their folded forearms on to the diaphragm. No doubt such cases of *tekan* as described to me by the Pakan physician exist, but such portrayals come to dominate the representation of this practice within the discourse of the medical profession. Through the biomedical rhetoric of risk, *tekan* is transmuted into something dangerous and feared by women.

Through childbirth and post-partum practices Iban women aspire to and express values that align closely with those usually assigned by researchers to Iban men, and aspired to through traditional institutions such as warfare and *bejalai*, or the practice of travelling away from the longhouse for extended periods in search of experience, employment and prestige. To be strong, able to withstand pain, to be able to endure discomfort, to be self-sufficient and brave continue to stand as values to which women also aspire. As a result of changes that have occurred through the advent of medical services and discourses of risk that emanate from biomedical practitioners and health workers, many women are being deprived of the opportunity to attain these qualities. Several Pakan women were proud that they had not resorted to using any additional methods to ease their pain during labour. Those who do weaken under the strains of childbearing are readily chastised by other women. Although women do talk about the pain and undesirability of much of childbirth with each other, a significant amount of value is placed on being strong and not crying out, and this stands as an important marker of difference between themselves and women of other ethnicities. Relating her experiences of giving birth in the hospital in Brunei to a group of women on the *ruai* one afternoon, One woman in her thirties said: 'In the room with me was a Malay woman and a Chinese woman. "Ahooooo! Ahooooo!" cried the Malay. "I'm ill! I'm ill!" cried the Chinese. But I made no sound.'

However, it is amongst the women at Rumah Nari that fear of giving birth in the hospital and clinic has been most markedly replaced by both fear and rejection of longhouse births and associated practices. These women even express a positive view of being 'cut', or undergoing episiotomies, and none whom I spoke to at Rumah Nari would consider giving birth in the longhouse these days:

W1 (40):   It's proper (*betul*) to give birth in the hospital. 'Do not give birth in the longhouse', say the people from the Department of Health. They don't want us to give birth here because it's difficult. They don't want it because there's no-one to give blood if we need blood.

W2 (80):   In the past many women died [in childbirth] in the longhouse. Now we give birth in the hospital.

W1 (40):   And there [in the hospital], if the baby can't get out, they know how to cut you.

W2 (80):   The baby comes out and they lift it up. In the past there was no understanding in the longhouse about how to lift the baby like that.

AH: Does the *manang* still perform *besudi* [in this instance a protective rite for newborns] for the child when it returns to the longhouse?

W1 (40):   No, not every time. There is not really any use for a *manang* in childbirth. We all give birth in the hospital. We have risen above the practice of *bekindu'*, as they did in the past. Now we take medicine from the hospital only.

Problems obtaining a birth certificate were of course not an issue for this community and never arose in conversation among these women. Among them, the biomedicalisation of motherhood gains a much greater acceptance, and is experienced without the negative repercussions in terms of self-perception evident among women outside this community. To Rumah Nari women, childbirth should occur in clinics and hospital, biomedical discourse informs arguments about risk, the skills of the *manang* are redundant and old post-partum practices are laughed about as quaint beliefs of the past. Older women at Rumah Nari were exceptional among their age group for having so entirely replaced a longhouse discourse of risk with that expounded by the medical profession. Neither do Rumah Nari women berate the conditions and service at the Pakan clinic in comparison with hospital as do women of other longhouses.

Bekindu' (post-partum heating): the endurance required and fortitude derived

Iban women of Pakan have been practising a form of post-partum heating known as *bekindu'* for as long as they can recall. Similar practices involving the application of heat to the mother (and often the child as well) after delivery have been common in Asia and Latin America, but usually in association with humoral theories of medicine (Manderson 1981), to which Iban notions of sickness and healing, it has been argued (Barrett and Lucas 1994), do not readily conform. The practice of *bekindu'* is defined in Richards' dictionary as follows: '(of a woman after childbirth, *ADA*) sit with a fire (of logs, *UNGGUN*) at her back: this often leads to burns and usu. debility from lack of normal food and sleep (feared as harmful)' (Richards 1981: 165).

Research over the last two decades has conveyed the impression that *bekindu'* is a practice of the past (e.g. Barrett and Lucas 1993, Sather 1978, 1988), and researchers tend to give voice to only negative recollections women have of this practice. Sather, for example, reports: 'The intensity of the heat of *bekindu'* is indicated by older women's recollections of the blisters raised by this procedure' (1988: 165), and Barrett and Lucas note: 'Reflecting on these former practices, an informant thought that the heating had sometimes been excessive and itself had caused death by congealing the polluted blood and preventing its escape' (1993: 579). According to Jensen, 'Burned backs are a common sight' (1966: 174). Similar recollections were also evident among Pakan women, but for many these were tempered, if not upstaged, by more positive perceptions of this practice. Such critical representations of Iban practices risk becoming examples of what McClain (1982, as cited in Jeffery and Jeffery 1993) has referred to as a biomedical perspective amongst researchers that can function to support and provide the criteria for Western-derived medical agenda of modernising the traditional. It is the broader social forces that underlie the distinction between women who reject the practice of *bekindu'* and those who view it in some degree as beneficial that are my central concern. It is, I argue, a misrepresentation to locate *bekindu'* simply and exclusively in the past, at least in regard to many of the women of Pakan, considering the ways it is talked about and integrated into a complex regime of post-partum self-care. Representations of changes in the practice of *bekindu'* in recent research literature are in terms of its diminution moving toward eventual and inevitable extinguishment, rather than its active reworking within current practices.

Encountering only one woman practicing *bekindu'* during my twelve months of field research does, however, suggest that it is far from a common practice. In October of 1995 Menti gave birth to her fourth child easily and unexpectedly one morning under a tree in her garden and in the company of another woman. The infant had arrived three weeks ahead of its due date. Menti was then in her late twenties and had given birth to all her children in the longhouse environment and claimed to have practiced *bekindu'* for approximately a month after the birth of each. She shared her *bilik* with her husband and children. It was the last on the upriver end of Rumah Tinggang with a window that looked over the river below where people bathed, and a floor fashioned from strips of split bamboo, making this *bilik* particularly light and cool.[11] I found Menti seated upright with legs straight out in front of her. Behind her a fire (*api unggun*) made from large slow-burning logs smouldered.[12] Menti held her baby in her arms as she fed it some cooked rice water mixed with a little sugar from a bottle. This, she said, she used in addition to breast milk. The infant looked healthy and alert, and a bright red from the heat of the fire and clothing it was wrapped in.

Menti was protected from the direct heat of the fire by a wide piece of bark wrapped in a sarong tied around her torso (a practice known as *balut*) that extended from immediately under her breasts to across her hips. This wrapping is generally put in place soon after the birth to help the woman's stomach regain its shape and aid the expulsion of 'bad blood'. It appears in most accounts of *bekindu'* from different regions of Sarawak. Pakan women say they remain upright to prevent this 'bad blood' from reaching the head (*enggai darah niki' pala'*) and causing *benta*, a type of debility and general weakness that affects women, marked in its initial stages by strong headaches. Sather aptly describes *benta* as 'a condition in which [the woman] becomes *layu'*, weak and pale . . . She may feel "giddy" . . . be forgetful or dreamy, and have difficulty walking . . . or seeing properly' (1988: 166). The ascent of blood is widely asserted in Pakan to be stimulated by the rising sun, rendering morning a particularly dangerous time of the day for post-partum women. Older women report that it was common not to lie down throughout night and day for the entire period of *bekindu'*. The head would be rested on folded arms over a bench placed in front of the woman. Some women, however, report lying down to the side during the night with their legs still stretched out in front of them, as Menti did. Many women I spoke to maintained that these days it is not a problem to lie down after 2 p.m. or 3 p.m. when the strong heat of the sun has passed.

To Menti's right lay a small woven mat and pillow, the sleeping place for the infant. Sweat dripped down her neck and shoulders and Menti exclaimed how hot and tired she felt, particularly in her legs. After feeding the infant, Menti dabbed Vicks – which she referred to as 'heating oil' (*minyak angat*) – on the child's head, abdomen and on each hand and foot to prevent the entry of debilitating cold wind (*angin celap*), according to some a form of *antu*. This done, she wrapped the infant in a soft cotton cloth and over that, a light towel. The child was placed on mat, hands in mittens and three loops of black cotton cloth (*ikat semengat*), one around each ankle and around one wrist. These provide protection for a child by rendering him or her invisible to potentially malevolent *antu*. Both the blackness of the cloth itself, and a substance (*engkerabun*) obtained from a *manang* which is sewn inside the black loops of cloth, act to blind *antu*. In addition to this function, the *ikat semengat* set off (*kejang*) and support (*tekal*) the flow of breastmilk (*penkalai tusu*).

Menti said she was planning to practice *bekindu'* for about a month, as she had with her previous three births, although she did not intend to follow the food restrictions that women heeded in the past. She ate all vegetables and fruit but fish was restricted to occasional consumption, possibly as fish are particularly implicated in women's ill-health through their manifestations as water residing *antu*. Neither could chickens or animals that had been killed by a member of Menti's household, or *bilik*, be eaten by her as this would risk illness or death of the child. Accordingly, Menti only ate pork, chicken and other animals which had been killed by people who were not of her *bilik*, and as an added precaution some time needed to have elapsed since the animal's death before consumption. This relatively open dietary regime represents a significant loosening of restrictions from former practices. Older women of Pakan tell of following a diet restricted almost exclusively to three types of vegetable – *daun sabong* (unidentified), *paku' keru'* (type of edible fern) and *upa' pantu'* (palm 'cabbage') and some fish if it has been prepared by being slowly smoked (*ikan salai*).[13] Department of Health education programmes are undoubtedly significant in effecting these changes.

In choosing to sit for such an extended period Menti was exceptional amongst women who reported practising *bekindu'*. Most women chose to sit for only a few days or maybe up to a couple of weeks, and often after returning from having given birth in the clinic or hospital. Most of the older women of Pakan recall long periods sitting in front of a fire after all of their deliveries. Sandin, writing in 1966, reported that *bekindu'* ranged from a month to forty-one days (1966: 2, cited in Sather 1988: 165). Sather reports that in the Paku region, 'for the few who continue *bekindu'*, warming generally lasts for only two or three nights' (1988: 166). In Pakan, reported periods of *bekindu'* range from three nights to over a month. Most common, however, in recent years, is the range from five days to two weeks. Many middle-aged women in Pakan report having practiced *bekindu'* for some births and not with others, while amongst the younger generation, there are those who say they have never and will never practice *bekindu'* and there are those who choose to continue its use. The present period is one in which there coexists a wide spectrum of experiences and views on *bekindu'* among Pakan women.

A number of post-partum practices used in conjunction with modified forms of *bekindu'* include drinking small quantities of alcohol, or *arak*, and taking heating medicine referred to as *ubat unggun*, both of which appear to be adaptations of practices among Chinese women. *Ubat unggun* – so named by Iban women by virtue of its shared function with *api unggun*, the smouldering fire traditionally used in *bekindu'* – is a Chinese herbal mix used to restore heat after childbirth. One woman in her early thirties describes her experiences of *ubat unggun*: 'The feeling is good, the same as after drinking arak, hot.' While we sat on the *ruai* one woman fetched her box of *ubat unggun* from her *bilik*, or longhouse apartment. After birth she mixed one small box of this powdered Chinese herbal mixture, labelled 'Ubat Ucing', with warm water and drank it four times each day for two weeks. Other women reported taking it once a day and others twice. In the following dialogue from a more upriver longhouse, women discuss some of their practices:

Bidan (50):   Women here take *ubat* [a term used in reference to a broad range of medicinal substances or methods] – *ubat unggun* and *ubat panjah* (poured over the body).

W1 (28):   made with banana palm leaves.

W2 (45):   many types of leaves are used, *puong* (unidentified) leaves – we soak them in water then pour that over the woman after giving birth. We use it to bathe.[14] Instead of practising *bekindu'*. It's not common now that women practice *bekindu'* here. Because of the fire.

W1 (28):   Women don't practice *bekindu'* here because they're not *nakal*.

Bidan (50):   They take *ubat* that's eaten – out of a bottle. Bought at a shop. Chinese medicine. *Nyamai isi'* (inside the body). Sweat. If we don't have sweat coming out then we'll get sick, *sakit celap* (cold).

W1 (28):   Sick in the stomach, sick in the bones, many types of sickness.

Bidan (50):   We're afraid of the stomach becoming cold.

W1 (28):   . . . of shivering.

W2 (45):   Yes, we must always be hot. The wind must not enter [through the stomach or head]. Wrap a piece of cloth around the head.

Women experience considerable personal agency as they devise their own regimes of post-partum care from the various resources available to them. But agency, although realised, seems to come at a cost. Women enter modernity as simultaneously empowered, able to reject or engage practices as they choose, but struck with their own failure to be as resilient (*nakal*) as their forbears, and having lost the source of post-parturient reinvigoration and strength. Two women at another longhouse reflect on changing practices:

AH: Do women here practice *bekindu'*?

W1 (32):   Sometimes. For two weeks. If it's for longer though, that's better. But if the mother is young they don't. In the past, sometimes for a month, sometimes two weeks, or a week. But if for longer, it's better and the body becomes healthy (*gerai*). People who are sick, who have headaches (*pedis pala'*) use *bekindu'*, as my mother did. But I've never practised *bekindu'*. I've always given birth in the hospital and used *ubat unggun*, taken arak and ginger water. My mother practised *bekindu'* with all her children, but I don't want to . . . *Bekindu'* is the most *senang* (pleasing) because we are *makai* (embraced/warmed, engulfed) by the fire from behind . . . *Bekindu'* is the most powerful.

W2 (29):   Yes, because we know we will become healthy.
AH: Then why do you use other methods?
W1 (32):   Because I'm not *nakal*! Because of the fire.

Most frequently women complained of the pain associated with having to sit upright for so long – an aching pain in the legs and arms usually, but on no occasion did anyone complain about being burnt. Alternative methods offered women an escape from these sufferances. For many women *ubat unggun* was a welcome alternative, and they found that it combined well with ginger and arak, or a shorter period of *bekindu'* for some. But even in the widespread shift to alternative methods, many of the women and men I spoke to expressed the view that, in comparison to these more recent alternatives, *bekindu'* remained the most effective method of abating the chances of the mother becoming cold, of becoming sick, suffering *benta* and, for some, preventing her transformation into an *antu koklier*. And rather than their movement away from *bekindu'* being expressed in terms of choice, it was expressed as being indicative of decreasing *nakal*. Those who choose not to practice *bekindu'*, like some who showed fear during childbirth, risk criticism from other women. During a conversation with a group of women and a few men, including the resident *manang*, at one longhouse, I was asked what method women in my country used to prevent them from becoming cold after childbirth. The conversation began with a discussion of giving birth at home:

W1 (41):   Does your race give birth in a hospital?
AH: Sometimes in the hospital and sometimes at home.
W1 (41):   In your own home?
AH: Yes. A woman usually comes to help.
W1 (41):   If we don't have time [to get to the hospital], we also fetch a woman [*bidan*].
W2 (52):   Do you have your own *adat* for giving birth at home?
AH: Yes, but we don't push on the stomach with our hands [*tekan*]. Sometimes we squat instead of lying down.
Manang: Like a chicken laying an egg. Women here will get sick if they're positioned like that. That's for producing eggs.
W1 (41):   It's better, more congenial (*nyamai*) at home because you can practice *bekindu'*.
AH: Well, women don't practice *bekindu'* in my country.
Manang: You don't?
W1 (41):   Well then what do you take instead? Medicine?
AH: No special medicine.
W1 (41) and Manang: Just arak?
AH: Not usually.
Manang: Well then what do you eat after giving birth?
AH: Usually women continue to eat as they usually do.

The conclusion W1 reached from this conversation was:

W1 (41):   See, they're healthy. They give birth and they don't take any med-
              icine. They don't suffer from headaches like us.
W3 (54):   If a woman here doesn't practice *bekindu'*, doesn't drink some
              arak, then she'll be in much pain. We of this longhouse, if we
              don't practice *bekindu'*, then we won't be hot and we'll be in much
              pain.
W1 (41):   They're not sick like we Iban.
W3 (54):   They have enough to eat.

My contribution to this conversation inadvertently served to highlight
women's perceptions of themselves as less *nakal* than women of Western
society but largely as a result of their economic impoverishment. To this
group of people, the longhouse is both a place where health can be maintained and the risks associated with childbirth in hospital avoided (as the
older woman state earlier in this conversation), but also a place where people
do not have enough to eat, are not as strong and need the healing powers of
bekindu' or its alternatives. To these women, the need for *bekindu'* symbolises
not only their greater propensity for debility but also their economic and
political marginalisation. Neither emerges clearly as the causative factor of
the other.

In contrast to the heterogeneity of views amongst these women, was the
widespread consensus evident at Rumah Nari. One elderly woman (referred
to as W(80)) reflected upon her experiences of childbirth and *bekindu'* as hard
and painful:

W (80):   In the past there weren't any doctors or hospital like there [in
              Sarikei]. We all practiced *bekindu'*. Women were worn out from
              childbirth in the past, those poor women were utterly exhausted.
              We had *api unggun*. Large logs were collected by someone. The
              head, pain in the head had to be prevented, so women used
              bekindu'. For thirty nights I sat, I felt so down! It was hot. I had
              bark and cloth wrapped around me – long long was the night – I
              took care of myself.
W (42):   But she shared the fire with another woman during *bekindu'*.
W (80):   Now, it's better, more congenial (*nyamai*) giving birth there [in the
              hospital].
W (42):   Much better, she says. The baby can sleep by itself and so we can
              also get some sleep. She and others who practised *bekindu'* didn't
              want to sleep during the night. They would always sit up, sit up
              against a post, without lying down. Never lie down. Can't, because
              they don't want blood to go into the head. That would cause a
              sickness in the head, *sakit benta*. That's what the older Iban say.

W (45):   It's much easier, childbirth now. We can eat pig, chicken, eggs!
W (80):   There was hardly anything that we could eat in the past.
W (42):   There'll be no more *bekindu'* in the future. Childbirth is at the hospital there.
W (45):   Yes, in the hospital in Sarikei.

These women of Rumah Nari had placed *bekindu'* firmly in the past. The practice is reconstrued as outdated 'belief', and women distanced themselves from it by presenting them as things the older women 'say' rather than as facts. The overriding feeling among these women was one of relief, that they are not required to endure that hardship. *Bekindu'* was practised out of necessity considering the lack of alternative and better facilities. Moreover, that women were not practising *bekindu'* now was not construed as a negative reflection on them. However, although these women emphasised the positive attributes of the hospital they continued to put together their own regimes of post-partum care – preparing and drinking ginger water, taking *ubat unggun* and drinking arak. The attitude of the Rumah Nari women was very much in accord with the medical profession, in sharp contrast to opinions expressed by Iban women elsewhere. As one woman at Rumah Lium said: 'After giving birth in the hospital we're not well and we become cold rapidly. There are not enough things at the hospital. Giving birth in the longhouse, *bekindu'* supplies what we need.'

Conclusion

Through the heteroglossia of women's voices emanating from Pakan longhouses, two dominant discourses that draw together perceptions of self and experiences of biomedicine can be discerned. Women for whom social, economic and political changes in recent years have manifested in tangible improvements in their material well-being and increasing economic autonomy do not tend to portray or conceive of the past as an era of greater well-being, and a time of stronger, healthier and more resilient individuals. Rather, *manang* are more likely to be spoken of as part of an institution whose time is rightly passing. Although these women appraise their biomedical options critically, their experiences and perceptions of the predominantly state-run biomedical institutions are generally favourable. For these women, childbirth under the jurisdiction of the biomedical profession has become a safer practice and women who gave birth in the longhouse in the past were not 'more *nakal*', they were merely less fortunate and had little choice in suffering far more than women today. For many Rumah Nari women, the social value of being *nakal* seems to have undergone a transformation. Instead of indicating prestige and status, having to be *nakal* has come to be indicative of lack of economic success, invoking more shame than pride. Similarly, women who practised *bekindu'* were not stronger, nor did they derive greater benefit from this practice, rather they lacked knowledge of and access to superior alternatives. For these women, life is, in many respects, becoming easier and they face the future with a certain amount of confidence. Yet, in Pakan, these women constitute the minority.

When women find that the rhetoric of development has failed to translate into significantly improved material conditions and access to avenues of power, they reflect on the past as an era of greater well-being. Depleted forest resources have not been replaced with easy access to market-bought goods. Cash crops have become increasingly unviable due to the time, energy and rising costs required to produce them and transport them to market without road access. Government agencies have not bestowed them with numerous rural development funds, due also to lack of road access and the difficulty these civil servants would face in overseeing and supplying the necessary materials to these communities. These conditions seem to be crucial in shaping women's perceptions of biomedical services as well as perceptions of themselves. Changes in childbirth and post-partum practices mark the decline of the strong, autonomous, fearless and pain-bearing Iban woman of the past. In comparison to their predecessors, contemporary Iban men and women of other races, these women perceive themselves as weaker, less resilient, less *nakal* and more fearful.

Many other women, however, whom I have not had time to discuss in detail here (see Harris 1998), express views that do not easily conform to the two broad groupings I have outlined. This suggests that the dimensions of experience discussed in this chapter are most appropriately conceived as existing on a gradient or continuum, but one in which economic and political status exert a significant polarising effect. Nevertheless, a consequence of this situation is an increase in divisions between Iban women of different communities; there are women in the less well-off communities who feel depleted and weakened and who find in the knowledge of past Iban a source of strength as well as a means to negotiate forces effecting their lives, and there are those who do not experience themselves as weakened in the more well-to-do communities, who turn away from much that is traditional Iban practice and align themselves more easily with the modern ideals of the developing state.

The other significant division that processes of modernity inculcate is that between Iban men and women. As women's talk about childbirth, illness and post-partum practice reveals, Iban women share with men aspirations to many common values including bravery, strength and the ability to withstand pain, even though they may express these values at times through different cultural practices. Biomedically shaped childbirth and post-partum practices deny many women the opportunity to experience themselves positively in these culturally salient terms. In contrast, men have available to them the opportunity to engage in newly emerging forms of power and leadership as Iban communities are increasingly tied into larger political contexts.

Pakan women see themselves as playing no part in this emerging domain of decision making (see Harris 1998).

Clearly the issue of rural healthcare is complicated by many factors which are beyond the scope of this chapter. However, the material presented here suggests that the delivery of healthcare services to rural communities in the most cost-effective and equitable manner requires attending to issues that extend beyond a limited notion of 'healthcare'. One needs to consider not only basic infrastructure such as roads and communications that allow people to access healthcare services but the consequences of rural development policies that lead to uneven economic development in rural areas, in terms of women's perceptions of and desire to utilise these medical services. It may also be productive to consider strategies that promote increased participation and meaningful involvement of rural women in the provision of health services, the creation of longhouse-based women's committees that work in collaboration with local healthworkers, and to look again at fostering relations between government midwives and local Iban *bidan* who often hold significant status in their communities, in ways that give consideration to their practices as reflective of the needs of longhouse women.

Notes

1 Several impressive essays addressing the experiences of Iban women appeared some years earlier, particularly those of Sather (1978 and 1988), but also Jensen 1966 and Sandin 1966.
2 People of Chinese descent constitute 28.9 per cent, Malays 20.8 per cent, Melanau 5.8 per cent, Bidayuh 8.4 per cent and Other Indigenous groups 5.5 per cent (King and Jawan 1996: 200).
3 Largely as a consequence of Brooke rule in Sarawak for about a hundred years, which failed to prepare the state adequately in terms of economic and political development prior to its incorporation into the Federation of Malaysia, Sarawak has remained dominated by federal authorities in Kuala Lumpur, largely comprising Peninsular Malays (King and Jawan 1996: 197; see also Pringle 1970). The mountainous and heavily forested terrain has also contributed to slower development in the eastern states.
4 Sarawak has the highest proportion of villages and population underserved by the government health-care delivery system and in 1990, the highest ratio of population per doctor among Malaysian states (Wee Chong Hui 1995: 115, 119).
5 These can include either the midwife, or *bidan*, *manang* or other community members. *Manang* have played significant roles in easing childbirth and performing rites before and after parturition (see Graham 1994).
6 More long-term data was unobtainable from Pakan but Sather notes that in Freeman's early work among Balleh Iban populations in 1950, he reports that the combined rate of still-birth and childhood mortality was 0.47, to mean that 'just under half of all births terminate in miscarriage or perinatal death or are followed by the loss of a newborn infant within early childhood' (1978: 351n). In Sather's opinion, 'Although currently available [1976] data suggest a substantial decline in mortality rates there is little reason to doubt that Freeman's figures are generally representative of traditional populations' (Sather 1978: 351 n. 2).

7 In 1995 an average of 11.25 births per month took place in the Pakan clinic, a 10.1 per cent increase on the figure for total births from the previous year. Between 1994 and 1995 the number of births occurring at home had dropped from 24 (10.8 per cent) to 10 (4.7 per cent), and births at the clinic had risen from 119 (53.6 per cent) to 135 (63.7 per cent). A concurrent drop occurred in the number of births occurring at the hospital from 79 (35.6 per cent) in 1994 to 66 (31.1 per cent) in 1995 which could be interpreted as indicative of an increased confidence and satisfaction in the clinic service among women.

8 The Iban *manang*, frequently translated as shaman, is the primary healer in traditional Iban society. However, childbirth and post-partum care are areas in which the role of the *manang* has probably undergone the most significant peripheralisation as a consequence of the advent of biomedical services. Previously, and continuing still in a number of Pakan communities, the *manang* performs rites to ease or hasten a difficult labour, as well as protective rites for the child after birth.

9 Ages of women are in brackets.

10 A similar practice is reported to occur, or to have occurred in the recent past among Malay populations (Laderman 1983), and Jeffery, Jeffery and Lyon 1989 report a similar method used by women in India. Critics of this practice amongst Malay populations maintained that pressure is applied with 'extreme violence' and is 'so brutal as to cause bruising of the gut' (Thambu 1971: 294 and Sambhi 1968: 348, both cited in Laderman 1983: 170). Hospital figures, reports Laderman, showed that rupture of the uterus from this practice was in fact a rare occurrence.

11 This presents a contrast to *bekindu'* scenes described by Sather where, 'Throughout the period, the interior of the *bilek* is generally kept in relative darkness by shuttering sky-lights and windows' (1988: 167). Sather suggests that this signifies the 'liminal' nature of the event, darkness and 'nightime being, significantly, the characteristic interval of Iban ritual activity' (1988: 167).

12 According to Sather, one of these types of wood was called *kayu' malam* (literally 'night wood'). 'In Iban ritual chants a living *kayu' malam* tree appears as a spiritual bridge, or ladder, used by the gods and spirit-messengers whenever they pass between *langit*, "the sky", and *dunya tu*, "this world"' (1988: 167).

13 Sather reports that in the Paku region 'throughout the period the mother is permitted to eat only special foods, such as smoked fish . . . and must avoid drinking ordinary water and consuming salty foods' (1988: 167).

14 Sather reports the use of steam 'baths' at the end of *bekindu'* (1988: 166).

References

Armstrong, D. 1986. The invention of infant mortality. *Sociology of Health and Illness* 8: 211–32.

Barrett, R.J. and R.H. Lucas. 1993. The skulls are cold, the house is hot: interpreting depths of meaning in Iban therapy. *Man* (NS) 28: 573–96.

Beck, U. 1992. *Risk Society: Towards a New Modernity.* London: Sage.

Campbell, R. and A. Macfarlane. 1987. *Where to be Born: The Debate and the Evidence.* Oxford: National Perinatal Epidemiology Unit.

Gifford, S. 1986. The meaning of lumps: a case study of the ambiguities of risk. In *Anthropology and Epidemiology*, edited by C. Janes, R. Stall and S. Gifford. Dordrecht: D. Reidel.

Graham, P. 1994 [1987]. *Iban Shamanism: An Analysis of the Ethnographic Literature.* Canberra: Australian National University.

Harris, A. 1998. Healing knowledge, healing power: the agency of well-being among Iban communities, Sarawak. Ph.D. thesis, University of Newcastle, NSW.

Jawan, J.A. 1994. *Iban Politics and Economic Development: Their Patterns and Change.* Bangi: Penerbit Universiti Kebangsaan Malaysia.

Jeffery, P., R. Jeffery and A. Lyon. 1989. *Labour Pains and Labour Power: Women and Childbearing in India.* London and New Jersey: Zed Books Ltd.

Jeffery, R.J. and P.M. Jeffery. 1993. Traditional birth attendants in rural North India: the social organization of childbearing. In *Knowledge, Power and Practice: The Anthropology of Medicine and Everyday Life,* edited by S. Lindenbaum and M. Lock. Berkeley: University of California Press.

Jensen, E. 1966. Iban Birth. *Folk* 8: 165–78.

Kaufert, P.A. and J. O'Neil. 1993. Analasis of dialogue on risks in childbirth: clinicians, epidemiologists and Inuit women. In *Knowledge, Power and Practice: The Anthropology of Medicine and Everyday Life,* edited by S. Lindenbaum and M. Lock. Berkeley: University of California Press.

Kedit, P. 1993. 'Meanwhile, back home . . .': *bejalai* and their effects on Iban men and women. In *Female and Male in Borneo: Contributions and Challenges to Gender Studies,* edited by V. Sutlive, Jr. Williamsburg: Borneo Research Council Inc. (Borneo Research Council Monograph Series, vol. 2.)

King, V.T. and J.A. Jawan. 1996. The Ibans of Sarawak, Malaysia: ethnicity, marginality and development. In *Ethnicity and Development: Geographical Perspectives,* edited by D. Dwyer and D. Drakakis-Smith. Chichester: John Wiley and Sons.

Kuching General Hospital. 1994. *Maternal and Child Health Service Report.* Kuching, Sarawak: Kuching General Hospital (Medical Department).

Laderman, C. 1983. *Wives and Midwives: Childbirth and Nutrition in Rural Malaysia.* Berkeley: University of California Press.

Lane, K. 1995. The medical model of the body as a site of risk: case study of childbirth. In *Medicine, Health and Risk: Sociological Approaches,* edited by J. Gabe. Oxford: Blackwell Publishers.

McClain, C. 1982. Toward a comparative framework for the study of childbirth: a review of the literature. In *The Anthropology of Home Birth,* edited by M.A. Kay. Philadelphia, PA: F.A. Davis.

Manderson, L. 1981. Roasting, smoking and dieting in response to birth: Malay confinement in cross-cultural perspective. *Social Science and Medicine* 15B: 509–20.

Mashman, V. 1993. Warriors and weavers: a study of gender relations among the Iban of Sarawak. In *Female and Male in Borneo: Contributions and Challenges to Gender Studies,* edited by V. Sutlive, Jr. Williamsburg: Borneo Research Council Inc. (Borneo Research Council Monograph Series, vol. 2.)

Padoch, C. 1978. Migration and its alternatives among the Ibans of Sarawak. Ph.D. thesis, Columbia University.

Pringle, R. 1970. *Rajahs and Rebels: The Ibans of Sarawak under Brooke Rule, 1841–1941.* London: Macmillan.

Richards, A.J.N. 1981. *An Iban–English dictionary.* Oxford: Clarendon Press.

Sambhi, J.S. 1968. Bomoh's abdomen. *Far East Medical Journal* 4: 347–8.

Sandin, B. 1966. *Tusun Pendiau* [Code of Conduct]. Kuching: Borneo Literature Bureau.

Sather, C. 1978. The malevolent *koklir*: Iban concepts of sexual peril and the dangers of childbirth. *Bijdragen tot de Taal-, Land- en Volkenkunde* 134: 310–55.

Sather, C. 1988. *Meri' anak mandi'*: the ritual first bathing of infants among the Iban. *Contributions to Southeast Asian Ethnography* 7: 157–87.

Sutlive, V.H. Jr. 1993. Keling and kumang in town: urban migration and differential efects on Iban men and women. In *Female and Male in Borneo: Contributions and Challenges to Gender Studies*, edited by V. Sutlive, Jr. Williamsburg: Borneo Research Council Inc. (Borneo Research Council Monograph Series, vol. 2.)

Sutlive, V.H. Jr. and G.N. Appell. 1993. Introduction. In *Female and Male in Borneo: Contributions and Challenges to Gender Studies*, edited by V. Sutlive, Jr. Williamsburg: Borneo Research Council Inc. (Borneo Research Council Monograph Series, vol. 2.)

Thambu, J.A.M. 1971. Rupture of the uterus. *Medical Journal of Malaysia* 25 (4): 293–4.

Tew, M. 1990. *Safer childbirth? A Critical History of Maternity Care*. London: Chapman & Hall.

Wee Chong Hui. 1995. *Sabah and Sarawak in the Malaysian Economy*, S. Kuala Lumpur: Abdul Majeed and Co. Publishing.

Wright, P.W.G. 1988. Babyhood: the social construction of infant care as a medical problem in England in the years around 1900. In *Biomedicine Examined*, edited by M. Lock and D. Gordon. Dordrecht: Kluwer Academic.

Chapter 12

Of *paraji* and *bidan*
Hierarchies of knowledge among Sundanese midwives[1]

Lynda Newland

Over the past twenty years, the biomedical treatment of childbirth has been broadly critiqued by both feminists and anthropologists because it operates as a field of power through which gendered and colonial/postcolonial interests can be maintained.[2] While many Western women feel alienated from a medical system which fails to give them autonomy and respect for their own decision making, such alienation is frequently intensified and multiplied in rural communities of developing nations, where Western medical practice founders, confronted with beliefs and practices that make no sense when the focus is on the physical body divorced from the wider socio-political and cosmological matrices (O'Neill and Kauffert 1993, 1995; Laderman 1983). At another level, the institutions of biomedicine introduce new hierarchies into local communities, displacing mystical knowledge and the power this brings to the people who wield it. Along with their clients, those who are displaced from their positions within their communities are often not free to resist openly as, in developing nations such as Indonesia, biomedical institutions are supported by the state and are enmeshed in ideologies of development and modernity. Local knowledges and practices, by contrast, are recast as traditional, superstitious and backward.

In West Java, village midwives (*paraji*[3]) were initially vilified. After an influential Dutch doctor had accused the *paraji* of being 'angels of death', claiming that they were responsible for the high maternal mortality rates, the colonial government set up programmes to train *bidan* (clinic midwives) with the idea that eventually demand for the *bidan* would eclipse the need for the *paraji* altogether (Niehof 1992). However, there continued to be such a shortage of *bidan* that the 'Purwokerto experiment' was implemented in the 1940s to upgrade and train the *paraji* in biomedical procedures instead. Indeed, over thirty years later, despite a growing system of clinics and hospitals, Niehof and Sastramihardja noted that the village midwife was 'far from extinct in Indonesia, and the shortage of modern midwives in the rural areas is still a problem' (Niehof and Sastramihardja 1978: 208; cf. Niehof 1992; IPPA 1971).[4]

While shortages of biomedically trained staff have long provided a major reason for the hospital system to continue tolerating the *paraji*, the *paraji* have since become strategically important to planners as a way of reaching the poorer population of village women. The possibility of turning the village midwife into a cultural broker has entered quite explicitly into development discourses. For example, a booklet put out in 1971 by the Indonesian Planned Parenthood Association called *Report on the Study of Dukuns in Central Java* explored the nature of the village midwife's role, whether she could be trained in biomedically accepted procedures (giving up practices such as massage), and whether she would be capable of taking the message of family planning to the community (IPPA 1971; see also Niehof and Hasyir 1975, for the last possibility mentioned). However, because biomedicine has international legitimacy and because it represents international business and humanitarian interests in the way that village midwifery practice does not, the idea of turning the village midwife into a cultural broker is inevitably loaded, and in a single direction. Indeed, this new role as cultural broker has grown in importance as the issue of effectively managing populations has become integral to development discourses (see Niehof, 1992, who endorses this).

Training programmes similar to the 'Purwokerto experiment' continue today. *Paraji* are rewarded with a complete kit which includes alcohol, gauze, Betadine, baby scales, brush, soap, plastic sheet and apron, cottonwool, scissors and a stainless steel basin packed in a stainless steel case if they train for two months with the Health Department. Much of the training revolves around issues of hygiene and attempts to change practices considered unhygienic, although not all of the suggested changes are supported by scientific evidence. Among other practices, *paraji* have been discouraged from using bamboo knives to cut the umbilical cord (Azwar and Prihartono 1978) and from using substances like kitchen ash to dry the bleeding at the infant's navel (Niehof 1992).[5] *Paraji* are now expected to wear rubber gloves at the time of birth, to use alcohol on the infant's navel and to reduce the number of massages which they give to the new mother (cf. IPPA 1971). After training, they are required to report to the *Puskesmas* every week to give information about how many pregnant women have been helped, to attend courses four times a year, and to disseminate family planning materials to post-parturient women. At the subsequent courses, the *bidan* demonstrates the preferred methods on a plastic doll and calls the *paraji* to repeat the demonstration one by one. The courses are rather lively events, giving the *paraji* a chance to socialise with each other as they begin to absorb their training while practising on the plastic doll. Beneath the liveliness, however, there is much ambivalence about replacing mystical knowledge with the practices of biomedicine. In this paper, I explore the attempt by the *bidan* to displace *paraji* from the village hierarchy and the impact this has on ideas and practices around childbirth.

The training of tradition

The *paraji* are usually older post-menopausal women who have completed their own reproductive lives (cf. Azwar and Prihartono 1978; Cosminsky 1976). In addition, despite Muslim notions of *aurat* which prohibit non-relatives from seeing the genitalia of the opposite sex, men with experience in animal husbandry may also be called upon by the poorest in the community or those in need of help (cf. Laderman 1983, who also records rare instances of male midwives in Malaysia). Both male and female *paraji* almost always come from the poorer section of the community. They often have little property of their own, and support themselves in part through the rituals around pregnancy and childbirth. Through the role of midwife, the *paraji* gain respect and a certain amount of influence which comes from their abilities to deliver healthy children with the aid and beneficence of Allah and the spirit-world. Their abilities to communicate with this world are often but not always dependent on following regular ascetic disciplines: fasts and feats of praying and not sleeping.

Usually *paraji* are called into midwifery as a vocation because their mothers or relatives have also been *paraji*. Ma Eha followed in the footsteps of her mother:

> This is a duty from my mother, and I took it on. I've been a *paraji* for seven years. I inherited it. She told me I had to be a *paraji*. I didn't want to but she said I must. I use *jampi* [incantation] and equipment – scissors, thread, *jamu* [medicinal tonic] to dry out the womb. When the baby comes out, there is a wound inside. In order to dry it I have to give *jamu*.
>
> You can't learn *jampi* in two months. You have to fast if you want to learn *jampi*. When you receive [mystical] knowledge in your heart, this is *jampi*. You have to fast on the day of your birth and Monday and Thursday as well. I did that for two years. You do this so that Allah fulfills the request. I learnt *jampi* while I fasted. And then I didn't sleep for a week, only ate banana – maybe a quarter of it – and water – one spoon a day. After a week, you can only eat a thumbful with a side dish. I learnt knowledge from my mother for about one year but I haven't learnt it all yet because I can't learn it all by heart.[6]

As with other *dukun* (healers), *paraji* may also be called into their vocation by dreams. The most mystical experiences were claimed by Ayah Enjum who was perhaps the poorest *paraji* I knew. When I was taken to visit him, he told me he had begun midwifery after being inspired by a dream in which a spirit appeared and took him to Medina. To show his magical abilities, Ayah Enjum showed us how his hands had been roughened by hard work in the fields, but, in preparing for a birth, he prays over oil and applies it to his hands to make them smooth. Later I was told somewhat facetiously by the family I stayed with that he also delivers cows. The family agreed, however, that it had become normal for neighbours to use him. While generous with his mystical knowledge, it seems that Ayah Enjum is a *paraji* of particularly low status and, when I visited him again in 1998, he said he had not been called upon very much in the recent past.

Women may also be first called upon simply because they are available and have seen the birth process before. Ma Juju's initial experience arose from an instance where a *paraji* was having difficulties assisting a birth:

> I recited the prayers three times [over water] and then she [the woman in labour] drank all of the prayer water. The baby came out. The placenta took three hours, the baby was already dry. They wanted to go to the hospital but they didn't have the money. [I studied my knowledge] from sentences [from the Qur'ān]. Nobody taught me. [My mother was not a *paraji*]. I liked to watch people assisting the birth and, *alhamdulillah*, how the difficult births became smooth. Since then I've been used.

While success rates may be construed as due to the effectiveness of individual *paraji* in dealing with the spirit-world, midwifery (like other forms of mysticism) is as much learnt as it is a gift. After their initial experiences, many *paraji* seek teachers from whom they learn the art. Ma Cucu, who no longer works in midwifery, was called upon when her older sister went into labour and the *paraji* had not arrived. Claiming that she had inherited the knowledge from her ancestors, she then went on and trained with other *paraji*. In the case of a difficult birth, other *dukun* or *orang yang pintar* ('clever people' who may not call themselves *dukun* but are known to be effective with their prayers) may also be called for assistance. In the instances described to me, the *orang yang pintar*, usually a man, sits reciting prayers over a glass of water in a room adjacent to where the parturient woman is lying.

The work of a *paraji* extends through the pregnancy and the birthing process, using a variety of skills from shamanship to practical application of massage, herbal remedies and corrective practices. However, late in my first year of fieldwork, I realised that many women gave birth without any assistance at all (cf. Harris Chapter 11 this volume). Sending for the *paraji* often involves sending out a party of relatives on foot late at night (as most labours seem to take place at night) to escort her the several kilometres along muddy paths back to their house. This may take considerable time. *Paraji* may also find that they have coexisting commitments, such as other women giving birth or the need to attend to the vegetable gardens, and therefore are often unable to attend births. Ibu Ecin described how she gave birth alone:

When I was about to give birth, I never waited for the *paraji*, so the *paraji* came after I'd given birth. I always gave birth by myself even for the last birth. That child was the smallest, he was born on Hari Raya, the evening of Idul Fitri at the opening of prayers. [With him] I was sick. I had a pain in the stomach. So I wanted the *bidan* [the clinic midwife] because I'd heard a lot [about what could happen] but, *alham-dulillah* [thank Allah], with the help of Allah I didn't have to wait for the *paraji*.

Ibu Ecin intimates that, while the non-attendance of the *paraji* appears to be fairly common, she went ahead with the birth rather than being forced to wait. If Ibu Ecin was nervous about the birth of her last child, Imas, mother of three, was confident of her ability to manage labour on her own: 'I wasn't troubled. If I felt like it I didn't call the *paraji*. I called her after the baby was born. It would just be me and my husband [at the birth].' In this way, women who are confident about their own capabilities have a certain level of freedom to decide whether they could manage on their own, at least after they have experienced the birth of their first child.

Sometimes, the *paraji* are also responsible for spacing pregnancies, although the level of these skills varies substantially from *paraji* to *paraji*. Such methods include contraceptive and abortive techniques. Elsewhere in West Java, a well-known method involved drinking young pineapple juice as an abortifacient, but it was reputedly only used by prostitutes. Apparently, *jamu-jamu* or herbal tonics are Javanese in origin but the Sundanese have their own recipes of herbs and spices for similar purposes, sometimes also called *jamu*. In Bandung, anthropologist Ibu Utja at Universitas Pajajaran told me that traditional contraception included: *jamu* or herbal tonics, *papalean* which is made from mahogany bark and boiled in water and then drunk twice a day, and the *lidi* or stick threaded with chilli, onion, turmeric and garlic which sits at the end of the mother's bed. As well as protecting the mother from the *kuntilanak* (spirit of a woman who died in childbirth), the *lidi* is said to represent the different stages of the mother's return to health and, while it is there, the husband is prohibited from sleeping with her for 40 days. Another researcher, Bapak Abdul Rodjak, gave me three recipes he had learnt from his mother: *rujak kesed* (a type of leaf) which is ground with sugar and salt and has to be taken after the birth for 40 days; *merang padi* made by baking a stalk of rice until it is ash, adding water and leaving it overnight; and *daun sembung* which is a leaf like tobacco that is immersed in hot water and drunk.

In Cipayun and its neighbouring villages, it was difficult to obtain much information about *kampung* contraception and abortifacients. Although Ma Eha explained several types of massage, she kept insisting that they should not be used to abort the foetus. Despite this, Ibu Mimin talked about how she had become afraid of falling pregnant because of her increasing discomfort in giving birth. After nine pregnancies where seven children had lived, Ibu Mimin chose to inhibit the likelihood of giving birth again:

> I didn't take *jamu* but I massaged my stomach every month when my periods didn't come until the blood came out. The *bidan* [biomedical midwife] said it might or might not have been a pregnancy because a woman is pregnant for two or three months when the menses stop and women aren't allowed to massage after that.
>
> I massaged by myself because then I could do it gently and slowly and get the blood to spurt out.

While Ibu Mimin eventually flouted convention and insisted on a hysterectomy, Sri explained how she avoided unwanted pregnancies:

> [I never joined the government's family planning programme because] I was organised by a *paraji* from the south. When my child was two months old, I went there to be massaged. So the child was 5 before I had another one [child]. [The midwife] was in C [village] but she's dead now. I was massaged and given a drink. Not *jamu*. [I was given the recipe and] I made it myself. [It was made from] *gambir*, yeast, pepper, garlic, egg yolk and mixed with hot water. After having periods, you drink it so that the womb's dry and you don't have children quickly. I was massaged three times after giving birth until the age of that child was 5. After the youngest child was born I was only massaged twice because that *paraji* died. It's already one and a half years since I stopped drinking [the solution]. Now I have a sick stomach so I'm not allowed to eat yeast and pepper.

Thus, while village forms of contraception and abortion exist, they do not appear to be common and nor are they widely talked about. The *paraji*'s role is more intensely focused on birth and the correct execution of the birth rituals.

However, all of her practices are now being contested by the clinic system. Brought under the national government's direction in the Five Year Plans, the *Puskesmas* (*Pusat Kesehatan Masyarakat* or community health centres) began providing general health care and mother and child health care, and later extended its services to provide 'the prevention and control of contagious diseases, hygiene and sanitation, and laboratory services. In addition, health education and collection of data for planning and evaluation also became tasks of the health centre' (Azwar and Prihartono 1978: 119).

By 1974, 2508 *Puskesmas* had been set up throughout Indonesia. On Java and Bali, one *Puskesmas* existed for every forty thousand inhabitants (Azwar and Prihartono 1978). In an effort to reach the poorer parts of the community, the concept of the *Posyandu* or Integrated Service Post was developed in 1984

(Hugo et al. 1987). Essentially an outreach programme, the *Posyandu* involves sending *Puskesmas* staff out into the villages to deliver services such as vaccinations, baby weighing, and the checking of pregnancies.

Hierarchy and the *paraji–bidan* relationship

While the clinic staff tend to assume that the hierarchy between *bidan* and *paraji* is natural – the educated teaching the ignorant or the progressive teaching the backward – there are individuals who attempt to soften these hierarchical differences in order to make the courses more effective. When I talked to Dr Anna Alisjahbana, who works in a Bandung hospital and who is widely known for her work in developing training programmes, she noted that medical bureaucracy operates as a top-down provider service. She explained how, within this context, she has worked to create a more even-handed dialogue between the *bidan* and the *paraji*. Over the years, these efforts have extended into the ethics of the *bidan*, so that, in one instance, a *bidan* new to the Cikajang area commented:

> The work's the same [between *bidan* and *paraji*]. We're like partners. For example, we train the *paraji* for normal pregnancies. Whenever the *paraji* aren't capable of doing it, they call the *bidan*. For my programme the *bidan* and *paraji* must assist the childbirth together so we can see how the training of the *paraji* is. So if there are mistakes we can do it together.
> [The *paraji* and the *bidan* can work together] by using the *bidan's* instruments: for example, when the baby has been born but the placenta has not come out. If it's more than half an hour, then they – the *paraji* – don't have the competence to do it by hand so by using the technical skills of the *bidan* we can help manually or before that we might inject oxytocin.

Despite the effort at collaborative approach, the hierarchy remains firmly set where the *paraji* is considered to have the inferior skills and must work under the gaze of the *bidan*. If complications occur Ma Eha among others noted, 'you must call the *bidan* and if the *bidan* can't do anything you must go to the hospital in Garut', as the *paraji* who has completed the courses is considered only sufficiently trained to deliver normal births, a trend that appears to be world-wide (cf. Pigg 1997). While this hierarchy is problematic because it discredits local knowledges, local hierarchies are also upended because older women who have given birth to many children like the *paraji* would normally expect deference from younger women who may not have been married like the *bidan* (cf. Cosminsky 1976). The village hierarchies are further confused by the bringing together of the urban middle-class *bidan* and the peasant-based *paraji* – two classes which are normally quite removed.

Altering village hierarchies has an impact on the way training is received. In other areas of the world it has been noted that 'once back in their villages, none of the certified midwives substantially changed their conceptions of childbearing or the type of care they provided' (Sesia 1997: 403 for Oaxaca, Mexico). This suggests that village midwives merely fall back into their old and bad habits. By contrast, among the *paraji* I worked with, there is a self-conscious rejection of many of the practices introduced by the *bidan*. For example, Ma Eha admitted that, 'If the woman is inspected by the *bidan*, the *bidan* uses gloves. I don't use them but according to the *bidan* I should always use gloves. If the *bidan*'s there, then I use them.' Her admission betrays her resentment of the new gauges of legitimacy – in this case, rubber gloves.

Often the *paraji* work to subvert or downgrade the new hierarchy. None of the *paraji* I knew thought the *bidan* were better than they were, but rather that their knowledge was a specific and restrictive type that was neither guaranteed nor any more specialist than their own. As Ayah Enjum pointed out, 'It's not definite that the *bidan* can do it.' Ma Eha described the *bidan–paraji* relationship in many ways, puzzling defensively about the popularity of the *paraji* in times when women could choose to go to the *bidan*:

> There's a lot of *bidan*, a lot of doctors, but most [pregnant women and their families] go to the *paraji*. Pak Harto [President Suharto and his family] also went to the *paraji*, not the *bidan*. The *bidan* are still new. Back then the delivery was done by the *paraji*, and there were also a lot who were blessed. There wasn't anything the matter. Now a lot say that the *paraji* should leave school an engineer [college-trained]. Back then, there weren't women who went to high school. Usually they were just *dukun kampung* [village healers] like me. Because of that, a lot [of pregnant women and their families] now feel strange if they go to the *paraji*. I also don't know why those who give birth still wish to go to the *paraji*. There are *bidan desa* [medically trained midwives allocated to the area], but [the women] still keep coming to me. Yet, I have to give reports to the *bidan* who are new and I have to join the courses. But I use *Gusti*'s [the Lord's] knowledge.

Ma Eha was also suspicious about the financial arrangements of the *bidan* who are increasingly asking that *paraji* inform their clients about family planning immediately after they have given birth. She felt that incentives given by the family planning programme[7] might provide a conflict of interest:

> I had to visit a woman because she wanted the IUD. I told her to join family planning and the woman went to the doctor. I told her but I didn't force her. If she wants to join family planning it's okay but it doesn't matter if she doesn't. But the *bidan* insisted that she had to because the *bidan* wants to sell the IUD and, if the IUDs are sold out, the government will give her a gift because women don't want to have IUDs.

For Ma Eha, the *bidan* is in the process of taking over the work of midwifery, changing the practice from a social and ethical one to a commercial enterprise. Meanwhile, the *paraji* are displaced not only in status and expertise, but also in income by biomedical knowledge and biomedical and state bureaucracies.

Yet *paraji* are also deeply aware that the training courses offered by the *Puskesmas* are now popularly perceived to legitimate their practice. Families are more inclined to call on *paraji* who have done the courses rather than those who have not. *Paraji* who remain untrained may find themselves edged out of midwifery.

Finding herself in this situation, Ma Cucu shifted her focus from midwifery to love magic and healing. Other *paraji* like Ayah Enjum refused to do the hospital courses. He said that he was busy enough, but his 'untrained' status has limited him to working only in his immediate village, and, as noted above, by my second visit his work appeared to have dropped off considerably. Ultimately, the training courses have been effective in creating new hierarchies between the *paraji* and between the *bidan* and the *paraji*.

Birth in the Kampung

While the courses have produced these new hierarchies, the local community has proven exceptionally resistant to accepting the *bidan* at the expense of the *paraji*. Table 12.1 is an indication of the relative popularities of the *bidan* and the *paraji*. I arrived at these figures by counting the entries in the handwritten records held by the *bidan* at the *Puskesmas*, but the accuracy of the number of births the *paraji* attend is questionable because the *paraji* do not always pass on complete information about their activities. Moreover, the *paraji* recorded here are only those who have been trained at the *Puskesmas* which means that the number of births attended by *paraji* are likely to be significantly higher.

While the *bidan* are making small but definite inroads into the community, there are also significant reasons why many prefer the expertise of the *paraji*. When I asked the *paraji* why they thought they were used more than the *bidan* one of the chief responses was the difference in the money which women and their families had to pay. Ayah Enjum, perhaps the poorest *paraji* I was acquainted with, contextualised fees and payments in terms of family income:

> If they have a lot of money then they never come to me – they like to be told what to do by the *bidan*. But if they have five children and only own a little: 'What's for the *bidan*? What's for the children's food?' then I help with gusto because they need the help. If they go to the hospital, how much does it cost them when they leave? For example, it's like this, in one day they might get Rp 2,000 [about US$0.80 at 1996] for their five children. If they are charged Rp 25,000 by the hospital [about US$10], how are they going to pay? That's why they come to me.

Table 12.1 The popularity of the *bidan* versus the *paraji* in Cikajang Shire

Year	Bidan-aided births		Paraji-aided births		Total
	Number	% of recorded births	Number	% of recorded births	
1984	72				
1985	94				
1986	84				
1987	48				
1988	110				
1989	101		482*		583
1990	104	12.1	753	87.9	857
1991	125	14.1	759	85.9	884
1992	120	15.5	654	84.5	774
1993	117	17.4	556	82.6	673
1994	212	20.6	815	79.4	1027
1995	200				

*Year incomplete in records
Source: compiled from *Puskesmas* records.

If the *bidan* are economically beyond the reach of many, the *bidan*'s demand for a set fee also differs from the gift given to the *paraji* in that it reflects a capitalist notion of value predicated on expertise and time rather than value according to the end result (which is judged by the well-being of both mother and child). Ma Eha, for example, said that she doesn't charge a set fee, but leaves it to the woman to decide how much to pay or if to pay at all. She explained that, 'You have to do it like this because maybe the *jampi* [incantation] is no good because Allah did not answer the request [and deliver a healthy baby to a healthy mother]' (cf. Whittaker Chapter 10 this volume).

This problem of payment has become a particularly acute embarrassment to the *paraji* because *bidan*, in a strategy to ingratiate themselves with the community, now ask to accompany *paraji* to births. Showing her frustration, Ma Eha exclaimed:

> When they are due to give birth you have to invite the *bidan*, but my objections are like this: when they are due to give birth [the family of the pregnant woman] don't order me to [fetch the *bidan*]. I'm not responsible for the costs. In any case, you have to pay the *bidan*. The *bidan* wants me to invite her but I'm not that brazen. 'Why do I have to take the *bidan*? I don't pay her.' My fear's like that. If there are difficulties then the family involved calls the *bidan*. They are welcome to do that but I don't want to order them to because some can pay and some can't. It's not me rebelling against the government but . . . I've already said at a

meeting at the *kecamatan* [shire office], 'What happens, *Neng* [polite title for a woman who has not had children], if they can't pay?' Because the *bidan* have been to school surely they wish to receive money from these women.

While Ma Eha's frustration may have a lot to do with being coerced into inviting competitors into her domain, the *bidan* also represent social relations predicated on the maxim of profit. This is a notion which directly conflicts with placing communal needs first and balancing one's wealth appropriately. In a peasant community where rituals constantly emphasise community and balance and yet where many barely subsist, fixed fees, meant to reflect the *bidan*'s specialisation, exclude all but the richest, providing fuel for resentment. In addition, if the practice of giving birth alone is as common as it was suggested, then the apparent obsfucation by the *paraji* (to the *bidan* and to me) about when women are due to give birth might be seen as an effort to allow the birth to happen in its own time as a natural event. In this light, the *bidan*'s pressure to accompany the *paraji* to births places the *paraji* in a difficult position because the *paraji* is coerced into attending births where once she was not required.[8]

Other reasons mentioned by the village women for preferring the *paraji* over the *bidan* include the problems of distance (the *bidan* invariably live in the town while the *paraji*, who might still have to walk for several kilometres, live in the villages), and the reluctance of the *bidan* to make journeys which might involve a long and muddy walk to people's houses in the middle of the night. In the unlikely event that women wanted to give birth in the *Puskesmas*, their families who are equally unlikely to own a vehicle would have to find motor transport to get them there. Difference in procedure also informs their choice. While women were eager to contract the *paraji* by holding the seventh-month *tingkeban* (Figures 12.1 to 12.3), they are apparently much less comfortable with the *bidan*'s internal examinations which are meant to be conducted four times during the course of the pregnancy. Moreover, as Ayah Enjum has already intimated above, class distinctions and familiarity also influence family decisions over whether the *bidan* or the *paraji* are more appropriate.

On the other hand, to use the *bidan* connotes a certain prestige, a fact not lost on the young women who see the *bidan* as modern, clean, efficient and reliable. For Wiwin, a young woman pregnant with her first child, disenchantment with the *paraji* (Ma Eha) came when she realised that the *paraji* had several coexisting commitments and would not stay with her for the duration of her labour. Her family called another *paraji* who arrived around midnight and insisted that they call the *bidan*, and before she left, the *mantri* (medical officer) made an appearance to inject oxytocin. Early the next morning, Ma Eha arrived and left again to massage another woman. Then, at 9 a.m., the *bidan* arrived and gave her a second injection, finally triggering the

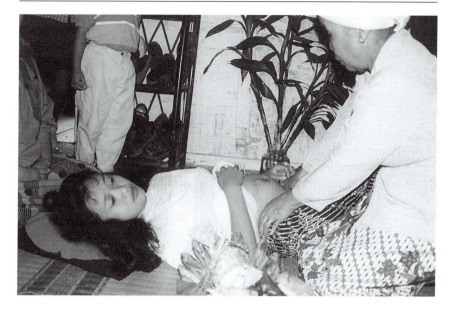

Figure 12.1 Massaging during pregnancy (photo by Lynda Newland)

labour. Wiwin concluded rather bitterly: 'After the *bidan* came and the injection was given nothing mattered to me. But with the *paraji* you just have to wait. With the *bidan* it's straight away. Ten minutes and it's finished.' Although Wiwin used the speed of the birth as an indication of whether the *paraji* or the *bidan* is more proficient, she also noted how much the birth hurt her (which may have been a result of the trauma induced by oxytocin).

In fact the different services offered by the *paraji* and the *bidan* point to the different priorities accorded to mother and child by the different knowledges. Ma Eha explained it this way:

> With the *paraji*, after the baby's born, the mother continues getting massages. With the *bidan*, the baby's first. With me, the mother is first. After being wrapped in a blanket, the baby is left. I worry about the mother. Has the placenta moved to where the baby was? It can be difficult. So the mother is the first person to be taken care of. After she's towelled and put to sleep, the baby. It is cleaned, washed, its navel is massaged, tied with thread, given Betadine, clothed, chatted to. With the *bidan*, the mother is left so only the baby gets organised. The *bidan* washes the baby. With me, the mother is first and she's massaged. I'm frightened of the womb coming out.[9] I don't wash her but towel her. Now you're not allowed to do enough towelling. If the mother discharges water after the birth she should be washed so that she's healthy but now you're not allowed to do it. That's the difference between the *paraji* and the *bidan*.

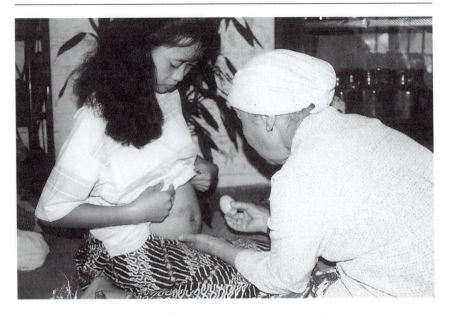

Figure 12.2 Sliding the egg down the belly at the seventh-month pregnancy ritual (photo by Lynda Newland)

This perspective accords closely with the view of village women who prefer the *paraji*. In separate interviews, Ibu Ida and Ibu Iroh explained their preference for the *paraji*:

> With the *bidan*, you only get an injection and can only use her for three days. You can use the *paraji* for forty days, so I had the *paraji*. With the *bidan*, before the birth you get an injection, after the birth you're given a sleeping pill. With the *paraji*, you're given *jamu* [a herbal tonic], and after the birth you're massaged and then bound with cloth. After three days you're massaged again.
>
> With the *bidan*, after giving birth, the woman is injected. With the *paraji*, she's massaged. After giving birth the mother's womb comes out. The *paraji* corrects it so they regain health quickly. So a lot have the *paraji*. But if it's difficult they have the *bidan* because the *bidan* has the instruments.

The time and physical attention the *paraji* gives to post-partum women is in striking contrast with the *bidan*'s focus on efficiency and access to technology. In Ayah Enjum's view, this attention is necessary so she can quickly return to the fields: 'After a birth I assist, the woman can hoe or dig up the earth after a week. She's healthy because she's massaged, and her nerves are straightened again.' In addition, if the *bidan* is perceived as caring only for the health of

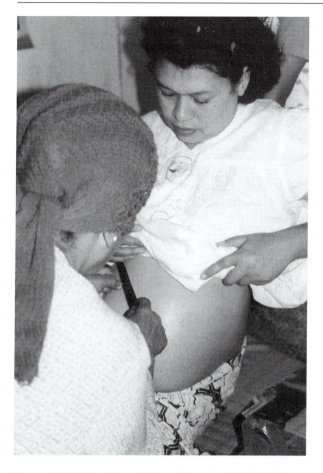

Figure 12.3 Tying the gold thread around the belly at the seventh-month
pregnancy ritual (photo by Lynda Newland)

the child, the style of care reflects differing objectives which relate directly
with cosmology. While the *paraji* protects women from the vital forces of the
spirits of the dead (Newland 1999), the *bidan* contains her concerns to the
organs of the living. The rationalising influence of the *bidan* did not escape
Ma Juju who noted: 'It's like this: the courses continue but I inspect difficult
births with religion [with religious power and requests to Allah]. If the child
is difficult coming out I say prayers and the child is born quickly. So I'm used
by everyone.'

As *bidan* are mostly urban and well-educated outsiders, the social and economic gap between them and the villagers is often vast. In order to gain clients,
the *bidan* have found themselves dependent on the *paraji* in gaining acceptance
into the village communities. Over the years, the *bidan* have attempted to

change this by initiatives such as organising meetings at the houses of family planning cadres which are designed to bring together the *bidan, mantri, paraji*, the family planning worker, the cadre and local women.[10]

One monsoonal day, Ibu Mimin and I slipped down to the cadre's house to a meeting with the new *bidan* from whom I quoted earlier. Despite the fact that they had been asked, Ma Eha and the family planning worker had not turned up. In their immaculate white uniforms, the *bidan* and the *mantri* handed around an exercise book to get everyone's names. Then they gave out six exercise books with columns prepared to record the name of the mother, father, ages, children's ages and number of children, the weight of babies just born, and immunisation as an example of the information they wanted to collect. This caused a great commotion. Two pamphlets about pregnancy, breastfeeding and babies with diarrhoea were handed around, and the *bidan* spoke about the risk of having children over the age of 35. Family planning came up briefly, but mother and child health were the priorities on the agenda. In the last hour of the meeting, a young unmarried friend of mine, Lina, was made responsible for recording pregnancies in the village for the *bidan*. (The problem, Lina told me, was that nobody was pregnant at the time. In the course of the following month, the *bidan* would arrive twice at her house for information but nobody seemed to be pregnant. The *bidan*, Lina reported, was angry, probably thinking she was being obstructed.)

Clearly the *bidan* had meant not only to introduce herself, but to position herself in relation to the villagers and the *paraji*. Set apart from the environment in uniform, she was attempting to create systems of surveillance new to the area in order to become known to the community and make her own position more efficient. Her readiness to show her frustration to Lina suggests that she was aware of the resistance she might encounter. While she had described the work between *bidan* and *paraji* as the same (as quoted earlier), her manner none the less suggested that she had a clear notion of hierarchy between the two and saw the latter as obstructive.

A further complication in getting the villagers to accept her is the *bidan*'s involvement with the family planning programme. Persuasion to accept family planning at these meetings tends to be strong. Ibu Engkoy, the family planning cadre, explained that women showed reluctance in coming for services such as weighing their babies because 'they are scared they'll also be forced to join family planning. If it's done by an official they're shy, but if it's done by me they're not.' Indeed, if the meeting attracted three potential acceptors of the IUD (a form of contraception not popular in the area) the *bidan* would come to insert them. Alarmed by the idea of the IUD being inserted in the volunteers' houses, I asked Ibu Eka, the family planning worker, about it:

> Back then [before 1991], the IUD could be inserted in the field, but sterilisation was less than guaranteed. So the medical experts agree that the

spiral should be done at the *Puskesmas* except if the women insist that, for example, they can't get there and then you can do it in the field. Before that, it was done on a bench at the *desa* office [the suburb office]. The bench had a mattress. Now you can't do that and must go to the *Puskesmas*.

While the insertion of IUDs in the field sometimes ended in complications, carelessness with the Depo-Provera injection resulted in paralysis in one woman and blindness in another. Explaining that these cases were due to the carelessness of the worker who may have hit a nerve when injecting the contraceptive, the *mantri* further noted:

> the *KB suntik* [Depo-Provera] caused a death . . . from abscess. It was not just from that, but because she had the injection they blamed the injection, whereas it was from other things. There was another sickness as well as the abscess from the injection: an infection inside.

As sickness rarely has an identifiable cause in village life, it is difficult to know when side-effects and contra-indications come specifically from contraceptive or other biomedical technology or when it arises from negligence by the people who insert it. In the case of negligence, the most damning repercussions, said the *mantri*, come 'not from organisations but from the community . . . There's already been censure from the community against that worker.' Such negligence also gives concrete justifications for suspicion about the practices of medical and family planning workers.

Despite the risks, the *Posyandu* meetings have been accepted in many villages, especially those which provide pickers for the tea plantations.[11] During my visit in 1998, I accompanied a team on a *Posyandu* excursion which seemed coordinated like a military operation. A *bidan* and her male off-sider, the *mantri*, were dropped off at each site where they met with the cadre and the gathering awaiting them. While babies were weighed outside in a length of cloth, the *mantri* and the cadre updated the books with the new weights. Meanwhile, the *bidan* prepared injections and injected women and their babies. When necessary, she took her client to an adjacent room containing a bed to check her pregnancy. Pamphlets were given out and problems discussed – in this case fairly speedily as the team was the last to be dropped off and had to be the first to leave (cf. Hunter 1996, for *Posyandu* in Lombok).

In this way, not only are the practical actions of the *paraji* under more intensive regulation and training, but the bodies of pregnant women are also caught directly in the medical gaze at the *Posyandu*. This, of course, is not to say that no women desire the advantages given by biomedicine nor that biomedicine is any more morally questionable than village midwifery. It highlights, however, the relations of power and the contestations of knowledge when biomedicine and village knowledge meet. Far from being an innocuous importation which improves community health, the introduction of biomedicine has far-reaching consequences, having the capacity to transform notions of self and the body, community and cosmology.

Biomedicine in the Kampung

The new technologies brought by the *bidan* and her offsider, the *mantri*, are perceived with a great deal of ambivalence by the villagers. Feminists have criticised biomedical practices used in Western hospitals for their assembly-line mentality where the body is viewed as a machine which has the tendency to go wrong (Davis-Floyd and Sargent 1997; Adams 1994; Martin 1987, 1990) or where pregnancy is laden with connotations of disease (Young 1990). Biomedical discourse has been criticised for interpreting the body as detachable pieces and separating reproduction into discontinuous steps where sperm, ova and embryo can be frozen, eggs can be farmed and fertilised *in vitro*, and body parts can be removed and replaced with those of donors (Braidotti 1994). Technology has been shown to alienate the parturient woman from her own internal processes in such a way that giving birth in hospitals can be an isolating experience (Fiedler 1997; Young 1990; Oakley 1984). Ultimately, the issue at the centre of these critiques is the nature of institutional control over the female body in childbirth.

The full impact of this mentality is yet to affect the villagers, who usually avoid hospitals. Yet the training courses for the *paraji* and the visits of the *bidan* and *mantri* are changing ideas about the body in quite palpable ways. For example, it is part of biomedical training to assume that the female body is unable to give birth unassisted and is vulnerable to complication when assisted by those who have no knowledge of biomedicine. Moreover, parturient women are expected to be assisted technologically and, indeed, all women are expected to submit to several of these technologies through the course of their lives.

However, the increasing biomedical assistance has given rise to confusion in the community. For instance, the recent initiative which insists on compulsory injections of tetanus toxoid for all brides is frequently confused with the contraceptive Depo-Provera. Mardiah told me, 'Now you must be immunised before you get married. You can't have children too fast.' Ma Eha spoke of this injection as causing the reverse: 'Here, if people are to be married, they have to be immunised in order to have a child quickly.' While this confusion is indicative of a hierarchy in which the women have little or no access to processes of consultation and negotiation, it also reveals their awareness that their lives are increasingly being dominated by the regulation of reproduction. In this case, the tetanus toxoid is meant to prevent disease in an infant which has not even been conceived. It is appropriate, then, that the word *suntik* which means 'injection' and which is used interchangeably to denote both immunisation (tetanus, polio, etc.) and injection of Depo-Provera and oxytocin has become the villagers' symbol for bio-medically assisted reproduction.

As tetanus toxoid, oxytocin, and family planning technologies such as implants, Depo-Provera injections and IUDs are all used for more effective control over reproduction, all of them can be considered as reproductive technologies and, while these technologies are intended to control the timing of the birth and the health of the mother and infant, they are being used increasingly extensively. The most desired injection is oxytocin, which speeds up the labour. In order to benefit from oxytocin, the families must call for the *mantri* during the girl's labour. In the area of my fieldwork, it seemed that, providing the family was able to afford it, calling the *mantri*[12] to administer the oxytocin was mandatory. In the words of Ibu Mimin, mother of seven adult children, oxytocin is necessary: 'The reason why many babies cannot be born is because there is no energy to push it out and you have to push.' The lack of energy comes from a condition referred to as *kurang darah* which literally means 'not enough blood' and roughly translates as anaemia. Women who suffer from *kurang darah* are feared to be too weak to proceed with the labour.[13]

Yet, the effects of oxytocin remain poorly understood. The fact that oxytocin has increased risks of prematurity, foetal distress, and neonatal jaundice, and that it tends to make the birthing process more painful and less satisfactory for the labouring woman (Oakley 1984) is not explained (and nor is it explained in Western hospitals – or commonly understood by doctors themselves). Studies in Western hospitals suggest that oxytocin has been linked with higher Caesarean rates and maternal infection (Dudley 1997; Kierse, Otterwanger and Smit 1996). Questions about its effects on the brain have only been asked recently (Curtis 1993). Oxytocin has also been criticised as one of many technological intrusions into the birth process which destroys the rhythm of the woman's labour in favour of doctors' (or *bidan/mantri*'s) rhythms (e.g. Fiedler 1997; Lazarus 1997; Szurek 1997), and the prevalence of its use suggests that women's bodies are perceived as unable to complete the birth process on their own.

The dominant village notions of the body represent it as vulnerable to shock, and the pregnant body is particularly susceptible to spirit possession and death. Yet pregnancy and birth are also considered natural and expected processes which every woman should go through to become a respected mother. Perhaps the ideal emotions were expressed by the granddaughter of Ma Eha, 18-year-old Rohanan, who, despite feeling hopelessness at the length of her (technologically unassisted) labour, described a feeling of immense pride immediately after the birth. By contrast, the injected birth appears to have an impact on women's sense of self-fulfilment after the birth. For example, Mardiah and Wiwin (both injected with oxytocin) both noted somewhat bitterly how much the birth had hurt them. Tuti, who also submitted to oxytocin, stated that childbirth was 'women's biggest burden'. While Rohanan had remarked on her inexperience in the sense that experience would have given her more control over the situation, experience for the other three young women seems to be more closely related to discovering how they have been duped.

While these views only give an impressionistic sense of how values about self-fulfilment in childbirth might be changing in the face of biomedicine, the different techniques used reflect different conceptualisations about the bodies on which they are performed. Biomedicine concentrates on the possible infection of the body parts of the living organism rather than the woman's well-being and comfort in a broader cosmological cycle (for more about this, see Newland 1999). Moreover, where the *paraji*'s responsibilities have been to ensure women's continuing fertility through care such as *jamu* (tonics) and massage, the role of the *bidan* is to manage fertility by containing it, so much so that the *paraji* are now asked to inform their newly post-parturient clients about family planning.[14]

Perhaps for this reason, *paraji* view biomedicine to be ineffective. Ma Juju who was considered by the medical profession as too old to continue practising midwifery insists (as all *paraji* do) that more women go to her than anybody else. She elaborated with a triumphant narrative of biomedical failure shared equally between family planning technologies and the *bidan*:

> A lot [of women] come here because they are on family planning but they still get pregnant. Nyi Heni . . . has had [the IUD] for four years. The fifth year she didn't get her period. She was inspected by the *bidan*. The *bidan* said she wasn't pregnant, and she kept getting inspected until the fifth *bidan* said the same thing. Then she went to Garut [city] to Pak I [doctor]. She was inspected by him. 'You're not pregnant', he said. 'Your stomach is pot-bellied because you eat a lot'. She came home again and stopped in at my place. It turned out that I inspected her and found she was already eight months pregnant. I said, 'You are going to give birth at the end of Jumadil [Islamic month]. If it's the fourth [date], a girl will be born. If the fifth, a boy.' She went back to Garut to get her spiral removed [at the hospital] and went to Pak I for another inspection. He was angry, 'Which *paraji*? Contradicting a doctor! I said there wasn't anything! And yes, there isn't anything!' And then she said the name of the *paraji*: Ma Juju from [a village near Cipayun]. 'Oh, Ma Juju! Let Ma Juju know that the spiral can't be removed because the baby's back is blocking it', he said after he inspected her, heh, heh.

Subjected midwives, subjected mothers and contested worlds

In conclusion, the *paraji* have unwittingly found themselves represented as oppositional to biomedical and state interests and, indeed, the aims of their practices position them as such. For, while the biomedical and state institutions aim to limit the population growth rate by containing the female reproductive capacity and justify this by recourse to health, the *paraji*'s role is to ensure the mother's physical well-being in order that all her labours are smooth and result in many children. In the efforts to bring the *paraji* under biomedical surveillance and control (which would also broaden the clinic's access to the local women), the *paraji*'s role has been recast by the authorities into that of cultural broker. After being trained in basic biomedical procedure, the *paraji* is expected to assist the *bidan* unproblematically in her dual role of introducing a regime of health to the villages and supporting the philosophy of reproductive containment. The underlying assumption here is that acceptance of the world-view propagated by biomedical and state discourses is merely a matter of being educated. Ultimately, transforming village practices and hierarchies in accordance with the state project of development is not just a matter of training the *paraji* with new procedures but requires their relinquishment of locally valued cosmologies and ontologies. This has resulted in a plurality of resistances from the *paraji* and the villagers. While these may be effective in the short term, they are also contested by an increasing number of young women who desire the trappings of modernity.

Notes

1 The material presented in this chapter was drawn from fieldwork conducted in the Shire of Cikajang, West Java, in 1995/6 and a subsequent visit in 1998. Much of it forms Chapter 7 of my Ph.D. thesis which analyses the impact of the Indonesian family planning programme on a rural Muslim Sundanese community in West Java (Newland 1999).
2 For examples see Ram and Jolly 1998; Davis-Floyd and Sargent 1997; Ginsberg and Rapp 1991, 1995; Adams 1994; Braidotti 1994; Shetty 1994; Martin 1987; Oakley 1984; McClain 1982.
3 *Paraji* is Sundanese for village midwife. The term in Indonesian is *dukun bayi* or *dukun anak*. Sometimes *dukun beranak* is also used although this has negative connotations as it is also used for animal husbandry (although even the Sundanese get confused over this one as the appropriate word may differ from region to region). The term used in the hospital system is TBA or Traditional Birth Attendant, a term first devised by WHO (cf. Whittaker Chapter 10 this volume). In Indonesian, if a village midwife has trained under the *bidan*, she is called a *dukun terlatih* or a trained healer. In Sundanese and Indonesian, singular and plural forms remain the same and I tend to refer to *paraji* as female because they usually are, but there are instances where men like Ayah Enjum take on this work. *Bidan* are always female.
4 The move to train village midwives was not confined to Indonesia, but has been part of a broader strategy in development encouraged by United Nations agencies like WHO (the World Health Organisation; cf. Whittaker Chapter 10 this volume). Until the 1970s, village midwives were largely ignored or condemned in countries as far-ranging as Mexico (Sesia 1997), Jamaica (Sargent and Bascope 1997) and Malaysia (Laderman 1983). In Malaysia, the Ministry of Health attempted to phase out village midwives by insisting that they had to be registered in order to

practise, and then closing the register in 1972. Yet, despite the fact that most midwives were over 60 and did not seem to face much of a future, rural midwives
continued to deliver just over half of all Malaysian births (Laderman 1983).

5   The use of such substances appears to increase chances of tetanus. However, the
change to metal knives and scissors has not always increased hygiene in the way
the *bidan* would like.

6   All interviews in this chapter were recorded on tape and then transcribed. They
were usually conducted in Sundanese with the help of my assistant, a student of
anthropology in Bandung.

7   While the family planning programme does offer incentives, I could find no evidence that this was one of them. However, the perception that the *bidan* receives
a financial advantage for her work in family planning is very important.

8   Of course, going through labour alone has its dangers. Ibu Mimin, who had
become disenchanted with *paraji* years before, noted that, with the *paraji*, 'when
the birth is very difficult the woman does it by herself. If she's unlucky she dies.'

9   This appears to be a reference to the possibility of a prolapsed uterus, commonly
cited as a problem to watch for, which *paraji* fix by kicking it back into place.

10 Normally, these are called *Posyandu*. However, while the meeting I describe here
seemed to be in the process of setting up a *Posyandu*, the locals were not calling it
by that name.

11 The villages which service the tea plantations were among the first to receive the
attentions of the family planning campaign.

12 In some areas the *mantri* is called the *tukang suntik* or trader in injections (Azwar
and Prihartono 1978).

13 Medical research shows that the infant mortality rate rises rapidly once the labour
exceeds thirty hours (Dudley 1997).

14 Because of the unavoidable pressure to change birthing practices (arising in the
forms of the *Posyandu* and other community meetings and the training courses for
the *paraji*), there are also transformations in the way births are now being managed. On hearing news of a birth in the neighbourhood, I arrived minutes after
Euis had given birth to a baby boy. A *bidan* who was liked among the *paraji*
(because her father was a *paraji* and she was indigenous to the district) was working alongside Ma Eha. While the *bidan* used her equipment to clean the baby, Ma
Eha chanted prayers over baby and mother. The baby was bound in swaddling and
propped on a cushion facing its mother. Ma Eha then left the room to clean the
placenta in preparation for burial. She stayed the night so she could bury it by the
first light of day and she would return to massage Euis on the appropriate days.
With the stick threaded with chilli, onion, garlic, ginger and a small knife to ward
off the *kuntilanak* beside her bed, Euis was up and sweeping the floors the next
day. For this particular birth, two traditions had fused successfully and without
embarrassment, but because many *bidan* completely reject the existence of the
kuntilanak and the other beliefs and practices of the *paraji* – and, indeed, the community – such occasions are rare.

References

Adams, A.E. 1994. *Reproducing the Womb: Images of Childbirth in Science, Feminist
Theory, and Literature.* Ithaca, NY, and London: Cornell University Press.

Azwar, A. and J. Prihartono. 1978. Healthcare in the subdistrict of Serpong. In *Family
Planning in Rural West Java: The Serpong Project*, general editor L.C.L. Zuidberg.
Amsterdam: Institute of Cultural and Social Studies.

Braidotti, R. 1994. *Nomadic Subjects: Embodiment and Sexual Difference in Contemporary Feminist Theory*. New York: Columbia University Press.

Cosminsky, S. 1976. Cross-cultural perspectives on midwifery. In *Medical Anthropology*, edited by F.-X. Grollig and H.B. Haley. The Hague and Paris: Mouton.

Curtis, P. 1993. Oxytocin and the augmentation of labor: human and medical perspectives. *Human Nature* 4: 351–66.

Davis-Floyd, R.E. and C. Sargent (eds). 1997. *Childbirth and Authoritative Knowledge: Cross-cultural Perspectives*. Berkeley and Los Angeles: University of California Press.

Dudley, D.J. 1997. Oxytocin: use and abuse, science and art. *Clinical Obstetrics and Gynecology* 40: 516–24.

Fiedler, D.C. 1997. Authoritative knowledge and birth territories in contemporary Japan. In *Childbirth and Authoritative Knowledge: Cross-cultural Perspectives*, edited by R.E. Davis-Floyd and C. Sargent. Berkeley and Los Angeles: University of California Press.

Ginsberg, F. and R. Rapp. 1991. The politics of reproduction. *Annual Review of Anthropology* 20: 311–43.

—— 1995. *Conceiving the New World Order: The Global Politics of Reproduction*. Berkeley and Los Angeles: University of California Press.

Hugo, G.J., V.J. Hull, T.H. Hull and G.W. Jones. 1987. *The Demographic Dimension in Indonesian Development*. Singapore, Oxford and New York: Oxford University Press.

Hunter, C. 1996. Women as 'good citizens': maternal and child health in a Sasak village. In *Maternal and Reproductive Health in Asian Societies*, edited by P.L. Rice and L. Manderson. London and New York: Harwood Academic.

IPPA (The Indonesian Planned Parenthood Association). 1971. *Report on the Study of Dukuns in Central Java*: Indonesia.

Kierse, M.J.N.C., H.P. Ottervanger and W. Smit. 1996. Controversies: prelabor rupture of the membranes at term: the case for expectant management. *Journal of Prenatal Medicine* 24: 563–72.

Laderman, C. 1983. *Wives and Midwives: Childbirth and Nutrition in Rural Malaysia*. Berkeley and Los Angeles: University of California Press.

Lazarus, E. 1997. What do women want? Issues of choice, control, and class in American pregnancy and childbirth. In *Childbirth and Authoritative Knowledge: Cross-cultural Perspectives*, edited by R.E. Davis-Floyd and C. Sargent. Berkeley and Los Angeles: University of California Press.

McClain, C. 1982. Toward a comparative framework for the study of childbirth: a review of the literature. In *Anthropology of Human Birth*, edited by M.A. Kay. Philadelphia, PA: F.A. Davis Co.

Martin, E. 1990. The ideology of reproduction: the reproduction of ideology. In *Uncertain Terms: Negotiating Gender in American Culture*, edited by F. Ginsburg and A.L. Tsing. Boston, MA: Beacon.

—— 1987. *The Woman in the Body: A Cultural Analysis of Reproduction*. Beacon Press.

Newland, L. 1999. Cosmologies in conflict: the politics of reproduction in West Java. Ph.D. thesis, Macquarie University.

Niehof, Anke. 1992. Mediating roles of the traditional birth attendant in Indonesia. In *Women and Mediation in Indonesia*, edited by S. van Bemmelen, M. Djajadiningrat-Nieuwenhuis, E. Locher-Scholten and E. Touwen-Bouwsma. Leiden: KITLV.

Niehof, A. and A. Hasyir. 1975. *The Traditional Midwife as a Motivator for Family Planning*. Serpong Paper No. 25, Universitas Indonesia and Leiden University.

Niehof, A. and H. Sastramihardja. 1978. The community-based channels for the diffusion of family planning. In *Family Planning in Rural West Java*, general editor L.C.L. Zuidberg. Leiden and Indonesia: Rijksuniversiteit Leiden, Universitas Indonesia.

Oakley, A. 1984. *The Captured Womb: A History of the Medical Care of Pregnant Women*. Oxford and New York: Basil Blackwell.

O'Neill, J.D. and P.L. Kauffert. 1995. Irniktakpunga! Sex determination and the Inuit struggle for birthing rights in Northern Canada. In *Conceiving the New World Order: The Global Politics of Reproduction*, edited by F.D. Ginsberg and R. Rapp. Berkeley and Los Angeles: University of California Press.

—— 1993. Analysis of a dialogue on risks in childbirth: clinicians, epidemiologists, and Inuit Women. In *Knowledge, Power and Practice: The Anthropology of Medicine and Everyday Life*, edited by S. Lindenbaum and M. Lock. Berkeley and Los Angeles: University of California Press.

Pigg, S.L. 1997. Authority in translation: finding, knowing, naming and training 'traditional birth attendants' in Nepal. In *Childbirth and Authoritative Knowledge: Cross-cultural Perspectives*, edited by R.E. Davis-Floyd and C. Sargent. Berkeley and Los Angeles: University of California Press.

Ram, K. and M. Jolly (eds). 1998. *Maternities and Modernities: Colonial and Postcolonial Experiences in Asia and the Pacific*. Cambridge and New York: Cambridge University Press.

Sargent, C.F. and G. Bascope. 1997. Ways of knowing about birth in three cultures. In *Childbirth and Authoritative Knowledge: Cross-cultural Perspectives*, edited by R.E. Davis-Floyd and C. Sargent. Berkeley and Los Angeles: University of California Press.

Sesia, P.M. 1997. 'Women come here on their own when they need to': prenatal care, authoritative knowledge, and maternal health in Oaxaca. In *Childbirth and Authoritative Knowledge: Cross-cultural Perspectives*, edited by R.E. Davis-Floyd and C. Sargent. Berkeley and Los Angeles: University of California Press.

Shetty, S. 1994. (Dis)locating gender space and medical discourse in colonial India. In *Eroticism and Containment: Notes from the Flood Plain*, edited by C. Siegel and A. Kibbey. New York and London: New York University Press.

Szurek, J. 1997. Resistance to technology-enhanced childbirth in Tuscany: the political economy of Italian birth. In *Childbirth and Authoritative Knowledge: Cross-cultural Perspectives*, edited by R.E. Davis-Floyd and C. Sargent. Berkeley and Los Angeles: University of California Press.

Young, I.M. 1990. *Throwing Like a Girl and Other Essays in Feminist Philosophy and Social Theory*. Bloomington and Indianapolis: Indiana University Press.

Chapter 13

Embracing modernity

Transformations in Sasak confinement practices

Cynthia L. Hunter

The onset of modernity and accompanying globalisation through the expansion and invention of communications technology creates a social development in which modern institutions are distinct and separate in form from traditional types (Giddens 1990: 6). Three features, the pace of change, the scope of change and the nature of modern institutions account for this separation and distinction (Giddens 1990: 6). Giddens also describes modernity as a double-edged phenomenon. Through the worldwide spread of modern social institutions, greater opportunities for humanity exist than ever before, but there is also a dark side in which capitalism, industrialisation and the expansion of bureaucracy can, for example, produce large-scale human degradation and destruction of the material environment. Central to any analysis of the above is the concept and notion of society.

Previous influential theorists, Marx, Durkheim and Parsons for example, have focused on the boundedness of social systems. Others, such as Foucault and Giddens, have focused on how to resolve the 'problem of order' in their explanations. Giddens, however, following Foucault (1984) reformulates the question of order as a problem of time–space distanciation, 'the conditions under which time and space are organized so as to connect presence and absence' (Giddens 1990: 14). This is based on a conceptual distinction between modern societies (nation-states) and the 'boundedness' of social systems. Because modernity is multidimensional on the level of institutions, he argues that 'such [modern] societies are interwoven with ties and connections which crosscut the sociopolitical system of the state and the cultural order of the "nation"' (Giddens 1990: 14). Such analysis is conceptually different from conventional structural-functional analysis of the kind which assumes the boundedness of social systems in which cultural elements such as traditional confinement practices are perceived as having an integrative function.

Giddens is not particularly interested in confinement practices (the topic of this chapter), but his analysis of modern institutions helps clarify, for example, the contrast between a state society and a society whose cultural order is derived from the local and ordinary knowledges of rural villagers. In addition, Giddens' work points to the criss-crossings which occur between the state and the cultural order.

My intention in this chapter is to examine local and ordinary knowledges about confinement practices and the criss-crossings between the state and the cultural order. Further analysis requires the articulation of three levels; the integration of (1) personal experience as in childbirth, with (2) the social values and realities of a 'cultural idiom' (the centrality of cultural meanings, as argued by Kleinman 1980 *inter alia*) and (3) the use of this explanatory system to mobilise social resources in order to reintegrate the mother and her reconstituted self into the social world and the established social relations.

In modern social environments which are marked by social fragmentation and social differentiation, there is no guarantee of cognitive homogeneity or social unity within the group. Groups and their members exist within and in relation to larger fields of discourse and power. It is a world characterised by the fragmentation of the organic unity and coherence of social life, one in which other voices resonate, often against a dominant discourse (Steedly 1988: 841). Fragmentation and different rationalities interweave in a complex process forming new fields of discourse in which the emergent tensions form disjunctions and resolutions as they address and confront each other. It is within this context that I locate my story of modern confinement practices, the strength of tradition (*tradisi* [I][1]) and its meaning for preserving cultural identity within the space and place of modernity.

This chapter is based on twenty months of ethnographic fieldwork researching the power relations between the state and village Indonesia, especially within the field of illness and healing. The research was conducted through participant observation within the village and the health clinic and subclinic. It also involved two surveys of villagers' ideas and practices regarding pregnancy, birth and post-partum periods, and several in-depth interviews with women and health clinic staff.

Lombok is a small island which lies to the east of Bali in the modern state of Indonesia and is a twenty-minute plane ride from Bali. The community of Elah, in which I lived during 1991/2, is situated in northeast Lombok, over 400 metres above sea level on the slopes of Mt Rinjani, a volcanic and holy mountain. The population of around 5000 people is homogeneously Sasak. It is a market village serving the four to five villages in its vicinity. The main income is derived from garlic and more recently tobacco and wet-rice agriculture, with the majority of landowners owning small plots of approximately half a hectare. Today, landlessness and unemployment amongst youth is becoming visible. Sasak kinship groupings are predominantly patrilineally based (Kitamura 1983), most land is inherited through males, although daughters in sonless families are also able to inherit land. Serial monogamy is a common marriage pattern and polygyny is practised by a few.

The state and development have provided Elah with several forms of modernity. The main roads are bitumenised, a private electricity company provides services to some homes, there are government primary schools in three of the four hamlets and one secondary school close by, as well as several schools run by religious organisations, and during my stay, a new television relay tower was being built to boost transmission to Sumbawa, the island visible to the east. There is a health subclinic (*pusat kesehatan masyarakat pembantu* [I] abbrev. *Pustu*) in the village, staffed by one paramedic and in 1992 a village midwife (*bidan di desa* [I]) was appointed. The health clinic (*pusat kesehatan masyarakat* [I], abbrev. *puskesmas*) at Labuan Sasak is 15 km away.

The majority of Sasaks, as well as other Indonesian ethnic groups throughout the archipelago follow the Islamic religion. Islam has (at least nominally) been the religion of over 90 per cent of Sasak since the fifteenth century. There are two main indigenous variants of Islam on Lombok (Krulfeld 1974; Cederroth 1981, 1993; Kitamura 1983). These are referred to as *wetu* or *waktu telu* [S] (literally, 'three times') and *waktu lima* [S] ('five times').[2]

Waktu telu is the older and more traditional of the two. It is a syncretic form of Islam and regarded by *waktu lima* reformers as heterodox and only nominally Muslim. According to Cederroth (1993: 4), one of the most important common elements shared by the *wetu* or *waktu telu* religion of Lombok, Balinese Hinduism and Javanese Islamic syncretism (*Agami Jawi*) is ancestor worship. The leaders of *waktu telu*, the *pemangku* [S], along with a group of indigenous healers called *belian* [S], have been the preservers of custom, tradition and cosmological beliefs (*adat* [S/I]) and constitute a group of village intellectuals. While once *pemangku* were found in all Lombok villages they are now only found in certain, more traditional villages. They have been displaced by modern *tuan guru* [S], a term implying 'great religious scholars'. The *tuan guru* have emerged since the 1930s as part of the pan-Indonesian Islamic revival. They live in the larger centres rather than villages, and are the leaders of *waktu lima*, the modern, orthodox Islamic variant. *Waktu lima* is proselytising, particularly austere, and modern in the sense that followers of *waktu lima* have created for themselves a Sasak identity within a much broader and wider Islamic world.

Village Sasak identify themselves with one or other of these variants, although *waktu telu* has been in decline for some time. Throughout the Indonesian archipelago the Sasak of Lombok are reputed to be *fanatik* [I], that is, strictly adhering to religion. This refers to the *waktu lima* ideology. Peasant villagers in Elah highly value going on the pilgrimage to Mecca because of the huge endowment of cultural, social and religious capital bestowed upon returning pilgrims. Few encourage their children along the costly path of education, preferring to use their economic resources for the *Haj* [I].

The sense of cultural identity which emerges in the Sasak of East Lombok is partially derived from these local cultural ideologies. Throughout Lombok there are variations in dialect, custom and cultural ideology as much as there are degrees of difference between villages in a subdistrict and between East, Central and West Lombok districts. What it means to be Sasak has become a contested issue, partly because, unlike in other regional areas, the local nobility became the orthodox followers of Islam rather than supporting custom (*adat*). As a consequence, Sasak commoners, who were usually loyal supporters of the nobility, became the upholders of Sasak cultural practices, at least up until the events of the mid-1960s.

In the rhythm of daily village life, there is a synthesis of tradition (*tradisi*) and the modern (*moderen*) in religious and cultural practices. If one relies solely on the spoken word of villagers, all Elah residents agree they are *waktu lima* and say 'we follow *agama* [religion] rather than *adat* [custom]'. None the less, indigenous healers (*belian*) still retain a significant role in illness and healing in all Sasak villages. By my count, there were at least thirty-seven indigenous healers in Elah.

Childbirth

Although villagers consider childbirth to be a natural event, and it normally takes place at home, it none the less contains elements of risk, fear and danger. The lack of a professional midwife in the health subclinic until May 1991 partly explains why women and men expect to call on the services of indigenous midwives at the time of confinement. Data collected in surveys of village men and women[3] revealed that few (8.0 per cent) used a health clinic or village professional midwife and most (92.0 per cent) used traditional midwives. Almost half (44.5 per cent) of these used state-trained indigenous midwives. The main reasons given for not using the midwife at the health subclinic referred to social, economic and distance barriers rather than cultural resistance. She was new to the village, she came without reputation, she was young and inexperienced, people were fearful of how much it would cost to use her services and were also concerned that she may not be able to attend a birth because of the lack of regular village transport.

Confinement is not considered in terms of illness. Consequently, unless complications arise, the services of health personnel or Western drugs are not considered necessary during confinement. Nevertheless, many of the women and men in the survey expressed their desire to call upon a indigenous midwife who had received health clinic training. Village women 'ease the passage' of childbirth by being attended by family members, neighbours and indigenous healers/specialists (*belian ranak* [S]) who possess spiritual and midwifery skills. Thus, until recently the only available delivery assistance was the services of an indigenous midwife. In Lombok they are all women, compared to Bali and Malaysia where midwives may be men or women (Connor 1983; Connor et al. 1996; Wikan 1990: 230–64; Laderman 1983).[4] The services of an indigenous midwife during the birthing process is twofold. She applies her medical/technical skills in assisting the mother during labour, cutting the umbilical cord using a bamboo knife, a razor blade or scissors, and attending to the neonate. She also, however, has ritual and caring responsibilities for mother and baby, which continue for some days after confinement.

One of the most important ritual responsibilities of a *belian ranak* is the spiritual cleansing of the birth space to ensure neither mother nor child will come into contact with harmful spirits. Another responsibility extends to caring for the afterbirth which is recognised as the spiritual birth sibling/siblings of the newborn child. These birth-sibling spirits have protected the baby in the womb throughout pregnancy and are born with it (Connor 1982: 260; Laderman 1991: 92–3). Both the *belian ranak* and the father of the newborn perform the preparation rituals and subsequent ceremony for the burial of the afterbirth. Childbirth is a space in which *adat* (custom) is persistent and embedded because Sasak cosmologies incorporate ancestral, supernatural and other non-manifest spirits which can affect humans in both positive and negative ways (Cederroth 1993). Until quite recently, Sasak indigenous medical practices and the rituals surrounding childbirth were the customary and acceptable forms of assistance for village women during confinement. These rituals represent an area in which close relations are of paramount importance, and *adat* or *tradisi* most persistent and embedded. Nonetheless, the ways in which villagers encounter modernity encompass modern (*moderen* [I]) forms of confinement practices.

Modernity brings transformations, not least of which is the monitoring in numerous ways of the populations contained within the state. The national health system had developed under the New Order government in the 1970s and 1980s with the establishment of health clinics (*puskesmas* [I]) throughout the country. With this development came the increased medicalisation of birthing (see also Whittaker, Harris, Newland, Chapters 10 to 12 this volume). In an attempt to decrease maternal and infant mortality rates, the Department of Health through the Primary Health Care Programme (established by WHO and adopted by Indonesia), encouraged health clinic training of indigenous midwives (see also Chapters 10 and 12). Indigenous midwives were given a two- to three-day training course at the health clinic. The course included instruction in hygiene, in recognising the danger signals of oncoming childbirth difficulties and where to go for help should any of these arise. On successful completion of the course, each midwife was presented with a kit for her use. In theory, though rarely in practice, she could replenish the kit with supplies from the health clinic (cf. Grace 1996, *inter alia*). Throughout Indonesia, the indigenous midwife belongs to one of only a very few indigenous categories of medicine recognised by the national health system. More recently, in the 1990s, the training emphasis has shifted away from indigenous midwives towards the planned provision of trained village midwives (*bidan di desa* [I]) in every village, with the intention that these latter people will gradually replace *belian ranak* (Grace 1996: 145).

The advent of the national medical services in the late 1980s in Elah village saw the development of medical pluralism (i.e., more than one set of medical practices operating at the same time). As I mentioned earlier, there has always been a group of indigenous healers who assist villagers through all manner of illnesses. Now the national health system has established a subclinic staffed by a paramedic who provides primary services. The new health services have made some, though not substantial, differences to childbirth practices. Elah village has at least eighteen indigenous midwives although their midwifery practices are not their only source of income. Nevertheless, only a few have had access to training programmes. Of the eighteen indigenous midwives I enlisted, only three had clinic training, all of whom are over fifty years of age. Unless a family history of complications in childbirth exists, it is rare for mothers to opt for health clinic confinements. In my survey of forty women of childbearing age, thirty-seven (92.5 per cent) reported being assisted by an indigenous midwife for their confinements (cf. Grace 1996).[5] Of the three who had some assistance from the state health system, two were local women married to wealthy villagers and the third was the wife of a school teacher stationed in the village. Thus, class or status appears to have an impact on whether the state system is used.

The low user rate of the state system is also partly explained by the uneven development of government infrastructure in rural Indonesia which has resulted in some villages having a resident trained village midwife while others have not. As I mentioned earlier, the first trained village midwife in Elah village arrived in May 1991, but six months later many women did not know of her existence and were, therefore, unlikely to call for her assistance. Customarily childbirth is a time to be safe amongst family members, sympathetic friends and trusted healers who will guide the woman through the birthing process.

Modernity also brings choices and some women are beginning to adopt different confinement practices. The choice of the majority remains with home deliveries assisted by indigenous midwives (trained or untrained). Other choices are combinations of the customary and modern: the indigenous midwife assisted by the trained village midwife, or the reverse – the trained village midwife assisted by the indigenous midwife. In the former case, the indigenous midwife delivers the baby, and the trained village midwife comes later to check mother and child and to give injections of tetanus toxoid and vitamins to the mother. In the latter, the trained village midwife attends to the medical/technical aspects of the birth, with the indigenous midwife as her assistant. The ritual aspects of confinement remain the domain of the indigenous midwife. To the villagers, it is the ritual domain of the indigenous midwife that defines her and is the magnet to which they are drawn.

The most modern and 'medicalised' choice, usually by women of means, is the clinic as an alternative space and place for their confinements. Nevertheless, their choice is often mediated by their husbands. It remains a moot point whether they have real choice or not because women remain sub-jugated by men. These women are the wives of men who have the means to be upwardly mobile, men and women who desire the visible trappings and social status which being modern means in Indonesia. They are better educated and are able to pay for the greater sense of security represented by confine-ment in a modern clinic. They are attended by the health clinic midwife, a trained nurse with midwifery qualifications.

Inaq Kariati's confinement

The rest of this chapter is devoted to the story of the health clinic confine-ment of Inaq Kariati, in whose household I lived for over a year. Inaq Kariati is forty-two years of age and she has had six children, four of whom are living. She is married to Mamiq Hamli, a retired government bureaucrat and a member of the lower aristocracy (*perwangsa* [S]). Mamiq's ascribed status and his previous career as a government bureaucrat partially explain why the health clinic was considered a possible choice for the confinement. Inaq's experience of being married to a government bureaucrat who was therefore familiar with the government's development plans for modernisation influ-enced their joint decision. Ideas of modernity, of what the government endorses, are easier to embrace when they are affordable. Inaq's age and a prior visit to the health clinic for a tetanus toxoid injection the previous month[6] probably also influenced her decision. At that time Inaq had a favourable encounter with the health clinic midwife, who showed concern for her well-being, talked about giving birth in the health clinic, told her what to bring with her if she decided to come and explained about her future family planning options. In the following narrative, I describe the event as it took place in the health clinic, some of the compromises which needed to be made by Inaq and her husband Mamiq, how Sasak *adat* was satisfactorily incorporated and carried out, and modernity embraced. I was reminded of the contrasts between this encounter with modernity and Clifford Geertz's example of a Javanese funeral (Geertz 1957: 32–54). In his ethnographic depiction of a Javanese funeral, Geertz draws together the tensions sur-rounding death and the funerary preparations involved in dealing with the corpse. I shall return later to the contrasts between the two encounters.

The persons involved

Inaq Kariati, a commoner woman married to a lower gentry man, Mamiq
 Hamli
Mamiq Hamli, a retired government bureaucrat, lower gentry
Baiq Kariati, their daughter, away at university
Lalu Jamaluddin, their son who works at the communication office
Baiq Hidayah, their daughter at junior high school

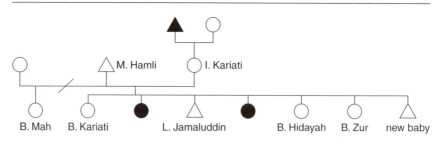

Figure 13.1 Family of Inaq Kariati and Mamiq Hamli

Baiq Zur, their daughter at primary school
new baby boy
Baiq Mah, the daughter of Mamiq Hamli and his first wife
Inaq Kariati's mother, grandmother to the children
Ibu Andi, a close neighbour, a Christian from Flores
Ibu Rohani, the midwife at the Elah village health subclinic
Ria, my research assistant
Zubaedah Amniah (Bidan Zubaedah), the health clinic midwife of Labuan
     Sasak
CLH, anthropologist living in Elah

Narrative

Inaq complained of *sakit tian* (a painful stomach), by which she meant that
the baby was on its way. She requested an examination by the village midwife
and asked me to call Ibu Rohani, who was in the health subclinic (*pustu*)
along the back lane from our house. Ibu Rohani came and confirmed the
baby probably would be born in the afternoon. Mamiq Hamli had already
gone to Lekong, a village two km away, to fetch Inaq's mother. Inaq said 'If
he is back in time and if he agrees, I'll go to the health clinic in Labuan
Sasak for my delivery. If he doesn't agree to that, I'll call *belian ranak* Papuq
Isah to assist.'
    An hour later, Mamiq returned and they decided to go to Labuan Sasak.
    My role was ill defined. I had not been asked to accompany them, yet
Inaq pressed me to eat *now*. I understood her to mean she wanted to make
sure I had eaten before she left, because usually it was she who cooked for me.
However, Ria came into my room and said, 'Inaq expects you to go with her'.
    Mamiq found a *bemo* (taxi). Inaq and I got in the front with the driver,
Mamiq, Ibu Andi, Mah, Jamaluddin and Zur in the back with the baggage,
which included woven sleeping mats, a pillow, a bag of baby clothes, several
lengths of batik cloth, a new needle and syringes,[7] soap and towel, a large
basin and a coconut.

We arrived at the health clinic at noon on Saturday to find it closed. The only health person around was Bidan Zubaedah who lives in the adjoining quarters. She ushered Inaq into the maternity room. The biomedical signs and symbols were in sharp contrast to the confinement space found at home births which take place in a room in the house and where there may be a normal sleeping bed, mats on the floor, some sarongs, the indigenous midwife's kit (if she is trained), soap and water. The maternity room contained two high plastic-covered beds (one with stirrups), two large cupboards, a humi-crib, baby bath, one large and one small steel bowl, obstetric examination instruments, a set of steps, a standard lamp, a small table and a broom. The contents of the cupboards included contraceptives, medical supplies and equipment.[8] Bidan Zubaedah examined Inaq internally using a rubber glove, gave her an injection of vitamin B12 and surmised that the baby would probably be born in the late afternoon at around 6.00 p.m. Inaq then rested on one of the beds. Mamiq, Zur and I stayed and the others went home.

It was extremely hot as the afternoon wore on, yet Inaq remained quiet and patient. The contractions were increasing in strength but were not becoming much more frequent. I fanned her face and wiped her forehead, face and neck with a wet cloth. She had a band of cloth tied up under her breasts. This, according to Sasak custom, discourages the baby from rising up to the stomach. Inaq frequently got up to urinate. She was drinking a little water. Bidan Zubaedah came and examined her again at about 3.30 p.m. and said that the baby was slow. Time crept by. Mamiq went home to collect Inaq's mother.

Zur collected bunches of flowers and talked with her mother. Inaq got up several times and walked around outside. By 6.00 p.m. things had not progressed much further and Inaq was becoming restless and a little stressed. Meanwhile Mamiq returned with Inaq's mother, a thermos of hot water and food. He pressed me to go home if I wanted to. He probably thought I was tired and the family could manage now Inaq's mother had arrived. I went home to bathe and eat, but later decided to return to the health clinic on my motorbike, arriving just before 9.00 p.m.

Inaq was standing outside. She had been lying down on a sheet of plastic. 'It's cooler out in the yard', she said. Her daughter was bedded down in the delivery room on a sleeping mat, while her grandmother sat nearby. It was suffocatingly hot and humid in the delivery room. The door to the room closest to the street was closed and therefore the only ventilation came through the double doors leading to the enclosed courtyard. Mosquitoes whined around us, both inside and out of the room. There was no sign of any repellent, coils or mosquito nets even though we were in a health clinic and the inhabitants of this region suffer malaria attacks.

Bidan Zubaedah came to examine Inaq after she came back inside. Things began moving quickly. Zur was moved out of the room on to a table on the verandah by her father and grandmother. They sat outside quietly waiting. I stood by Inaq's head fanning her. Up until now Inaq had only grimaced in pain with each new contraction, now she uttered a few cries. She pushed hard and long once. Then she pushed again and out popped the baby, a healthy boy. Bidan Zubaedah dealt with the umbilical cord. She called authoritatively for me to hurry up and bring the *obat merah* (mercurochrome), to soak cotton wool with it and hand it to her. It was necessary that I assist her because there were no other health personnel present. She used surgical instruments to cut the cord and tied it off with thick white thread. My next job was to find a cloth, blanket and clothes for the baby from the bundle we had brought from home, then the baby soap in readiness for his bath. The baby was wrapped in the cloth and placed on the small side table.

Bidan Zubaedah attended to Inaq first, massaging her abdomen to expel the afterbirth. This was placed in a basin under the bed. There is a customary Sasak ritual for the afterbirth which is performed by family members. More clean cloth was required, this time one from the batik bundle, to wrap around Inaq. After Bidan Zubaedah had sponged her down we bound her stomach with the traditional *songkak* (S), a long band of woven cotton used by women to bind the abdomen immediately after childbirth. This cloth is wound tightly around the body several times to encourage the uterus to return to its normal size. Traditionally women follow this practice for forty days or more (see also Laderman 1983: 176). Then Inaq rested.

Mamiq was called to fetch the baby's bath. Hot water was added and the baby bathed. Bidan Zubaedah got a small rubber tube and sucked out his mouth and nose to get rid of any remaining liquid and mucus lodged there. Then he was dressed and weighed. He weighed 3 kgs 40 grams, a healthy weight. He was placed in the crib, wrapped up in his blanket. Inaq changed her sarong again and rested quietly.

Throughout the birth, Inaq's mother had remained outside. She now came in to view the baby. Zur stayed sleeping. Bidan Zubaedah suggested we go and buy milk and a bottle in case the baby wanted nourishment before morning and until Inaq's milk came. I thought this an odd suggestion. It was late at night; there were no shops open! Perhaps if one lives in the town you wake up a shopkeeper to fulfil this perceived need. Bidan Zubaedah left for the night.

Mamiq and I chatted. He was overjoyed, especially because the baby was a boy and they only had one son. 'And he waited for you to return. Wasn't that wonderful!' he exclaimed. 'We didn't know you were coming back to the health clinic, but he knew and he waited. As soon as you returned he was ready to be born.' We all retired to try to sleep.

At midnight I checked on Inaq, who was resting quite well considering the humidity, and I went out to the back to chat with Mamiq. He had been busy! He'd washed all the cloths and had them drying on the line. Normally, a husband has nothing to do with these chores; in the Islamic tradition there are pollution taboos about menstrual blood, the blood of childbirth and lochia. He had found the afterbirth, cleaned it and then wrapped it in the customary fashion, in white cloth, placed it in the coconut and buried it in the corner of the garden to the right of the door, the traditional place for boys. He said, 'I didn't know what to do with it, whether to throw it in the sea or take it back to Elah or what.' Having decided neither was appropriate he had proceeded with the burial. 'I've washed all the cloths. Usually the *belian* [*ranak*] attends to the washing but as there isn't one, I've done it.' He was still excited, happy, proud of himself to be so organised. He said that Inaq had liked being in the health clinic; it was quiet, whereas at home people kept coming around and it was not as restful. He said that I must help with choosing a name for the baby. Inaq called and wanted a clean sarong. Mamiq washed the soiled one immediately.

When the baby began to cry everyone got up to check on him. Inaq held him to her breast and he was sucking strongly. Inaq was tired but had no temperature. Everyone settled down again until the crackling loudspeaker call for morning prayer from the market mosque across the road penetrated any early morning slumbers with its loudness. From a Westerner's viewpoint, the sick are required to have peace and quiet. In Indonesia, health clinics are usually located on busy thoroughfares. This one, an in-patient health clinic is built on the main north–south connection of East Lombok, immediately opposite the mosque and the town market.

Mamiq went over the road for some more hot water and we all had some coffee.[9] Zur slept on. At 6.00 a.m. Bidan Zubaedah came and gave Inaq an injection of vitamins, an antibiotic and some *obat* (pills) to take. She thought she could go home at about 10.00 a.m. Bidan Zubaedah's responsibility and treatment ended here. Any further problems could be attended to by Rohani, the village midwife.

It was early morning when I returned to the village to spread the news. Mah was still in bed and others had only just begun to stir. They were tired and said they had been watching Inaq's mango trees most of the night to stop thieves stealing the fruit. An hour later, Mamiq arrived with Zur and told the full story, with all its excitement and how the baby had waited until my arrival to be born. Family and neighbours shared his excitement. He returned to fetch baby, Inaq and her mother at about 11.00 a.m. The event was reiterated, this time by Inaq's mother. Everyone shared the happy news, people visited to view the baby, there was talk about names for the child and more talk about how the event had gone.

Inaq Kariati reflects on the experience

Two weeks later I had a chat with Inaq Kariati about her health clinic experience. She repeated what Mamiq Hamli had already told me, saying:

> I hadn't given birth in a health clinic before. It was *baik sekali* [I] [very good]. I felt safe and it was quiet. There weren't too many interruptions. The *bidan* [midwife] was good because she had come in several times to

see me [four times]. Several women from Elah have gone to Pare for delivery. But there it's noisy and the *bidan* leaves them for long periods, only visiting once. People have said that sometimes she [the *bidan*] comes, does an examination and then goes out [leaves the health clinic]. Previously people didn't want to go to the health clinic in Labuan Sasak because there was a shortage of water. This isn't the case now. It [the experience] was good. It cost Rp25,000 [about US$10 at 1996 rates], including transport.

This fee is in contrast to a delivery with an indigenous healer who charges whatever people can afford. For example, they may give her some cash – Rp4,000 to 5,000 [US$1.60 to $2] plus other items, a chicken, thread, betelnut, a piece of cloth. Payment in cash or kind can be made over a long period of time.

Analysis

Inaq Kariati's health clinic confinement represents a favourable experience of 'modern' health care services. Inaq and her husband's choice of the health clinic confinement was based on experience and knowledge of childbirth constituted in a time and space prior to the availability of modern health services in the village and her access to others with different knowledge and experience. New perspectives on childbirth were offered by her neighbour Ibu Andi (the Christian from Flores), the few women known to her who had had health clinic confinements, myself who had been living in her household for eight months, and the health clinic midwife. During our discussions Inaq Kariati had expressed concern about her age and the safety of the confinement, and the fact that she wished this to be her last baby. Her last two children, including this one, were 'mistakes' (her account was that Mamiq forgot to buy the pill). Her favourable encounter with the health clinic midwife provided an opportunity to fulfil her desire for knowledge about health clinic confinements and more reliable forms of contraception. She had not felt let down by the experience; on the contrary, it had been favourable.

The couple's choice can be considered precautionary, rather than curative or preventive. Their choice represents a willingness to try something new where there is concern for safety and health on the one hand, and on the other, sufficient knowledge and positive reinforcement from those with different experiences of time and space (i.e., those who had experienced childbirth in a biomedical setting where medical monitoring and technological apparatus is used) to quell any fears of the unknown. It was not a haphazard, spur-of-the-moment decision, but one based on a collective knowledge of childbirth experiences in the village and a favourable encounter with the health clinic midwife. If the latter had been out of the question in terms of the proximity of the birth, there was a contingency plan. It was

Inaq's wish to call on Papuq Isah, the best-known and most popular of the three clinic-trained indigenous midwives of the village. The services of the new village *bidan* were not called for, except in the initial stages, to confirm the birth was in progress. This was probably because she was new to the village, she came without a reputation and she was young and relatively inexperienced.

Inaq Kariati's favourable experience of the modern health system differs from the encounters with the modern health system that many other people have had. In everyday life, people describe unfavourable encounters about all manner of sicknesses from treatment for a cough, broken limbs, intestinal problems, skin irritations. Whereas the health clinic offers curative services, with successful and unsuccessful results, childbirth services are considered precautionary or preventive. The mother chooses to place herself, her body and the baby in a situation in which, if unforeseen complications arise, bio-medical expertise is on hand to assist.

Prior to the introduction of the health clinic or village midwife, seeking the national health services for confinements only occurred in emergency situations, that is, when there was a high risk of medical intervention failing. These are times when events are unforeseen, that is, they occur when difficulties arise during the birthing process. With the increasing level and accessibility of modern health services, childbirth is becoming medicalised and monitored. The population of pregnant women attending trained midwives for antenatal care examinations is increasing, and therefore women with high-risk conditions are becoming visible. Appropriate steps are being taken to ensure their deliveries are monitored and accompanied by the most modern medical servicing available.

On the whole, those who choose the health clinic service are wealthy or *perwangsa* (aristocracy) (or both). These groups are less socially distant from the professional health personnel than the *kaula* (commoners). The aristocracy have had greater access to education and bureaucratic jobs. They have more social experience with the middle classes, are likely to be more mobile, speak Indonesian and high Sasak well and are thus more at ease with government bureaucrats and the machinations of government than the lower classes. They are more likely than their poorer, *kaula* neighbours to enjoy an economic status which gives them greater access to modernity and choice.

Modernity embraced

Modernity is often accompanied with a disregard for the more traditional and customary rituals of people's lives. In the confinement, the realm of *adat* rituals is incorporated within modern space and technology. The coconut and dish, both items necessary for the traditional rituals were taken to the health clinic as part of the baggage. There was no questioning of change to *adat* in the modern setting. The health clinic midwife silently supported and

292 Cynthia L. Hunter

reinforced this ritual. After expelling the afterbirth, she placed it in a bowl under the bed and left it. Mamiq found it there and only then, as he exclaimed himself, did he query what to do with it. With pragmatism he decided to bury it in the courtyard, to the right of the door, as is customary for boys. The question arises as to where he might have buried it had it been a girl, as there was no ground to the left of the door. Would he have thrown it away in the sea, buried it someplace else, or taken it back to the village for burial?

Although Inaq's mother was present and could have washed the blood-stained cloths, it was Mamiq who took responsibility for the task. This is highly unorthodox; it is a task left to the women because of the taboos about men touching or coming into contact with menstrual blood, the blood of childbirth and lochia (the discharge from the uterus and vagina which follows childbirth) (see also Laderman (1983: 74 for Malaysia). During confinement and afterwards, it is usual for the woman to get someone in to help her with cooking because taboo prohibits her from cooking for her husband. There are, however, other reasons too: she may still be weak and unable to manage for some time. According to one young male informant,

> Islamic doctrine contains strict taboos about men handling the after-birth (*adiq adiq* [S]) or washing any bloodstained cloths, or in any way coming into contact with menstrual blood and lochia. However, in prac-tice, it depends on the attitude of a woman's husband to the prohibitions and it depends on circumstances.
>
> (Fieldnotes 10/08/1992)

This vignette is a case in point. There were no others to assist except myself and Inaq's mother. Inaq's mother had a problem with the sight of blood and no-one else is as suitable as a close relation or the *belian ranak*. Pragmatism prevails over customary law.

Inaq's mother's role in these rituals was also highly unusual. She remained subdued throughout. She would usually be one of the women assisting her daughter in childbirth. However, in this case, she looked after Zur and attended to the food and drinks. Mamiq explained to me why. 'She did not participate because she is frightened of the sight of blood', he said. Maybe she felt uncomfortable in surroundings as strange as the health clinic. Or maybe her perceived passivity resulted from the presence of the midwife (a symbol of modern health care) and myself (an outsider, and someone she might suppose to be more familiar with modern confinements, since she knew I had two children of my own), both people trusted by her daughter. Regardless of the reasons, Inaq, Mamiq and Inaq's mother all expressed sat-isfaction with the tasks of the health clinic midwife and their experience of the health clinic.

Modernity in this confinement has positive outcomes. The experience is a representation of the 'opportunity side' of modernity (Giddens 1990: 7) in which individuals who are willing to take risks and maintain trust can enjoy the benefits of modern institutions such as health. The family (particularly Mamiq Hamli) successfully finessed the transformation from traditional to modern of a life-cycle event, incorporating symbols and cultural meanings from both with an outcome which was pleasing and integrative. In contrast, Geertz's (1957) analysis of a Javanese funeral represents the dark side of modernity (Giddens 1990: 8). Geertz illustrates the disintegrative and dis-ruptive aspects and the disorderliness of a life-event ritual (a funeral) in a small community at a time when social, political and cultural changes were emerging (Geertz 1957: 32–54). The analysis reveals the unsettling disjunc-tions which relatives and officials experience at a time of personal grief coupled with the desire to fulfil duties with regard to and respect for the dead. Where once *adat* prescribed an indisputable procedure in funerary rites, now new, disturbing and confusing procedural elements emerge as part of modernity. The fragmentation of social and kin relations is evident through the rural–urban divide; the fact that the parents of the dead boy live in the city and must travel to the village for the funeral. Geertz's example is now forty years old but in my view, there is a resonance with changed social real-ities in the two examples. Both events are illustrative of the mediation of change towards modernity and both reveal the double-edged character of modernity, that is, it provides both opportunities for reward as well as disin-tegration and disruption.

Elah is a rural village that still maintains cultural traditions from the past, especially surrounding life-cycle events, such as childbirth and death. Any form of modern health care has only appeared in the last ten to twelve years and has been received by many villagers with mixed feelings. So far, only the rich farmers or the few professionals living in the village have had much experience with the health services outside the village. Childbirth remains the most embedded tradition, so for a family to opt for a health clinic confine-ment displays elements of risk as well as trust. In Geertz's example of the funeral, the outcomes appear disastrous. In the confinement they are not, but may well have been because the tensions created by mediation were poten-tially as much disintegrative and disruptive as they were integrative. In contrast to the funeral, there are no political or ideological tensions dividing the community. The importance of ritual for both the parents and child are elements of all birth and death events. To the villager the ritual appears to be a pattern of cultural meaning and a form of social interaction. Birth ritual (and death) is territorially based and the primary ties are between families of residential propinquity. The potentially disruptive elements emerge because of the new space and place for confinements, the new set of social relations (contractual) which follow and the lack of precedence in how to maintain the customary birth rituals. Clinic confinements are representative of another ordered system of meaning, one in which individuals are still tentative in their actions. There is some displacement of the patterned social interaction.

Mamiq is able to resolve his moments of tension and his confusion over elements of procedure: what to do with the afterbirth, how to incorporate the prescribed *adat* surrounding its burial, who is to wash the blood-stained cloths. Inaq's mother's role in the health clinic confinement is also resolved. Both successfully finesse the disjunctions with pragmatism, and thus embrace modernity with the joy and excitement the birth of a new child brings.

The health clinic midwife and village midwife are representatives of modern Indonesia. Their professional lives are spent operating in a biomedical setting with the rituals of biomedicine learned through their training. These are embedded in a scientific tradition which emphasises objective rather than subjective criteria as described by Foucault's (1973) medical gaze, through which parts of the body are reified and objectified with the loss of subjectivity of the whole person. The health clinic midwife's procedures of examination, the instruments she relies upon for difficult cases, the clinic organisation and the bureaucratic structure of the state health system all correspond with what Giddens (1990: 27) describes as expert systems. The health clinic midwife contracts professional relations with clients. Her primary responsibility to the mother is a medical one in which the patient's subjectivity is eclipsed by the objectivity of the birthing process. If a patient dies, the health clinic personnel is required to take professional responsibility as a consequence of the medical or bureaucratic code, rather than taking personal responsibility. Unless the patient is a personal friend, therefore, the social relations required to assist confinement are minimal. The relationship between health clinic personnel and client is defined and bounded by a rationality based in a scientific and objective paradigm in which the patient presents her/his body or part of it for examination and treatment.

A rationality of this kind is in contrast to the rationality of indigenous medicine that subscribes to a holistic view of the body. People's encounters with indigenous midwives are personal and dyadic (Wolf 1966), based on trust, informality and give-and-take information. The indigenous midwife is a source of authoritative knowledge within a discourse which is socially and culturally embedded in village life. The indigenous midwife has a social and curing responsibility to patients which continues beyond any one encounter because of the similarity in social space, because of the close social networks in everyday life and the social embeddedness of aetiologies, and cosmologies.

In contrast, 'disembedding', the 'lifting out' of social relations from local contexts of interaction and their restructuring across indefinite spans of time-space' (Giddens 1990: 21), becomes an issue once a confinement is located in a medicalised environment. For most villagers, the clinic is locationally and spatially distant from any given situation of face-to-face interaction. The social context is replaced by a biomedical, cartographic and objective reality in which persons become things. There is no further social commitment required of the doctor or nurse to the patient within this context. In the clinic setting the midwifery assistance is of a medical-technical nature only, as is the assistance of the village midwife, her counterpart in the village. She takes no part in the social rituals performed with the birth siblings *(adiq adiq,* afterbirth), though as a Sasak and an Indonesian, she is aware of and complies with these practices.

Nor does the midwife or the health clinic supply accommodation or refreshments for the mother or accompanying family. Because it was the weekend, she relied on whoever else had come with Inaq to assist her. Thus, close relations remain important in each of the social spheres encompassing confinement because, without close kin, neighbours and/or ritual specialists to oversee the significant social and spiritual rituals, the life-cycle event would be marked with tension, uncertainty, indecision and disjunction. Giving birth in a health clinic is a very different social experience from giving birth at home. The 'social' is a powerful signifier of identity in this context.

The transformations required in adopting a health clinic confinement have embedded within them sufficient Sasak ritual to preserve a continuity with the village-world space. This embeddedness ensures a Sasak social and cultural identity while simultaneously satisfying villagers' desires to embrace modernity. The new baby representing a new generation of Sasak is protected by the continuing rituals which ensure his spiritual well-being is taken care of.

Transformations in the relations between gender, power and modernity are also represented in the health clinic confinement. The knowledge and experience of the outside world empowers men, as the carriers of modernity, to take their wives with them. Villagers with greater economic and social resources at their disposal recognise they have more choices. Theirs is a calculated decision based on greater knowledge and resources, particularly economic and social power. It is probable that an element of this is the deliberate, though not necessarily articulated, setting up of difference from the poor and those of lower status. Nevertheless, those of lower status can afford to make a similar choice if they have the funds, though for women access to funds is through men. In Bourdieu's terms, the experience in the health clinic is in a different social space from that of the home birth (Bourdieu 1989). Clinical intervention creates a social distance and greater social, economic and cultural differentiation between clients and between clients and medical personnel. Different social fields are engaged and different cultural and economic capital is utilised compared with village confinements, for example a field of biomedicine, education, formalised professions, contractual relations, *Gesellschaft* relations.

Medicalised environments tend to be disembodying. They erode social and cultural identities while at the same time reinforcing stratification. The power and knowledge of the health clinic midwife is based in the field of modern medicine. The technological differentiation offered in the medical space is modern, and beguiling, because it offers perceived greater security. It therefore becomes a factor in the choice of confinement care, space and place. Thus, the entry of the national health system into villagers' lives elicits a range of options hitherto unknown, but the decision-making process with regard to care, and the preservation of cultural identity, remains within a social context of close relations. Nevertheless, had this confinement taken place in a hospital ward rather than a local clinic, it is uncertain whether such positive transformations from a traditional to a modern life-cycle event would have been possible.

Notes

1   Terms in Bahasa Indonesia are indicated by [I]; terms in the Sasak language by [S].
2   In popular parlance 'three times' and 'five times' refer to the number of times people pray a day. There is a different, more academic explanation which I will not discuss here.
3   I carried out two surveys. The first was of forty women, the second of forty men (mainly the husbands of the women in the first survey).
4   The austere form of Islam on Lombok does not allow men to attend women in childbirth.
5   Grace (1996), who did fieldwork in the same district but in a different village, reports that twenty-nine of thirty women surveyed planned to deliver at home.
6   The previous month I accompanied three pregnant women to the health clinic (*puskesmas*) in Labuan Sasak for tetanus toxoid injections, an unusual event. Usually one waits for the next integrated health post (*posyandu* [I]) session (scheduled for each month). *Posyandu* sessions, however, do not always happen according to schedule, so Inaq Kariati and the other women did not want to take the risk of not having a complete antenatal course (two injections) before their respective impending confinements.
7   As mentioned earlier, some of these items had been requested by the health clinic midwife. The new needle and syringes had been suggested by Ibu Andi (Inaq Kariati's closest neighbour, a Christian from Flores), and myself. We were both aware of the possible supply shortage of these items in the health clinic.
8   Contraceptives included the injectible Depo Provera, Norplant insertions, IUD spirals and oral contraceptives. Supplies included kidney bowls, gloves, needles and syringes, pincers, tweezers, scissors, gauze in sterile solution, glass jars of cotton wool, cotton swabs, a sterile steel box for needles and syringes, glycerine, ampoules of vitamin B1 and diphenhydramine.
9   Health clinics do not provide any canteen facilities. Patients who stay must provide their own food.

References

Bourdieu, P. 1989. Social space and symbolic power. *Sociological Theory* 7 (1): 14–24.
Cederroth, S. 1981. *The Spell of the Ancestors and the Power of Mekkah: A Sasak Community on Lombok.* Göteborg: Acta Universitatis Gothoburgensis.
—— 1993. Aspects of Sasak cosmology: binary oppositions and sacred cloths among *wetu telu* Sasak (Lombok, Indonesia). Unpublished paper presented at the 9th European Colloquium of Indonesian and Malay Studies, July 1993.
Connor, L.H. 1982. The unbounded self: Balinese therapy in theory and practice. In *Cultural Conceptions of Mental Health and Therapy*, edited by A.J. Marsella and G.M. White. Dordrecht: D. Reidel.

—— 1983. Healing as women's work in Bali. In *Women's Work and Women's Roles*, edited by L. Manderson. Canberra: ANU Press (ANU Development Studies Centre Monograph No. 32.)

Connor, L.H., P. Asch and T. Asch 1996. *Jero Tapakan: Balinese Healer: An Ethnographic Film Monograph*, second revised edition. Los Angeles: Ethnographics Press.

Foucault, M. 1973. *The Birth of the Clinic: An Archaeology of Medical Perception*. Translated by A.M. Sheridan-Smith. New York: Tavistock Publications.

—— 1984. Nietzsche, genealogy, history. In *A Foucault Reader*, edited by P. Rabinow. London: Penguin Books.

Geertz, C. 1957. Ritual and social change: a Javanese example. *American Anthropologist* 59: 32–54.

Giddens, A. 1990. *The Consequences of Modernity*. Cambridge: Polity Press.

Grace, J. 1996. Healers and modern health services: antenatal, birthing and postpartum care in rural East Lombok, Indonesia. In *Maternity and Reproductive Health in Asian Societies*, edited by P. Rice and L. Manderson. Australia: Harwood Academic Publishers.

Kitamura, T. 1983. Village organization and patrilineal kin groups in east Lombok. *Minzokugaku Kenkyu (Japanese Journal of Ethnology)* 48: 217–35.

Kleinman, A. 1980. *Patients and Healers in the Context of Culture: An Exploration of the Borderland between Anthropology, Medicine, and Psychiatry*. Berkeley: University of California Press.

Krulfeld, R. 1974. The village economies of the Sasak of Lombok: a comparison of three Indonesian peasant communities. Unpublished Ph.D. thesis, Yale University.

Laderman, C. 1983. *Wives and Midwives: Childbirth and Nutrition in a Rural Malay Village*. Berkeley: University of California Press.

—— 1991. *Taming the Wind of Desire: Psychology, Medicine and Aesthetics in Malay Shamanistic Performance*. Berkeley and Los Angeles: University of California Press.

Steedly, M. 1988. Severing the bonds of love: a case study in soul loss. *Social Science and Medicine* 27 (8): 841–56.

Wikan, U. 1990. *Managing Turbulent Hearts: A Balinese Formula for Living*. Chicago: University of Chicago Press.

Wolf, E. 1966. *Peasants*. New Jersey: Prentice-Hall.

Index

Note: Contributors have sometimes used differing spellings for the same name or term, reflecting dialectal or language differences or differing transcription practices. Where possible, these forms have been grouped together (e.g. Bhairav and Bhairu; *jhad poonk* and *jharfuk*)